The Nomadic Alternative

World Anthropology

General Editor

SOL TAX

Patrons

CLAUDE LÉVI-STRAUSS
MARGARET MEAD
LAILA SHUKRY EL HAMAMSY
M. N. SRINIVAS

MOUTON PUBLISHERS · THE HAGUE · PARIS
DISTRIBUTED IN THE USA AND CANADA BY ALDINE, CHICAGO

The Nomadic Alternative

Modes and Models of Interaction in the African-Asian Deserts and Steppes

Editor

WOLFGANG WEISSLEDER

MOUTON PUBLISHERS · THE HAGUE · PARIS

DISTRIBUTED IN THE USA AND CANADA BY ALDINE, CHICAGO

General Editor's Preface

A traditional subject matter for anthropology is a continental area, like Africa, Asia, Oceania, and South America, or a subcontinental area like South Asia, the Far East, the Andes, and the Caribbean. In one such area interdisciplinary scholarship has studied peoples and cultures in their broad geographic and historic interrelation. The present book began with a proposal to cut boldly across the continents to define and explore "new" contiguous areas. Scholars who had never faced each other would get new perspectives on old subjects even as they together defined new ones. Credit certainly belongs to the editor of this volume, Wolfgang Weissleder, who extended his vision from his personal scholarly center in Ethiopia westward across the deserts and grasslands of Africa to the Atlantic and eastward and northward through all of those fabled lands to the Pacific. The occasion for this effort and its climax in a meeting of scholars had to be a great international congress.

Like most contemporary sciences, anthropology is a product of the European tradition. Some argue that it is a product of colonialism, with one small and self-interested part of the species dominating the study of the whole. If we are to understand the species, our science needs substantial input from scholars who represent a variety of the world's cultures. It was a deliberate purpose of the IXth International Congress of Anthropological and Ethnological Sciences to provide impetus in this direction. The *World Anthropology* volumes, therefore, offer a first glimpse of a human science in which members from all societies have played an active role. Each of the books is designed to be self-contained; each is an attempt to update its particular sector of scientific knowledge and is written by specialists from all parts of the world. Each volume should be read and reviewed individually as a separate volume on its own given subject. The set as a whole will indicate what changes are in store for anthropology as scholars from the developing countries join in studying the species of which we are all a part.

The IXth Congress was planned from the beginning not only to include as many of the scholars from every part of the world as possible, but also with a view toward the eventual publication of the papers in high-quality volumes. At previous Congresses scholars were invited to bring papers which were then read out loud. They were necessarily limited in length; many were only summarized; there was little time for discussion; and the sparse discussion could only be in one language. The IXth Congress was an experiment aimed at changing this. Papers were written with the intention of exchanging them before the Congress, particularly in extensive pre-Congress sessions; they were not intended to be read aloud at the Congress, that time being devoted to discussions – discussions which were simultaneously and professionally translated into five languages. The method for eliciting the papers was structured to make as representative a sample as was allowable when scholarly creativity – hence self-selection – was critically important. Scholars were asked both to propose papers of their own and to suggest topics for sessions of the Congress which they might edit into volumes. All were then informed of the suggestions and encouraged to rethink their own papers and the topics. The process, therefore, was a continuous one of feedback and exchange and it has continued to be so even after the Congress. The some two thousand papers comprising *World Anthropology* certainly then offer a substantial sample of world anthropology. It has been said that anthropology is at a turning point; if this is so, these volumes will be the historical direction-markers.

As might have been foreseen in the first post-colonial generation, the large majority of the Congress papers (82 percent) are the work of scholars identified with the industrialized world which fathered our traditional discipline and the institution of the Congress itself: Eastern Europe (15 percent); Western Europe (16 percent); North America (47 percent); Japan, South Africa, Australia, and New Zealand (4 percent). Only 18 percent of the papers are from developing areas: Africa (4 percent): Asia-Oceania (9 percent); Latin America (5 percent). Aside from the substantial representation from the U.S.S.R. and the nations of Eastern Europe, a significant difference between this corpus of written material and that of other Congresses is the addition of the large proportion of contributions from Africa, Asia, and Latin America. "Only 18 percent" is two to four times as great a proportion as that of other Congresses; moreover, 18 percent of 2,000 papers is 360 papers, 10 times the number of "Third World" papers presented at previous Congresses. In fact, these 360 papers are more than the total of *all* papers published after the last International Congress of Anthropological and Ethnological Sciences which was held in the United States (Philadelphia, 1956).

The significance of the increase is not simply quantitative. The input of scholars from areas which have until recently been no more than subject matter for anthropology represents both feedback and also long-awaited theoretical contributions from the perspectives of very different cultural, social, and historical traditions. Many who attended the IXth Congress were convinced that anthropology would not be the same in the future. The fact that the next Congress (India, 1978) will be our first in the "Third World" may be symbolic of the change. Meanwhile, sober consideration of the present set of books will show how much, and just where and how, our discipline is being revolutionized.

The Congress produced books on a variety of geographic areas, both on land (different parts of Africa, Asia, and the Americas) and sea (the maritime Atlantic and Pacific separately) and combinations such as the circumpolar region. Readers of the present book will also be interested in a variety of volumes in this series on related archaeological, ecological and historical subjects and on a range of topics from religion, aesthetics and folklore to the politics, economics, and social problems which cut across continents.

Chicago, Illinois   SOL TAX
September 2, 1977

Table of Contents

Introduction: Notes on a Discussion

WOLFGANG WEISSLEDER

The ICAES session on pastoral and nomadic peoples of the hot and cold steppelands of Africa and Asia was faced with the organizational problem of assuring an orderly presentation and discussion of widely disparate material, deriving from a vast expanse of the earth's surface and dealt with under a variety of scientific orientations. What seemed at first hopeless – and what may, in the end, prove to have been impossible – was approached through a clear-cut, if sometimes arbitrary, division of topics into four major subject headings. For each of these, one scholar present at the session volunteered to act as sectional chairman and discussant.

As the four sections gradually gained definition, they also established the table of contents of this volume. Ecology, a matter of first-line contemporary concern, was dealt with in its widest sense, ranging far beyond narrow definitional confines of environment and technologies. Professor Charles Frantz, U.S.A., conducted the discussion. Professor T. A. Zhdanko, U.S.S.R., dealt with questions of ethnic development and with sedentarization as process and policy. In a third section, relationships of peripheral nomadic societies with centralized power structures and their orderly integration and safeguards of subgroup autonomy were taken up by Mr. Jean Bigtarma Zoanga, Upper Volta. Finally, cognitive determinants of nomadic culture were discussed under the guidance of Dr. K. C. Malhotra, India.

A contrasting, not to say contradictory, pair of principles reemerged throughout the discussion, reminiscent of a dichotomy of approaches to nomadic societies once stated by Professor Willy Kraus (1969:8). At one end of a continuum of attitudes, nomadism might be viewed as a socio-economic stage totally out of tune with the requirements of modern developmental policy. Where it still exists it must be considered an obstacle or countercurrent to a path of change generally accepted to be inevitable as well as desirable. Nomadism is characteristically pre-industrial and inherently at odds with its institutions. Seen in this light, nomadism is something to be overcome, and serious discussions of its intrinsic merits as a way of life become academic at best but futile in any practical sense. As a topic of policy, nomadism could then be treated rationally only with emphasis on methods of promoting sedentarization and establishing the most effective means of transition to agriculture or stationary forms of animal husbandry, keeping specific time and space factors in mind. (In fact, it was stated that the nomadic way of life does not promote high levels of cultural activity, as it does not promote the improvement of health or of hygienic conditions.)

The polar opposite of this attitude was expressed, overtly and covertly, with equal frequency and weight of conviction. In a variety of ways the point was made that wide regions of the world are most effectively exploited by nomadic peoples whose technology, in arid and semiarid zones, can play an important part in the production of animal proteins. The frequently mentioned incapacity of nomads to become successfully integrated into larger political communities was viewed with doubt. To the contrary, the spontaneous and gradual modification and transformation of nomadic society was accepted as a distinct possibility, while the expedient of forcible sedentarization to achieve permanent structural change and abandonment of the nomadic life style was treated with scepticism or was rejected outright.

Both programmatic points of view, stated above in their more extreme forms, reentered the discussion in a more-or-less guarded manner, whether ecology, power and authority, ethnogenesis, or cognition and value systems was the ongoing topic. Concern with the direction which the transformation of pastoral nomadism is to take in the future is an undercurrent through many of the papers of this volume and was evident in the background of all scholarly discussion of its existential realities. Thus, for instance, the ecological approach taken by several authors and discussants reached beyond the exclusive consideration of ecological variables to take up the cause of nomadic populations squeezed in the trammels of a marginal environment and a hostile or un-understanding policy. As thought was given to ways in which peoples more fortunately endowed could come to the aid of those faced with recurrent or endemic crises, the definition of ecology was readily expanded to encompass social and political factors. This was held to accord well with traditions of anthropology, leading back at least as far as the anthropogeography of F. Ratzel. Ever since, there has been a return to the inclusion of noncultural and nonsocietal variables closely interrelated with culture and society. The most recent wave of interest merely restates old definitions of ecology in a broader, more inclusive sense. Physical anthropologists, archaeologists, and social-cultural anthropologists are thought to be able to converse with one another precisely because of a common interest in events at the subhuman, subsocial, and subcultural level of phenomena. Everything in man and in the environment which supplies his subsistence must in some way be considered relevant in anthropology. Ultimately this must include everything from landform, rainfall, runoff patterns and the storage of precipitation in wells, lakes, rivers, or canals, and diseases of soil, plants, and animals to human physical constitutions, disease, and metabolic success or failure. Ecology can hardly be regarded as a discrete and separate field of study. As anthropologists we can lay a preemptive claim to most of the crucial variables which to others may seem to coalesce into a new science.

Anthropology, however, having contributed much, also has much still to do, especially in the area of nomad studies. The hope was therefore voiced that the broadest possible coverage be given to the biological as well as the sociocultural dimensions. This hope was realized in a number of the papers, which interrelate classical ecological variables of the natural environment, i.e. biotic and biological factors, with social and cultural data.

Limitations of time permitted no more than identification of levels of phenomena that relate to the pastoral-nomadic way of life or mention of a few of the ideas that have been expressed in the literature of the last decade. More definite answers were demanded to the question of whether specific pastoral life styles and their social, economic, political, or even ideological systems correlated with the domestication of and the pasturing practices with regard to specific herd animals, so that sheep raisers, for instance, would predictably exhibit some general distinctions of social structure when compared with reindeer or camel nomads. This question was addressed at various stages of the discussion, frequently tied to another: is nomadism dead or moribund everywhere or should it be treated as a still-viable alternative in ecological situations which favor or are best exploited through spatial mobility? A case from South America, where large-scale herding of domesticated animals has not been part of traditional cultures, was mentioned. The nomadic or at least seminomadic pattern is making an appearance among certain groups of Quechua (Aymara) Indians who raise llamas. Inhabitants of some small Caribbean islands, where attempts to grow cotton have met with little success since the days of slavery, are turning more and more to cattle raising. The implication is that a move toward pastoralism or even seminomadism in areas of poor or depleting soils should come as no surprise.

Though none of the papers in this volume deal with it specifically, discussion expanded and elaborated the previous point beyond pastoral nomadism itself. Forms of mobility for which an adequate terminology still seems lacking in anthropology are represented in modern industrial society by population sectors engaged in such activities as dam building, pipeline construction, or oil drilling. This work force tends to move from site to site, creating a new kind of nomadism in which huts, trailers, cabins, or prefabricated housing represent a new form of habitat. When accepted as a distinctive type of exploitative relationship to primary resources, such practices might constitute a new variant of nomadism. In this regard, the Middle East, where resource-industrial nomadism is very topical, would commend itself to anthropological research. For instance, would traditional forms of nomadic life permit themselves to be grafted onto the contemporary expressions of an emerging technologizing society?

The broadening of the term nomadism to include industrial mobility was not accepted without objection. Industrial mobility, it was stressed, is basically opportunistic in nature and lacks some of the salient characteristics of nomadism: the rhythmical and cyclical, almost predictable, shifts of location, with territorial limits or band or lineage structure defining the migrating group.

Nevertheless, there remains the signficant fact that industrial society is not as fully sedentary as we may be tempted to regard it, but that it generates its own form of mobility. Seen over the long course, world populations may in fact be on the road to increasing rather than diminishing geographical mobility. While millions of nomads are being sedentarized in some regions, other millions of historically sedentary people are becoming at least partially nomadic. Hitherto sedentary individuals have left their places of residence to work abandoned mines in the US and Canada, urged on by the inflated prices of gold and other metals and minerals. Thus, even mineral exploitation can have its variable and cyclical phases. Industry, especially resource industry, is developing a growing need for an adaptive labor force, in a sense, as nomadic populations adaptively relate to their changing resource availability, be it grass or water, or agriculturalists relate to the requirements of seasonal crops. For some time, industrial societies have tended to produce stable labor forces and less-stable residential patterns. We used to call this "neo-locality," but it may reflect a more pervasive ecological dimension. Though the shift should be expected to be most noticeable at the level of the proletariat, it is no less apparent in high managerial and administrative strata.

In absolute numbers, with a world population doubling every fifteen to twenty years, there will be more millions of nonsedentary peoples than there ever were in the past. In time, we may find the experience of traditional nomads to have held lessons and models for far more complex societies.

Spatial proximity and symbiosis between sedentary and nomadic peoples took on the weight of a *sine qua non* for the definition of pastoralism or even nomadism in some of the contributions. Not only in the realm of economic exchanges but also in the political sphere, a measure of balance and equilibrium between the two was seen as a potential outcome of continuous interaction, even though it would take the form of ongoing competition and contest.

The discussions generated a verbal contribution, not included among the submitted papers, by Dr. K. C. Malhotra, who offered it as an example of symbiotic interaction between fixed and mobile peoples, taking place mainly in the realm of cognitive determinants. Some little-reported nomadic Indian subcultures function as necessary adjuncts to sedentary societies. They embrace a great variety of occupations: hunters, trappers, fishermen, blacksmiths, basket weavers, and entertainers such as acrobats, magicians, snake charmers, puppeteers, monkey trainers, singers, and dancers, as well as philosophers, teachers, fortune-tellers, palmists, and lowly beggars. Only a few of these groups, such as sheep raisers and cattle breeders, directly contribute to the food inventory. The integrative role of these traditionally mobile population groups within a, for the most part, immobile society is little understood. We do not know how to range them on the functional-structural scale of food-producing, semiparasitic, or parasitic members of the greater society. Nor can they as yet be assigned a place in the *jajmani* system, that essential aspect of caste organization in traditional and modern India. No serious studies tell us of the role which these wanderers play in the life of village India, and no data indicate what impact changing social and political atmosphere, directed industrialization, and improving means of communication have upon them. It is very apparent, however, that the present forms of their nomadism are fast disappearing and that a process of settling down is under way as traditional modes of occupation are threatened.

Fairly representative of the problem is the case of the Nandiwalla, whose involvement in the life of settled communities also sheds light on ideological reciprocity in their relationships with members of a complex peasant society. The Nandiwalla moved from Andra into Maharashtra about eighty years ago. Their language is Telugu but they are also fluent in Marathi. Though nomadic and economically dependent on cattle, they cannot be called pastoralists. Their main income-producing occupation is the display of bull oracles: Nandiwalla buy bulls from farmers and train them to respond with simple "yes" or "no" signals to any question that is put to them. Bulls are, of course, sacred vehicles of the Lord Shiva and are worshiped as such, especially by the women. They ask very specific questions of the oracle, such as whether they will give birth to a son, a matter of great importance in a patrilineal or virifocal society. If the bull's answer is borne out, in the future the women will receive its oracular pronouncements with all the more respect and esteem. A larger amount of money or possibly a cow will be given to the Nandiwalla who trained it.

The migrations of some of the Nandiwalla groups have now been mapped and can be predicted. Each group controls a territory inherited from its ancestors. Incursions into the territory of another group are punished through a very powerful caste system. The economic gains which the Nandiwalla derive from the villagers among whom they move flow back into the community in which they originate. Excess money earned through the oracles is lent at interest to farmers, who can then use the capital for sinking wells or for other small agricultural-improvement projects. This ethnographic example was chosen to present the case for "nonecological" nomads in the fuller context of a total economic and ritual network, in a symbiotic rather than a competitive relationship with sedentary population sectors. Unanswerable so far is the question of what the future holds for such integrational networks and whether they can be successfully modernized and absorbed into the mainstream of sociocultural changes. If not, will the result be more landless laborers, increasing the already staggering number of unemployed?

The nature and organization of the ICAES sessions on African and Asian nomadic peoples precluded any degree of prescriptive programming. For this, if for no other reason, this volume must submit to Neville Dyson-Hudson's reproach that nomadic studies seem always to have had a "curiously inchoate, noncumulative character" (1972:2). The contributions to this volume stand as a repertoire of evocative themes awaiting convincing systematization, a lexicon with little grammar or syntax. The papers and the discussions which they generated could do no more than underscore the need for ever more rigorous research into the total ambience of nomadic/sedentary life on the one hand, and the creation of a powerful and unifying theory of the nomadic alternative on the other. Can this be accomplished before the problem disappears with the demise of the last nomadic society – or before nomadism has shown itself to be the predominant life-style of the future?

REFERENCES

DYSON-HUDSON, NEVILLE
1972   "The study of nomads," in *Perspectives on nomadism*, edited by William Irons and Neville Dyson-Hudson. International Studies in Sociology and Social Anthropology. Leiden: E. J. Brill.
KRAUS, WILLY
1969   "Nomadismus als entwicklungsgeschichtliches Problem," in *Nomadismus als Entwicklungsproblem*. Bochumer Symposium 14/15, July, 1967. Bielefeld: Bertelsmann Universitätsverlag.

SECTION ONE

Ecology

The Culture Areas of the Middle East

RAPHAEL PATAI

I. In recent decades a consensus has crystallized among anthropologists and other area specialists concerning the landmass to which the designation "Middle East" should be applied. To put it as briefly as possible, the Middle East is today understood to comprise the territory bounded by the Atlantic Ocean in the west; the Mediterranean, the Black Sea, the Caucasus, the Caspian Sea, the Kara Kum and the Kyzyl Kum deserts, and the Alai Range in the north; the Indus Valley in the east; and the Arabian Sea, the Ethiopian highlands, and the southern reaches of the Sahara in the south. When I first suggested in a 1952 paper that these should be recognized as the appropriate boundaries of the Middle East (Patai 1952), my suggestion was at variance with the dominant, much narrower, view of the delimitation of the area. Subsequently, however, the basic cultural unity of the area in question became more and more generally accepted, and thus the Middle East came to be considered as comprising all of North Africa down to the Sudan, the Arabian Peninsula, the Fertile Crescent, Asia Minor, the Iranian Plateau, and the adjacent lands as indicated above. This is the sense in which the term "Middle East" is used by, among others, anthropologist Carleton S. Coon (1965), sociologist C. A. O. van Nieuwenhuijze (1971), historian Sydney N. Fisher (1968), and political scientists Benjamin Rivlin and Joseph S. Szyliowicz (1965).

Ten years after the publication of the aforementioned paper I returned to a discussion of the subject (Patai 1962). In the intervening decade, continuing study of the Middle East convinced me that the term "culture area," borrowed from the well-known work of Americanist Clark Wissler (1922) and Africanist Melville J. Herskovits (1924), cannot properly be applied to the Middle East as a whole for two reasons: (1) the Middle East, occupying some seven million square miles, is not much smaller than the continents within which the anthropologists mentioned distinguished numerous culture areas; (2) beneath the overall similarity characterizing "Middle East culture" there are too many strongly pronounced local variations, which become most apparent if one compares widely separated parts of the Middle East, e.g. Río de Oro (the "Golden River") with the Turkmen-Uzbek area traversed by the poetically famous "Golden Road," or Asia Minor with the southeastern part of the Arabian Peninsula. Because of these considerations, as well as an overall structural comparability between the Middle East and continental Europe, I suggested in 1962 that the former be designated a "culture continent," which term would indicate both the huge size of the geographical area concerned and the existence of internal variations among its constituent regions (Patai 1962: 15, 40–47).

Once it is agreed that the Middle East is a culture continent comparable to Europe or to the aboriginal continent of America, the question inevitably arises as to whether it is feasible to present portraits, or at least thumbnail sketches, of the culture areas contained in it. In general, the problem of how to subdivide culturally the vast land area of the Middle East has received scanty attention. As to that part of the Middle East which lies in Asia, it is so small in relation to the huge Asian continent that in an all-Asian perspective it can easily appear as one single culture area. In any case, only one relatively recent study is known to me which discusses the possibility of determining the culture areas of Asia. This study, by Elizabeth Bacon (1946), distinguishes only two areas, which cover the Asian part of the Middle East as well as much of the rest of Asia. One of the two, termed "Southeast Asian Sedentary," was stated to extend "from the Mediterranean to central India, and [to be] also found in the oases of Turkestan." The other, the "Pastoral Nomadic," was defined as extending "from Manchuria to Palestine and from Siberia to the Arabian Sea" (Bacon 1946: 122–123). The untenability of thus lumping together Central Asian and Middle Eastern nomadism into one single culture area was pointed out by me (Patai 1951: 401–414) and subsequently readily admitted by Miss Bacon (1954: 44, 53ff.).

The African part of the Middle East received attention from Africanists who, however, were somewhat at a loss as to how to treat this part of Africa, which is so evidently different from black Africa south of the Sahara. As early as 1894, A. de Préville attempted to divide North Africa into a northernmost belt of *cavaliers* [horsemen], a belt of *chameliers* [camelmen] comprising most of the Sahara, a third narrow belt of *chevriers* [goatmen] to the south of the former, and a belt of *vachers* [cattlemen] occupying roughly the area between the 12th and the 16th parallels north, across the whole width of Africa (de Préville 1894). More than a decade later came Jerome Dowd's superficial division of North Africa into a "camel zone" and a "cattle zone," which deserves no more than passing mention (Dowd 1907).

The first serious attempt to delineate the culture areas of Africa was made by Melville J. Herskovits in 1924. Although he called his study "A preliminary consideration of the culture areas of Africa," he seemed to have considered it satisfactory enough to repeat it with practically no change in 1930 and again in 1948. As far as the division of the northern part of Africa is concerned, Herskovits's attempt is far from satisfactory. To mention only one detail, he draws a dividing line right across the middle of the Sahara, thereby assigning the Tuareg to two different culture areas. Like Herskovits, the German Africanist Richard Thurnwald paid little attention to North Africa in his classification of African social systems into nine types, two of which, he found, had representatives also in North Africa (Thurnwald 1929).

Wilfrid D. Hambly's mapping of the culture areas of Africa in 1937 represents some advance, inasmuch as he divides the Sahara into three subareas: (1) the Tuareg, (2) the Tebbu, Tibbu, and Teda of Tibesti, and (3) the Arabs of the Libyan oases (Hambly 1937: 325ff.). George P. Murdock (1959) does not map culture areas but attempts an ecological classification, on which basis he finds that North Africa comprises three types: (1) "north African agricultural civilizations" (Berbers and Saharan Negroes), (2) "east African pastoralism" (including the Beja), and (3) "north and west African pastoralism" (Bedouin Arabs, Tuareg, Baggara, and Fulani) (Murdock 1959: 111–133, 314–318, 392–421).

The unsatisfactory nature of all these attempts to classify North Africa into culture areas becomes evident as soon as one has a closer look at the actual situation (see Figure 1). It becomes readily apparent that, apart from one or two areas, no region in the Middle East exhibits the cultural and ethnic homogeneity which formed the basis for delimiting culture areas in America or black Africa. In the Middle East, each culture area (perhaps with the exception of areas 1 and 15, and to a lesser extent area 6) is characterized by the presence of several ethnic groups with different languages, religions, and/or life patterns. A Middle Eastern area is a patchwork quilt composed of irregular assortments of different materials, with pieces of the same material appearing in several different parts, alternating with one or more other types of patches. Given this configuration, the *degree* of internal variety becomes a significant characteristic of every area, over and above the differences in culture between one area and another. Thus, to mention only one example, apart from the obvious cultural differences between areas 1 (the Nile area) and 23 (the Turkmen-Uzbek area), the fact that area 1 is almost entirely homogeneous while area 23 shows a patchwork-like pattern of at least five different ethnic groups becomes an important characteristic differentiating the two. In other cases two areas may be distinguished by different proportions of

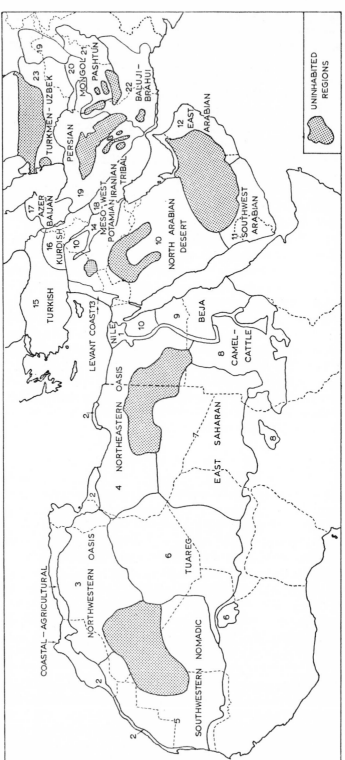

Figure 1. The culture areas of the Middle East

the same two or more ethnic elements found in both, just as in human genetics the incidence of two or more antigens (e.g. in blood groups) is used to differentiate between populations. Thus the proportion of settled versus nomadic populations or of Arabic-speaking versus Berber-speaking groups can be factors distinguishing between neighboring culture areas.

Secondly, it will soon be noted that the differences among Middle Eastern culture areas are far less pronounced than those within the culture areas of native America or black Africa. The latter two continents did not have the historical experience of being politically and culturally dominated by one single ethnic group. Yet this is precisely what happened in the Middle East. Not merely once, but several times in its long history, the Middle East, or major parts of it, were ruled by *one* power and exposed to what today could be called the "cultural imperialism" of one ethnic group. Assyria, Babylonia, Egypt, Phoenicia, Persia, Greece, Rome, and Byzantium, one after the other, filled this role of politico-cultural dominator in the Middle East. Surpassing them all, the Muslim Arabs, emerging from their arid peninsula in the seventh century, not only conquered and ruled practically the entire Middle East, imposing upon it their religion and to a more limited extent their language, but also settled there and intermingled with the local populations. Hence, what is surprising when one looks at the Middle East from this historical viewpoint is not that its many areas are as culturally similar as they are, but that despite these unifying influences so many differences have survived. It is the historical sequence of influences, emanating one after the other from a series of cultural and political centers, that stamps the Middle East with the character of a culture continent.

II. What, then, in concrete terms, are the cultural features which make for this overall similarity? Obviously, only a very brief enumeration is possible in the present context. Moreover, such an enumeration is made especially difficult by the unprecedented cultural changes which are taking place today all over the Middle East, albeit at greatly disparate rates. In presenting such a list of features, I am following, with certain modifications, a list I presented in 1962. These, then, are the consistent cultural features of the area:

1. A basic ecological dichotomy, corresponding to the geographical dichotomy of the desert and the cultivated land: on the one hand, camel- or sheep- and goat-breeding tribes following a pastoral nomadic mode of life, and, on the other, settled villagers practicing agriculture.

2. The presence of transitional or intermediary types of societies ranging from seminomadic tribes in various stages of sedentarization to almost completely settled tribes.

3. The use of the black hair tent by all nomadic and seminomadic

tribes and the presence of tightly clustered villages all over the settled parts of the Middle East.

4. Patrilineal descent, whether actual or assumed, as the basis of social organization among the tribes as well as in the villages.

5. Rudimentary occupational specialization among both nomads and villagers: almost all of the former are engaged in pastoral pursuits, while almost all of the latter are agriculturists.

6. Much of the interrelationship between nomads and villagers taking the form of raids by tribal groups who regarded the villagers as their legitimate prey, at least in the past; recently, this form of interaction has been suppressed by the state governments and replaced by commercial exchange with the local towns as its focus.

7. A monopoly on leadership in all fields (religion, education, art, politics, business, etc.) held by the numerically small urban upper and middle classes, resulting in a considerable cultural gap between town and country.

8. A triple class structure, pronounced in the towns, rudimentary in the villages, and almost nonexistent in the nomadic tribes. However, among the nomads there is a great emphasis on rank differences between "noble" and "vassal" tribes.

9. Westernization centered in the towns and strongest in the upper class, less advanced in the middle class, and incipient in the lower class.

10. The extended, patrilineal, patrilocal, patriarchal, endogamous, and occasionally polygynous family as the basic social and economic unit in nomadic camp and village, with the individual subordinated to the family. In the city, the Western-type nuclear family becomes more and more prevalent.

11. In traditional circles (as above), participation by the individual in social groupings larger than the family not on an individual basis but through his family membership.

12. In the town, such associations as guilds (now largely defunct) based on occupation, though membership is often inherited.

13. Indications everywhere of a dual organization.

14. On he local level, in camps and villages, social control and political leadership based on family ies and influence, with the powers divided between headman and council.

15. On the higher level, in the capitals and other central towns, the spectacle of the traditional feudalistic, oligarchic, and at times despotic rule slowly being either mitigated by newly introduced Western forms of government or transformed into dictatorships with capitalistic control and a disproportionate accumulation of wealth in the hands of a few "great" families.

16. General poverty, subsistence-level life, and a high incidence of disease, high birth and death rates, and low life expectancy, with the situation somewhat better in the Westernized sectors of the towns.

17. Very high rates of illiteracy, which still stamp the Middle East as an illiterate culture.

18. A great preoccupation, on the other hand, with folklore: folk poetry, folk song, folk tales, folk music, riddles, and proverbs, and great emphasis on oral expression in general.

19. The tribal population's adherence to the old, local, traditional, customary law (known as *'urf* in the Arabic-speaking areas) rather than the Muslim religious *sharī'a* law, which, however, is gradually being displaced in the more Westernized countries by modern Western law.

20. A strongly marked double standard of sexual morality, with great emphasis on premarital virginity, female chastity, and modesty.

21. Veiling of women, practiced sporadically but most prevalent in conservative urban circles.

22. Honor, hospitality, generosity, kin-group loyalty, sensitivity to shame ("face") and insistence on revenge; these are predominant values which strongly influence behavior patterns in direct proportion to the general conservatism.

23. The esthetic element permeating everyday life, its forms and areas of expression being determined by local tradition.

24. An all-pervasive religiosity, comprised of elements of belief, ritual, custom, and morality.

25. Intense belief in and reliance on the one and only God, accompanied by a belief in demons and spirits, and by saint worship in the towns and villages; ancestor worship is absent.

26. Finally, a widespread broad outlook on human existence, comprising a firm belief in reward and punishment in the afterlife, an acceptance of one's fate, and a relative indifference to adversity.

III. The Middle Eastern culture continent as a whole is characterized by the foregoing twenty-six common features. Unless otherwise stated, these features can be assumed to be present in each of the culture areas discussed. In attempting to characterize the culture areas of the Middle East, I must point out that, in order to make the description of the individual areas manageable, only a few basic features could be selected for presentation. The features selected include the political control to which the area is subject; the estimated number of its inhabitants; the ethnic groups; the subsistence economy; the religion(s); the language(s); and, finally, those special features in which the area differs from the general Middle Eastern pattern.[1]

[1] The approach utilized by Murdock (1967) in his *Ethnographic atlas* in determining his "classification by clusters" could not be used because most of the very large number of features (some 50) listed there are identical for either the entire Middle East or major parts of it; or data are unavailable for most of the ethnic groups of the area. Moreover, Murdock's classification by clusters lumps together such far-apart and disparate groups as, for example, Egyptians and Moroccans, or Jordanians and

1. *Nile Area*

Political control: Egypt (the Arab Republic of Egypt) in the north and the Sudan in the south. The population of the area can be estimated at 39 million, of whom roughly 35 million are in Egypt, and 4 million in the Northern and Blue Nile provinces of the Sudan.

Ethnic groups: in the north, Arabic-speaking Egyptians, including 7 percent Copts. In the south, Nubian-speaking Barābra (singular Barbarī), numbering some 200,000 and including the Kunūz (singular Kenūzī) between the First and Second Cataracts in southern Egypt, and the Sukkūt and Maḥas between the Second and Third Cataracts in northern Sudan. The Danāqla (or Danāqīl, singular Danqalī) between the Third and Fourth Cataracts are linguistically and physically related to the Kunūz but do not consider themselves Barābra. South of the Fourth Cataract live the Gaaliyyin (Jaʿalyyīn), Shayqiyya, and other Arab tribes with a strong Nubian component. The ancestral home of the Nubians in the Wadi Halfa area south of the Egyptian frontier has in recent years been inundated by Lake Nasser, created by the Aswan High Dam, and the people have been relocated along the Atbara River near the Ethiopian border. In the Northern province of the Sudan some 20 percent of the total population is Nubian and 80 percent Arab. In the Blue Nile province, to the south, more than 86 percent is Arab, with the remainder West African speaking a variety of African languages.

Subsistence economy: this is one of the world's oldest and most intensively cultivated areas of irrigated riverain agriculture. The high fertility of the land, annually replenished (until the construction of higher and higher dams) by the silt deposited during the summer floods of the Nile, made possible an extremely dense population concentration, with villages many times larger than in any other area of the Middle East. This, moreover, is the only area in the entire Middle East in which nomads are totally absent. Paralleling the huge triangle of the Nile delta in the north is a similar triangle in the south, to the south of Khartoum between the Blue Nile and the White Nile, the so-called al-Jezīrah, with irrigated agriculture practiced in both.

The religion of the people is Sunnī Islam, whose Ḥanafī School enjoys official status. Popular religion stresses the veneration of saints, whose birthdays are celebrated at their tombs in great annual festivals (the so-called *mawlīd*s). The Copts of Egypt are monophysite Christians who represent the remnants of the country's pre-Islamic Christian population and, on the whole, are more educated and urbanized than the Muslims.

The language of the area is predominantly Arabic as far south as the First Cataract, and again south of the Fourth Cataract. Arabic is spoken

---

Yemenis (Murdock 1967: 19, 21), and is thus not useful in an attempt to delimit smaller areas.

by both Muslims and Copts (the latter gave up their Coptic language centuries ago) in the special Egyptian Arabic colloquial which differs to some extent from the Arabic of areas 10 and 13, and more so from that of the North African Maghrib (areas 2, 3, and 4). The Nubian peoples inhabiting both banks of the Nile between the First and Fourth Cataracts speak Nubian dialects. Nubian is an east-Sudanic language belonging to the Nilo-Saharan family.

2. Coastal Agricultural Area

Political control over this very narrow and very long area is exercised (from west to east) by Mauritania, Morocco, Algeria, Tunisia, and Libya. A population estimate is very difficult to arrive at, since the area comprises minor parts of no less than five political entities whose total combined population in 1970 was about 15 million. However, as a guess one can say that probably at least two-thirds to three-quarters of this number live within the area.

Ethnic groups: there can be little doubt that genetically most of the present-day inhabitants of the area are descendants of the Berbers, the original native inhabitants of North Africa, whom the Greeks called *barbaroi* and the Romans *barbari*. The Berbers, in general, are lighter in color than the Arabs. After the Arab occupation of the North African Maghrib all Berbers adopted Islam and most of them gave up their original language for Arabic. Today only those groups are called Berbers who have retained their old language, spoken in many different dialects. Most of the present-day Berbers live outside our area (assimilation has always been less strong in the hinterland than on the coast; see areas 4, 5, and 6).[2] Within our area, where the Arabization of the Berber speakers still proceeds quite rapidly, the major ethnic groups are as follows (again from west to east): Imragen (or Hawāta, or Shnāgla), Oulād bū Ayta, Foykat, and Lammiar of the coast of Mauritania and the former Spanish Sahara; these are Arab or Arabized Berber tribes engaged in sea fishing and paying dues to the nomadic Moorish warriors and *marabout*s who own the fishing grounds. The southwestern Atlantic coastal plains of Morocco, the Anti Atlas, the High Atlas, and the Sous River region are occupied by 3 million Shluh (Shlöh), who are sedentary cereal cultivators or seminomads and partly or wholly Berber-speaking. The Atlantic coastal region of northern Morocco is inhabited by about 1.3 million sedentary Arabic speakers, with another 1 million detribalized Arabic speakers in the urban areas. To the east of them, in the mountains of

---

[2] The total number of Berbers, i.e. groups whose colloquial is or until recently was Berber, in all of the North African part of the Middle East can be estimated at about 10 million.

central Morocco, live the transhumant Berāber (approximately 500,000), who speak a dialect of Tamashek Berber. Near the northernmost tip of Morocco, down to the Mediterranean, are several Berber sedentary agricultural or mountaineering tribal groups who are in a rapid process of Arabization and are known under the names of Jebāla, Ghumāra, Ṣenhāja, and Riffians. East of the Riffians, as far as the Algerian border, are located several Berber Ruāfa or Tamashek-speaking groups commonly referred to as Zenāta. Along the entire coast of Algeria live sedentary Arabized Berber Algerians, in whose midst the Berber Kabyles, also sedentary cultivators, constitute a compact sector along the coast. In the Aures mountain area of eastern Algeria live the Berber Shawiyya (Chaouia), who are sedentary cereal cultivators. In Tunisia the Arab Tunisians in the north and the Sahel (also the name of the northeastern coastal plain of Tunisia) are sedentary cultivators. In southern Tunisia many of the Arab Arad are likewise sedentary cultivators. In Libya a settled agricultural Arab population lives along the Tripolitan coast in the west and the Cyrenaic coast in the east, but not on the central Sirtican coast. Berbers live in the Jebel Nefūsa of Tripolitania near the Mediterranean.

This area occupies that narrow coastal belt of North Africa extending from Mauritania to Libya, in which sufficient rainfall makes dry-farming possible. Thus the subsistence economy in the area is based primarily on extensive cultivation of rainfed lands with irrigation applied only exceptionally. Nomads, few in number, practice transhumance and thus utilize lands unsuited for agriculture. The majority of the people live in villages, the minority in cities, the largest of which are strung along the seashore.

The religion is predominantly Sunnī Islam of the Mālikī school. A small group of Ibādhis lives on the Tunisian island of Jerba, where they form about half the population and call themselves Wahbīs. They are an austere, puritanical sect. In the eastern, Libyan, part of the area, Senussi sectarianism is strong, although its influence is on the decline in the modernizing sector of Libyan society. In the west of the area there is widespread veneration of saints, with annual pilgrimages to their tombs. All over the area among untutored people, old folk-beliefs survive, expressed in a fear of *jinn* [spirits] and the evil eye, and a belief in *baraka* [mysterious beneficial power] possessed by *marabouts* [Muslim holy men]. Religious brotherhoods (*tarīqas*), with centers (*zāwiyyas*) which are a combination of monastery and clubhouse, exist all over the area, but are increasingly discouraged by the respective governments. In Algeria the Ramaniyya, Qādiriyya, and Tijāniyya brotherhoods have a combined membership of close to 400,000 in a total population of about 2 million adult male Muslims.

The language generally spoken in the area is the Maghrib Arabic dialect. Berber languages are still spoken by many of the Berber inhabitants of the area, especially in the former Spanish Sahara, the Rif region in Morocco, and the Qusūr Mountains and the island of Jerba in Tunisia. However, the Arabization process of the Berbers is proceeding everywhere. As a result of the decades of French domination of Morocco, Algeria, and Tunisia, much of the instruction in schools is still in French, and French is still the language of the urban elite. French culture vies with Arab culture for the loyalty and sentimental attachment of the upper classes, and the major cities, notably Algiers, exhibit a high degree of French-oriented Westernization.

3. Northwestern Oasis Area

Political control: Morocco, Algeria, Tunisia, and Libya. A population estimate of this area is even more difficult to arrive at than one for area 2. Perhaps 2.5 million may not be too far off the mark.

Ethnic groups: the Berber–Arab dichotomy (see area 2) exists in this area as well. Since most of the area falls within Algeria, it can be mentioned that the 1966 Algerian census listed more than 3 million, or 17.9 percent of the total population, as Berber speakers. An earlier (circa 1960) estimate by French experts put them at 30 percent.

Perhaps more important than the linguistic dichotomy is the nomadic/settled division in the area. Among the nomads, who graze their camels, sheep, and goats in the desert and steppe, there are more Arabs than Berbers; among the settled cultivators, who concentrate on date culture in the oases, the majority are Berber. The most important pastoral nomadic tribes are the Atta, the Dwī Menīa, the Benī Gīl, and other Berber tribes of southeastern Morocco and western Algeria; the Hamyan, the Oulād Sidi Shaykh, and other Bedouin Arab tribes of the Algerian steppe near the Moroccan frontier; the Bedouin Arab Oulād Na'īl of the central Atlas region of Algeria; the Hamāma and related Bedouin Arab tribes of the interior steppe of Tunisia; and the large Bedouin Arab Chaamba (comprising many tribes which differ in rank) and others of the Algerian Sahara.

Among the settled cultivators in the oases and along a few rivers, the most important are the Berber Drāwa and Filāla of Morocco; the Berber Figuig (Fajīj), who inhabit a group of seven walled villages (*qṣūr*) in southeastern Morocco near the Algerian frontier and cultivate date palms and fruit trees; the Berber Touat, Mzab, and Wargla (Ouargla) in Algeria; the Arab Laguat (Laghouat), Ziban, Ruārha, and Swāfa in Algeria; the Arab Gafsa (Qafsa) and Jerīd of Tunisia; and the Berber Benī Wazīt, Benī Ulīd, and Oulād Bellīl (the latter consider themselves of Arab origin) tribes of the Ghadames (Ghdāms) oasis in the western Libyan Sahara. In the past, many of these oasis peoples owed their fortunes more to the trans-Saharan caravan trade than to cultivation.

The subsistence economy of the area, as indicated above, is partly nomadic herding and partly oasis cultivation. The latter is generally irrigated agriculture and arboriculture. In the past, the oases were often worked by Negro slaves for their nomadic masters. The slaves have long been officially liberated, but many of them still work the oases as *harāṭīn* [agricultural serfs] for absentee masters.

The religion of the area is Sunnī Islam; however, several of the Berber groups belong to the Ibādhi sect, notably the inhabitants of the Mzab and Wargla oases. Among the nomads, Islamic observance is rather lax. The Qādiriyya and Tijāniyya brotherhoods (compare area 2) have adherents here as well.

Family structure differs from the general Middle Eastern type in that most of the Berbers are monogamous.

4. Northeastern Oasis Area

Political control: Libya in the west, Egypt in the east. The population can be estimated only very roughly at about 1 million.

Ethnic groups: the Berber speakers constitute a smaller proportion than in area 3, perhaps 10 to 20 percent. In Tripolitania (western Libya) live the nomadic Arab tribes of Riyāh (Ria), Busayf, Hasāwna, Hutmān (Hotma), Megārha (Maqārha), Urfilla (Ourfellah), Zintān, and others; on the Sirtican coast and to the south of it, the nomadic Arab tribes of Jamāʿāt, Qadhāghfa, Oulad Solimān, and others; and in Cyrenaica (eastern Libya), the Senussi, who are mostly nomadic Arab tribes. The Western Desert of Egypt is the domain of, among others, the nomadic Arab Saʿadī tribes with their tributary Murābiṭīn. The population of the large oases includes the Berbers of the Libyan Forgha, Jofra, Zella, and Jalu oases, and of the Egyptian Sīwa oasis (circa 4,000 inhabitants); and the Arabs of the Libyan Fezzan, Kufra, and Wanyanya, and the Egyptian Bahariyya, Farāfra, Dakhla, Kharga, and Selīma oases.

The subsistence economy is the by now familiar dual one of nomadic pastoralism and irrigated cultivation. In the east (in Egypt) the buffalo makes its appearance, but it is unknown west of this area.

The religion of the area is Mālikite Sunnī Islam with Ibādhis found in the west in Tripolitania, in Jebel Nefūsa and Zwāgha, and the Senussi sect or religious order predominating in the central part, including the Sīwa oasis. The Senussiyya was founded as recently as the middle of the nineteenth century, but by the eve of World War I, it had achieved effective political and commercial control over the whole eastern half of the Sahara, and after World War II (in 1950) its head became the king of Libya. Since the overthrow of the Libyan monarchy in 1969 the sect has lost influence. Nevertheless the Senussi *zāwiyyas* (compare area 2) are still important centers of religious life, and in many places replace the mosques. The *marabouts* are as influential here as in area 2, and the belief in their *baraka* remains strong. Many Berbers of the area still adhere to the Khārijī sect.

The language is predominantly Arabic, which has almost entirely replaced the Berber languages. In Libya 90 percent of the population is Arabic-speaking. The Arabic spoken in Tripolitania and Fezzan belongs to the Maghrib group (compare area 2). In Cyrenaica the Arabic resembles the dialect of Egypt. In the south of Libya (area 7) some Sudanic languages are still spoken. The inhabitants of the Sīwa oasis and of Sokna and al-Foqa in northern Tripolitania speak Berber.

The family structure is of the general Middle Eastern type but is modified somewhat due to the greater prevalence of homosexuality in some oases (e.g. in Sīwa).

5. Southwestern Oasis Area

Political control: Mauritania, Mali, and Algeria. The number of inhabitants cannot be estimated with any reliability, but it seems to be around 600,000.

Ethnic groups: this area is much poorer in oases than areas 3 and 4, and consequently its total population is both smaller and more nomadic. Enumerating counterclockwise the major tribes of this horseshoe-shaped area surrounding one of the largest uninhabited desert regions of the world, we find in the north the totally Arabized and largely sedentarized Tajakant (singular Jakānī) and associated tribes of western Algeria and northern Mauritania; the Berber nomadic Tekna of southern Morocco and the northern part of the former Spanish Sahara (Río de Oro); the Bedouin, fully Arabized Oulād Delīm and the powerful, noble Regeybāt (or Rguibat, singular Rguībī) of Mauritania; the Bedouin Arab Trārza and Brākna, including the Tasumsa, still partly Berber-speaking, and other minor groups in southern Mauritania; the largely Arabized Berber semisedentary sheep-herding and millet-cultivating Duwaysh in southeastern Mauritania; the Arabized Berber Bedouin Zenāga in the Hodh region of Mauritania and east-central Mali; and the Bedouin Arab Berābish and Kunta in Mali north of Timbuctoo. All the population elements identified in the above listing as Arabs are actually Maure, or Moors, who are basically of Arab-Berber origin with varying degrees of Negroid admixture, increasing toward the south. They constitute about half the area's population, with one-third Berbers in the northwest (the Tekna) and one-sixth Negroid peoples in the south, including the Fulbe or Fulani, who number some 50,000.[3]

[3] The total number of Fulani, scattered all over the western Sudan, is about 5 million.

The subsistence economy of the area is based primarily on animal-herding (mostly sheep and goats, camels and cattle), with 70 to 75 percent of the population nomadic or seminomadic – one of the highest percentages in the Middle East.

The religion is Islam, with the Qādiriyya and Tijāniyya brotherhoods quite strong (compare areas 2 and 3).

The language is the Ḥasaniyya Arabic dialect, which manifests varying degrees of Berber influence. Some tribes still speak only Berber, others are bilingual.

This area is characterized by hierarchically structured social systems, most pronounced in the south. At the top is the white Moor warrior nobility (designated as *ḥasan*); next come the primarily Arab religious groups (*zwāya*); then follow the white Moorish commoners, primarily Berbers with an admixture of Negro blood; and at the bottom of the ranking order are the black Moors, mainly Berbers, but with a greater proportion of Negro blood due to interbreeding with Negro slaves. In the whole of Mauritania 54 percent of the population are white Moors, called *bīdān* [whites], and 27.5 percent are black Moors. The remaining 18 percent are black agricultural people living along the Senegal River just to the south of the border of our area.

6. *Tuareg Area*

Political control: Algeria in the north, Mali in the southwest, Niger in the southeast, and Libya in a small eastern corner. The population of the area can be estimated at less than 1 million, of whom the Tuareg (singular Targūī) account for 300,000, while the rest are Negroid serfs and slaves.

Ethnic groups: this sparsely inhabited central part of the Sahara desert and the Sudan belt is dominated by several Berber-speaking Tuareg tribal confederations: the Azjer or Ajjer (numbering about 6,000) and the Ahaggaren (about 5,000) in the north; the Ifora or Ifogha (about 5,000) in the southwest; the Aulliminden or Iullemmedden (about 100,000) in the south; and the Asben or Kel Air, embracing the Kel Geres and other groups (about 30,000), in the east. Several additional tribes occupy smaller areas along the bend of the Niger River: the Antessar and the Tengeredif (about 40,000) along its north bank, and the Wadalan, the Gossi, and others (100,000) south of the river. The Tuareg groupings in general comprise two hereditary classes of nomads: the noble, ruling Tuareg (*imajeghen*), and the vassal Tuareg (*imghad*) who pay rent or tribute to the former. Outnumbering them are the Negro slaves (*iklan*), at least two or three of whom are owned individually by each Tuareg family and used as house-workers, with the females also serving as concubines; and groups of Negroid serfs, known as *ḥarāṭīn* (singular *ḥarṭānī*), who are engaged in sharecropping, cultivating the oases for their nomadic noble or vassal overlords, or living with the latter in their tribal groups and camps as herdsmen.

The subsistence economy of the Tuareg is based on camel (or sheep and goat) herding. It is supplemented by the products of the oases, their property, worked for them by serfs or slaves. In physical type the Tuareg are taller, slimmer, and lighter-colored than their Arabic-speaking neighbors (areas 3 and 4). In fact, they are among the tallest people in the world and are thin and sinewy. However, a large minority among both nobles and vassals show signs of Negroid admixture as a result of Negro concubinage.

The religion of the Tuareg is Mālikī Sunnī Islam, adherence to whose tenets is, however, rather lukewarm. Moreover, their religious practices incorporate numerous unorthodox magical elements.

The language spoken by the Tuareg is Tamashek, a form of Ṣenhājan Berber, which comprises various dialects. This is the only area in the entire African Middle East in which Berber languages still predominate. The Tuareg language is unique in possessing an old script, called Tifinagh, which is generally known and used only by women for such purposes as sending love messages or writing love poems.

The relationship between Tuareg men and women is also unique in the Middle East. Women enjoy a higher status there than elsewhere. There is great freedom as far as premarital relationships between young men and women are concerned, and romantic love affairs, in which women, as a rule, take the initiative, are frequent. It is the men who wear the veil (the *lithām*, usually dark blue or black), while the women go unveiled. Ritualized social gatherings (called *tendi* and *ahal*) take place with the participation of large numbers of men and women. Descent is matrilineal. Monogamy is universal, the preferred marriage is within the clan, outside the first degree cousinship, and outside the camp community. Divorce is unusual. All this suggests pre-Islamic survival. Other archaic features include the use of animal hides dyed yellow or red as tent coverings, rather than the black hair tent cloth generally used by nomads all over the Middle East.

7. *East Saharan Area*

Political control: Libya in the north, Niger and Chad in the south, and the Sudan in the east. The population can be only very roughly estimated at 2.3 million, of whom more than half live in the Sudanese part of the area.

Ethnic groups: this is the only area in the Middle East which is inhabited almost entirely by Negroid peoples, the so-called Saharan Negroes. Some Arab tribes are found near the southern border of the area, and, for the last 150 years or so, also in the Kufra oasis in its north, which until 1813 was occupied by the Saharan Negro Teda. Most of the area constitutes the wandering territory of the nomadic Saharan Negro Teda (in the north) and Daza (to the south of the Teda). These two tribal groups, also referred to as Toubou (Tūbū), number about 200,000 and roam freely across the frontiers of Niger, Chad, and Libya. One-third of the Teda are fully nomadic; two-thirds of them and all the Daza are seminomadic and regularly return to their villages during the rainy season (from July to September). The Teda mainly tend camels; the Daza also raise horses, donkeys, sheep, and goats. Both of them comprise several subgroups, which, however, do not consider themselves (as Arab tribes usually do) descendants of a single, often mythical, ancestor, but rather trace their origins to one single locality. Close to the southern borders of the area are found the Daza tribes of the Kreda (the most numerous), the Bulgeda, the Kanemba, and the Kawar. In the southeastern corner of Libya are located the Bideyāt, a Sudanese group of Daju origin which, however, has largely adopted Arabic speech. Across the Sudanese frontier are the non-Arab tribes of the Zaghāwa, the Nubian Midobi, and the Berti, the Berkid, the Fūr, and the Daju, about 54 percent of whom speak Arabic and 42 percent Darfurian. North of Lake Chad are found the Arabic-speaking Solimān.

The subsistence economy of the area is determined to a large extent by the amount of rainfall. In the north, rain is minimal, and the scanty vegetation of the desert enables only camel nomads to exist, with the exception of the Kufra and other oases, in which irrigated agriculture and arboriculture are pursued. Toward the south, rainfall increases, favoring seminomadism based on sheep and goats, with the raising of cattle gaining importance farther south. The southernmost outskirts of the area receive sufficient rain to make them savanna rather than desert, and in their eastern and western extremes considerable numbers of people engage in agriculture.

The religion of the area is almost entirely Islam, although some groups adopted it as late as the eighteenth century. Some tribes, moreover, in the northeast of the area (e.g. the Bideyāt), are still partly pagan, partly rather indifferent Muslims. In the southern tier of the area, pagan elements are still found interspersed with Islam.

Language, side by side with religion, is an important differentiating factor in the area. While Arabic, together with Islam, continues to spread, and constitutes the *lingua franca* of the area, some tribal languages still hold their own. These as a group are called "Kanuric" by Murdock (1959: 129) and "Central Saharan" by Greenberg (1955). Language and tribal identification go hand in hand: the Toubou groups which speak the Tedāga dialect refer to themselves as Teda; those who use the Dazāga dialect call themselves Daza.

8. Camel–Cattle Area

Political control: almost the whole of this area lies within the Sudan, except for a disconnected small western section located in south-central Chad and inhabited by the seminomadic Arab Hemat (Haymad) and related tribes, all of which show a substantial Negroid admixture. The population can be estimated at a few hundred thousand. Of the total population of the Sudanese Northern and Kordofan provinces, the Arabs constitute some 60 percent, or about 2.5 million.

Ethnic groups: in the Dongola region to the north are the Arabized Nubian Kerārīsh, camel nomads; between the 18th and the 15th parallels to the west of the Nile live the Kabābīsh, the Hawāwīr, the Keriat, and the Shayqiyya; to the east of the White Nile live the Battāhīn and the Shukriyya. All of these are camel nomads and reveal varying degrees of Negroid admixture; they occupy a large area in the Kordofan province of the Sudan. To the south of them are the Anag and other Arabized Nubian tribes of the hill country of central Kordofan; the Fezāra and related groups who are cattle and sheep nomads in central Kordofan; the seminomadic Hamar (Homr), Bedāwiyya, Ḥasaniyya, and Gimma to the west of the White Nile, and the Rufā'a to the east. South of the former live the cattle nomad tribes of the Habbāniyya, the Messiriyya, and the Selīma. The cattle tribes are collectively referred to as *baqqāra* (also spelled *baggara*) [cattle herders], whose traditional weapon is an extremely long-bladed spear. In contrast, the camel nomads who predominate in the north are called *jammāla* [camel herders]. Most of the Sudanese Arabs claim either Guhayna or Gaaliyyin affiliation, the former being primarily nomadic and the latter mostly settled (see also area 1).

The subsistence economy, depending on climatic conditions, makes a greater population density possible as one proceeds from north to south. On the southern fringes of the area, as in neighboring area 7, agriculture plays an increasing role.

The religion is Islam, and, in contrast to their western neighbors, the *baqqāra* are fanatical Muslims and a warlike people.

The language of most of the tribes (over 90 percent) is Sudanic Arabic, which differs dialectically from the Egyptian Arabic of the north.

Family life differs from the general Middle Eastern pattern in that there is a higher incidence of polygamy and an initial matrilocal residence, both features indicating persistent pre-Islamic African influences. The Middle Eastern black hair tent is frequently replaced among the nomads by other types of temporary shelter.

9. Beja Area

Political control: Egypt in the north and the Sudan in the south. The population was estimated in 1969–1970 at 1.67 million, of whom only 40,000 live in the Egyptian part of the area; the rest inhabit the Sudanese part. The Beja speakers, who numbered about 650,000, or 50 percent of the total in the Kassala province of the Sudan in 1955–1956, are the dominant group in the area.

Ethnic groups: the northern, or Egyptian, part is occupied by the 'Abābda (singular 'Abbādī), numbering about 20,000. They are Muslim nomadic pastoralists, mostly Arabic-speaking. To the south of them, in the Sudan, are the Beja people, most of whom belong to one of three groups (from north to south): the Bishārīn, the Amarār, and the Hadendowa. These descendants of the original indigenous inhabitants of the area have lived there ever since early Pharaonic times. Most of them are nomads, herding sheep, goats, camels, and cattle, although one of the two divisions of the Bishārīn are settled along the Atbara River on the southwestern border of the area.

The subsistence economy is nomadic, with sheep and goats tended all over the area, supplemented by camels in the north and by more cattle than camels in the south. Due to the generally poor grazing conditions, the tribes must break up into small groups in search of pasture. In addition, some occasional cultivation is practiced by the women.

The religion is Islam. The conversion of the Beja peoples to Islam took place between the thirteenth and the fifteenth centuries. Following Muslim custom, the Beja adopted Arabic personal names and took to claiming Arab descent.

The language spoken by the 'Abābda in the north is mostly Arabic, which has replaced their original Cushitic tongue. The Beja, on the other hand, have largely retained their old northern Cushitic (Hamitic) language, designated by the Arabic term tu-Beḍāwiyye. This language, used by half the total population of the Kassala province, is spoken by each of the three Beja groups in a different dialect. About 36 percent of the province's population speak Arabic, and about 11 percent speak various West African languages.

In physical type, the Beja are Caucasoid, with copper red or deep brown skin. They display some pre-Islamic or non-Middle Eastern cultural features, such as the use of grass or palm-leaf mats to cover their tents, initial matrilocal residence, and bride service. Their social organization is relatively egalitarian: there are neither slaves nor nobles. On the other hand, the Beja are characterized by extreme conservatism and pride.

10. North Arabian Desert Area

Political control: mainly Saudi Arabia; minor parts are controlled by Egypt, Israel, Jordan, Syria, Iraq, and Kuwait. Population estimates are extremely difficult because of the area's political fragmentation and because no census has ever been taken in Saudi Arabia. The total population of Saudi Arabia can be estimated at 7 million, to which must be added about 1.5 million nomads and seminomads in the other six countries named, resulting in a total estimate of 8.5 million.

Ethnic groups: the area is inhabited almost exclusively by Arabs, i.e. by people whose mother tongue is Arabic and who consider themselves Arabs. Apart from this general awareness of being Arab, there is an almost equally important feeling of loyalty to the specific tribal group of which one is a member by birth. This loyalty is most pronounced among the nomads, less so among the villagers, and least among the townspeople, many of whom have become Westernized and minimize the importance of genealogical identification.

The Arabian Peninsula is the original home of the Arab tribes who, beginning in the seventh century, conquered all the countries which today form the Arab world and, in the process, imposed much of their own tradition upon the native populations. Tribal identification and loyalty were two of the foremost elements of that tradition and, to a considerable extent, they still are. In our area the number of tribal groupings is so large that only some of the most important can be mentioned.

In the Syrian desert two major tribal confederations rank first, both of them comprising noble camel nomads: the 'Aneze (or 'Anaza), whose tribal territory extends over parts of Syria, Jordan, and Saudi Arabia, and the Shammār, in Iraq and Saudi Arabia. Important tribes in Jordan are the Benī Ṣakhr and Benī Ḥasan; on the Iraqi–Saudi border, the al-Zafīr; in the Kuwait–Saudi region, the Muṭayr; in Ḥijāz Province of Saudi Arabia, the Ḥarb and the Hudhayl; in the central Nejd, the ʿUtayba; in southern Saudi Arabia bordering on the uninhabited Rub al-Khālī [Empty Quarter] desert, the Yām, and to the east of them the 'Awāmir. In addition to these noble tribes, there are numerous smaller, weaker, nonnoble tribes who are their vassals, as well as tribal splinter groups of the generally despised Heteym (Hutaym) and Ṣolubba, who serve the noble tribes as tinkers, smiths, etc. On the outskirts of the desert, close to the cultivated and better-watered regions, are the sheep and goat nomads, considered as ranking beneath the camel nomads but above the vassal tribes.

The entire tribal population of the area and many of its settled inhabitants claim either southern (Yamanī, Qaḥṭānī, or Ḥimyarī) descent or northern (Qaysī, 'Adnānī, Ma'add, Nizar, or Muḍar) genealogy. These dual descent traditions influence alliances and allegiances.

The nomads in general look down upon the settled people (the so-called *ḥaḍarī*) because the latter have submitted to the yoke of agricultural labor, while to the nomad the only activity befitting a free man is tending his herds and flocks.

The subsistence economy of the nomads is based mainly on their animals. Each group of related extended families moves from place to place within its own territory, the migration being determined by the seasonal conditions of rain, pasture, and well water. Theirs is a unique adaptation to the hot desert and steppe region which occupies the major part of the Middle East and which, without them, would be entirely un-inhabited and unutilized (see also areas 3 through 9). The deserts and the steppes can, of course, support only a very sparse nomadic population. The oases in the desert are like green islands inhabited by settled people practicing agriculture and arboriculture. In recent decades efforts have been made by the governments to settle the nomads and induce them to switch to sedentary cultivation by providing them with deep wells in areas formerly arid and uncultivable. Many of the major cities of the area are located on or near the borders between the desert and the cultivated land.

Following World War II, an entirely new economic dimension developed in the area, especially in Saudi Arabia, Kuwait, and Iraq, as well as in area 12, with the exploitation of oil by large American and European companies. This resulted in the industrial employment of tens of thousands of local tribesmen, in billions of dollars in revenue for the governments, and in an inevitable modernization for considerable segments of the population.

Religion: the peninsular core of this area is the birthplace of Islam and of Arab culture, which spread from here throughout the Middle East from the seventh century onward, the religion reaching farther afield than the Arabic language. The holy cities of Mecca and Medina have remained the religious centers of Islam and attract hundreds of thousands of pilgrims annually from all over the Muslim world. In Saudi Arabia, Sunnī Islam is the ruling religion, with the puritanical Wahhābī sect of the Ḥanbalī School predominating. Saint worship is found only on the outskirts of the area.

The southern part of this area, together with areas 11 and 12, contains the least Westernized and most conservative population elements of the Arab world, retaining such features, outmoded or discarded elsewhere, as slavery, large harems maintained by rulers and the rich, an autarchic monarchy, punishment by bodily mutilation, and the like. Only Muslims are allowed to set foot in Mecca – a unique restriction among the holy places of the world.

11. Southwest Arabian Area

Political control: the Arab Republic of Yemen and the People's Democratic Republic of Yemen (better known as Southern Yemen). Although no census has ever been taken, the area has an estimated population of 7 million, of whom 5.5 million are in Yemen and 1.5 million in Southern Yemen.

Ethnic groups: most of the people of the area are Arab in both descent and language. The tribal traditions are still very strong, and the genealogical claims of being either of southern or of northern descent (compare area 10) play an important role in political affiliations, tribal alliances, and the like. In Yemen, the most important upland tribal groupings are those of the Ḥāshid and Bakīl confederations north of Ṣanʿa (both claiming southern origin). Other "southern" tribes are the Hamdān, the Khawlān, and the Murra. "Northern" tribes are the ʿAbsiyya, the ʿAnaza, the Benī Ismāʿīl, and the Benī Qays. In Southern Yemen, the Yāfaʿ (Yāfiʿ) and Hamdān confederations are both of "southern" stock, as are the ʿAbdalī, the Aqrabī, the Faḍlī, the ʿAwlaqī, the Dhiaybī, and others. The Hadhramaut Valley, one of the most fertile regions of Southern Yemen, is inhabited by a large number of tribes (some estimates run as high as 1,300) of whom the Kathīrī and Qaʿaytī groupings are among the most important. All these groups claim "southern" descent. Among the tribes, but not a part of them, live the Sayyid, who claim descent from the Prophet Muḥammad and wield great influence as religious leaders, keepers of the shrines of saints, and mediators in conflicts.

Subsistence economy: the hot, humid, and sandy coastal lowlands are very sparsely populated except for a few seaside towns. Most of the population live in the highland region in numerous towns and villages, where they practice agriculture, made possible primarily by the summer monsoon rains in Yemen and by irrigation in the Hadhramaut Valley in Southern Yemen. Farther inland, on the edges of the great Rubʿ al-Khālī desert, live nomadic tribes herding sheep, goats, camels, or cattle.

The religion of the tribes and townspeople inhabiting the mountains and valleys of central, eastern, and northern Yemen is Zaydī Islam, a Shīʿite sect. In all other parts of Yemen and in all of Southern Yemen, the Shāfiʿī School of Sunnī Islam is followed. The Shāfiʿīs comprise a servile class, the *akhdām*, descendants of African slaves, among whom African religious customs, such as the *zār* exorcism, survive.

The language of the area is Arabic, spoken in the specific Yemeni and related South Arabian dialects. Only the camel-breeding Mahra tribes, living in the desert on the borders of area 12, speak a number of languages unrelated to modern Arabic. The Mahra differ from the rest of the population in garb and customs also. They are, however, of "southern" descent.

Physically the people differ from those of area 10 in that they have darker skin and are smaller of stature. In the Tihāma coastal lowlands of Yemen the population exhibits a strong Negroid admixture.

Among the specific features of the culture of this area can be mentioned the addiction to chewing qāt (*Catha edulis*), a mildly intoxicating shrub grown in the hills of Yemen and enjoyed daily in separate circles by men and women. The tribesmen wear a large curved dagger, shaped like a capital J, in the front of their belts. There is an old architectural tradition of building high houses, with up to six stories. Among some tribes of the interior, the men wear only loincloths and no head coverings.

12. *East Arabian Area*

Political control: Oman, United Arab Emirates, Qatar, Bahrein. The estimated population is about 1.3 million, of whom 750,000 are in Oman, 350,000 in the United Arab Emirates, and 200,000 in Bahrein.

Ethnic groups: the majority of the population is Arab, claiming "northern" descent in the Emirates, partly "northern" and partly "southern" descent in Oman. Among the most important tribal groups are the "northern" Ghāfirī, who are partly Sunnī or Wahhābī, and the "southern" Hināwī, who are Ibādhis, both in Oman. Among the important tribes of the Arab Emirates are the Banī Yās, al-Manāsir, al-Dhawāhir, and al-'Awāmir of the sheikdoms of Abu Dhabi and Dubai. In the two coastal cities of Muscat and Matrah, Indians, Negroes, and Baluchis predominate. Baluchis are also found in the villages around the town of Mazim in the Dhahira section of northern Oman. The Qara of the Qara Mountains of Dhufar and the Shihūh of the Rās al-Jabal mountains of the north of Oman seem to be remnants of pre-Islamic aboriginal tribes.

Subsistence economy: this area, which lies between the desert and the sea, has traditionally based its economy on desert nomadism, on subsistence agriculture along parts of the seashore and in a few oasis villages, and on some maritime activity including pearl fishing. Only the southwestern part of the area, Dhufar, which lies in the monsoon belt, receives enough rain between June and September to sustain perennial streams and ponds. The nomadic peoples of the area wander from sheikhdom to sheikhdom and cross the frontiers between Oman and the Emirates and Saudi Arabia in search of pasture for their animals. The discovery of oil in about 1960 completely changed the economic picture (as it did in area 10) and thrust this remote and conservative corner of the Arabian Peninsula suddenly into the turmoil of modernization.

The religion is Islam, with the Ibādhī sect predominating in southern Oman and the Mālikī Sunnī and Wahhābī sects in the north and in the

Emirates. In Qatar, the native-born half of the population follows the Wahhābī sect (see area 10).

The language is Arabic.

The physical type is Mediterranean, with some Negroid and Baluchi admixture along the coast and in the towns.

13. Levant Coast Area

Political control: Syria, Lebanon, Israel, and Jordan. The population can be estimated at 11 million, of whom about 3.5 million live in western Syria, 2.5 million in Lebanon, 3 million in Israel, and 2 million in the northwestern part of Jordan.

Ethnic groups: ethnicity and religious affiliation go hand in hand in this area. The great majority of people in the Syrian part of the area, about 25 percent of the population of Lebanon (circa 650,000), all the Muslim Arabs in Israel (circa 220,000), and practically the entire population of Jordan are Sunnī Muslim Arabs. The Shī'ite Muslims are strongly represented in Lebanon (circa 600,000), with smaller groups in Syria (circa 20,000) and in Jordan (1,000 Chechen from the Caucasus). The Christians fall into numerous sects, mostly in Syria and Lebanon: some 265,000 Greek Catholic Arabs and 500,000 Greek Orthodox Arabs; some 520,000 Maronite Arabs; some 35,000 Syrian Catholic Arabs and 85,000 Syrian Orthodox Arabs; some 50,000 Armenian Catholics and 300,000 Armenian Orthodox; as well as several other Arab and non-Arab Christian denominations. The total of 1.75 million Christians represents 16 percent of the population, as against 7 percent Christians (Copts) in Egypt (see area 1).

The Alawis or Nuṣayrīs, a heterodox Muslim sect, number some 500,000, most of whom are concentrated in the Latakia province of Syria. The Druze, a semi-Muslim sect, number a total of 300,000, of whom 150,000 are in Syria, 120,000 in Lebanon, and 30,000 in Israel. In Lebanon there are also some 25,000 Sunnī Muslim Kurds, who differ from the other Sunnī Muslims of the country because of their Kurdish language (see area 16). Around the town of Hama in Syria there are some 50,000 Ismā'īlīs, a Muslim sect whose main center is in India. In the Golan area of Syria live some 35,000 Circassians, who are Sunnī Muslims and have only recently assimilated to the Arabs linguistically.

The majority of Israel's population (circa 2.7 million) are Jews, comprising ethnic groups differentiated from one another not by religion but by country of origin and cultural background. Some 40 percent of them are of European origin, some 50 percent are of Middle Eastern origin, and some 10 percent are the so-called Sephardim, who came mostly from the Balkans and Turkey and trace their descent to medieval Spain or

Portugal. The language of Israel is Hebrew, a Semitic tongue related to Arabic and Aramaic. Adding Christians and Jews, we get a non-Muslim population of close to 4.5 million, representing some 40 percent of the total of the area and making it by far the least Islamized area in the entire Middle East.

The subsistence economy has traditionally been agricultural, mostly rainfed but occasionally irrigated, with only a sprinkling of nomadic pastoralists. Cities (some of them, such as Jerusalem or Damascus, of great renown) have existed of old, either on the seashore or farther inland in the mountains. In recent decades, Jewish immigration into Israel has brought about large-scale industrialization and the introduction of a Western type of culture, which have had an impact on other parts of the area. Lebanon is the most Westernized, most urbanized, most industrialized, and most literate country in the entire Middle East apart from Israel, with an emigrant population overseas whose number is estimated to almost equal that of the Lebanese at home.

The religious and linguistic diversity of the area has been touched upon in connection with the ethnic groups. One may add that in this area a higher percentage of the people speak a European language in addition to their own than in any other part of the Middle East (primarily English in Israel and French in Lebanon).

14. *Mesopotamian Area*

Political control: Iraq and Syria. The estimated population is about 8 million, of whom about 7 million live in Iraq and 1 million in Syria.

Ethnic groups: the population is divided between Sunnī and Shī'ite Muslim Arabs. The Sunnīs are found in the Syrian part of the area and in the *līwa*s [districts] of Baghdad, Diyāla, and Dulaym in central Iraq; the Shī'ites predominate in southeastern Iraq, in its Kūt, Diwāniyya, Karbala, Hilla, Amara, Muntafiq, and Baṣra *līwa*s. There is a traditional distrust between the Shī'ites, who are the majority in Iraq, and the Sunnīs, who, although in the minority, occupy more leading positions in official and professional circles. While almost all the population is settled, nomadic traditions are strong and tribal identification stressed even in urban groups.

The subsistence economy of the area is primarily riverain irrigated agriculture, similar to but less developed and systematized than that of area 1. Date cultivation is an important branch of Iraqi agriculture; Iraq's 20 million date palms produce about three-quarters of the world's dates. The only industry of consequence is oil production, a recent development. The farmers working the alluvial plain of southern Iraq are mostly Shī'ite Arabs, who are, on the whole, less literate than the Sunnīs of the area, who constitute the farming population above Falluja and Baghdad.

A special subarea is that of the Shī'ite Marsh Arabs of Muntafiq and Amara provinces of southern Iraq, with an estimated population of 350,000. The Marsh Arabs, so called because they live in the extensive marshes of the Tigris–Euphrates river system north of Baṣra, dwell in reed huts, are farmers, herd buffalo from shallow-draft canoes, and engage in fishing.

The religious dichotomy between the Sunnīs and Shī'ites has been indicated above. The religious minorities, of whom Iraq has an ample share, live mostly outside our area, in those parts of Iraq which belong to areas 10 and 16. In our area are found the four important Shī'ite shrines of the towns of Samarra, Kadhimayn, Karbala, and Najaf, to which Shī'ites come in pilgrimage from as far away as India. During the first ten days of the month of Muḥarram, passion plays, commemorating the death of Ḥasan ibn 'Alī in the battle of Karbala in 680 A.D., are performed at these shrines and are usually accompanied by outbursts of mass hysteria.

The language of the area is Arabic, spoken in several dialects.

15. *Turkish Area*

Political control: Turkey. According to the 1965 census, the number of people inhabiting Turkey was 31,391,000. The 1970 estimate is 35,230,000. Deducting the 2.5 million Kurds who live in southeastern Turkey (see area 16), we reach the figure of an estimated 32.7 million for the population of the area in 1970. Some 150,000 Turks live on the island of Cyprus, where they constitute about one-quarter of the total population, the rest being Greeks.

Ethnic groups: the area is solidly homogeneous, with Sunnī Muslim Turks constituting the overwhelming majority. Some 375,000 Arabs, mostly farmers but still tribally organized, live in the Hatay province (the *sanjak* of Alexandretta) in the northeastern corner of the Mediterranean which was annexed by Turkey in 1939. There are some 230,000 Christians and about 40,000 Jews. Among the Muslim ethnic minorities are the Yürüks (variously estimated at 50,000 to 1 million), most of whom live in the Taurus Mountain region in southwestern Turkey; many of them are still true nomads, others seminomadic cultivators, both of whom retain some archaic cultural features. There are also some 10,000 unassimilated Tatars in the area, settled in villages west of Ankara.

The Turks themselves differ in origin and physical features from their Arab and Kurdish neighbors. They hail from Central Asia, and, while they exhibit a variety of types, most of them (some 75 percent) are brachycephalic (broad-headed). Only 30 percent have dark hair, only 5 percent have slanting Mongoloid eyes. Some have blue eyes and light coloring. In contrast to most areas of the Middle East, in which tribal identification and loyalties are still important in the thoughts and emotions of the people, such tribalism has been superseded among the Turks by a general Turkish national consciousness. This development was brought about partly during the four centuries of Turkish minority domination over large areas of the Middle East inhabited by other peoples (primarily Arabs) when Turkish cohesion was essential, and partly as a result of the modernization which followed the establishment of the Turkish Republic in 1923.

Subsistence economy is still largely agricultural, with less than one-quarter of Turkey's land area under cultivation, as against 36 percent used for pasture. About 70 percent of the people live in villages, 30 percent in cities. In the planned modern economy of Turkey, the great efforts made towards industrialization have been crowned with considerable success.

The religion of the area is Islam, to which more than 99 percent of the population subscribe. Of the Muslims, some 87 percent are Sunnīs and 13 percent (or about 4 million) Shī'ites. In the more tradition-bound rural regions, these sectarian differences are still sufficiently strong to preclude intermarriage. In the 1925–1935 decade, far-reaching reforms were carried out with a view to transforming Turkey from a Muslim into a secular state. The fez, for long a symbol of Turkdom, was outlawed; Islamic law was replaced by new civil, penal, and commercial codes; polygyny was declared illegal; and only civil marriage and divorce were recognized. Women received the right to vote, surnames were introduced, and Sunday was declared the weekly holiday. Despite all these reforms, however, Muslim religious sentiment has remained strong, especially in rural areas.

The language of the area is Turkish. Turkish is the western branch of the Turkic family of languages, other branches of which are found in areas 18 and 23 and, outside the Middle East, in adjacent regions in Soviet Central Asia.

The religious, legal, economic, and cultural reforms have put a distance between Turkey and the rest of the Middle East and brought Turkey close to the Western prototype of a political entity. Educated Turks today like to think of themselves as Europeans and insist that Turkey be counted as a European country.

16. Kurdish Area

Political control: Turkey, Iran, and Iraq. Some Kurds live in the north-eastern corner of Syria and in Soviet Transcaucasia. Their total number is estimated at 5.75 million, 2.5 million in Turkey, 1.5 million in Iran,

1.5 million in Iraq, some 250,000 in Syria, 25,000 in Lebanon, and 20,000 in Soviet Transcaucasia.

Ethnic groups: the Kurds are traditionally and culturally one people, despite their political fragmentation. Apart from the Kurds living in Lebanon and Soviet Russia, they are a compact minority concentrated in one contiguous area, known as Kurdistan [Land of the Kurds]. The ties binding them together are a common language, a common religion, and above all a strong ethnic tradition and a consciousness of being Kurds. At the same time, until their recent large-scale uprisings, which had a unifying effect on the Kurds within at least some of the countries in which they live, they lacked all centripetal tendency, were fragmented into small tribal or village groups, and perpetually fought among themselves. Nevertheless, their fierce desire for independence led to periodic uprisings whenever the states in which they lived tried to assert control over them. Thus they revolted against Turkey in 1925, 1930, and 1936; and against Iraq in 1922–1923, 1931–1932, 1944–1945, and almost continuously in the 1960's. In 1946, under Soviet sponsorship, a short-lived independent Kurdish republic was set up at Mahabad in Iranian Kurdistan. These revolts bore out the Kurds' long-standing reputation for physical prowess, temper, and violence. The rugged mountainous area of Kurdistan has favored the emergence among them of local cultural variants in language, costume, and custom, in addition to the major differences which separate them from their neighbors.

Inside the Kurdish area there are (or, rather, were) two historically established, ancient, indigenous minorities: the Assyrians, or Nestorian Christians, around Lake Rezaiye (Lake Urmia), numbering some 20,000; and the Kurdish Jews, scattered among the Kurdish villagers. They spoke neo-Aramaic dialects and were treated by the Kurds as a second-class, low-ranking people. After the creation of an independent Israel in 1948, all Kurdish Jews moved to that country. Most of the Nestorians still live in Kurdistan.[4] On the borders of the Kurdish area are transitional regions inhabited by both Kurds and Turks (in Turkey), Kurds and Azerbaijanis or Kurds and Persians (in Iran), and Kurds and Arabs (in Iraq and Syria).

Subsistence economy is nomadic or agricultural or a combination of the two. Many Kurds are still pastoral mountaineers, either practicing transhumance or living in various stages of seminomadism or sedentarization in villages. A typical Kurdish tribe or village is largely self-sufficient as well as independent, with a headman (called *aga* or *agha*). In recent decades several localities have grown into sizable towns.

The religion of the Kurds is Sunnī Islam, an additional factor separating them from the Shī'ite Iranians.

[4] The total number of Nestorians (Assyrians) can be estimated at 40,000, of whom 20,000 live in Kurdistan and 20,000 in villages in Syria along the Nahr al-Kabbur in the northeast and on the western slopes of the Anti-Lebanon mountains.

The language is Kurdish, an Iranian tongue not intelligible to Persian speakers and, of course, differing entirely from Turkish and Arabic. Kurdish itself is, however, spoken in three very different dialects.

17. Azerbaijani Area

Political control: Soviet Russia in the north, Iran in the south. The northern part forms the Azerbaijan S.S.R.; the southern, the East Azerbaijan province of Iran, which in 1945–1946 had a brief period of autonomy under Soviet sponsorship. (The Iranian province of West Azerbaijan belongs to area 16.) The population of the area is estimated at 6.83 million, of whom about 4.23 million are in the north and 2.6 million in the south.

Ethnic groups: the majority of the population (three-fifths in Russian Azerbaijan and a higher proportion in the Iranian part) consist of Muslim Azerbaijanis of Iranian origin who, since the eleventh century, have spoken a Turkic tongue called Azeri. They are mostly settled farmers and herders and in physical type are larger and heavier than either the Persians or the Arabs. Important minorities are the Russians in the north, the Kurds in the south, and the Armenians in both areas. The Russians in the Azerbaijan S.S.R. number 16 percent of the total population and are employed primarily in modern industries (of which oil production is the most important) and administration. The Armenians account for 12 percent (or 500,000) in Russian Azerbaijan and number about 110,000 in the south and in other parts of Iran.[5]

An important element in the area is represented by the 200,000 Shāhsavan [king's guards], half of whom occupy about a hundred villages north of Menab and near Khoy on the borders between East and West Azerbaijan, while the other half are seminomadic, practice transhumance, and spend the summer in the lower reaches of the Savalan Mountains (some eighty miles east of Tabriz) and the winter in the Moghan (Mūqān) steppe. The yurt-like dwellings used by the latter testify to their Central Asian extraction. To the north of them, on the Russian side of the Moghan steppe, live other seminomadic tribes.

The subsistence economy of the area, apart from that of the few nomadic tribes mentioned and the modern industries introduced by Russia in the north, is based primarily on dry-farming. The members of the minority groups are more frequently craftsmen and traders.

---

[5] One and a half million Armenians live in the Armenian S.S.R., the western neighbor of the Azerbaijan S.S.R., where they constitute 88 percent of the population (the remaining 12 percent being Azerbaijanis, Russians, and Kurds). Another 500,000 Armenians live in the Georgian S.S.R. and 190,000 in Iran. Smaller groups of Armenians live in Turkey, Iraq, Syria, Lebanon, and Israel, as well as in Europe and North America. The total number of Armenians can thus be estimated at 2.5 million.

The religion of the Azerbaijani majority in both the Russian and the Iranian parts is Shīʿite Islam.

Azeri, the language spoken by the Azerbaijanis, is a Turkic tongue which differs considerably from the Turkish spoken in area 15 and which shows Persian influences. In the Soviet north it is written in the Cyrillic alphabet, while in the Iranian south Arabic script is used. Azeri has been the vehicle of an important literary movement which began in the nineteenth century, and it has been the medium for dramatic works and numerous periodicals in the twentieth century.

18. West Iranian Tribal Area

Political control: Iran. The area covers most of the provinces of Kermanshahan, Khuzistan, and Fars, and the governorates of Ilam, Luristan, Chahār Mahal-Bakhtiyārī, and Kukilua-Boyar Ahmadi, whose combined population according to the 1966 Iranian census was 4.6 million. If we exclude the eastern fringes of Luristan, Chahār Mahal-Bakhtiyārī, and Fars (which belong to area 19), as well as the major cities of Isfahan and Shiraz with their environs (which lie just east of our area), we get an estimated population of 3.5 million for the area. It is even more difficult to estimate the number of tribal nomads. In the census mentioned, 642,000 is given as the total nomadic population of Iran. Students of Iran, however, estimate the nomadic population of this area alone at more than 2 million.

Ethnic groups: while the area comprises a large settled Persian population living in numerous villages, it is one of the few areas in the Middle East in which the nomadic population constitutes more than half the total. The most important tribes are (from northwest to southeast) the Shīʿite Lūr (estimated at 300,000); the Bakhtiyārī (nearly 400,000), consisting of two subgroups, the Haft-Lang and the Chahār-Lang; the Kuh Galu (150,000) and the Mamassani (55,000), who speak various Persian dialects; the Turkic-speaking Sunnī Qashqai (625,000); and the Khamseh (525,000), who fall into several (originally five, hence the name) tribal groups, of which the Bāṣirī are Persian-speaking, the Jebbāra and the Shaybānī speak Arabic, and the Aynalū, the Bahārlū, and the Nafar are Turkish-speaking. Along the seashore, all the way from the Iraqi border to Pakistan (except for a part of the Persian Gulf coast held by the Qashqai), are Arab tribes, either sedentary or nomadic, including the two largest, the Āl Kathīr and the Benī Lām. These tribes are Shīʿite, except for the Benī Lām, which is Sunnī. Finally, on the easternmost part of the coast are seaside villages inhabited by Arab seamen.

The subsistence economy of the tribes is based on sheep and goats (with few other animals), whose pasturing requires transhumance. The tribes spend the summer months in the mountains; in the fall they move their flocks and herds down to the warmer low-lying regions where they spend the winter; in spring they return to the mountains. Some, like the Lūr, have permanent villages in both places. Others move with their black hair tents. The migration pattern of the Qashqai, who specialize in horse breeding, takes them a distance of 350 miles each way, from the coast of the Persian Gulf to points deep inland south and north. Their tribal headquarters is in Shiraz, where the chiefs occupy a palace. The Bakhtiyārī khāns [chieftains] also have their residences in town, and several years ago they began to send their sons to Europe for an academic education. The nontribal sectors of the population generally practice agriculture in the villages and craftsmanship and commerce in the towns.

The religious and linguistic variety of the tribes has been touched upon above. The nontribal sectors are Shī'ite Muslims who speak Persian (see area 19).

Special features characterizing the tribes include the greater freedom accorded to women. The Bakhtiyārī women, for instance, wear no veil and walk about freely within the tribal area. During the khān's absence, his wife substitutes for him in adjudicating cases. Divorce is almost unknown. The women weave the tent cloths and the well-known *kilīm* rugs, while the men make their characteristic footgear, the *gīwa*. Healing through incantation is practiced by tribal herb doctors. The nontribal population belongs culturally to area 19.

19. *Persian Area*

Political control: Iran, Afghanistan, and Soviet Russia. The population can be estimated at 22.5 million, of whom 18.5 million live in Iran, 2.5 million in Afghanistan, and 1.5 million in the Tajik (Tadzhik) S.S.R. Several thousand live in adjacent regions of China.

Ethnic groups: the solid majority consists of Shī'ite Iranians in Iran who speak Persian (Fārsī) and closely related Tajiks in western and northeastern Afghanistan (where they are also known as Pārsiwān) and in the adjacent Tajik S.S.R. Other Tajiks occupy some of the most fertile agricultural sections in the Ghazni and Kabul regions of eastern Afghanistan. The Persians of Iran are generally settled urbanites and villagers. Among the latter, the primary form of cultivation is dry-farming, in which about 80 percent of the people are engaged. Along the southern shores of the Caspian Sea live the Gilanis and the Mazenderanis, rural people engaged in farming and fishing, who differ from the other Persians in language, costume, and custom. Scattered all over the Iranian part of the area are found smaller religio-ethnic minorities, such as the 35,000 Zoroastrians (Parsis) adhering to the old pre-Islamic religion of their ancestors; the 190,000 Christian Armenians (see area 17); the 65,000 Jews; the 35,000

Catholics; the 25,000 Protestants; and the 500,000 or more Bahá'ís, whose
religion is not recognized by the government. The Tajiks of Afghanistan
are usually considered as comprising four geographically differentiated
groups. Most of them are either sedentary cultivators or else urban
dwellers (e.g. in Kabul) engaged in commerce, handicrafts, or administrative occupations.

The subsistence economy of the area has been touched upon already.

The religion of the great majority in the area is Shī'ite Islam of the
so-called Twelver School, which venerates twelve *imām*s [charismatic
religious leaders]. The first of these was 'Alī, the son-in-law and cousin
of Muḥammad, while the remaining eleven were his descendants. The
twelfth and last *imām*, it is believed, did not die but went into hiding and
will return as the *mahdī* [guided one]. Shī'ite Islam, as followed in Iran,
encourages *taqiyya* [dissimulation] as a means of self-protection in the
face of enemies. The annual performance of passion plays is an important
feature of popular religion, eliciting the same emotional response as in
area 14. Shī'ite Islam permits temporary or term marriages (*mut'a*). Pilgrimage to the holy places of Shī'ite Islam in Iraq (see area 14) and in
Meshhed, capital of the Khorasan province of northeastern Iran, generally
takes the place of the Sunnī *ḥajj* [pilgrimage] to Mecca and Medina (area
10). Despite the prohibition by the *sharī'a*, the traditional Muslim religious
law, wine is enjoyed by the Shī'ites, especially by the nomadic tribes
among them, and the pictorial representation of human beings has been
practiced for centuries. Ṣūfī dervishes, a traditional feature of Iranian
Islam, have in recent times declined in both numbers and influence. The
Tajiks are almost entirely Sunnīs.

Language: Persian (Fārsī), spoken in various dialects, is the language
of the Iranian part of the area. The Gilani and Mazenderani local dialects
spoken on the southern shores of the Caspian Sea are unintelligible to
outsiders. Among the Tajiks, various Darī dialects are spoken. Persian is
considered an extremely beautiful language (by Persian speakers), and
listening to the recitals of classical Persian epic and lyric poetry is held
to be the noblest pleasure.

Among additional special features of the area are the love of physical
exercise (*zūrkhāne*s [houses of strength], the traditional athletic clubs,
flourish) and of hot baths. Both seem to be survivals from pre-Islamic
times. In the towns, also, nineteenth-century Russian influences are dis-
cernible, e.g. in the love of tea and the use of Russian-type samovars.

This area has a highly developed traditional urban civilization of great
refinement in the visual, literary, and musical arts, including architecture,
miniature painting, calligraphy, ceramics, embroidery, silverwork, brass-
work, rugs, garden arrangement, poetry, story-telling, instrumental music,
etc. The ancient cities, dispersed all over the area, have been important
cultural centers for centuries.

20. *Mongol Area*

Political control: Afghanistan. The population is estimated at 1.5 to 2 million.

Ethnic groups: the area is inhabited by numerous tribes, all of which exhibit a more or less pronounced Mongoloid appearance or a mixture of Mongoloid and Iranian features. In central Afghanistan west of Kabul is the Hazārajāt region, inhabited by the Hazāra Mongols (also known as Barbarīs), who claim descent from the armies of Genghis Khan (thirteenth century). Their number is estimated at 1 million. They are Shī'ites and speak a Darī dialect of Persian, closely related to the Darī spoken by the Tajiks (see area 19) but containing Persian and Mongolian words. The Hazāra are mostly settled people who live in numerous, occasionally fortified, villages and who engage in intensive irrigated agriculture in the valleys and some dry-farming in the uplands, as well as animal husbandry and some hunting. Considerable numbers of them live in the urban centers of Afghanistan, while others, in the northern plains, are seminomadic and use the Central Asian yurt tents in summer. The Hazāra comprise a number of tribes differentiated by dialect and cultural variants, but their tribal cohesion is not strong and some intermarriage with the Tajiks and the Pashtuns (area 21) occurs.

To the west of Hazārajāt, on both banks of the Harī Rūd river, live the seminomadic Chahār Aymaq ["four tribes"], who are of Turko-Mongol origin and have a rather Mongoloid appearance. Their number is estimated at between 300,000 and 900,000. They are Sunnī Muslims but, like the Hazāra (with whom they are closely linked), speak Darī dialects. They comprise the four basic groups of (1) Jamshīdī (some of whom practice dry-farming) northeast of Herat; (2) Fīrūz-Kūhī, seminomadic farmers and cattle raisers around the upper reaches of the Murghab river (Badghis and Ghor provinces); (3) Taymannī, north and south of the Harī Rūd and its tributaries, divided into a northern group, resembling the other Chahār Aymaq and engaging in irrigated agriculture, and a southern group, living in black hair tents and having affinities with the Pashtun nomads (see area 21) farther south; and (4) Hazāra Aymaq, engaged in seminomadism and agriculture, vigorously rejecting any suggestion of a connection between them and the Shī'ite Hazāra discussed above. Apart from the southern Taymannī, the rest of the Chahār Aymaq seminomads live in yurts in the summer and permanent villages of flat or dome-roofed houses in the winter. They herd sheep, goats, and cattle. Some Chahār Aymaq groups, notably the Taymūrī, live in Iran to the west of the Afghan border.

The customary beverage of the area is tea.

21. Pashtun Area

Political control: Afghanistan and Pakistan. The population can be estimated at 11 million, of whom 8 million live in Afghanistan and 3 million in Pakistan.

Ethnic groups: the dominant ethnic group is that of the Pashtun, called "Pakhtun" in the northeast, while in Pakistan the Indian form "Pathan" is used. In Afghanistan, where the term "Afghan" denotes any citizen of the country, the Pashtun constitute about half the total population (for the rest see areas 19 and 20). The Pashtun fall into numerous groups, all of which maintain tribal traditions, albeit to varying degrees. Some 2 to 2.5 million of them are nomadic or seminomadic. The most powerful tribal group is that of the Durrānī (formerly called Abdālī), who number more than 2 million and are divided into two groups, one of which included the royal tribe of the Sadōzay. The Durrānī occupy the southwestern part of Afghanistan as far south as the uninhabited desert which separates this area from area 22. More numerous than the Durrānī but second to them in importance are their long-time rivals, the Ghilzay or Ghalzay, about 2.5 to 3 million strong, also comprising two groups. They occupy the southeastern part of Afghanistan, and their annual migrations took them across the Pakistani frontier until 1961, when it was closed by the Pakistani government. Several tribes live on both sides of the frontier, e.g. the Wazīr in the mountains between the Kuram and Gumal rivers, the Mahmand north of the Kabul river, and the Afridī around the famous Khyber Pass and the adjoining regions to the north of Wazīristan. Numerous other Pashtun tribes inhabit the barren and isolated hill country of the Northwest Frontier region of Pakistan, where they constitute the overwhelming majority and used to be termed "problem tribes" or even "criminal tribes" because the British government of India was unable to control them.

Most Pashtun value their tribal traditions highly; they have a fierce spirit of independence and a strict code of honor similar to that of the Bedouins of area 10. Among their traditions is the claim to descent from King David (some regard themselves as the Lost Tribes of Israel) or from the soldiers of Alexander the Great. Many of them have fair skin and blue or gray eyes. In the north and west of the Pakistani part of the area, the Pashtun are all nomadic; in the southeast, around and to the south of Peshawar, they are settled. However, whether they are nomadic or settled in villages and towns, an extremely complex tribal structure and a tribal way of life remain the most outstanding Pashtun characteristics.

The religion of the entire area is solidly Sunnī Muslim of the Ḥanafī School. The conversion of the tribes of Kāfiristān (renamed Nūristān) in northeastern Afghanistan from an ancient polytheism of the Indian type to Islam took place only in the late nineteenth century. To this day, the rugged and inaccessible mountainous nature of the area enables several unorthodox groups to maintain themselves in isolated localities.

The language spoken by the Pashtun is Pashto, an Iranian tongue which comprises two major dialects: a southwestern or Qandahārī and a northeastern or Peshawari. The Kabul and Ghazni regions are mainly Darī-speaking due to the presence of large numbers of Tajiks. Pashto is written in a modified Arabic script.

22. Baluchi–Brahui Area

Political control: Iran and Pakistan. The population is estimated at 1.3 million, of whom about 500,000 Baluchis live in the Iranian, 330,000 in the Pakistani, and 70,000 in the Afghanistani part of the area. Some 366,000 Brahuis live in Pakistan, and a few thousand live in Iran.

Ethnic groups: the Baluchis, who are the dominant majority of the area, gave their name to the southeastern part of Iran and the adjacent southwestern part of Pakistan; both are called Baluchistan [land of the Baluch]. We include in the area the Sistan province of Iran, the northern neighbor of Iranian Baluchistan, because it is inhabited by a strong Baluchi element. Outside this area, Baluchis live in Sind and Punjab to the east and near Merw in the Turkmen S.S.R., where they are nomads. The Baluchis are mainly nomadic and seminomadic peoples organized into tribes and eking out a living in the arid and mountainous area they inhabit. Some of them have become settled farmers and have given up the tribal social system. They are among the poorest and least advanced peoples of both Iran and Pakistan. They comprise roughly sixty-four tribes in Iran alone and about a dozen in Pakistan.

The Brahuis form a large island in Pakistani Baluchistan extending from Quetta in the north to Las Bela in the south. They are primarily sedentary farmers who used to be subject to the Baluchis.

Both the Baluchis and the Brahuis are Sunnī Muslims.

The language spoken by the Baluchis is an Iranian tongue, closer to Pashto than to Persian, which falls into two dialects, one spoken to the west and one to the east of the Brahui region. The language of the Brahuis is Dravidic, related to the languages of southern India.

In addition to these two major groups, the area is inhabited by smaller ethnic groups. Among these can be mentioned the Negroid people in the coastal zone of Iranian Baluchistan, the Jāts, and other Indian minorities farther to the east.

23. Turkmen–Uzbek Area

Political control: the Turkmen S.S.R., the Uzbek S.S.R., Iran, and Afghanistan. The population can be estimated at 12 million.

Ethnic groups: the predominant ethnic elements are the Turkic-speaking Sunnī Muslim Turkmen and Uzbek tribes, both of which are of Central Asian origin. Most of the Turkmen and Uzbeks live within the boundaries of the Soviet Union, but smaller contingents are found south of the Soviet frontier, in the northern parts of Iran and Afghanistan. They are predominantly of Mongoloid physical type. In the Afghanistani part of the area, the patchwork-like pattern of ethnic configuration is very pronounced, with small regions inhabited by alternating groups of Turkmen, Uzbeks, Pashtun, Tajiks, and Hazāra.

The Turkmen number about 1 million in the Turkmen S.S.R., 400,000 in Afghanistan, and 100,000 in Iran to the east of the southeastern corner of the Caspian Sea. Since some 80 percent of the land area of the Turkmen S.S.R. is taken up by the uninhabited Kara Kum desert, most of the Soviet Turkmen live near the Iranian and Afghan frontiers, concentrated in oases along the foot of the southern mountains. Many of the Turkmen are still nomadic, organized into tribes, and possess large herds of sheep, goats, horses, and camels. In all parts of their territory they have maintained much of their separate identity and tribal traditions. Under Soviet rule the Turkmen have been exposed to pressure to sedentarize, and many have become farmers.

The Uzbeks number about 6 million in the Uzbek S.S.R., which extends to the northeast from the Amu Darya (Oxus) river, from the Aral Sea to the Afghan frontier. They constitute three-quarters of the total population of their republic. Along the northern border of Afghanistan live another 1 million Uzbeks. The Uzbeks tended, more than the Turkmen, to give up their tribal traditions, to become settled villagers and townspeople, and to intermarry with outsiders, notably their eastern neighbors, the Tajiks (see area 19).

As to subsistence economy, the entire area is primarily a desert, steppe, and oasis region, which, however, can be partly irrigated from the waters of the ample rivers flowing through it. Consequently, many of the formerly nomadic inhabitants could be, and actually were, induced to turn to agriculture and to take up at least a seminomadic existence, living in permanent villages in the winter and in their traditional yurts in the summer. Among the animals herded are the famous Karakul sheep. In Afghanistan, most Uzbeks are settled in villages and towns and engage in such crafts as pottery, weaving, carpentry, and copper and ironwork, as well as in commerce and farming.

This area includes the old Muslim feudal city-states of Khiwa, Bukhara, Kokand, and the famous Samarkand, the center of Tamerlane's empire.

The religion of the area is Sunnī Islam. The languages spoken are Turkic dialects.

The culture of this area is differentiated from that of area 19 by the persistence of old features of Islam, by the retention of elements of old shamanistic religion, and by other features of Central Asian origin.

To the east of the Uzbeks live the Kirghiz, another Mongoloid, Sunnī Muslim people speaking a Turkic dialect. Some 15,000 of them live in the eastern panhandle of Afghanistan, the Wakhan mountain region, where they move in seasonal migration back and forth across the Soviet and Chinese frontiers. In the Soviet Union the Kirghiz number close to 1 million.

REFERENCES

BACON, ELIZABETH
  1946   A preliminary attempt to determine the culture areas of Asia. *Southwestern Journal of Anthropology* 2: 117–132.
  1954   Types of pastoral nomadism in central and southwest Asia. *Southwestern Journal of Anthropology* 10: 44–68.
COON, CARLETON S.
  1965   *Caravan: the story of the Middle East* (revised edition). New York: Holt, Rinehart and Winston.
DE PRÉVILLE, LOUIS ARMAND BARBIER
  1894   *Les sociétés africaines: leur origine, leur évolution, leur avenir.* Paris: Firmin-Didot.
DOWD, JEROME
  1907   *The Negro races,* volume one. New York: Macmillan.
FISHER, SYDNEY NETTLETON
  1968   *The Middle East: a history* (second edition). New York: Knopf.
GREENBERG, JOSEPH H.
  1955   *Studies in African linguistic classification.* New Haven: Compass.
HAMBLY, WILFRID D.
  1937   *Source book for African anthropology.* Field Museum of Natural History, Anthropological Series 26. Chicago.
HERSKOVITS, MELVILLE J.
  1924   A preliminary consideration of the culture areas of Africa. *American Anthropologist* 26: 50–63.
  1930   The culture areas of Africa. *Africa* 3: 59–77.
  1948   *Man and his works.* New York: Knopf.
MURDOCK, GEORGE P.
  1959   *Africa: its peoples and their culture history.* New York: McGraw-Hill.
  1967   *Ethnographic atlas.* Pittsburgh: University of Pittsburgh Press.
PATAI, RAPHAEL
  1951   Nomadism: Middle Eastern and Central Asian. *Southwestern Journal of Anthropology* 7: 401–414.
  1952   The Middle East as a culture area. *Middle East Journal* 6: 1–21.
  1962   *Golden river to golden road: society, culture and change in the Middle East.* Philadelphia: University of Pennsylvania Press.

RIVLIN, BENJAMIN, JOSEPH S. SZYLIOWICZ, *editors*
1965   *The contemporary Middle East.* New York: Random House.
THURNWALD, RICHARD
1929   Social systems of Africa. *Africa* 2: 221–243, 352–378.
VAN NIEUWENHUIJZE, C. A. O.
1971   *Sociology of the Middle East.* Leiden: Brill.
WISSLER, CLARK
1922   *The American Indian: an introduction to the anthropology of the New World.* New York: Oxford University Press.

The Ecology and Politics of Nomadic Pastoralists in the Middle East

EMANUEL MARX

Only in recent years have the nomad tribes of the Middle East become the subject of intensive anthropological and sociological research. Today, with the help of this work, it is possible to obtain a clearer picture of the ecological conditions under which these societies exist, their social organization, and their relationships with the outside world.

In attempting to formulate some generalizations regarding the factors which influence the size of territorial and political units and the concentrations of power in them, it will become clear that the commonly accepted sociological picture of the tribe as a political organization is incomplete and that these societies are in fact much more complex than was thought. Alongside the tribe – which fulfills important functions in the society – exist other organizational forms which, although perhaps not as prominent, are nevertheless very important.

The travelers, missionaries, and administrators of the nineteenth and twentieth centuries wrote profusely about the Bedouin. Most of this literature is tinged with romanticism and enlarges on the personal qualities of the male Bedouin. He is described as an individualist; a lover of freedom who struggles heroically with nature's forces; a lover of adventure and war who behaves chivalrously to the defeated, who keeps his word and fulfills the obligations of hospitality even unto his last crust of bread. These characteristics are assumed to be found in the "true" Bedouin – the camel breeder belonging to strong aristocratic clans, who, in his wanderings, penetrates the heart of the desert. Tribes which breed sheep and goats are regarded as morally and physically inferior, and those who

An earlier paper on this subject, "The political organization of nomadic animal breeders in the Middle East" (in press), was prepared for a colloquium on Arab society organized by the van Leer Jerusalem Foundation in 1971. I am grateful to Dr. S. Deshen, Dr. Y. E. Eilam, Dr. E. Eilat (Epstein), Professor E. L. Peters, Dr. M. Sharon and Dr. R. P. Werbner for their helpful comments.

cultivate the soil, beneath even them.[1] Such classics as the works of Niebuhr (1799), Burckhardt (1830), Palgrave (1868), Doughty (1937), Jaussen (1908), Musil (1928), and Lawrence (1935) influenced generations of readers and also left their mark on scholarly works dealing with the nomads of the Middle East.[2]

The portrait drawn in these descriptions is, of course, not entirely imaginary but rather represents the Bedouin as he sees himself. Some of the authors did have long and continuous contact with the Bedouin but did not examine the working of their society and were content with reporting what the Bedouin told them about it. Others attempted to describe the Bedouin but did not show interest in depicting the gray reality; they generally preferred to present the more exotic aspects of nomad life in order to amuse their readers. Even the most acute observers emphasized those aspects of society which the Bedouin themselves regard as the most important. They largely relied on Bedouin informants, whose statements were often normative and culture bound. The few scholars who lived with the Bedouin for longer periods also write about the other aspects of nomad life, but wherever actual behavior contradicted the accepted norm, they regarded such behavior as exceptional.[3]

This duality is apparent in the works of both Doughty and Musil – two travellers who knew the Bedouin better than others. For example, the picture painted in Musil's book, *The manners and customs of the Rwala Bedouins*, is very different from the one reflected in his journals, published in several volumes, among which *Arabia deserta* is probably the most interesting. Although both books deal with the same tribal group, the reader gets the impression that they concern two different peoples. The difference between them is that the former is based on what Musil considered to be proper methods of ethnographic research and the second on unedited observations of the reality. In his travelogue, Musil describes how he collected the material for his book on Bedouin manners and customs:

... from sunrise until four o'clock in the afternoon I sat in my round tent. In the morning Mhammad usually brought me some informant, with whom I closeted myself. Often I found it impossible to question him, for he would not answer me until he had told me all that was in his mind ... he would ... gaze longingly at the exit of my tent. How gladly would he have disappeared through that exit to avoid the torment of my questions! Only when he was explaining something to his own liking would he show more animation [1917:17].

Musil was convinced that the personal concerns of the Bedouin were not a part of the basic system of customs and beliefs which – in his opinion – guide the Bedouin's way of life.

---

[1] H. R. P. Dickson (1951: 108–113) naively describes this system of ranking.

[2] For example, the account of the Bedouin in C. D. Forde (1934: Chapter 15) is based mainly on Musil's material.

[3] This approach was not confined to the literature on the Middle East. Compare M. Gluckman (1963: 246–247) on the early work on African societies.

There is no hint of such methods of research in *The manners and customs of the Rwala Bedouins*; there Bedouin ideology is presented as a living reality and a scientific truth. The result of such an approach can already be seen in the opening sentence of the book (1928: xiii) in which the author asserts that "The Rwala are recognized by all their neighbours as being the only true Bedouin tribe of northern Arabia." Not many Bedouin would agree with such a partial statement and Kennett is right in saying that "Although various tribes vie with one another in their claims to be the oldest, and so on, yet as a rule one tribe will recognise the just claims of another to be 'out of the top drawer'" (1925: 23).

The common belief that our knowledge about the Bedouin is extensive and that we understand their society better than other sectors of the population of the Middle East is unfounded.[4] We know less about Bedouin society than about the Arab rural population. The rich raw material to be found in the books of Doughty, Epstein, Jaussen, Musil, and others still has not been properly exploited,[5] in spite of the efforts made by various writers to marshall the information available on Bedouin society in various fields: Oppenheim (1939–1968) on the history of the tribes; Gräf (1952) on law; Henninger (1943) on the family; Sweet (1965) on ecology; Feilberg (1944) on the tent. Most of these authors give systematic accounts of the situation in the particular field which each of them chose to examine but, to my mind, the information does not yield many striking new theories. Several attempts were also made to analyze the characteristic traits of Bedouin society, e.g. by Bacon (1958), Chelhod (1971), Montagne (1947), Patai (1969), and Coon (1951). These are thorough and important works, and some of them show brilliant insights. However, they also hold a hidden danger: as they use the existing literature and are not based on independent investigations, they continue and even reinforce the distorted traditional image of Bedouin society and thus restrain the "well-read" researcher from making new departures. I myself have experienced this. Before entering this field of research I had definite ideas about Bedouin society, and even in the face of contrary evidence I found it hard to free myself of them. This is probably true of other students. In all the works on Middle Eastern nomad societies, one will find that the scholar consciously struggles with the traditional image of Bedouin society, and in most of them traces of the nomad's viewpoint still remain. But in recent years a more factual, if less impressive, picture of these nomad societies has begun to emerge. Several new monographs have appeared which, perhaps, do not yet permit us to redraw the picture of the Middle Eastern nomad, but at least permit us to attempt a tentative reanalysis.

[4] This opinion is also expressed by J. Gulick (1969: 3).
[5] An exception is a paper by H. Rosenfeld (1965), which is based to a great extent on Musil's material. It is significant that Rosenfeld uses Musil's travelogue extensively but refers only rarely to the book on manners and customs.

How does this recent work differ from that of earlier writers? It can be seen immediately that most of it does not deal with the Bedouin in the narrow traditional sense of the word. Thus it does not examine a tribe of nomadic camel breeders. I presume that the scholars did not reach these tribes, both because of the physical difficulties involved in such an operation and because the number of such Bedouin has dropped considerably in recent times. The new work also differs in that it is written by trained anthropologists, it is based on other types of data, and it pays attention to subjects not discussed extensively in previous work. The new type of researchers lived for comparatively long periods in their chosen societies. They did not collect their material at random but in a systematic and concentrated manner. For the most part they limited themselves to examining a well-defined region and a limited number of people. Unlike their predecessors, they relied less on information given by informants from the society under investigation and more on personal observation; they thus depended less on norms and *post facto* accounts and more on behavioral data. They also attached importance to the collection of standardized data covering the universe of research. I refer to the work of Asad, Barth, Cunnison, Marx, and Peters, all of which appeared during the decade 1960–1970. The concern with a set of common problems is evident in all these monographs and papers, and as a result they give a new impetus to the thinking on several subjects in anthropological theory.

Two subjects to which these researchers have given a great deal of attention are the ecological influences on the life of the nomads, and the interrelationships between the nomads and the settled population. Both these subjects are intimately related and cannot be separated even for the purpose of an analytical exercise. Society must be looked at as a whole whose parts are interlinked, and this viewpoint is reflected in the analysis, where seemingly irrelevant subjects will intrude and the same ground will be covered repeatedly. Even if we are aware that a society must be described as a closed system, we have no choice but to start the analysis at some point and from there lead on to others until eventually a composite picture emerges. This serves as a firm foundation for the analysis of particular aspects of the society.

According to the *Encyclopaedia of Islam*, "Bedouin are 'pastoral nomads' of Arabian blood, speech and culture [who] are found in the Arabian Peninsula proper and in parts of Iran, Soviet Turkestan, North Africa and the Sudan" (Coon 1960). Since my interest is not in questions of language or origin but in ecological problems, I shall depart from the customary definition and confine myself to one trait: pastoral nomadism. I shall discuss Middle Eastern tribes who exploit dry (and other) regions for animal breeding. Thus I shall not deal with Bedouin who do not engage in breeding animals, as for example some of the tribes of southern Sinai, nor with Bedouin who have ceased wandering, such as the Iraqi

Shabana (Fernea 1970). The analysis does relate to tribes who are not regarded as Bedouin according to the accepted meaning. I shall discuss not only Arab-speaking tribes, but also the Persian-speaking Basseri of the district of Fars in Iran; not only those that raise camels, sheep, and goats but also the Sudanese Baggara, who are Arab-speaking cattle breeders. The analysis can also be applied to other nomad tribes which will not be explicitly discussed, such as the Nuer of South Sudan or the Turkana of Kenya. In order to avoid confusion, I shall henceforth use the concept pastoral nomads, and not Bedouin.

It should be noted that the breeding of animals is not always the sole or even main occupation of the nomads. Salzman is right in arguing that "the economies of most peoples are not based upon a single resource but rather upon multiple resources: this is just as true of so-called pastoral nomads" (1971: 186). These "pastoralists," however, take the raising of animals very seriously and often regard it as the principal economic activity and as the mainstay of their culture, and, incidentally, sometimes transmit this belief to the unsuspecting anthropologist. Pastoralism also affects the territorial and political organizations and the patterns of movement of those who engage in it, even where it is not the major source of income.

Throughout the discussion I shall touch upon the differences between various nomad societies. I see no point in giving a detailed catalogue of such differences, except as an indicator of the range of a social trait. Differences must be studied in their wider context, and meaningful comparisons can be made only where there are broad underlying similarities between societies. Although the anthropologist cannot create laboratory conditions, he has a tested method for isolating variables: he compares several descriptions or case studies of similar social phenomena in roughly comparable social contexts. Since reality is infinitely varied, the anthropologist expects to find differences between similar cases and will then attempt to isolate the variables which may account for the differences. If he arrives at the conclusion that the difference must be ascribed to certain factors, he then tries to unravel their complexities and to sharpen the analysis by extending his series of cases.

In this manner, an anthropologist may sometimes study processes which extend over many years, although his fieldwork usually only continues for a year or two. By arranging a series of synchronic descriptions in logical order, he may gain insight into the nature of continuing processes. I intend to apply this method to the study of pastoral nomads.

THE TERRITORIAL ORGANIZATION

There is considerable ecological variety in the areas frequented by pastoral nomads. Some regions have fertile soil and an abundant supply of water, and, if these resources were exploited more intensively than for grazing, they could adequately support a densely settled population. Other regions are blessed with fertile soil but suffer from a serious limitation: a shortage of perennial water sources. Consequently they can support only a small settled population. In the absence of sophisticated technology, the water supply cannot be increased; and part of the population is therefore forced to wander in small groups over the area in order to draw water when and where it is available.

One of the characteristics of the nomad's habitat is the rather sharp division of the year into rainy and dry seasons. In the rainy season the abundant supply of water often allows some of the nomads to farm the land and to stay for several months on one site, perhaps even to construct permanent dwellings (like the wealthier members of nomadic tribes in southern Sinai), while others continue to move. This specialization may temporarily separate the members of a family, as among the Kababish; the extreme example is probably that of the Turkana of East Africa, whose households are for most of the year divided between two homesteads, one for the cattle and the other for the camels and goats (Gulliver 1955). Or it may temporarily separate the households of a group, some of whom may opt for staying on their farmland and hand over their herds to the care of households who decide to move with their animals, or to hired herdsmen, as among Bedouin of the Negev. In the dry season all these people revert to the nomadic way of life. Nomadic pastoralism is thus mainly an adaptation of people with an undeveloped technology to the scarcity of water in the dry season. People utilize water wherever it may be found. When the reserves are exhausted in one place they move to another site, usually in a fairly regular annual cycle.

Most of these areas do not lack pasture during ordinary years. As the population grows and the herds increase – and sometimes this process is accompanied by an expansion of the settled population, which in itself causes a further decrease in pasture areas – the pasture also becomes a scarce commodity. Such changes are liable to end the nomadic way of life, since the continuous coordination of two scarce factors of production, neither of which has a substitute, is beyond the capability of the nomad. Even in regions which usually supply all the nomad's needs, such situations may occasionally arise and cause a crisis. Musil describes such a situation which caused the Rwala great consternation: "Hmār avowed that he had no memory of any such egregiously unfavorable season in thirty years. Where pasturage was abundant, water was absent, and where there was water, there was no pasturage" (1927: 110).[6]

Shortage of water is due to inadequate rainfall and the many fluctua-

---

[6] A romanticized account of such a crisis can be found in C. R. Raswan (1936: 85ff.). Spurred on by the sight of their starving camels, the Rwala Bedouin invaded the territory of a neighboring tribal group, and in the resulting fighting numerous lives were lost.

tions therein. The pastoral nomad needs a minimal amount of rain even in areas of winter pasture and certainly in summer grazing grounds. The claim that he lives in almost arid zones ignores the basic fact that the whole area of his wanderings – and not only the region considered to be his undisputed tribal territory – must be regarded as one unit of living space. The data assembled in Table 1, from various monographs, indicate

Table 1. Average annual rainfall in nomad regions (in millimeters)

Tribe/Region	Country	Rainfall on	
		dry season pastures	rainy season pastures
Cyrenaica	Libya	400	50–100
Kababish	Sudan	200+	100
Ẕullām	Israel	200–400	100–200
Basseri	Iran	250	250
Baggara	Sudan	900	450

Sources:
Cyrenaica: E. E. Evans-Pritchard, *The Sanusi of Cyrenaica* (1949: 30–32).
Kababish: T. Asad, *The Kababish Arabs* (1970: 13).
Ẕullām: E. Marx, *Bedouin of the Negev* (1967: 20–21).
Basseri: F. Barth, *Nomads of South Persia* (1961: 3).
Baggara: I. Cunnison, *Baggara Arabs* (1966: 30–32).

that in the nomad areas the annual average amount of rainfall does not drop below 100 millimeters approximately, and that nomad areas also include enclaves with an annual rainfall of 900 millimeters, which are unquestionably suitable for agriculture.

Today it is generally accepted that an average annual rainfall in excess of 250–300 millimeters is an adequate precondition for growing grain on a regular basis. Regions where rainfall is low but does not fall below 100 millimeters per year can support farmers on condition that there are water resources not directly dependent on rain; or they can provide a living to men engaged in a combination of economic activities, e.g. agriculture, grazing, and hunting, and who, by so doing, reduce the risk of becoming the victims of local droughts. Regions where rainfall is less than 100 millimeters per year cannot support farmers, and their inhabitants become entirely dependent on pastoralism. As the spring vegetation lasts for a short period, sometimes only a few weeks, they can be exploited economically only when they form part of a larger territory also comprising areas blessed with more abundant rainfalls.

These norms may be modified by additional ecological factors such as the quality of the soil, the proximity to wells and roads, and the availability of other sources of income, all of which influence the possibilities of practical utilization of any particular region. Modern technology can, of course, overcome natural disadvantages and erect a permanent settlement on a site where rainfall is sparse.[7]

Even in arid regions it happens that a particular geological formation drains the rainfall of a considerable area to one locality. Thus oases are formed, which depend only to a very small extent on the frequency of rainfall and which can support permanent settlement. However, not all the oases in Bedouin areas are settled permanently, some oases never becoming more than wells at which the nomads water their herds. In order for an oasis to support a permanent settlement, it must be large enough to support a population capable of defending itself against groups of nomads wishing to exploit its resources. This implies that the point at which an oasis will become a permanent settlement differs from place to place. Since the power concentrations of the nomads change from generation to generation, oases may be deserted even when the natural conditions remain unchanged.[8]

A rainfall of 100–200 millimeters, in the climatic conditions of the Middle East, not only moistens the soil in pastures and fills water holes and wells but will also, in the "normally" dry years (those without severe drought), cover the temporary deficits in water that can result from irregularity of anticipated rain. This irregularity comprises annual fluctuations in quantity of rain, variations in distribution of rain during the season, constant differences in quantities of rainfall in various parts of the region caused, for instance, by its topography, and also the varying geographic distribution of rain from season to season. For example, in the Ẓullām region of the eastern Beersheba plain, average annual rainfall fluctuates between 200 millimeters in the west and 120 millimeters in the southeast, over a distance of only thirty-five kilometers. Annual fluctuations in rainfall are striking: the maximum registered in Beersheba was 336 millimeters in 1933–1934 and the minimum forty millimeters in 1962–1963. Even a year in which a normal quantity of rain falls can end in drought. This happened in the year 1960–1961 in the Negev, when 185 millimeters were measured; after the first rains in November, there was a pause for six weeks during which none of the autumn sowing germinated. In the months of January and February there occurred heavy showers, most of which ran off into the wadis and were not absorbed in the soil. Following these rains many Bedouin sowed their land a second time, but in March scorching east winds caused the second sowing to wither. Many Bedouin harvested only straw and no grain that year.

Every year there are showers which cover areas of a few square kilo-

[7] D. W. Lockard (1970: 400) describes the process of settlement of Saudi Arabian Bedouin around pumping stations of the Tapline Company. A regular supply of water brings about a significant change in the way of life of the Bedouin.
[8] In the Negev there are numerous examples of well centers which sometimes supported a settled population and at others only served as watering places, like Beersheba, Tel al-Milh, and 'Ar'arah.

meters and leave adjacent areas dry. One never knows where these rains will produce good pasture and where they will fill the waterholes.

In other regions, too, rainfall poses severe problems for the nomad. Musil describes how the seasonal fluctuations and the geographical distribution of rain make the life of the Bedouin difficult (1928: 8–16) and force the Rwala tribe to operate an intelligence network to keep the sheikh informed on the state of pasture (see Musil 1927: 110). Doughty notes that a guest among the Bedouin is safe from the questions of those assembled in the tent until after he finishes the meal "...yet after some little discoursing between them as of the rain this year and the pasture, they may each commonly come to guess the other's tribe" (1937: 624).[9] Apparently these Bedouin take a keen interest in information on the distribution of rainfall, if questions about rain and pasture precede those on personal matters.

Another means by which nomads overcome the difficulties of coordinating their scarce resources is the conservation of their late-summer water supply and the adjacent pasture. They try to delay their advance on these last critical reserves as long as they can. This rule is respected by all the tribesmen, so that only in late summer do their herds and households slowly converge on the main well centers, and even then they try to keep the herds at a distance and bring them to the wells only for watering (Asad 1970: 22; Musil 1927: 351–353).[10]

The main method by which the nomad attempts to overcome the irregularity of rainfall is by occupying a territory sufficiently large to cancel out the influence of geographic distribution and annual and seasonal fluctuation of rainfall and including areas rich in water. In such a territory he will find pasture and water for his herds throughout the seasons of the year and can even reserve an area to which he can retreat in the last hard days of summer. The type of rainfall to a large extent determines the annual range of his wanderings. In the Negev, the Bedouin will range up to 60 kilometers, in Libya up to 100 kilometers and more, and the Rwala moves up to 800 kilometers. Among the Bedouin of the Negev, only a part of the region of their wanderings is under the direct control of the tribes, since the better areas have been settled in recent generations. The tribes of Libya and the Rwala control practically the whole range of their pastures. In order to overcome fluctuations of rainfall, they were compelled to form big organizations which were strong enough to retain control over areas, parts of which were suitable for agricultural settlement. The big Bedouin tribes are territorial organizations which provide their members with pastures suitable for their needs throughout the seasons of the year. The occupation and protection of such a territory often requires

[9] Doughty (1937: II, 662) illustrates the many fluctuations and irregularity of the rains. See also Asad (1970: 13).
[10] For instance, the Rwala enter the settled area in the vicinity of Damascus at the end of June.

an organization comprising a large number of men. Bedouin tribes in Libya fluctuate in size between 6,000 and 30,000; the Rwala confederation in the Syrian desert numbers 35,000 persons and some 350,000 camels.[11] The fact that the Bedouin who desired to exploit the Wadi Sirḥān area for pasture were obliged to assure themselves of permanent access to pasture during all seasons of the year and to insure themselves as far as possible against fluctuations in rainfall was crucial in determining the size and organization of the Rwala tribe. I do not wish to argue that the Rwala tribe did not exist before it moved to Wadi Sirḥān. It is known that they previously lived in northern Arabia together with other tribes of the 'Aneze Arabs, and Doughty found, even in his day, tribesmen who remembered that they had in the past lived in the neighborhood of Khaibar (1937: 376–377). It is probable that they moved to the new territory in the mid-eighteenth century and drove before them the Mawali tribe (von Oppenheim 1939–1968: I, 68–70; Ma'oz 1968:137). However, as sociologists we are not so much concerned with this proven historical continuity. The Rwala in the neighborhood of Khaibar lived in ecological conditions different from those of the Wadi Sirḥān, and the new area required a different kind of social organization and influenced every aspect of their culture. We know that even the historical traditions and genealogy of the tribe changed under the influence of their migration.[12] Climate and pasture, neighboring tribes, and governments were the factors that dictated to these men, who wished to find their livelihood in the Wadi Sirḥān, the form and scope of their political organization and the size of the territory which they were compelled to control. Membership in this organization gave each tribesman a formally equal right – that could not always be realized under equal conditions – to exploit the pasture and the water sources of the whole area. That the tribe is mainly a territorial ecological organization becomes evident from the fact that the largest tribal units do not necessarily have a leader. Sometimes the tribal group or confederation bears the name of an ancestor, denoting its unity, but possesses no territorial center or locality in which the leaders of the subunits would assemble. Such a tribal confederation has no established leader and there are no formal arrangements for coordination between its groups. Unity exists primarily in the consciousness of the members, to whom it is self-evident that their livelihood depends on their gaining free access to the whole territory. Whenever necessary, a number of leaders of the autonomous political groups – but never all of them – meet to discuss arrangements for grazing and coordinated exploitation of water sources. They often

[11] Raswan (1936: 20) refers to 7,000 tents. M. von Oppenheim (1939: 1, 120–122) mentions 4,630 tents. If we accept von Oppenheim's estimate that an average of seven persons live in each tent (1939: 12) we arrive at a population of 32,410 souls.
[12] E. E. Bacon (1958: 125) has charted the changes in the genealogy of the Rwala over the course of a hundred years by comparing the information collected by Burckhardt, Doughty, and Ashkenazi.

succeed in reaching agreement, but occasionally they also argue over resources. Whichever be the case, the tribe that has the formal right to exploit the territory continues to exist.

The right to utilize resources in the territory is granted in normal times to tribes that are not members of the confederation. Jaussen, for example, relates that in the area of Kerak during the summer a number of tribes of different confederations gather together and pasture their herds in common (1908: 117). But the best tribe retains the privilege of first access in the event of shortage; whether it is capable of safeguarding this right is a different question, and, as Jaussen puts it, "the pastures are open to all the nomads, with a certain priority right to the tribe in whose territory they happen to be" (1908: 240).

When observers of Bedouin and other pastoral societies define the tribal confederation as a loose association of tribes (see, for example, Shimoni [1947: 13]),[13] they usually refer to a territorial unit such as described above. Such a unit may under certain circumstances develop political leadership and organs of government, but the history of the Arabian Peninsula provides numerous examples of ephemeral Bedouin states which crumbled as rapidly as they appeared. When leadership arises in the tribe, its scope is likely to expand very quickly beyond the organization of pasture and water. Out of a desire to guarantee the tribe's livelihood, the leadership will attempt to gain control over other resources that are used by its members, such as transport routes and caravan traffic, and the market towns in which the nomads exchange their animals and produce for the products of the settlers and for trade goods. In due course the leadership of the tribe moves to the occupied town, which then becomes the capital of a small kingdom.[14]

The need for pasture and water alone never brought about the rise of a strong tribal leadership, and certainly not the formation of a Bedouin state. The economic advantage of permanent and guaranteed control over territory does not weigh in Bedouin eyes against the burdens imposed by a central authority in the form of compulsory military service[15] and payment of taxes. Doughty shows that although the annual tax collected by

[13] V. Müller (1931: 200–202) gives his own interpretation of this phenomenon; in his opinion the whole political organization of the Bedouin is based on kinship relations. As these become more distant, the contact between tribesmen gets weaker. Only at the level of the tribe does this process cease "and only due to the personal authority of the sheikh at its head." Müller does not realize that the groups he refers to are territorial alignments, expressed in an idiom of kinship. Nor does he touch on the fact that the tribe is for the most part the largest political unit, while the confederation is no more than a territorial unit. On the other hand, Bacon (1958: 127) clearly perceived that "the genealogical segments larger than the tribe do not operate as political units."

[14] H. Rosenfeld (1965: 79–85) illustrates the beginnings of this process among the Rwala and its more advanced stages in the Shammar kingdom of Ḥāil.

[15] Rosenfeld (1965: 176–182) cites sources showing that the Bedouin cooperated, sometimes involuntarily, in the military ventures of Ibn Rashid; some of them served in lieu of payment of tax.

Ibn Rashid only amounted to "...eight or nine shillings for every household: yet the free-born, forlorn and predatory Beduw grimly fret their hearts under these small burdens; the emir's custom is ever untimely, the exaction, they think, of a stronger, and plain tyranny" (1937: 394). Doughty immediately goes on to explain why the Bedouin are nevertheless ready to accept the burden of the ruler: "Yet yielding this tribute they become of the prince's federation, and are sheltered from all hostility of the Aarab in front" (1937: 394). So under the pressures of hostile neighbors, the Bedouin are compelled to seek the patronage of a ruler or to create for themselves a political association that can match that of their enemies. The source of these pressures is not in the Bedouin tribes but in the permanent settlement, since only it can maintain comparatively large regular military forces. When the rulers or neighbors exerted constant military or administrative pressure on any group of tribes, they compelled it to organize within a large framework and brought about the development of aggressive leadership. This was necessary both for negotiation with the powers that be and for defense against attack.[16]

The tribesmen knew, of course, that it was beyond their power to match the government's military forces, but they could by these means prevent harassments and small punitive actions. The authorities had to realize that only serious military operations could take on the Bedouin. Whenever a Bedouin tribe instituted a more powerful tribal government, this brought about a chain reaction since it placed its neighbors in the position of having to make the awkward choice between creating another, perhaps even stronger, organization to combat the aggressive neighbor, joining other large tribes, or seeking the protection of the government authorities. Whichever it was to be, the tribe merged in a bigger and stronger political framework.

This was the process undergone by the Rwala confederation in the nineteenth century due to the pressure of the Ottoman authorities in Damascus on the one hand and the kingdom of Ibn Rashid in Ḥāil on the other. The Rwala tribes ranged over the Wadi Sirḥān and thus at various times entered the sphere of influence of both rulers. Toward the end of the summer, they approached Damascus and were open to pressures from its ruler, while in the spring they reached the southern limits of their wanderings, Jauf and Taima, where they came under the authority of Ibn Rashid. In order to protect their independent existence, the Rwala were compelled

---

[16] I take issue here with M. D. Sahlins (1968: 37) who, following Krader (and, incidentally, Durkheim), argues that "degrees of political integration [of pastoral nomads] vary directly with population density, thus ultimately with the natural abundance of water and pasture." The Rwala Bedouin, to be discussed later, live in a poorly endowed environment. Their spatial density is low, and yet they developed some degree of political concentration in response to political pressures from the outside. Abundance of material resources and density of population do affect political concentration, but their weight differs from case to case.

to join forces, thereby making the sheikhs of the Sha'alān family their leaders. Even then the number of their slave warriors was not more than a few tens. Because of their dependence on the two rulers, the Rwala did not usually come down in support of either side, but kept up constant negotiations and intrigues with both sides.

These historical developments are illustrated by the history of Jauf. Musil records that "from about 1820 to 1853 the inhabitants of al-Gowf were tributary to the Rwala. Then the oasis was seized by Talal eben Rašid" (1927: 553). When the house of Ibn Rashid rose to power and, among other exploits, brought Jauf under their sway, they forced the Rwala to build up more concentrated power in order to protect their grazing grounds against encroachments. Therefore we are told at about the same time that the Sha'alān family became the acknowledged leaders of all the Rwala tribes, who until then had spent as much time fighting each other as fighting other groups.[17]

Even then the Sha'alān did not rule the Rwala but became a focus of communication between their constituent tribes. They could coordinate migrations and other joint activities and, with the support of other leaders, could recruit forces for limited short-term military exploits. But they never sought to establish a standing army or permanent control over territory beyond their grazing requirements. Even the two attempts of the Rwala to gain control of Jauf, first in 1870 and later in 1909, were not carried out on the initiative of the Rwala chiefs but, in the opinion of Philby (1955: 228, 251), at the instigation of the Ottoman authorities. In the opinion of Musil, the second attempt was due to the private initiative of the Rwala chief's son.[18]

The same phenomenon recurs, on a more modest scale, in the Negev. Here the Israeli military government confined the tribesmen to a closed area for the greater part of the year, and all the inhabitants became dependent on the economic resources available in it. The Bedouin became subject to indirect rule by the tribal chiefs, and in this manner the tribe was strengthened and the sheikh became a very influential leader. The edge of this political organization was directed both against the government, to prevent it from encroaching on Bedouin land, and against the "peasants," landless Bedouin who earned a living as sharecroppers. Every peasant

[17] Musil (1928: 57–58) quotes Rwala informants who assert that Faisal al-Sha'alan (killed 1864) "established the power of the Rwala to the south of Damascus in the late 1850's...Fejsal waged war successfully and became the supreme lord of northern Arabia." We can interpret this statement to mean that the rise of the house of Ibn Rashid forced the Rwala to establish a stronger central leadership and to keep armed men ready for fighting in order to protect their traditional pastures.

[18] We possess a detailed description of the first abortive attempt of the Rwala to take control in J. Euting (1896: I, 131–134); and of the second attempt, which gave the Rwala control of Jauf for a few years up to 1922, in Musil (1927: 162ff.). According to Musil, even though some of the leaders of the divided house of Rashid invited the Rwala to take Jauf, the Rwala sheikh opposed his son's occupation of the settlement.

depended for his livelihood on the Bedouin landowners and knew that if he established strong political groups, this could not improve his economic lot. Nevertheless, the peasants were organized in minimal political groups similar to those of the Bedouin, since by doing so they could prevent unnecessary annoyances and react to Bedouin provocations (Marx 1967: 77–80, 206–209).

Although in one respect there is a parallel between the Bedouin of the Negev and the tribes of north Arabia, they differ greatly in other matters. The ecological conditions of the Negev do not require such a large territorial organization as that of the Syrian desert and north Arabia. Furthermore, the territorial organization of the Negev Bedouin extends over only part of the regions which supply them with pasture and water. It covers the spring pasture on the desert hills east and southeast of Beersheba and the early summer pasture in the Beersheba valley. Thus the Ẓullām tribal group secured access to all the pastures in the hills east of the Beersheba plain and down to the cliffs overlooking the Dead Sea. All the members of the tribal group and, in normal times, members of other tribes as well, have equal rights to exploit these grazing grounds. At the beginning of summer the flocks pass through the harvested fields of their owners and graze on the stubble left on them. Thence they continue westward to the stubble fields of villages. They graze on vacant state land or on areas belonging to the western Negev settlements and sometimes continue northwards up to the Ramleh area.

The Negev Bedouin thus belong to territorial organizations which control only part of their water and pasture requirements. In the literature these territorial organizations, such as the Ẓullām, the Qderāt, and the Ḥkūk, are called tribal groups, but the Bedouin themselves have no special term for them and do not regard them as political groups in the sense of such active groups as the tribe. In other cases such groups may be called confederations (qabīla), such as the Jahalīn or the Taʿāmrah of the Judean Desert. The tribal groups are just territorial units without a center of government or supreme leader. Tribes coordinate their activities by means of contacts between the sheikhs, whose marriage links create convenient channels of communication, and by means of individuals belonging to the various groups who have also established marital links with other groups. The confederations are homologous to tribes, and even if they have a central meeting place and a formal leader (sheikh of sheikhs), their tribal government is usually very limited. The territorial organization is not necessarily a large one; often a small territory will supply all the resources needed for the yearly cycle of wandering. The Jahalīn tribe numbers less than 1,000 souls, but the ʿAzāzmah, who, despite their being a confederation, had no central meeting place or supreme leadership, numbered (up to 1948) 12,000 souls. The Ẓullām group of tribes numbers 5,000 and also has no formal supreme leadership.

Territorial organization permits the Bedouin to cope with most of the ordinary annual and seasonal variations in water and pasture but does not protect them from the more serious fluctuations. Connections with neighboring units at the level of tribal groups and above can help, up to a point. Genealogical connections between neighboring tribal groups reflect, among other things, the desire of the groups to extend their control over rainfall fluctuations even further, by opening up additional possibilities of movement. However, such "kin relationships" between the tribal groups do not always stand the test of the harsh reality of a drought year, much less oblige the relatives to go to war together, as some scholars assumed in the past.

Both the relation to the land and the political organization are reflected in the histories and genealogies of the pastoral nomads. The Bedouin conceptualize the territorial organizations as a kind of political group whose membership is based on agnatic descent. They usually relate how a named forefather acquired rights to the area of land which they occupy. Members of the tribe inherited these rights through their fathers, who were the sons and grandsons of this ancestor. Since, according to Bedouin custom (which, incidentally, contradicts *Shari'ah* [the official Moslem law]) only sons can inherit the lands and flocks of their father, this is unassailable evidence, in their eyes, of their territorial rights. Patrilineal descent and the ideological connection between the ancestor, whether male or female, and the ownership of land are common to all the pastoral nomads.

Thus, the four Z̧ullām tribes have a genealogy which, although not identical in all its details, does support the claims of the tribesmen to the territory. Their belonging to a group of tribes serves as justification and a kind of charter for their ownership of the territory. The tribesmen explain that their forefather came some 200 years ago from the north of the Arabian peninsula to the Negev and settled in its eastern part, which was then uninhabited. This forefather was called "Z̧ālem" and the Z̧ullām are literally "Z̧ālem's people." The sons of Z̧ālem are the ancestors of the present-day tribes. According to one interpretation of the genealogy, Abu Jwe'id's daughter married Z̧ālem, and their descendants acquired their right of occupancy on the land (see Table 2).

That Z̧ālem, at variance with Bedouin custom, acquired his right to the land through a woman does not bother anybody. Z̧ālem had the right of the first comer and was not yet subject to the rules intended to guarantee continuity of control of an area and the balance of power between the various groups. A member of the Abu Jwe'id tribe explained the matter by saying that in actual fact Z̧ālem had not arrived in a completely deserted country: he found already in it the father of Abu Jwe'id and he, Z̧ālem, only acquired his right to the land by marrying his daughter. Thus the Bedouin explained to his own satisfaction his tribe's right of ownership of the area, but he did not explain how a woman inherits land.

Table 2. The origin of the Ẓullām tribes according to the Abu Rbeʻah tribe

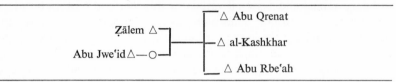

Legend:
Woman ○
Man △
Relationship through marriage ⊐
Relationship through descent ⊏

Note:
I have replaced the traditional names of the ancestors by the names of the tribes as used today.

When a group considers some neighboring groups to be genealogically closer to it than others, this may indicate either that these groups are linked by joint interests over and above proximity and common use of territory, or that the topographical boundaries between them are not as clearly demarcated as those with other groups. Thus, while each of the three big Ẓullām tribes usually conceptualizes the others as descendants of their eponym, they consider the Abu Rqaiq tribe, which borders on all three of them, as nonrelated members of the same tribal group, the Tiāha. While the three Ẓullām tribes intermarry a great deal, they do not contract marriages with Abu Rqaiq tribesmen. The genealogical conception reflects a situation in which the three Ẓullām tribes jointly control extensive spring pasture in the hilly eastern part of the territory and can effectively bar the Abu Rqaiq tribe to the west from entering this pasture. As a rule, the Abu Rqaiq herds use the Ẓullām spring pastures on equal terms, and only when there has been too little rain and the vegetation is scanty are they not welcome in the hilly area. The Ẓullām get nothing in return and cannot even use the pasture in Abu Rqaiq territory when their herds move westward in summer: the stubble fields there cannot even satisfy the hunger of the Abu Rqaiq herds, so all the herds wander further westward and out of Bedouin territory to seek pasture in the settled districts. It follows that, while the Abu Rqaiq depend on the Ẓullām, these do not depend on the Abu Rqaiq. All the Ẓullām need is good neighborly relations with the Abu Rqaiq, who therefore can be considered distant relatives.

The version of the origin of the Beni Sakhr (also called Dahamsheh) tribe east of the Jordan reported by Jaussen is similar in various ways to the genealogy of the Ẓullām. A man named Dahamsh found an abandoned baby in the desert, brought him up, and gave him his daughter in marriage. The four sons born from this union are regarded as the forefathers of the Beni Sakhr tribe (Jaussen 1908: 107). Apparently the fore-fathers of the Skhūr (plural of Sakhr) also did not inherit their land from their primeval ancestors; rights of ownership came to them only through their mother, the daughter of the original owner of the land. The Skhūr are divided into three groups of tribes, each headed by a sheikh. There is no supreme sheikh for the whole tribe, and the tribes even war with each other (Jaussen 1908: 114). Only the territory of the confederation is con-sidered to belong to all the tribes, and every tribesman has equal rights of access to it.

In Cyrenaica, all the "aristocratic" landowning Bedouin claim to be descended from a common mother called Saʿada. The nine large aristo-cratic tribal confederations are her descendants, and through her they acquired rights to the land (Peters 1960: 29–30).[19] Except for Saʿada, mother of all the tribes, no women figure in the genealogy. Robertson Smith brings together examples of tribal ancestresses from early Arabia (1903: 29–30) and remarks that "there is no tribe with a female eponym in which the main groups have not male eponyms" (1903: 37). It would be possible to cite many examples of present-day Bedouin tribes where women appear at the apex of the genealogy as owners or inheritors of the land (Murray 1935: 245–246, 307), thereby contradicting the rules of in-heritance practiced today, while all the offspring of these mothers appear-ing in the genealogy are male, thereby confirming the validity of these rules of inheritance. It will shortly become clear that the female connec-tion with the land in apparently patrilineal societies is not only meant to confirm ownership of the territory, but also refers to a specific type of political organization.

All Bedouin groups claim to be descended from the male or female eponym of the tribe. Bedouin are unable to give the names of the ances-tors intervening between the eponym and the last few generations and therefore are never certain whether the line from the forefather is direct and how many generations have passed since his time. In this manner all the groups of landowning Bedouin in a tribe, whether they be large or small, and even those whose origin may be outside the group, may claim descent from the eponym and thus assert their right to the land.

In the Negev, groups which own either very little or even no agricultural land are considered by the landowning Bedouin to be, paradoxically, "peasants" (*fellahīn*). These peasants do not claim descent from a named ancestor who settled in the tribal area, although membership of the group

---

[19] Rifʿat al-Jauhari (1947: 223) gives another version, according to which all the Saʿadi tribes are descendants of one man, Abu Dib of the Quraish tribe, who married Saʿada, the daughter of Jāziah of the Bani Hilāl tribe. The invasion of the Bani Hilāl and Bani Sulaim tribes in the eleventh century turned Libya into a predominantly Bedouin country. Today's Bedouin still view these tribes as conquerors of the land. As Bedouin see it, the marriage of Abu Dib to Saʿada of the Bani Hilāl gives his descendants a right to the land.

is based on the common origin. For example, the Abu Ṣaʿalūk group of peasants contends that *Ṣaʿalūk* [The Beggar] was the nickname of their ancestor, whose real name has been forgotten, and who dwelt in their country of origin, Morocco. The descendants of Ṣaʿalūk wandered through Egypt to the Gaza Strip until they reached the Ẓullām around 1910. They add that "the first to come here were six men who were brothers and cousins to each other" and who bought a little land in the region (Marx 1967: 114). The Abu Ṣaʿalūk who live in the Ẓullām area have therefore no common ancestor through whom they could link up with the tribal ancestor and claim rights to the land.

The Kababish are a tribe only in name, for they do not corporately control their pastures but are directly administered by the government. "Land is owned by government and pastures are free to all" (Asad 1970: 31). Each citizen, whether a Kababish tribesman or not, may freely use the pastures, for "although the Kababish are divided into a number of named clans these do not possess any rights to territorial resources" (Asad 1970: 13). The situation with regard to water is similar. The permanent wells have become public property and:

Rights of access are held by individuals and not by whole sections or subsections. Tribal custom (as administered by Local Courts and recognised by the Rural Council authorities) insists that all established users are equally entitled, that no prerogatives are held by "original owners" (Asad 1970: 27).

The formal appellation of "tribe" is retained only because the leading families act as tax collectors for the government and have appointed prominent tribesmen from the larger groups as their representatives. Even "tribal custom" is being interpreted to conform with government policies. As there is no tribe:

Elaborate agnatic genealogies as such are considered unimportant and rarely remembered. In answer to [the anthropologist's] questions on the subject, young men would almost invariably reply: "I can tell you the names of my mother's kin and my father's mother's kin, but I cannot tell you the names of our distant ancestors. Our elders never bother to tell us who they are" (Asad 1970: 106).

This is the one end of the continuum, at the other of which stand the Libyan Bedouin, who are "proud to the point of boastfulness of their genealogical knowledge, and...wherever the anthropologist travelled the first request he had to comply with was to take down a large proportion of a tribal genealogy" (Peters 1960: 40). It appears that pastoral nomads who are in full control of territory and capable of defending it, like the Libyan Saʿadi tribes, show detailed genealogical knowledge that explains their territorial and political divisions and their relations with their neighbors. Pastoral nomads who have lost control over their territory and are no longer corporately organized, like the Kababish of the Sudan, have no need for tribal genealogies. In between these extremes range groups like the Abu Ṣaʿalūk "peasants," whose corporate organization has been set up in response to outside pressures but who do not control territory. The genealogies indicate various peculiarities in the territorial and political organization. One of these was discussed in detail: whenever there is a female eponym, this indicates that the widest territorial boundary required by a group of pastoral nomads has no political counterpart and no constituted leadership.

The tribal genealogies are certainly inaccurate from a historical viewpoint. Even small groups usually have difficulty in tracing the kinship ties between all their members. It is therefore even harder to rely on details of ancestors who lived, according to the nomads themselves, some seven or eight generations ago. Memory works very selectively, so that significant names may be remembered, but the biological links between their bearers and the people living today may be completely forgotten. However, the genealogy does represent reality of a kind: it is the nomads' conceptualization of their distribution on the land and gives some indication of the political structure. It thus says very little about the past but a great deal about the present. This illustrated by the Bedouin who view the distribution of tribal lands as a patrimony to be divided among brothers. Each brother gets a portion of the property, and after the division the brothers are not obliged to manage the assets jointly but to help each other in time of need. As the membership in agnatic groups is acquired at birth and is therefore "permanent," and since a person cannot belong to two groups at the same time, the arable land is neatly divided between the groups and acquired chiefly by inheritance. The genealogical connections between the groups also represent their joint ownership of pasture that is accessible to all their members. Even while speaking of cooperation between agnatic groups such as these, Bedouin stress the differences between them, such as in their often quoted saying "I am against my brother, my brother and I are against my cousin, my cousin and I are against the stranger" (Yehudah 1932: I, 75). Eliahu Epstein describes the situation as follows:

Each and every tribe has its land in the desert and has the sole right of exploiting it and its springs, rights which over the course of time have become the accepted law of the desert. When two Bedouin tribes are on good and friendly terms one may occasionally camp as a guest on the other's land with its consent. But encroachment on another's land causes arguments and is one of the most common causes of desert wars (Epstein 1933: 14).

It may be added that in some cases a tribe will collect a payment for the right of pasture on its lands.

So far the tribe and the confederation have been viewed as organizations that secure and hold the territory necessary for the livelihood of pastoral nomads. They protect it both against the invader from outside and against the tenants or clients from within who wish to gain control of the land. The tribe is structured much like a military organization: it comprises a large number of small close-knit groups, capable in time of need of coalescing in a predetermined manner into larger units. At the head of each unit stands a leader. The members of the small groups live and wander at no great distance from each other and consider themselves to be agnates even if they cannot trace the relationship. Members of such groups believe that they are the descendants of a common father whose name they bear. The genealogy also serves as a rough guide to their potential amalgamations into larger groups, according to the (disputable) logic that two neighbors living in adjacent areas with similar ecological characteristics have common interests. The common interest is translated into the idiom of kinship; agnation signifies the unity of the members of the smaller corporate groups. This solidarity is also expected of the relations between groups linked in a larger framework, and, accordingly, the ancestors of these groups are represented as agnates of each other.

When viewed as a series of fighting units, the Bedouin tribal organization is segmented, embodying many of the characteristics which appear in the classic description by Evans-Pritchard (1940: 142–144),[20] the most important being that the units amalgamate for common action only in times of emergency, and in times of tranquility break up into small segments. However, as opposed to the sociological model, in real life the units do not necessarily amalgamate according to the genealogical scheme; the amalgamation proceeds always according to the governing interest of the particular moment. In normal times, when no external enemy threatens the groups, they are free to engage in disputes between themselves which occasionally lead to bloodshed. A conversation held between Musil and one of the leaders of the Rwala shows how far matters can go; the sheikh told him, "The Fed'ān are unbelievers to us, hence we fight them." When Musil reminded him that the Fid'ān were of the same origin as the Rwala and that both were of 'Aneze stock, the sheikh replied, "I know that they are related to us through their blood and faith, but they have deceived us, hence they are worse than all the foreigners and Christians and we are in holy war against them" (Musil 1927: 426).

He who looks upon Bedouin society in a tranquil period will perceive a series of discrete and disputing groups, clearly demarcated territorial frontiers, acts of violence, and blood revenge between related groups. He will find it difficult to understand how Bedouin belonging to the various groups are capable of jointly managing and exploiting pasture and water sources. This is difficult enough even when there is political coordination. There is evidence that the Sha'alān, the well-known chiefly family of the Rwala confederation, could not prevent banditry even between the tribes

[20] This is the simplest and clearest exposition of the theory of segmentary organization. Evans-Pritchard emphasizes that each segment is a territorial unit, that the small segments are the elements in a larger organization, and that the large units are activated only for war.

under their supervision.[21] Such supreme sheikhs cannot overcome the discord since they have no means of control apart from the agnatic units and maintain only minute military forces of their own. The situation should be even worse in tribal confederations which do not have a senior sheikh.

How can units which are constantly at such odds as these divide between them the pasture land and the water in an equal and fair manner and permit members of rival groups to live side by side? This is a problem with which most of the descriptions of nomadic society have not dealt. Many of the authors were not even aware of the existence of such a problem. Only Sweet points out that "though it is logical to suppose that freedom of access to adequate pasturage is a condition of tribal life, how this is regulated within the tribal structure of north Arabian Bedouin society has not been fully understood" (Sweet 1965: 136). We lack detailed information on this subject on all but two Bedouin societies: the Zullām tribes in the Negev and the tribes of camel breeders in Libya. We know how the land is divided in these societies both in ordinary years and tranquil periods and in drought years when the area becomes insufficient for all the population and their flocks. Normally, pasture areas are not divided permanently between the various groups, but in practice the strong groups that are settled in proximity to these lands control access to them. Other Bedouin are entitled to use the pasture areas when there is sufficient grazing. When grazing is restricted, access is given to Bedouin from the outside only through marital relationships created especially for this purpose. These marriages create a close-knit network of contacts spread all over the tribal territory.

In both the Bedouin societies there is an "inferior" sector which bears most of the suffering caused by drought or increase in population and flocks. These are the *fellahīn* in the Negev or the "clients" in Libya, who do not have a share in the land and are not absorbed in the tribal military organization and who can therefore be driven off when space becomes tight. The distinction between the owners of land and the landless is essential for the understanding of many pastoral societies.

A detailed examination of these and other phenomena shows that the corporate organization based on quasi agnation is only part of the structure of pastoral nomad society. It is just the showcase of this society, desiring to appear to the outside observer as a warrior society. The nomad, steeped all his life in this ideology, sincerely believes that this is the real essence of his society and that the other aspects are coincidental, atypical, or exceptional. While he is capable of interpreting various aspects of his society in an entirely objective fashion, he possesses only one model, or conception, of his total society, namely that of a segmentary political

[21] Musil (1927: 24–25) tells how he was robbed by members of a clan "attached" to the Sha'alān. When he complained that he was a member of the household of the sheikhs, the robbers were not at all impressed, even though they did believe him.

organization. Therefore, for him, all economic marriage links are private arrangements and every agreement with a tenant or a client is made only in order to give him a personal economic benefit. It is even more surprising that until recent years scholars accepted the same ideology and did not diagnose the part played by marriage links and by "clients" in nomadic society.

Among the Negev Bedouin, each marriage serves the interest of a small group of real agnates, including brothers and cousins, who together decide how to match their sons and daughters. Since the weight of whole groups stands behind these marriages, they are stable, and the number of divorces is infinitesimal.[22] Intimate and frequent contacts are maintained particularly between the two men closest to the woman: her husband and her brother or father, both of whom are responsible for her, though in different ways. The woman frequently visits her family of origin, sometimes for several weeks, and during such long visits the husband comes to visit her. The members of the family of origin on their part return these visits. The woman provides a link between the two groups, carries information and requests in both directions, and cares for the continuing relationship. It has already been noted that the heads of the Ẓullām tribal group are connected through marriage. Even when the chiefs of the tribes quarrel over tribal interests, their wives keep up regular contacts with their families of origin and do not cease the exchange of visits. Occasionally the husbands accompany their wives on these visits, and it then becomes clear that the heads of disputing tribes are in-laws who treat each other with respect and friendship.[23]

Even more impressive is the fact that practically all marriages of tribesmen are contracted inside the common territory. All the 130 marriages between the Bedouin of the tribe of Abu Jwe'id which I studied in detail were effected in the Ẓullām region. Some of these marriages took place within the tribe and others with other Ẓullām tribes. Only three women married Bedouin of a neighboring group of tribes, and the three husbands permanently resided among the Ẓullām. All the marriages took place between Bedouin, and I did not hear of any matches between Bedouin and peasant sharecroppers; thus all the matches created links between land-

---

[22] This holds true even though (in accordance with the Koran) the argument can be heard that there is nothing easier than divorce, since it is enough for the husband to pronounce the formula of divorce in order to cast off his wife. This contention contributed to the mistaken view, held by some scholars, that the rate of divorce in Arab society is high, as in R. Patai (1969: 106–206).

[23] Musil (1927: 22) records the sheikh of the Rwala tribe as saying to the heads of the 'Amarāt, another tribe of 'Aneze Bedouin, "We as the chiefs of our tribes are enemies but as men we are the best of friends." I suggest, though I cannot find documentation for this in the literature, that marital connections existed between the two families of sheikhs, as is common among the great sheikhs. Thus, for example, there has been a connection for generations between the heads of the Rwala and the heads of the Fid'ān confederation. (See von Oppenheim 1939–1968: I, 103; Raswan 1936: 88.)

owners. All these marriages serve the various interests of the parties as individuals and as groups. Such close-knit links permit the Ẓullām to jointly exploit the pasture and water in the territory under their control and also serve them in the pursuit of other interests. In tranquil times, these connections play an important part in daily life. However, the Bedouin also attach considerable importance to the interests of their groups. Therefore they do not exploit all the marriages in order to create economic contacts but use a number of them for the maintenance of political connections within and between the corporate groups. The over-all result of these marriages was the creation of a network of kinship relationships involving most of the Bedouin groups of tribes, and through these relationships the Ẓullām became a "group of tribes," capable of cooperating economically and politically.

CAUSES OF CHANGE IN NOMAD SOCIETY

The lack of any marital connections between the Ẓullām Bedouin and their peasants underlines the united front which the owners of land have put up against their sharecroppers. The Bedouin know that kinship re-lations between them would break down the fence separating the two economic classes. In any case, approximately half the population in the Bedouin areas is composed of peasants, some of whom have succeeded in acquiring a bit of land, although no peasant group has reached a point where it can do without additional land. Even the AbuʿArār, the wealthiest of the *fellaḥīn* groups, still lease 40 percent of their land from the Bedouin. The head of every peasant family establishes a personal relationship with a Bedouin landowner. In order not to give the peasant rights of tenure and in order to keep the right of grazing on stubble in summer, the Bedouin do not lease their lands for more than a season. The terms of lease are equal everywhere. Although the peasant is allowed to lease from a new landowner every year, he cannot expect to improve his terms of lease; at most he will receive slightly better land. Obviously the uniform and short-term contracts are intended to leave the Bedouin with a free hand in the management of the land. The peasants were given a foothold as long as land was plentiful and as long as the Bedouin themselves could not cultivate the agricultural lands of their regions. By leasing surplus land to tenants, the Bedouin received welcome additional income without investing any effort. Any change in the Bedouin population necessarily influenced the situation of the peasants. A small Bedouin population could absorb a large number of peasants, but an increase in the number of Bedouin immediately caused some peasants to be pushed out. The peasants thus served the Bedouin landowners as a tool for efficient exploi-tation of the economic resources in their region, notwithstanding changes in the demographic situation. It was therefore important for the Bedouin not to tie the *fellaḥīn* either to themselves or to the soil.

It must be added that for several decades this unintended but useful arrangement operated well in the Negev, but since the 1940's the system has been upset for various reasons. During World War II the Allied forces offered employment in the erection of army camps and airfields in the Negev, and many youngsters, both pastoralists and peasants, found work in the camps. As a result of the fact that the income from such work was much higher than the income of a sharecropper, a part of the fields in the Negev remained uncultivated. During the first years after the establishment of the State of Israel in 1948, the opposite situation was created. The military government restricted movement into and out of the Bedouin area and issued only a limited number of short-term movement permits. In this way the authorities wished, among other things, to prevent cheap Bedouin labor from competing with new Jewish immigrants for the few jobs available at the time. The military government thus cut off the Bedouin from the national labor market. The authorities dealt with the Bedouin through the tribal chiefs, and anyone registered with one tribe generally remained attached to it. Accordingly, peasants of the Ẓullām tribes were forced, as in the past, to cultivate the Bedouin lands as sharecroppers, in spite of the fact that better-paid work was available outside the area. These peasants remained attached to the Ẓullām tribes and to the traditional terms of lease and were unable to benefit from state land given to the landless Bedouin of other tribes at nominal rents. During all that time the population grew rapidly, and with it mounted the demand for land. The Bedouin themselves needed larger areas for cultivation, while the peasants, who were increasing at the same rate, were left with less land. As a result, the area of land under cultivation increased year by year, until all the 175,000 *dunam* considered as cultivable in the Ẓullām area were sown, and tenants were found even for the less fertile lands.[24]

In approximately 1960, a change occurred which prevented a further deterioration. The employment situation in the country improved and the granting of exit permits from the Bedouin area was liberalized. Thus the state in its turn used the Bedouin as a whole for absorbing fluctuations in the supply of manpower in the national economy, much as the Bedouin landowners had exploited their peasant tenants. As a result of this change, the young Bedouin and peasants again went to work outside, and the area under cultivation in the Ẓullām area was reduced drastically. Some peasant households even left the region for good.

Several parallels exist between the Bedouin of the Negev and the

---

[24] The continuing cultivation did not cause a great decrease in crops in spite of the fact that the Bedouin do not improve their soil nor rotate crops. Because of the frequent droughts, good harvests are attained on the average only once in every four years and thus the fertility of the soil is preserved.

Bedouin of Libya. The nomadic population of Cyrenaica is divided into aristocratic landowning Bedouin and "clients" with no right to land or water, who use these resources only with the permission of their owners. Only the aristocratic clans figure in a genealogy that encompasses all their confederations and tribes. Peters states, "descent from Saʿada...in theory gives [a man] rights to land in Cyrenaica, [and] his genealogical position in a particular group gives him rights in a particular strip of territory, but not in all" (1968: 175).

Peters attaches significance to the choice of Saʿada as ancestress of all the tribes:

Female names can be used to show a greater notion of cohesion than the mere use of male names, and the significance of a female name placed at the apex of the Cyrenaican genealogy is that it is a symbol of full brother unity at the highest political level (1960: 29).

If we were to place in this quotation the word "territorial" in place of "political," we would arrive at the same concept already described above: Saʿada, the ancestress, represents the participation of all the aristocratic tribes at a level that encompasses the whole area exploited by the Bedouin; by right of this participation every Bedouin is entitled, in theory, to enjoy the natural resources of the whole territory. There is no political association of the tribes at this level, and if there were, it would become a serious rival to the state.

The Bedouin population in Libya was decimated during twenty years of war against the Italian conqueror, and all the aristocratic Bedouin tribes needed reinforcements in order to exploit their territory. Each aristocratic Bedouin group therefore attempted to draw in clients, both in order to exploit the resources and to prevent encroachment by larger groups of aristocrats. Nevertheless, they did not want to grant the clients ownership rights on the resources and therefore abstained from accepting them into their agnatic political association.

The landless clients formed between 10 and 16 percent of the Bedouin population (Peters 1968: 169), and the aristocratic Bedouin were therefore not afraid of the clients' ever being able to create a united political front against them. They therefore did not prevent marriages with the clients. On the contrary, Bedouin gave their daughters to clients in order to bind them. By right of kinship clients were permitted the use of cultivatible land and water, but, in the opinion of Peters, the kinship never became membership in the corporate organization that held the rights on the territory. Each and every year the clients were obliged to renew their agreement for the use of agricultural land and water (there was never shortage of pasture), and some of them were told to leave (Peters 1968: 175, 186).

The Bedouin of Cyrenaica, like the Ẓullām tribes, created a network of marital relationships through their territory. Agnatic groups systematically married into other groups. But they skipped over adjacent groups with resources similar to their own and preferred to marry into more distant groups and ecologically differentiated areas (Peters 1967: 274). These Bedouin also created marriage links with residents of the oases, and they specifically stated that they were "marrying dates." The efforts of individuals and of sections of agnates to secure access to economic resources of various types here too produced the network of kinship relations covering the length and breadth of the Bedouin territory and making for contacts between the members of all the political groups.

The Bedouin's intention to exploit the clients without granting them rights was frustrated here as well. The Italian authorities had already demanded equal access rights to the wells for all the citizens, and the order was carried out at wells close to permanent settlements (Peters 1968: 177). Peters mentions a case, certainly one of many, where a group of clients gained control over the territory and water of the aristocratic group to which it belonged. The small aristocratic group was forced to stand aside while the clients watered their flocks at its own well (1968: 173). It may be supposed that the authorities justified such actions as the right of a Bedouin group to benefit from public property. It appears that in Libya no pressure of population on territory has as yet developed, and, following the discovery of oil wells during recent years, it may be assumed that the surplus population will be drawn to better-paid work with the oil companies. A considerable number of young Bedouin have possibly already begun to leave the tribes in order to accept regular work at the oil installations or in the towns.

On the other hand, in the Basseri tribe of south Iran, a serious situation of surplus population and overgrazing has developed. Here the authorities exercise full control over the tribe and even regulate its movements. At the same time, the tribe's population has increased rapidly. According to one version it has tripled during the course of the last thirty to forty years (Barth 1961: 115). At present the Basseri do not have tenants from inferior groups who can be pushed out, since the tribe grazes its flocks on land belonging to the state, which will not permit discrimination between groups. They are therefore obliged to draw off the surplus population. Barth is of the opinion that there are two mechanisms which balance the relation between land and flocks: such a balance is possible, he claims, when the flocks belong to an individual and not to a large group – in such a case, various mishaps can strike the individual, force him out of the game, and make him settle on the soil (Barth 1961: 124). The implicit, but probably correct, assumption is that sheep raising gives quite a good income as compared with agriculture.[25] A herdsman whose flocks have been so far reduced that he can no longer support his family leaves the tribe

[25] U. Mor (1971: 17) claims that this is true also in the Negev.

and becomes a farmer. In the conditions of the Fars province, a man apparently has no choice but to work in one of these two primary occupations. However, owners of large flocks can also be cast out for another reason: the social pressures on a wealthy man increase, and he becomes afraid of investing all his capital in animals liable to be afflicted by epidemics, acts of banditry, etc. Therefore he invests part or all of his capital in the acquisition of land and in this manner either leaves the game or at least reduces his flocks.

Barth is of the opinion that these two processes have prevented the uncontrolled growth of population and flocks. However, it can be safely assumed that the mechanisms are not so well adjusted as to maintain a perfect ecological balance. It may rather be assumed that, as with the Rwala tribe, an impoverished man can get a new flock either as a gift or a loan.[26] Since there is no central authority that supervises the size of flocks, every family head is liable to find it more difficult each year to find grazing but will still try to increase his flock. This is what happened in the Negev. Only a very serious situation is likely to cause a reduction in the flocks.[27]

Among the large Bedouin tribes of north Arabia, demographic pressures express themselves in a different form. For as long as they maintain effective control over their lands and there are no outside forces interfering in their affairs, men and herds spread out relatively evenly over the face of the territory. The good pasture attracts larger herds than the bad pasture, and the distribution proceeds on the basis of thorough and continuing intelligence operations. When the population grows and the herds multiply in a specific region, they spread over a greater area. When the territory is large, small demographic fluctuations are absorbed without being noticed. However, fundamental demographic changes are not amenable to simple solutions and cause the tribes to spread out beyond their own territories. Changes such as these happened from time to time among the large tribes and caused intertribal warfare. We have, for example, detailed historical descriptions of the expansion and contraction of tribal territories in the Negev in the nineteenth century.[28]

---

[26] In Musil (1927: 463) a Bedouin reports that fifty camels were demanded of him as blood money. The head of the tribe gave him twenty-five camels as a gift and the remainder were given him by other tribesmen.

[27] The problem of traffic congestion in cities can be explained similarly: everyone wishes to own a motorcar but finds that driving and parking in the city are becoming increasingly difficult.

[28] One of these is al-'Arif (1934). A large section of the book is devoted to a description of the tribal wars in the Negev. The accounts were given by the Bedouin and according to good Bedouin traditions the wars were explained as personal arguments between leaders over wives and horses or as a result of insults to elders. Since there are no full figures on the size of the tribes and their herds, it is almost impossible to reconstruct the ecological and demographic factors in these wars.

CONCLUSIONS

It has been shown that pastoral nomads do sometimes exploit land that is not fit for cultivation and which, without this exploitation, would remain unused. But they prefer to pasture their herds on good rain-soaked land; furthermore, part of the pasture must always be of this type in order to maintain the herds at the end of the dry season. Therefore the nomads are interested in controlling agricultural land or at least in exploiting underpopulated agricultural areas. Periods of political turmoil, when settlements are abandoned and destroyed and agricultural land is released for pasture, are convenient for the nomads. However, they are interested in destruction of agricultural settlements only up to a certain point; they need the settlements in order to sell their animals and produce and to purchase foodstuffs and industrial products. The method of exploitation of land by the nomad is extensive and becomes possible only when there are wide unsettled spaces. Under such conditions the breeding of animals by the pastoral method is profitable, as the labor force employed is relatively small: one herdsman can control a camel herd of 70 to 80 head (Musil 1928: 366), or a flock of sheep of 150 head, and where conditions of production are primitive his product will be of greater value than that of the farmer. But when land is scarce and becomes an expensive economic factor, the breeding of animals loses its relative advantage.

The confederation of tribes is a territorial unit, extending over areas of pasture and water sources sufficiently large to permit the pastoral nomads to cope with the ordinary environmental hazards. As long as the state does not seek to control the nomads, the size of the territory required and the outside political forces brought to play on the tribe by settled populations and by neighboring tribes are the factors which determine the number of its members. If the tribe's population is small, then it is unable to maintain full control over the territory; the pasture areas shrink and its chances of overcoming the ecological difficulties decrease. Then one of two processes takes place: either the whole or a part of the area is taken over by other and stronger groups, or the tribe increases its strength by absorbing additional population. In either fashion land is redistributed. All this changes when a central government assumes control over the nomads.

The terms "confederation" and "tribe" are somewhat misleading, as they convey the impression that they are military units standing at the apex of a political organization controlling territory and defending it and its members. Where the state does not administer the nomads, the confederation, and often the tribe as well, may only be a territorial unit, without a corresponding chiefship or military organization. The military organization of pastoral nomads is based on small agnatic groups, capable, in time of need, of uniting with other groups, for short-term and mostly small-scale military exploits. In ordinary times, this capacity to unite and fight is enough to deter would-be invaders of their territory. Consequently, there are long periods of respite when the nomad looks after his own business which, in any case, is exhausting enough. It leaves him little time for political activity and all he does in this respect is to stay close to his agnates, the members of his minimal group. Each small group establishes links, usually through intermarriage, with other groups with whom its own movements intersect at various times. These links break down the discreteness of agnatic groups.

The nomad is loath to allocate much of his limited resources to a permanent administration that would coordinate the activities of various groups and always be ready to deal with invaders. Sometimes there is no permanent leader at the head of a confederation and the constituent groups may even be constantly at odds with each other. When that is the case, practical control over the area and coordination between groups moving about in it are achieved by an extensive network of personal links that operate at various levels: the links established between small groups of agnates, the personal marriage links between the leaders of the larger political groups, the communications borne by strangers residing in the tribal territory, and, last but not least, the personal economic links that almost every nomad maintains with affines and cognates in other parts of the territory – all these contribute to the creation of a network of relationships spread out over the territory of the confederation and almost co-extensive with it. The acephalous tribal confederation is then the cumulative end result of the efforts made by individuals and small groups to cope with problems of pasture, water, and self-defense. A large number of personal links crisscross a territory that is large enough to satisfy the requirements of men and animals throughout most of the year and through "ordinary" environmental variations, including "normal" droughts. These links cover a defined territory and form the framework within which a dense network of relationships and interaction exists. They determine the access to the territory of some groups to the exclusion of others. Even so, the nomads conceptualize their territorial control, in customary fashion, as a grouping of agnates based on a defined genealogical relationship. This indigenous theory has for a long time obscured the rather more complex social reality.

In this context marital links must be viewed as channels of communication between interested parties, through which they can cooperate, carry on arguments, and settle them. Where older agnates control the marriages of young members of their groups, usually assisted by their control over the group's or household's property, as well as enforcing strict premarital sexual abstention for both sexes and particularly for women, the links are mainly, but not exclusively, those of kinship and marriage. But there are also links institutionalized as friendship and brotherhood, and in some societies these may predominate.[29] Since the nomads live on land which is at least in part suitable for cultivation, it is not surprising that some of them engage both in pastoralism and in agriculture. In this way they guarantee themselves a complementary livelihood and reduce the danger involved in failure of one branch of the economy. Besides, they can thus vary the diet. They organize their cycle of movement in such a way that in the plowing and harvesting seasons they pass close to their cultivated areas (e.g. the Zullām and Baggara). Only those tribes whose range and route of movement does not permit an arrangement whereby each family of herdsmen also engages in agriculture make use of one of the following solutions: either the tribal population is divided into shepherds, camel nomads, and farmers (Libya), or a nontribal population cultivates the soil in the tribal territory and the nomads take a part of the produce (Rwala, and to a certain extent the Basseri).

Two extraneous factors, which often appear in concert, have far-reaching effects on pastoral nomadism: a strong central government and a growing population. Each government sees in the tribal organization an independent concentration of power (notwithstanding the fact that these concentrations of power develop in response to government pressure), attempting to enforce its own law, trying to evade payment of taxes and other civil obligations, and causing harm to the settled population. Governments wish to settle farmers on the agricultural lands held by the nomads, on the one hand, and on the other to secure control of water sources. By means of settling the land and opening access to water for all, they restrict the nomad's movements and may also be taking from him essential pasture lands. Reduction of pasture land turns the breeding of animals into a less worthwhile business, fraught with greater risk, and, in order to balance their economy, the nomads themselves may increasingly turn to agricultural cultivation. Under the protection of the government, agricultural land becomes the property of the individual, and by this means the pastoralists close off to themselves additional areas which are required for efficient grazing. The owners of extensive areas of land do not suffer from this situation. But nomads whose agricultural land is limited or who do not own land are unable to find the summer pastures that they need. By this means, central governments weaken the pastoralist economy even without taking any direct action against the breeding of animals.

Parallel with the growth of the state's centralized power, there often occurs a rapid growth of population, both of the nomads and of the settlers. The pressure of population on the land therefore increases

---

[29] Among the Marri Baluch, for instance, marriages are not stable, and permanent economic and political links become established as "friendships." The friends address each other as *bradir* [brother] (Pehrson 1966: 16).

quickly, and while more and more land comes under cultivation, either by settlers or by the nomads themselves, and the pastures become more and more limited, the number of nomads and their herds increases in the remaining area. If, at the same time, the external economy develops and opens access to new forms of livelihood, it is to be assumed that many pastoralists will give up the breeding of animals. These are the main causes of the decline of the pastoral way of life. The explanation often heard, that the decreasing value of the camel as a beast of burden and for riding is the chief cause, is mistaken.[30] Camels become less important for transport, but meat prices are high; and if the pastoral nomad had at his disposal the large area required for breeding animals, then the business would still be worthwhile today. Only the reduced size of the nomad's territory, the growing pressure on the land, and the advent of new types of employment yielding higher income bring about a decline in the breeding of animals by the pastoral method.

REFERENCES

AL-ʿARIF, A.
    1933   *Al-qada bain al-badu.* Jerusalem: Bait al-maqdis.
    1934   *Taʾarikh Bir al-sabaʿ wa-qabailaha.* Jerusalem: Bait al-maqdis.
AL-JAUHARI, R.
    1947   *Asrar min al-sahraʾal-gharbiyah.* Cairo: Dar al-maʿarif.
ASAD, T.
    1970   *The Kababish Arabs: power, authority and consent in a nomadic tribe.* London: Hurst.
ASHKENAZI, T.
    1938   *Tribus semi-nomades de la Palestine du Nord.* Paris: Geuthner.
BACON, E. E.
    1958   *Obok: a study of social structure in Eurasia.* Viking Fund Publications in Anthropology 25. New York: Wenner-Gren Foundation.
BARTH, F.
    1961   *Nomads of south Persia: the Basseri tribe of the Khamseh confederacy.* Oslo: Oslo University Press.
BURCKHARDT, J. L.
    1830   *Notes on the Bedouins and Wahábys.* London: Coburn.
CHELHOD, J.
    1971   *Le droit dans la société bédouine: recherches ethnologiques sur le ʿorf ou droit coutumier des Bédouins.* Paris: Rivière.
COON, C. S.
    1951   *Caravan: the story of the Middle East.* New York: Holt.
    1960   "Badw" in *Encyclopaedia of Islam* (new edition). Leiden: Brill.
CUNNISON, I.
    1966   *Baggara Arabs: power and the lineage in a Sudanese nomad tribe.* Oxford: Clarendon Press.
DICKSON, H. R. P.
    1951   *The Arabs of the desert.* London: Allen and Unwin.

[30] This is the explanation advanced by al-ʿArif (1933: 224).

DOUGHTY, C. M.
1937   *Travels in Arabia deserta.* New York: Random House. (First published 1888.)
EPSTEIN (EILAT), E.
1933   *Ha-beduim hayeihem u-minhageihem.* Tel-Aviv: Shtibel.
EUTING, J.
1896   *Tagbuch einer Reise in Inner-Arabien.* Leiden: Brill.
EVANS-PRITCHARD, E. E.
1940   *The Nuer: a description of the modes of livelihood and political institutions of a Nilotic people.* Oxford: Clarendon Press.
1949   *The Sanusi of Cyrenaica.* Oxford: Clarendon Press.
FEILBERG, C. G.
1944   *La tente noire.* Nationalmuseets Skrifter, Etnografisk Række 2. Copenhagen.
FERNEA, R. A.
1970   *Shaykh and effendi: changing patterns of authority among the El Shabana of southern Iraq.* Cambridge, Mass.: Harvard University Press.
FORDE, C. D.
1934   *Habitat, economy and society: a geographical introduction to ethnology.* London: Methuen.
FORTES, M.
1949   "Time and social structure: an Ashanti case study," in *Social structure: studies presented to A. R. Radcliffe-Brown.* Edited by M. Fortes. Oxford: Clarendon Press.
GLUCKMAN, M.
1963   *Order and rebellion in tribal Africa.* New York: Free Press.
GRÄF, E.
1952   *Das Rechtswesen der heutigen Beduinen.* Walldorf-Hessen: Verlag für Orientkunde.
GULICK, J.
1969   The anthropology of the Middle East. *Middle East Studies Association Bulletin* 3 (1): 1–14.
GULLIVER, P. H.
1955   *The family herds: a study of two pastoral peoples in East Africa.* London: Routledge and Kegan Paul.
HENNINGER, J.
1943   Die Familie bei den heutigen Beduinen Arabiens und seiner Randgebiete. *International Archives of Ethnography* 42.
JAUSSEN, A.
1908   *Coutumes des Arabes au pays de Moab.* Paris: Adrien-Maison Neuve.
KENNETT, A.
1925   *Bedouin justice: law and customs among the Egyptian Bedouin.* Cambridge: Cambridge University Press.
LAWRENCE, T. E.
1935   *Seven pillars of wisdom.* London: Jonathan Cape.
LOCKARD, D. W.
1970   Book review. *American Anthropologist* 72: 400.
MA'OZ, M.
1968   *Ottoman reform in Syria and Palestine 1840–1861: the impact of the Tanzimat on politics and society.* Oxford: Clarendon Press.
MARX, E.
1967   *Bedouin of the Negev.* Manchester: Manchester University Press.
MITCHELL, J. C.
1956   *The Yao village.* Manchester: Manchester University Press.

MONTAGNE, R.
1947　*La civilisation du désert*. Paris: Hachette.
MOR, U.
1971　"Ha-Beduim ba-negev–seqirah klalit," in *Ha-beduim*. Jerusalem: Prime Minister's Office.
MÜLLER, V.
1931　*En Syrie avec les Bédouins: les tribus du désert*. Paris: Leroux.
MURRAY, G. W.
1935　*Sons of Ishmael: a study of the Egyptian Bedouin*. London: Routledge.
MUSIL, A.
1927　*Arabia deserta: a topographical itinerary*. New York: American Geographical Society.
1928　*The manners and customs of the Rwala Bedouins*. New York: American Geographical Society.
NIEBUHR, C.
1799　*Travels through Arabia*. Perth.
PATAI, R.
1969　*Golden river to golden road: society, culture and change in the Middle East* (third edition). Philadelphia: University of Pennsylvania Press.
PEHRSON, R. N.
1966　Article in *The social organization of the Marri Baluch*. Edited by F. Barth. Viking Fund Publications in Anthropology 43. New York: Wenner-Gren Foundation.
PETERS, E. L.
1960　The proliferation of segments in the lineage of the Bedouin in Cyrenaica. *Journal of the Royal Anthropological Institute* 90: 29–53.
1967　Some structural aspects of the feud among the camel-herding Bedouin of Cyrenaica. *Africa* 37: 261–282.
1968　"The tied and the free: an account of patron–client relationships among the Bedouin of Cyrenaica," in *Contributions to Mediterranean sociology*. Edited by J. Peristiany. The Hague: Mouton.
PHILBY, H. ST. J.
1955　*Sa'udi Arabia*. London: Benn.
RASWAN, C. R.
1936　*The black tents of Arabia: my life amongst the Bedouins*. London: Hurst and Blackett.
ROSENFELD, H.
1965　The social composition of the military in the process of state formation in the Arabian desert. *Journal of the Royal Anthropological Institute* 95: 75–86, 174–194.
SAHLINS, M. D.
1968　*Tribesmen*. Englewood Cliffs, N.J.: Prentice-Hall.
SALZMAN, P. C.
1971　Movement and resource extraction among pastoral nomads: the case of the Shah Nawazi Baluch. *Anthropological Quarterly* 44: 185–197.
SHIMONI, Y.
1947　*'Arvei Erets-Israel*. Tel-Aviv: 'Am 'Oved.
SMITH, W. ROBERTSON
1903　*Kinship and marriage in early Arabia*. Edited by S. A. Cook. London: Black.
SWEET, L. E.
1965　"Camel pastoralism in north Arabia and the minimal camping unit,"

in *Man, culture and animals: the role of animals in human ecological adjustment.* Edited by A. Leeds and A. P. Vayda. Washington: American Association for the Advancement of Science.

VON OPPENHEIM, M.
1939–1968   *Die Beduinen.* Leipzig: Harrassowitz.

YEHUDAH, I. B.
1932–1934   *Mishlei 'Arav* (parts one and two). Jerusalem: Hasefer.

The Environmental Adaptation of Nomads in the West African Sahel: A Key to Understanding Prehistoric Pastoralists

SUSAN E. SMITH

Archaeologists obtain reasonable pictures of the physical settings of the prehistoric populations they are investigating by analyzing floral and faunal remains and the geomorphology of the areas. However, they are then faced with the following question: given this type of environment, what adaptations enabled the people to extract from it their basic requirements of food, water, and, perhaps, shelter? Ethnographic analogy cannot describe the relationship between man and the land that existed in a particular case, but it can suggest a range of alternatives that may provide clues for further archaeological investigation.

The following discussion is intended as an example of one of these alternatives. It is based on nine months of fieldwork undertaken by the writer in southern Mali among the nomadic Kel Tamasheq,[1] who exploit an environment and illustrate a life-style similar in many important respects to that of the post-Paleolithic inhabitants of the same area.

The physical setting to which they are adapted borders the southern Sahara and is known as the West African Sahel. This region is characterized by an annual rainfall of 50 to 150 millimeters (*Annuaire Statistique* 1967), which allows the survival of a vegetation pattern dominated by such grasses as *Cenchrus biflorus* and *Tribulus terrester* and such trees as *Ralanites aegyptiaca* and *Acacia* sp. The fauna includes *Gazella dorcas* and *Gazella dama* as well as ostrich, warthog, and giraffe; recently, however, these wild populations have been drastically reduced due to the use of firearms and motorized vehicles (Nicholas 1950: Plate 1; Richer 1924: 9). Three seasonal extremes can be distinguished: a cold period from

The majority of this time was spent with the Oulliminden tribe, who inhabit the area between Gao on the Niger River and the Niger border. These people are one of the most isolated of Tamasheq groups, and the lack of outside influence is reflected in both material culture and diet.

December through February, a hot dry period during April and May, and a wet season beginning in mid-June and lasting to September, during which violent storms and the only measurable precipitation during the year occur. Temperatures during the day reach highs of 115° Fahrenheit in May and at night may dip as low as 40° Fahrenheit in December. The Sahel dwellers have adapted to this environment by utilizing almost all the available natural resources, either directly or through the medium of animals: they obtain these resources in amounts sufficient to sustain life by moving from area to area.

The nomads do not form a homogeneous society, although they have a common designation as Kel Tamasheq [Tamasheq speakers] or Kel Esuf [people of the bush].[2] They comprise five distinct social categories: *imajaren* [nobles]; *imrad, debakar, chamenamas* [their vassals]; Kel Essouk [*marabout* tribes]; *iklan* or *bella* [slaves]; and *inadan* [artisans].[3] Details of occupation, ritual, physical type, and kinship patterns vary among these groups, but on the whole their adaptation to their environment is quite similar. All are pastoralists, with herds including camels, cattle, sheep, and goats (household animals include donkeys and dogs); they are all traditionally "pure" nomads, i.e. never sedentary; they are Muslim; and they speak a common language, Tamasheq.

DIET

Although diet varies according to the season and to the wealth, age, and social position of the individual, milk is the basic item for all. It is drunk either fresh or soured. For the latter, a culture is placed in fresh milk (preferably cows'), which is then allowed to stand for fourteen hours. It may then be drunk plain or mixed with water. Dried and pulverized fruit of the *Ziziphus* species, flour made from millet or wild grains, cheese, or dates may be added. These preparations, translated as *crème*, are considered very fortifying. Butter is made from cows' milk and is churned in a goatskin each morning. Cheese is only made during the rainy season when there is a surplus of milk; after drying it can be kept for more than a year. Donkeys' milk is used only for medicines.

In principle, the milk supply available to each family at any one time depends upon (a) the number of milk animals it owns, or, as in the case

[2] Many authors have used the Arab term Tuareg in reference to this group, but since it is sometimes used to refer only to noble classes and because the nomads never use it, their own designation for themselves, Kel Tamasheq, will be followed. Recently non-Tamasheq speakers have been moving into this area, mainly Peul (Fulani) and Arabs. The adaptation pattern of the Arabs is very similar to that of the Tamasheq, but the Peul life-style differs considerably.

[3] Slaves and artisans may reside either independently or, as is traditional, in the camps of the wealthier nobles, vassals, and *marabouts*; the latter three groups may visit each other for long periods but do not live together permanently.

of *iklan*, the number allotted to it, and (b) the type of animals – this factor determines when lactation begins, how long it continues, and the amount of milk produced. (See Tables 1, 2, and 3.) An individual family is likely

Table 1. Average number[a] of lactating animals per household, according to social class and animal type (example drawn from one camp, June 1972)

	Imajaren (5 households)	*Iklan* of cows (7 households)	*Iklan* of camels (5 households)	Artisans (4 households)
Camels	3.0	0	3.5	1.3
Cows	2.4	3.2	0	4.0
Goats	0	9.0	5.0	6.0
Sheep	0	b	0	0

[a] Ratio changes as new animals are born.
[b] Only one household has lactating sheep (10).

Table 2. Approximate yields of milk (in liters) at evening milking according to animal type

	Cold season	Hot season	Wet season	Number of milkings per 24 hours
Camel	5–7	2–4	7–9	3
Cow	3–4	2–3	4–7	2
Goat	0–$\frac{1}{2}$	1	2	2
Sheep	2	0	3	1

Table 3. Lactation patterns according to animal type

	Months gestation	Months between gestations	Births per 2 years	Months lactation
Camel	12	10–12	1	18–24
Cow	10	2–4,[a] 12[b]	2	10–15
Goat	5	2	8 (twins)	7–8
Sheep	6	2[a]	6 (twins)	7

[a] If pasture is extraordinarily good.
[b] If pasture is extraordinarily bad.

to have only one or two types of milk animal. However, these social and economic variations are minimized through a system of redistribution operating both between the households and between the social categories within a camp. The common mechanisms are trading (e.g. tobacco for milk, camels' milk for cows' milk), sharing, and "stealing." *Imajaren* households are an exception in that they cannot share the milk itself with others of the same rank, but they may instead either borrow a lactating animal or send their children to drink with a family that has a surplus.

Except during the wet season, milk is insufficient to nourish adults and is therefore supplemented with wild and domesticated grains. The former, gathered by the slaves and poorer vassals, consist primarily of *ishiban* (*Panicum* sp., which can be further separated into *akasof* and *asaral*) and *wajag* (*Cenchrus biflorus*) (see Tables 4 and 5 for additional species).

Table 4. Commonly used wild grains

Name	Collection	Preparation	Importance or use
Ishiban			
asaral	August to June in watered plateaus and valleys; by *iklan* or *imrad*	Cook, always needs sauce (milk or butter)	First grain to ripen; light, no diseases; "good against diarrhea"
akasof	Drier plateaus; is smaller than *asaral*	Same as *asaral*	
tegebart	Found in same places as *asaral*, often mixed	Cook or eat raw as *crème*, does not need sauce	Is considered best of *ishiban*
Wajag	Needs heavy rain before growth starts, must wait until straw is dry before gathering; by all *iklan*; found on dunes and plains	Cook or eat raw as *crème*	Considered more nutritious than *ishiban*; was main feed for horses with milk; if eaten excessively can cause diarrhea
Agarof	During wet season when still slightly green; on dunes	Pound to break off spines (vicious!); eat cooked or raw	Flavorful; especially "good for old people as tonic, and against blood diseases"
Afazo	On dunes in same areas as *ishiban* during October	Harder to pound than *ishiban*; eat raw or cooked	Can be found in great quantities but is only harvested if *ishiban* is lacking; famine food, low status
Tajite	Red grain found in clear spaces after rain; collected by ants; can be scraped up with hands	Difficult to pound; eat cooked or raw	One of the few grains available at this time; "keeps stomach full till next day, good for men"; medicinal

Table 5. Commonly used foods

GRAINS:

asaral   = *Panicum laetum* Kunth
akasof   = *Panicum laetum* Kunth
tegebart = *Echinochloa colona* Link
wajag   = *Cenchrus biflorus*
agarof   = *Tribulus terrester*
afazo   = *Panicum turgidum*
tajite   = *Eragrostis* sp.

FRUITS:
amalaja = *Acacia raddiana* Savi
tadant   = *Boscia senegalensis* Lamk.
abora   = *Balanites aegyptiaca*
terakot = *Grewia populifolia* Vahl.
tabakot = *Ziziphus saharae*

VEGETABLES:

eshako   = *Glossonema boveanum*
agar   = *Maerva crassifolia*
tagoya   = *Citrullus colocynthis* Schrad.
alikid   = *Citrullus colocynthis* Schrad.
ibellawent = *Rumex*?
abedebit   = *Boerhavia agglutinans*
tamasalt   = *Limeum inducum* Stacks

GUMS:
tamat   = *Acacia Seyal* Dil.
afaja   = *Acacia raddiana* Savi

Panicum is the most important wild grain, since it is the most abundant, is the first to ripen after the rains, requires very little preparation (pounding), and does not cause digestive upsets. It is harvested at three different stages in the ripening process; the first, beginning in August or September, lasts only ten to fifteen days and involves cutting the heads from the standing grain. This harvest is especially important if the milk supply is low. The second follows in mid-September when the grain is ready to fall and can be harvested by bending the stalks over a basket and beating the grains into it. This *ishiban* is considered the cleanest and is preferred. The final harvest begins in October and lasts until the next rains in June or July; it consists merely of sweeping up seeds which have fallen naturally after the straw has been cut, eaten by animals, or burned off. Grain gathered in the latter manner is considered of lowest quality, because it requires considerable preparation to remove the sand before eating. After harvesting, the grain is dried and stored in leather sacks, in mud-brick granaries rented in towns, or in holes in the sand (diameter 0.5 meters, depth 1.5 meters) lined with matting. Grain stored in the latter fashion is usually conserved for times of scarcity. With the first harvests in September these reserves are immediately replenished; whatever old grain remains is either eaten or sold. The grain is said to suffer little loss in quality for at least two or three years. The location of the holes is secret, but they are often placed near the wells frequented by the group, beside the stands of grain, or on the edge of a village. (Table 6 lists the harvest periods of the primary grains.)

Domestic grains (wet rice, millet, and occasionally sorghum), grown by sedentary agriculturists along the Niger River, were traditionally supplied

Table 6. Harvest periods of major domestic and wild grains

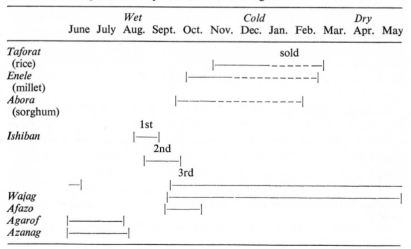

to the nomads as tribute; now they are purchased by the nomads when the wild grains are unavailable or for special occasions. Domestic forms constitute roughly one-half of the grain eaten by nobles, but only one-quarter of that of the *iklan*; this depends on the size of the harvests, however. During the months from September to January *ishiban* and *wajag* are eaten by everyone, but as the supplies diminish, the wealthy nomads and *imajaren* eat an increasingly greater proportion of domesticated grains, whereas the poorer people resort to the less common wild grains, e.g. *agarof* (*Tribulus terrester*) (see Figure 1).

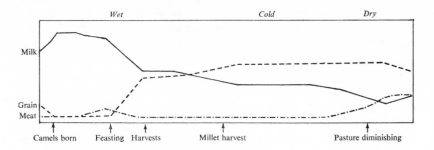

Figure 1. Proportion of milk, meat, and grain in diet according to season

Both domestic and wild grains are pounded in wooden mortars[4] to remove the bran, which is then separated from the grain by shaking from one flat basket to another; this process is also used for removing sand. The bran is frequently given to slaves and is eaten either raw or cooked. The cleaned grain is boiled in open metal pots, then eaten with butter, pounded meat, or sour milk and salt.

Vegetables are consumed mainly when other foods are lacking or by children of lower-status groups. This is largely due to the fact that higher-class Tamasheq, as well as the slaves and artisans who live with them, are prohibited from eating them, and perhaps also to the relative scarcity of vegetables in the Sahel. Vegetables are usually cooked in water, although the *tilagarzen* [melons] may be roasted in hot ashes. Some (e.g. *tatola*) are eaten raw, but this is rare.

Fruits are generally taboo, but *tabakot* [small dried berries of *Ziziphus* sp.] and *terakot* (*Greia populifolia*), which are both gathered by *iklan* during August and September, are sometimes used as a sweetening for sour milk. *Iklan* and artisan children also collect and enjoy *aborak* (*datte sauvage*)[5] and the gums of several trees. Dates are also used for sweetening,

---

[4] No stone querns, pestles, or grinding stones were observed among the Tamasheq Sahel dwellers although Nicolaisen (1963) and Gast (1968) note their use in the northern Sahara.
[5] This is the fruit of *Balanites aegyptiaca* and not that of the wild date palm *Phoenix reclinata*.

but they are scarce because they are not found in the Sahel and must be acquired through trade with northern oases. Some leaves used as medicines, e.g. *agargar* (*Cassia obovata*), may impart some nutrition; they are usually chewed or brewed as tea. The commonly used species of vegetables, fruits, and gums and their modes of preparation are listed in Table 7.

The *imajaren* are prohibited from eating fish and insects as well, but other groups, especially those whose nomadic patterns bring them close to the Niger River, eat fish. Use of locusts has been noted among the Tamasheq tribes of the Sahara by Foley (1930: 209) and Gast (1968: 251).

Meat of domesticated animals is generally eaten only on special occasions, such as for religious festivals, at arrival of visitors, during major camp movements, and for medicinal purposes; Tamasheq, however, believe that meat should be eaten at least every one to two weeks in order to maintain health, and they have been known to stage a "special occasion" to justify butchering an animal. Goats are most frequently used because they are least valuable and are generally kept near the camp. A larger animal may be butchered when meat is scarce, when there are many visitors, or when the animal is too weak – from thirst, hunger, or travel – too old, or too sick to continue, though the latter depends on the type of infirmity: victims of pleuropneumonia, for example, are not eaten.

Wild animals are seldom eaten; this may be due partly to their present scarcity, or to food taboos, or possibly to the lack of means or expertise for hunting. Weapons consist only of knives and throwing spears; no bows are used except as toys.

An animal is killed by slitting its throat. Blood and stomach contents are the only parts not used, and the meat is divided according to strict social rules: the chest is given to *marabouts*, if present; ribs to the man of highest rank; head to the shepherd or owner of the herd; neck to the elders in the shepherd's family (if he is young); stomach and intestines to *iklan*; lower legs to children; and the rest to the owner of the animal. This pattern differs slightly according to the type of animal. Large animals such as camels or cows must be partitioned among the whole camp; sheep and goats are primarily for the family that butchers them, although almost anyone may come to eat with that family or ask for some of the meat. Organ meats (liver, heart) are roasted on hot coals immediately after butchering and are eaten with salt by the family head and respected guests. Later, the haunch and meaty portions are prepared in any of the following three ways: (1) roasted by burying in sand with a fire built on top; (2) boiled in water, after which the meat is removed from the bones, pounded in a mortar to break up the fibers, and then served with grain or, very rarely, with butter only; (3) cut from the bones, divided into thin pieces, and hung inside the tent to dry. Bones are discarded.

Fresh milk is the first meal of the day for children and is taken at dawn; the adults drink only sweet tea and chew tobacco. At midmorning *crème*

Table 7. Commonly used vegetables, fruits, and gums

Name	Collection	Preparation	Importance or use
VEGETABLES:			
Eshako	At end of wet season, in stony ground	Pull off leaves and boil in water	Important food plant in barren areas
Agasse	Short plant found after rains beside lakes	Remove thick stems, boil leaves in water	Eaten in great quantities by children
Akowat	Parasite growing usually on *afagag* or *tazite*	Eat raw (leaves), never cook; slightly bitter	
Agar	Leaves of tree are picked	Cook twice, discard first water	Not very tasty, only for emergencies
Tatola	Thick woody vine that grows up trees; eaten after rain	Eat root raw, cook leaves in three waters or roast	A sweet famine food
Tagaya	Melon seeds taken from excreta of cow	Wash, pound, add *tabakaten*	Sweet "like dates"
Alikid	Fruit of melon; after wet season found "everywhere"	Put fire in hole in sand, remove, insert melon; or boil in water	Food source; water source (juice); medicine
Ibellawent	At end of hot season, on dunes	Eat raw	A sweet
Abadebit		Fruit: eat raw; grain: pound, boil; leaves: boil	Food source
Tamasalt	Grain found in ant hills or beaten out of husk with stick	Grain: pound, boil, mix with *ishiban*; leaves: cook in water	Food source
FRUITS:			
Amalaja	Shake from trees at end of dry season	Pound, sieve, add sour milk and *ibakaten*	"Very good for getting fat"; enjoyed by sheep
Tamint	Fruit of *tadant*	Dry near fire, pound, put in cloth in water 10 days, cook with meat; can also eat raw	Food source; a sweet
Ebelekunt	Fruit of *agar*, black when ripe	Eat fresh; or dry, then add water	Sweet, good for journeys
Aboragen	Fruit of *abora*, gathered from ground during dry season	Eat fresh or cook green fruit	A favorite sweet of children; nut is important medicine
Tamont	Picked from bush in wet season	Eat raw, discard skin, suck nut	Eaten only by children
Terakot		Grind, discard seeds; or eat as is	For sweetening sour milk
Tabakot	Picked by *iklan*	Eat as is or grind, mix with water, bake	The most important fruit for sweetening
GUMS:			
Awarwar		Eat raw	Antisorcery
Tamat		Eat raw	Tonic
Afaja		Eat raw	Sweet
Ibalugalug		Suck	Medicine for mouth sores

is eaten by men and children and less frequently by women. In early afternoon, if grain is available, a major meal of grain with either meat, butter, or milk is prepared. In the evening fresh milk is drunk by all, occasionally supplemented by a small dish of grain if milk is scarce. Visitors are usually given a meal of meat and grain, preferably millet or rice, in the evening.

Food is served in wooden bowls, four or five people partaking from each, using either the hand or a wooden spoon. Bones are cracked with knives or Neolithic stone axes to obtain the marrow and are then thrown out of the tent. If the camp remains in one place for more than a few days, such debris is swept farther away from the tent (eight to ten meters).[6] Bones seem to accumulate on the west side of the tent during the cold season and the east side during the hot months. (At other times, camps are not stationary long enough for the debris to become concentrated.) This difference may be due to the fact that in winter meat is eaten to celebrate the arrival of visitors and is served at the evening meal, when people sit on the west side (perhaps for protection against easterly winds). During the hot season, however, meat is most frequently eaten at the main afternoon meal, when the tent occupants gather on the shady east side. Meat has less of a ceremonial function at this time of year because visitors are not common; it is more important as a food source because milk and grain are insufficient. Also, many animals are dying of starvation or thirst and have to be slaughtered.

DETERMINANTS OF MOVEMENT

The nomads' most common response to pressures from the physical and social environment (hunger, thirst, political hostility) is to move. It is one of the most effective means of exploiting widely scattered and scarce resources. The precise nature of the movement (its time, frequency, direction, and distance) is the result of a complex interplay of the needs of people and animals and the availability of food and water, the latter being the most critical commodity.

Kel Tamasheq do not wander randomly but circulate in general "home" regions; within these, they follow a habitual route, e.g. south to north to south again, although both the region and the route can change in response to unusual political or seasonal situations. The nomadic pattern is oriented to seasonal water points and key pasture areas (see Map 1).

In the first months after the rains, September to December, water is obtained from shallow hand-dug wells, which are usually surrounded by adequate pasture. Locating camps near the water enables them to remain

---

[6] Occasionally dogs, one or two of which are present in most camps, will scatter bones farther. However, scavenging is not their main means of obtaining food; they are fed on milk and grain when it is available.

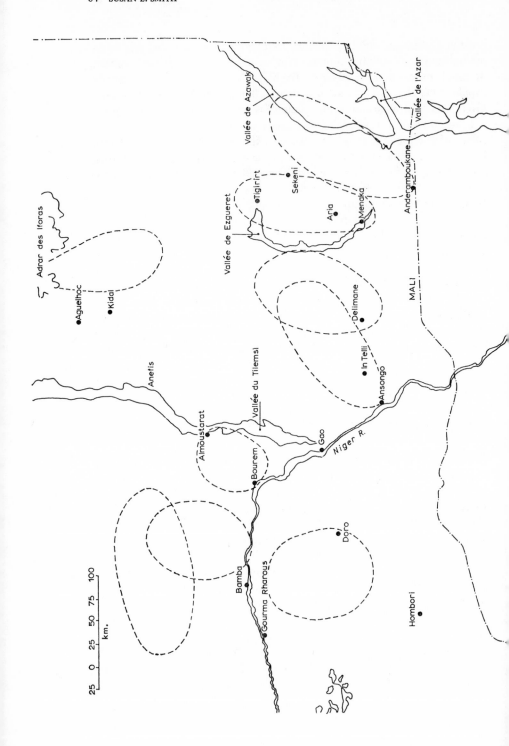

in place for as much as a month at a time. As this water dries up, usually in January and February, groups move toward more permanent sources, such as bored or pump wells or the traditional hand-dug wells in beds of now-dry lakes. As pasture is consumed in all directions around these wells, the camps gradually move outward, spending not more than a week in one spot, until the distance between water and pasture is the limit that mature cows and caprines can travel (see Table 8). At this point, which

Table 8. Resistance of animals to thirst, hunger, and fatigue

	Maximum number of days without water,[a] cool season	Maximum number of days without water,[a] hot season	Maximum number of days without food, hot season	Maximum kilometers per day
Camel	90	5–7	5–7	80
Cow	3	2	2	20
calf	1	1		10
Goat	15	2	2	20?
Sheep	30	1–2	2	30?
Donkey		4		

[a] Depends on quality of pasture.

occurs at the height of the dry season, the camp is literally tied to one water source and remains immobile, positioned between the well and the pasture, for several weeks. The exact placement of the camp itself at this time and all others is determined by the water requirements of the young animals that remain inside the camp, as well as those of the people them-selves. Lambs, kids, and humans do not require great quantities of water (amounts sufficient for two days can be carried in leather water bags), but because calves drink more, they must be taken directly to the water source every day. The extent of the daily travel depends on age and physical con-dition, but it is unlikely to exceed ten kilometers one way. It can be postu-lated, then, that the calves determine the exact distance of the camp from its water source.

On the other hand, the crucial decision of *when* to move appears to depend on the food needs of mature animals, specifically of those which are lactating. They must return to the camp each evening to be milked and to feed their young and therefore cannot travel more than twenty kilometers (the maximum for cows) in search of pasture.[7] When the pas-ture is consumed beyond this limit, camp and herds must move to another permanent water source; or, possibly, if it is near the usual end of the dry season or if the distance to the new source is too great for the animals to

[7] To insure their return, herders send the mothers in one direction and their young in another, on the principle that in the evening both will converge on the camp, the young being hungry and the females seeking relief; if, however, the two somehow meet in grazing (a not uncommon occurrence), neither comes back to camp.

walk, they may remain and try to eke out a living until the rains come. In either case, and especially when the rains are delayed, a considerable toll is taken of animals.

Such extreme conditions do not occur every year, but they serve to illustrate the critical balance that exists between man and land at all times in a marginal environment. Nomadic life requires a sensitive evaluation of the needs of animals and an awareness of where the optimum supply of water and pasture can be found. Increase in population or change in environmental conditions may bring nomads into competition for these limited resources. It seems likely that these mechanisms were at work 4,000 years ago when the prehistoric pastoralists were being forced out of the Sahara to find new and more permanent water sources.

During the wet season an entirely different set of considerations dictates the location of camps and the time of movement. The needs of animals are no longer critical because new grass is growing and water is available everywhere in streams and shallow lakes. At this time, the mature nonlactating animals, which until now have been totally independent of the camps and wandering freely in search of food and water, are rounded up; this process may take several weeks. When all the animals have eaten enough new grass to regain the strength lost during the hot season, the camp and its consolidated herds embark on a month-long journey to areas of *terre salée* [salt earth], generally located to the north on the edge of the Sahara (the precise area differs for each region). This trek has both a health and a social function. It allows the animals to graze on salt grasses and drink water of high mineral content, which the nomads believe is necessary for the health of both their animals and themselves. Secondly, because related tribes usually frequent the same *terre salée*, this is a time of feasting, competitive sports (camel racing, wrestling), and, above all, courtship.

During the wet season, the camps usually move each day or every other day; the exact speed and frequency of movement, however, is dependent upon the strength of the young animals, usually born at this time; for example, young camels must rest for at least a day after birth before they can travel; even then they may not be able to keep up with the herd, and a herder will often drop back to walk with the mother and infant. Progress is often slowed also by the need to retrieve each morning the animals that have wandered during the previous night. During the seasons when movement is infrequent, the trek animals are collected and hobbled the day before the camp moves, but when camp is being moved each day, the animals must be left free to graze at night. A minor factor affecting the speed with which the salt areas are reached is the search for appropriate routes. Large lakes must be skirted; and in the Saharan region, good water and pasture again become a problem. The northward journey, then, is not direct but follows a zigzag pattern (see Map 2).

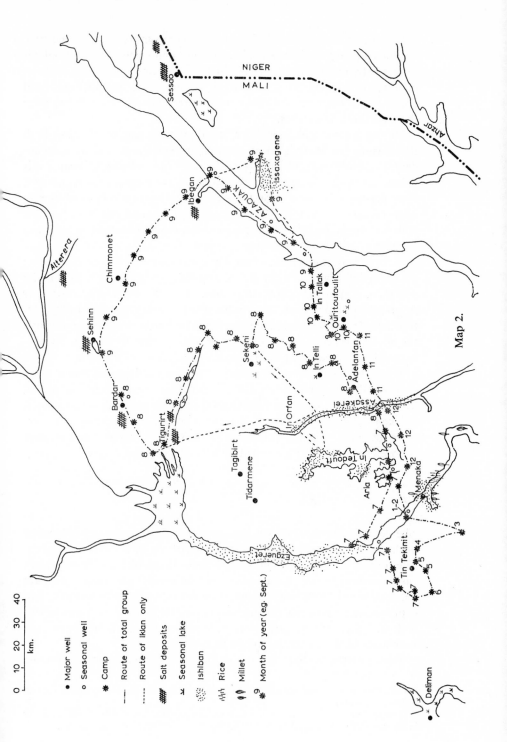

Map 2.

During all seasons the distance that a camp moves at any one time depends directly on the availability of water and pasture, but normally it ranges between two and thirty kilometers. Movement begins at dawn (it takes approximately half an hour to break camp) and continues only until noon. If still more territory must be covered, the journey resumes after the day's heat diminishes.

During August and September, the movement pattern of *iklan*, both those who are a component of other camps and those who are independent, is slightly different from that of nobles and *marabouts*, because it is influenced by their search for wild grains. At the time of the first harvest, *iklan* groups will converge on the areas which have been favored by rain or soil conditions. If the yield is abundant, the second and third harvests will be limited to collecting grain encountered while herding and will affect their movements to a lesser degree.

A local variation of the general movement pattern is found among groups living near the Niger River, especially those between Timbuctoo and Gao. At the end of the hot season, especially if it was prolonged or severe, the groups reverse their pattern of following the diminishing pasture away from the river and make a forced march back toward it, through the now barren country, in order to let their animals feed on the *bourgou* [river plants] exposed by the lowered water levels.

Movement of all groups is influenced by death and disease. Nomads are aware of the danger of contagion and isolate the tent of one who has an infectious illness. When traveling they try to pass on the upwind side of a stricken camp. When a person dies, he is buried several hundred meters from the camp, oriented to the east in the Muslim fashion, and the grave is covered with straw; afterward, ideally, the camp is moved.[8]

CAMP ORGANIZATION

The necessity for more or less constant movement has greatly influenced both the material culture and the living pattern of the Kel Tamasheq. The former is restricted to household necessities which are light and not easily broken; for this reason little pottery is used[9] and most vessels are made of wood. With superfluous items cut to a minimum, esthetics are expressed in such functional items as carved tent poles, beds, and bowls, and intricately woven mats, as well as in personal decoration – hair styles, necklaces, swords, charms, and leather wallets.

Tents are the logical response to the need for a shelter that can be

[8] Tamasheq do not condone amputation, surgery, or mutilation of the body even in order to save life.
[9] The only item of pottery noted in one of the camps was a large broken pot (one meter in diameter), in which hides were soaked to remove the hair prior to tanning.

Plate 1. Tent layout looking northeast. Note small tent of household *iklan* beside noble's tent

Plate 2. Camp prepared for storm. Note tent flaps being tied to supports at ground level. Herds of goats and mature camels have already returned although it is still daylight (4 p.m.)

Plate 3. *Iklan* milking a camel. Bowl is balanced on his raised right knee

Plate 4. Camp scene looking northeast. Tent at left being prepared for evening (flaps thrown back across roof of tent). Tent at right still with flaps extended for maximum shade (5 p.m.)

Plate 5. Typical scene of camp, looking west, with young camels tethered to post and donkeys loose but hobbled (4 p.m.)

quickly and easily dismantled and rebuilt during seasons of rapid move-ment. Tents are placed over a framework of wooden poles lashed together with ropes made from the bark of *afagag* (*Acacia raddiana*). They are fashioned from goat or cow hides sewn together with thongs. The number of hides depends on the wealth or social status of the occupant and ranges from as few as four to as many as sixty (see Plate 1). The tents constitute the heaviest and bulkiest items of gear, but this weight is necessary if a tent is to withstand the high winds and torrential rains of the wet season. During storms the tents are secured by tying their edges to the bases of the auxiliary tent supports (see Plate 2) and by throwing ropes, the ends of which are knotted around bundles of straw buried in holes one meter deep, across the tents. Tents have an average life of ten years and are easily repaired by stitching circular patches of leather over rips or holes. During the hot season, when the camps are stationary for weeks at a time, straw huts, cooler than the dark tents, are constructed; the tents are then stretched out on the ground, where they are mended and butter melted into the leather by the hot sun in order to soften and preserve it. *Temesgeit* [red ochre] is then rubbed in as an additional preservative.

Camps are located in relation to natural features according to the season. In the cooler months (September to November and February to March) camps are placed near areas of small trees or bushes that provide fodder for young goats. In the cold months of December and January, camps are moved into the shadow of an acacia "forest" or, if that is unavailable, a large dune, for protection from cold winds. During the hot and rainy seasons, camps are made on top of high dunes to take advantage of cooling breezes during the former and to avoid the mosquitoes and water runoff associated with the latter. The nomads explain that at no time are camps placed within 100 meters of a water source because it is prohibited to eat in such places.

Within the camps there appears to be no pattern regarding the place-ment of tents other than personal preference: some family heads prefer higher ground, others like to camp beside a tree, and some families habitu-ally camp near each other because they get along well or have herds in common. The exceptions are that tents of *iklan n iminas* [slaves who care primarily for camels] are placed to the east of the master's tent and the tents of *iklan n tess* [those who are slaves of the cows] are always to the west. Also, the tents of artisans are generally situated in a cluster to the west of the camp. The chief or most respected person chooses his place first and the others follow, apparently in order of seniority. Tents appear to be always situated toward the east,[10] i.e. baggage is piled on the north and south sides, allowing the east and west sides to be opened when the sun, or sometimes the wind, is not coming from those directions. At noon

[10] This is contrary to the observations of some other writers, e.g. Briggs (1960) in the northern Sahara and Nicolaisen (1963) among the Kel Ayr.

tents are opened on both sides to give maximum shade and ventilation. The distance between tents varies according to the terrain. On small dune tops, the major family tents of nobles, for example, may be within ten meters of each other, with the household slave tents clustered within two meters (Map 3); on open plains, however, they may be separated by fifty meters (Map 4), obliging the women to ride donkeys when visiting friends on the opposite side of the camp.

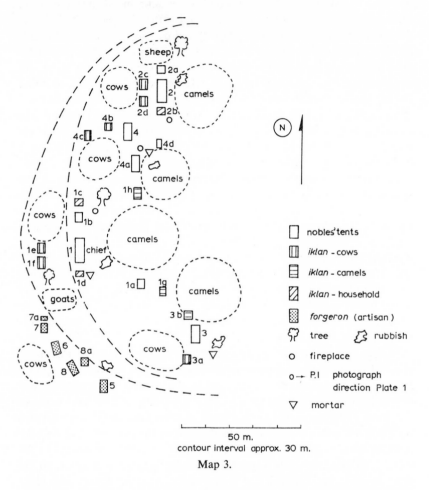

50 m.
contour interval approx. 30 m.

Map 3.

Camps as a whole are vaguely crescent- or U-shaped. At night when the animals return to the camp for milking (see Plate 3), the camels are placed on the inside and goats, sheep, and cattle lie outside, though there is no rigid rule and it is largely a matter of what is most convenient for those who care for them. Newborn sheep and goats are kept inside the tents. Older ones are allowed to run free in the camp during the day but

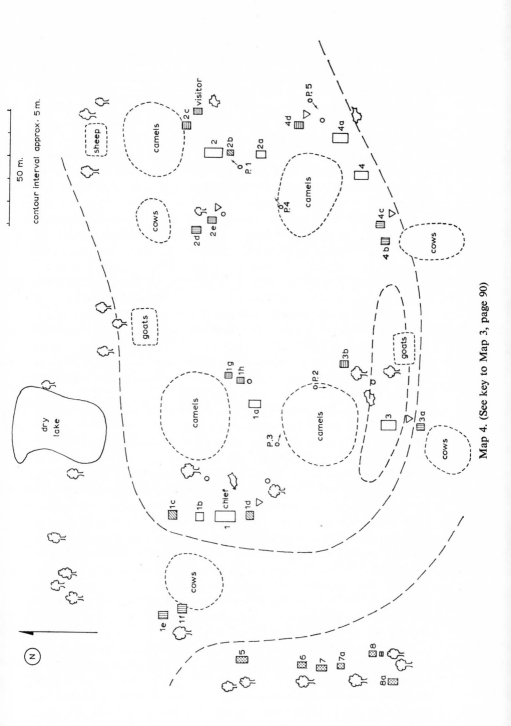

Map 4. (See key to Map 3, page 90)

are tied by their necks to a rope stretched between two stakes at night. Brush enclosures are sometimes made to protect goats and sheep from jackals. Newborn camels are tied by one foreleg to individual stakes in the middle of the camel yard (Plate 4); when older ones come back from pasture, they are tethered in a group to one stake (Plate 5). Calves are tied individually by the neck at night and are sent to pasture during the day. Donkeys' front feet are hobbled when they are likely to be needed, but otherwise they are allowed to roam freely. It must be emphasized that usually only young animals and mature lactating females are found in the camps; the others are brought in only when camp is about to be moved, and even then not all are found.

Because material culture is limited among the nomads, abandoned cool-season campsites are indicated only by trampled earth, dung, the lack of grass in the surrounding area, and a few branches used as auxiliary tent supports. Hot-weather sites may show traces of straw huts, and rainy-season camps often have remains of "nests" that children build in trees to escape the mosquitoes or occasional bed supports that lift sleeping mats 1 to 1.5 meters off the ground for the same purpose. Sometimes there are remnants of charred branches left from the huge bonfires that are built during wet-season storms to keep goats from stampeding. In the section of the camp inhabited by artisans, iron staples and small pieces of brass used in mending chips and cracks in wooden bowls may be found. There are also discarded pods of *tagart* (*Acacia scorpioides*), used for tanning hides, as well as numerous strips of leather and pieces of matting. Nearby trees may have scars where strips of bark have been removed for use in medicines, tanning, or rope-making, depending on the type of tree. In nobles' camps the pounding and winnowing of grains is done by *iklan* beside their tents; seeds and chaff may remain in these areas. Cooking fires are usually near the tents of the household *iklan*, whereas fires for warmth, used only during the cold months, are located directly in front of the *imajaren* tents. Perhaps because of the scarcity of rocks in the areas observed, no stones are placed around campfires, and such places are indicated only by darkened sand, charcoal, and ashes. The precise location of tents is indicated by areas swept free of dung and straw. The debris from the tents, such as cooked grains, seeds of *terakot*, excreta of babies, camel dung, pieces of wood used for games, and pieces of charcoal used for heating tea are accumulated about ten meters to the east or west of the tent site, where the bones are also thrown.

The population of camps varies from over 100 people to fewer than ten, with an average of five to six people per tent. The population per square kilometer is approximately 0.3.[11] The size of camps depends primarily on the social class of the members, because a camp of noble Tamasheq includes their slaves and artisans as well as their own families. Size also

[11] Computed from figures in *Annuaire statistique* 1967.

depends on the availability of pasture; a large camp may split if there is insufficient food for the animals. Some nomads maintain that in the past camps were considerably larger, perhaps several hundred people, because pasture was more plentiful. Others insist that this only appears to be the case because either individual camps of one hundred were more common, as slaves who now travel independently formerly lived with their masters, or because small camps would migrate as a group for protection against enemies rather than in dispersed units as they do now.

An example of the layout and demographic composition of a large Tamasheq camp (Oulliminden) is presented in Maps 3 and 4 and in Table 9, respectively. The sexual distribution varies with the season, because during the months of February to May and September to November the males often make journeys to sell animals and buy necessities, collect taxes and tribute, conduct raids on enemies, or just visit. Recently, major epidemics of smallpox, measles, pneumonia, and meningitis have been

Table 9. Demographic composition of a Tamasheq camp (June 1972)

Tent	Social category	Total persons per tent	Adults m	Adults f	Children living	Children dead	else-where	Others *iklan*	artisan
1	*Imajaren*	7	1	1	3	2	3	1	1
1a	*Imajaren*	3	1	1	0	0	0	1	0
1b	*Imajaren*	3	2	0	0	0	0	1	0
1c	*Iklan* (tent)	3	0	1	2	1	1	0	0
1d	*Iklan* (tent)	4	1	1	2	0	0	0	0
1e	*Iklan* (cow)	7	1	1	5	3	1	0	0
1f	*Iklan* (cow)	8	1	1	6	1	0		
1g	*Iklan* (camel)	4	1	1	2	0	1		
1h	*Iklan* (camel)	8	1	1	6	0	0		
2	*Imajaren*	5	1	1	3	1	0		
2a	*Imajaren*	2	1	1	0	0	0		
2b	*Iklan* (tent)	2	0	1	1	0	0		
2c	*Iklan* (camel)	4	1	1	2	2	3		
2d	*Iklan* (cow)	2	1	1	0	0	0		
2e	*Iklan* (cow)	5	0	1	4	1	2		
3	*Imajaren*	5	4	1	0	0	0		
3a	*Iklan* (cow)	6	1	1	4	2	0		
3b	*Iklan* (cow)	4	1	1	2	0	1		
4	*Imajaren*	6	1	1	4	2	0		
4a	*Imajaren*	4	1	1	2	1	0		
4b	*Iklan* (cow)	5	1	1	3	3	0		
4c	*Iklan* (cow)	6	1	1	4	3	0		
4d	*Iklan* (camel)	5	1	1	3	3	0		
5	Artisan	9	1	1	7	0	0		
6	Artisan	4	1	1	2	2	2		
7	Artisan	5	1	1	3	3	0		
7a	Artisan	1	0	1	0	0	1		
8	Artisan	5	1	1	3	2	0		
8a	Artisan	2	0	2	0	0	0		

decimating the youngest and oldest age groups. In the past, war appears to have been a more significant factor in mortality than disease. A few small groups differ significantly from this model; their social codes have inhibited marriage and consequently they are suffering major population declines.

Herd size reflects the wealth of the owner but not his social status; at present, there are slaves and vassals who have more animals than the nobles. Traditionally, however, the noble was considered to own the animals of his slaves and to have access to those of his vassals. The number of *iklan* tents associated with an *imajaren*, vassal, or *marabout* tent is, on the other hand, an indicator of status. For example, the largest herds among the Tamasheq are owned by the vassal tribe, Daousahak, but they do not have *iklan* and care for the animals themselves.

SUMMARY

This description of the habitation and exploitation pattern of a nomadic pastoralist group in a marginal environment with relatively harsh climate and scarce resources suggests that its situation is possibly analogous to that of post-Paleolithic herding peoples, who inhabited the Saharan and Sahel zones around 4000 to 1300 B.C. This pattern utilizes almost all the resources of the environment, either directly or through the medium of animals, and obtains them in sufficient quantities to sustain life by movement from area to area.

In terms of nonfood resources, wood is the major element drawn directly from the environment. It provides heat for cooking and is used to make tent supports, beds, vessels, and eating utensils.

The food resources directly available are vegetables, fruits, birds, fish, and wild grains. Food taboos restrict the use of a number of these items, especially among the noble classes, but wild grains are an important source of seasonal food for all. The primary subsistence sources, however, are the domesticated animals. In addition to supplying food, they may be traded for other goods, such as clothing, knives, and domesticated grain. They also provide many of the raw materials necessary for nomadic life – hides for tents, sandals, and saddles, urine and excreta for medicines – and they are the means of transportation for both people and camp gear (see Table 10). The animals, thus, are the primary link between the Kel Tamasheq and their environment, the West African Sahel; and the animals' welfare largely determines the welfare of the people.

Table 10. Comparison of uses of various domestic animals

Type	Transport	Meat	Milk and products	Hides	Social function	Occasion when sold
Camel	(a) Tent, large utensils (b) Men, small boys, traditionally women also (c) Grain in leather sacks (d) Salt slabs (e) War drum	Rarely (sick or weak animal)	Fresh milk	Camel whips	(a) Prestige (from number and form of animals) (b) Bridewealth (c) Camel dance for celebration and healing	Dire need: tax, fines
Cow	a	(a) For large groups (b) Weak animal	Sour milk, butter, cheese	Tents, sandals	Indication of wealth	Large purchases: tax, grain, clothes, saddles
Sheep		(a) Religious sacrifice (b) Visitors (c) Celebration	Fresh and sour milk, butter	Pouches, wallets (wool not used)		Small purchases: grain, butter, leather work
Goat		(a) Visitors (b) Hunger	Fresh milk, cheese, medicine	Water bags, milk churns, cushions		Smaller purchases: tea, sugar, tobacco, salt
Donkey	(a) Women and children (b) Pots, tent poles, small camp gear (c) Water		Medicine			
Horse	Respected elders					
Dog		?			Chiefly status Guarding of camp and herds, hunting, as pets	Usually given as gift

a Apparently bovids are used for transport in the northern Sahara, but this was not observed in the Sahel.

REFERENCES

Annuaire statistique
1967   *Annuaire statistique.* Gao, Mali.
BERNUS, EDMOND
1967   Cueillette et exploitation des ressources spontanées du Sahel nigérien par les Kel Tamasheq. *Cahiers ORSTOM, Série Sciences Humaines* 4: 31–52.
DORST, J., P. DANDELOT
1970   *A field guide to the larger mammals of Africa.* London: Collins.
GAST, MARCEAU
1968   *Alimentation des populations de l'Ahaggar.* Mémoires du Centre de Recherches Anthropologiques, Préhistoriques et Ethnographiques. Algeria.
NICOLAISEN, JOHANNES
1963   *Ecology and culture of the pastoral Tuareg.* Copenhagen: National Museum.
NICHOLAS, FRANCIS
1950   *Tamesna. Les Iullemmeden de l'est ou Touareg "Kel Dinnick."* Paris: Imprimerie Nationale.
RICHER, A.
1924   *Les Oulliminden.* Paris: Emile Larose.
SCHMIDT-NIELSEN, KNUT
1964   *Desert animals.* Oxford: Clarendon Press.

Ecology and Social Organization Among Nigerian Fulɓe (Fulani)

CHARLES FRANTZ

The ecological approach has been employed increasingly in anthropology during the last quarter century. Using concepts borrowed from biology and geography, the sociocultural approach to ecology views human societies as adapting or adjusting to such factors as diseases, parasites, humidity, water supply, topography, soil conditions, temperature, and plant and animal life. Most ecological studies have focused on societies whose basic subsistence derives from hunting, gathering, fishing, or shifting cultivation. A growing number, however, have concentrated on societies in which animal herding or husbandry are of primary importance (see Netting 1971), and several inquiries have examined cattle-raising societies, most of which are found in Africa. Regardless of the subsistence base, the general point of departure assumes that cultural patterns and social organization are always affected by ecological factors. Steward (1955), in what he termed a cultural ecological approach, postulated the emergence of a core of institutions related to the fundamental processes of adaptation. Following his suggestions, many writers have paid special attention to the significance of natural resources, the techniques by which they are exploited, and the systems of production and exchange that develop. This cultural core is said to influence or largely determine such things as residential patterns, inheritance practices, the size and organization of local communities, and other economic, political, and religious institutions.

The new perspectives of cultural ecology have helped to advance our

The author spent five months in Mambila District, Sardauna Province, and was assisted at various times by Mahmoud Hamman, Salihu Dogo, and A. B. Jauro, students from Ahmadu Bello University. Data from other districts were collected by the following students: Donald Hamman, Mohammed Dahiru, Suleiman G. Balami, Sa'ad Alkali, A. G. Aminu, and Musa M. Dede. I wish to express much gratitude both for their assistance and for the financial aid given by Ahmadu Bello University, the Research Foundation of the State University of New York, and the Smithsonian Institution.

understanding of the dynamic relations between physical environment, the use of domesticated food animals, and human organization. The non-social factors in the ecosystem are often thought to affect the number and size of domesticated animals, the age and sex structure of herds, their rates of reproduction, morbidity, and mortality, the size of flocks, and their location during the year. Each domesticated species has peculiar capacities and requirements that facilitate survival in areas (or niches) where dependence on other species, or on nonherding kinds of subsistence activity, is less probable. Conceptual refinements have now made it clear that pastoralism and nomadism do not necessarily occur together (Jacobs 1965; Salzman 1971); that herding and husbandry involve different activities and expectations (Paine 1964); and that pastoralism and herding are not identical (Krader 1968).

A society whose subsistence depends primarily upon cattle, therefore, will be likely to develop a core of institutions adaptive to the raising of animals, which themselves are constantly adapting to the physical-biotic milieu. Schematically, the general postulate would arrange the variables in the following fashion, assuming the centrality of a particular species of animal as the source of food:

	Environment		
	X	Y	Z
	1	4	7
Groups	2	5	8
	3	6	9

The general postulate would predict the following:

Groups 4, 5, and 6 will have the same social organization (or core institutions), because they live in the same or an equivalent natural environment.

Groups 3, 6, and 9 will have different social organizations, since they live in dissimilar natural environments.

If Group 8 moves from environment Z to environment Y, it will develop a social organization like that found in Group 5, and vice versa.

Group 4 will retain its social organization if it migrates from one location to another one with the same or an equivalent natural environment.

Before considering the Nigerian data, it may be useful to delineate the main characteristics commonly attributed to African societies whose principal subsistence base is cattle.[1] This is difficult because of the variation between nonsedentary, semisedentary, and fully sedentary cattle-raising societies. Nevertheless, the following portrait seeks to identify the adaptive responses in social organization made by societies for which cattle provide the chief source of subsistence.

[1] In addition to various monographs and articles, this composite picture draws upon the African data provided in Murdock (1967) and subsequent additions or modifications in the journal *Ethnology*. See also Jacobs (1965) and Monod (i.p.).

Settlements are impermanent; or, alternatively, residence in permanent structures is only seasonal. The mean size of local communities is quite small, usually less than 200 inhabitants. Its composition in terms of kinship is quite flexible and variable. The minimal herding unit is a nuclear family, although commonly there is periodic cooperation with other families or units not based upon kinship (e.g., age grades, stock associates, or friends). Cattle are predominantly cared for by males; females may assume responsibility for some tasks, particularly milking. The animals are more important for their milk than for their meat. There are few, if any, techniques for preserving and storing meat. Owners seek to maintain or increase their herds rather than to conserve grazing ranges and water resources. They also seek to achieve the same goal by gifts, exchanges, loans, and retaining herd ownership within the family or lineage. Symbiotic ties with agricultural peoples or traders are necessary to obtain foodstuffs. First marriages invariably involve the giving of bride payments, usually in cattle, by the groom and/or his kinsmen. Polygynous families are common, or at least occasional. Residence after marriage is generally patrilocal, less frequently virilocal. Divorce and remarriage are relatively easy and frequent. Descent groups are generally organized patrilineally but have only shallow generational depth. Each herding unit and local community has a high degree of political autonomy, at least seasonally. Political leadership is based on several criteria, including knowledge, personality, seniority, and patrilineality. Administrative hierarchies are weak or absent, and councils are informal or nonexistent. Judicial activity is generally the responsibility of elders and/or political and religious headmen.

I now turn from the logic of cattle and human adaptation to the empirical interrelations of physical environment, cattle raising, and social organization among the Fulani of the North Eastern State of Nigeria. Ideally, this should involve both complete spatial and lengthy temporal data, but unfortunately the information is too limited to permit this. Significant contributions have been made by Stenning (1957, 1959), Fricke (1964), Forde (1945), and various government surveys, but a full and coherent analysis of the interrelations of ecological components in cattle raising remains to be written both for particular areas and for the whole of Nigeria.

The North Eastern State, located between 7° and 13° north latitude and 9° and 14° west longitude, embraces four of the provinces in the former Northern Region of Nigeria. It is the largest state in the republic, having an area of 271,799 square kilometers (104,942 square miles). An estimated 9,678,869 people, about 14 percent of the national total, inhabited the state in 1972.[2] The state has greater variation than any other in rainfall,

---

[2] This figure, based on 1963 census data, was projected by the Federal Office of Statistics, Republic of Nigeria, in December 1971.

temperature, vegetation, and altitude. The sun reaches its zenith at 10° north latitude on approximately April 10 and August 20, and there are well-defined wet and dry seasons. Annual rainfall varies from 400 to 2,000 millimeters (15 to 80 inches), the minimum in the north where the shortest growing season and the highest temperatures are also found. Altitudes range from approximately 120 to 2,225 meters (400 to 7,300 feet).

Estimates of the number of cattle in Nigeria vary between eight and eleven million, and it is thought that slightly more than 50 percent are found in the North Eastern State (Fricke 1964: 79). Approximately 80 to 90 percent of these are said to be owned by Fulani, although they make up perhaps no more than a fifth of the human population. Two other peoples, the Kanuri and the Shuwa Arabs, raise most of the remaining cattle, although individuals of many ethnic groups have traditionally owned small numbers.

Fulani populations are widely scattered in the sudanic and savanna zones of West Africa. Their gradual spread from a putative homeland in the western Sudan over many centuries was generally by means of migratory drift (Stenning 1959), although it was sometimes associated with Islamic holy wars (*jihādi*). Today Fulani are extensively scattered throughout the six northern states of Nigeria, and a growing number reside at least seasonally in other states as well.

In the North Eastern State, Fulani communities have adapted to diverse environmental, economic, political, and religious conditions by developing a variety of settlement and subsistence patterns (Stenning 1959; Fricke 1964; Malumfashi 1969; van Raay 1970; Frantz 1972b, i.p.). These range from full-time pastoralism to permanent settlement. The degree of dependence on cattle varies from extremely high to almost nil, a variation which cannot be easily correlated with the degree of residential stability.

To examine the significance of differing natural environments upon social organization, I will present data on Fulani populations in five different areas (see Map 1):

1. Madagali District, Sardauna Province. Elevation 450 meters, with seasonal pastures above 1,000 meters. Rainfall 750 to 1,000 millimeters. Sudanic parkland and mixed annual grasses. Most horticulture at subsistence level although cash crops are increasingly grown. Population sparse.

2. Yola District, Adamawa Province. Elevation 185 meters, with seasonal grazing areas going up to 1,000 meters. Rainfall 750 to 1,000 millimeters. Vegetation principally acacia or sudanic savanna and mixed annual grasses, with open parklands; savanna woodlands in the hills. Areas of shifting and permanent cultivation, some of which are intercropped year-round. Population dense in some areas only.

3. Yamaltu and Nafada districts, Gombe division, Bauchi Province. Elevation 200 to 300 meters, with hilly grazing areas going up to 600

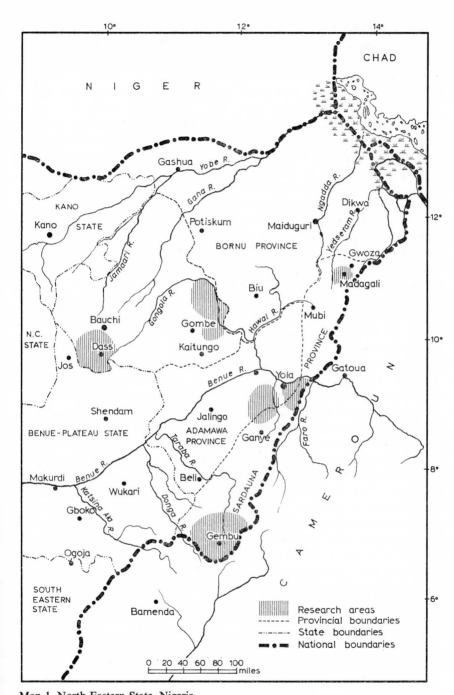

Map 1. North Eastern State, Nigeria

meters. Rainfall 1,000 to 1,250 millimeters. Acacia savanna and mixed annual grasses. Scattered horticulture, except east of Gombe City, where intensive cash cropping is found in the Gongola Valley. Population in these two settings respectively sparse and dense.

4. Dass, Lere, and Toro districts, Bauchi Province. Elevation 900 meters, with seasonal grazing areas going up to 1,500 meters. Rainfall approximately 1,250 millimeters. Savanna vegetation with predominantly perennial grass cover. Seasonal grazing areas frequently have sparse trees or shrubs. Mostly subsistence horticulture, with cash cropping on the increase. Population sparse.

5. Mambila District, Sardauna Province. Mean elevation 1,500 meters, with higher grasslands rising to 2,000 meters and river valleys as low as 1,100 meters. Rainfall between 1,650 and 2,100 millimeters. Vegetation montane grassland with perennial grass cover, although woodlands are found on steep slopes and water-courses. Subsistence agriculture and extensive year-round grazing. Low population density. District mostly an extension of the Adamawa Plateau in the Republic of Cameroun.

It is obvious that cattle raising is carried on at significantly different altitudes and in varying rainfall and vegetation zones. Higher densities of cattle are likely to be associated with nutritionally more favorable settings, such as on the Mambila Plateau, in well-watered valleys, and at the base of hills, rather than with marginal environments. Contrary to popular belief, many Fulani do not migrate southward in the dry season and northward in the rainy season. Those in Mambila and a sizeable percentage in other districts remain in the same or contiguous territories throughout the year.

Since all these groups have the same technology, their locations tend to reflect one or more nonenvironmental factors, such as the presence or absence of competing farm communities, agreements with horticulturalists to allow cattle access to crop residues, embarkment upon agriculture themselves, and the attraction of markets in which to sell dairy products. Agreements between graziers and farmers regarding dry-season pasturage are quite varied. In Yola, Mambila, and Madagali, farmers grow dry-season grains, vegetables, or other nitrogenous fallowing plants that preclude opening the land for cattle to browse. In other areas, the extension of agriculture has made available additional crop residues, which cattle prefer to grass (van Raay and de Leeuw 1970). There is considerable variation in the management of dry-season stubble grazing: in some districts there is no fee charged to graziers by farmers, but more often Fulani pay either cash or cattle for the farmers' crop residues. Yet in some areas, the farmer pays the Fulani for bringing a herd into his harvested fields. In Madagali, all three types of land-use agreement occur. Southeast of Yola, a Verre farmer does not pay the Fulani herd owner to bring his cattle to consume crop residues, but he provides tributes or gifts to the Fulani lineage or clan head (*ardo*) and to the chief (*lamido*) of the emirate.

The location of cattle herding is also affected by government initiatives to control endemic and epidemic diseases, to demarcate areas solely for grazing, agriculture, or forestry (especially in Mambila, but also in Gombe and elsewhere), to construct waterholes and dams and improve grassland ranges, to encourage beef production, to tax cattle, to control the burning of bush in the dry season, to terminate raiding and theft, to adjudicate farmer-grazier land disputes, to develop a more comprehensive system of land tenure laws, to expand cash cropping, and to sedentarize nomadic Fulani. The spread of Islam has also generated increasing interaction between religious teachers, traders, farmers, and graziers, thereby exerting a pull toward permanent residence or association with towns or villages that have mosques.

The size of herds and their age and sex compositions have increasingly been affected by these nonphysical environmental factors. Government veterinary services and the regulation of grazing land have been particularly significant. This is most noticeable on the Mambila Plateau, where grazing has rapidly expanded in the last fifty years because of large, unused areas of verdant grassland. Several individual Fulani now own more than 1,000 head of cattle, and even some non-Fulani have larger herds here than do most Fulani living in other parts of Nigeria.

Throughout the state the cattle population has been expanding, as increased agricultural activity has resulted in additional crop residues and as more non-Fulani have begun to raise cattle. The gradual sedentarization of Fulani has also been accompanied by enlarged herd size, because the cattle can be fed with greater regularity and at less cost by using residues from the Fulani's own farms.

The composition of herds also reflects the differential acceptance and exploitation of natural resources. In general, herds now include cattle owned by persons other than kinsmen or neighbors, although in Mambila the number of cattle owned is so large that herds have to be split into subfamily grazing units. In all districts, cows belonging to migratory, semisedentary, and sedentary Fulani are frequently herded together, even though nomadic Fulani sometimes decline to permit this in order to control the spread of epizootic diseases. Similarly, cattle owned by other ethnic groups and by civil servants, traders, and townsmen are often herded jointly with those owned by Fulani (Frantz 1972a).

The mean size of local cattle-owning communities has tended to increase, mainly as a result of political and economic factors, and a growing number of permanent buildings are being constructed in all the districts studied. An increasing number of Fulani camps have seasonally or permanently attached themselves to the villages of horticultural ethnic groups, either as neighboring hamlets or as wards within the main settlements. As an ever-expanding agricultural population converts rangeland into farmland, nonsedentary pastoralists realize increasingly that the principal sanction to claims upon land is continued use.

The size of the cattle-herding unit has changed as the number of animals has increased. This is most dramatic in Mambila, where herds are so large that non-Fulani herdsmen must often be employed, even though a high incidence of Fulani polygyny would logically seem to make this unnecessary. The minimum size of the Fulani herding unit, then, seems to correlate with the number of cattle rather than with the physical environment per se.

The division of labor found in the diverse ecological zones has been modified more by nonenvironmental than by environmental factors. Islamic conversion has withdrawn many adult women from milking and marketing activities, particularly among the nonnomadic Fulani. The freeing of former slaves and serfs has also eliminated an automatic source of labor in some areas. On the other hand, non-Fulani males have increasingly been employed to herd animals, collect firewood, provide transport across rivers, do horticultural tasks, and construct camps or permanent houses. This is particularly true in Yola, Mambila, and Gombe, either because of unusually large herds or because Fulani have become more sedentary and have thus begun to raise crops. In Mambila, the government restricts herds to 120 cattle, which require two full-time herdsmen. (A man with 1,400 cows thus needs twenty herders available at all times to tend his animals.) Payment for labor in cash and/or cattle has become common among Fulani in all districts; such wage relations are sometimes even found between fathers and sons. The influence of Islam and perhaps economic necessity have brought an increase in the fosterage or adoption of non-Fulani children, who complement an owner's kinsmen in herding responsibilities (Frantz 1972a).

The growth of towns, the use of money as a medium of exchange, and the spread of Western consumer products (e.g. bicycles, radios, and bottled beer) have also led many young Fulani men to leave their pastoral camps or sedentary hamlets. On the other hand, many Fulani herders have been employed by non-Fulani cattle owners. In one sense, the pastoral Fulani are becoming a specialized occupational category, in addition to being distinct ethnic groups; however, this category of labor is actually becoming transethnic since a growing number of non-Fulani are also employed as herdsmen.

Among the nomadic Fulani in all districts, cooperation in herding continues to involve not only kinsmen but also nonkinsmen chosen on the basis of friendship, age, and proximity. The government's veterinary services and the regulation of grazing lands, however, have reduced the degree of Fulani cooperative activity. The introduction of cattle taxation and the absorption of headmen into nonethnic administrative structures have also changed the ways in which Fulani manage their labor resources. It may also be noted that some of the labor involved in husbanding and disposing of cattle (e.g. controlling disease, slaughtering for ceremonial purposes, market selling, and settling estates) are being performed by nonkinsmen or non-Fulani.

Fulani cattle are increasingly owned by individuals or families rather than by lineages and clans. I found no area in which descent groups larger than extended families normally hold collective title to animals. In some cases, a father is the *de facto* owner while his children or wife/wives are *de jure* owners. In other cases, the father is both the controller and the owner of the family herd. It is clear, therefore, that ownership cannot be associated automatically with the right to dispose of cows. In Mambila and Madagali the progressive division of a man's stock among sons upon their marriage has generally ceased. Sons may now be given money rather than cattle, and they may have to await their father's death before acquiring enough animals to allow them to be self-sufficient.

The disinclination to eat their cattle continues among Fulani in all ecological zones. Owners of larger herds are likely to kill more beasts at betrothals, weddings, and naming ceremonies, but frequently rams are substituted. Nonphysical environmental factors have resulted everywhere in an increased dietary reliance upon grain, whether produced on Fulani farms, obtained through market exchange, or received as payment for grazing cattle in non-Fulani fields.

The giving of cattle as bride payments has decreased[3] in all districts studied, most of all perhaps in Mambila. Cash payments are more commonly used in marriage transactions, political tributes, and religious almsgiving. The sale of cattle or skins in order to obtain money to pay taxes and to obtain foodstuffs, salt, clothing, and other necessities has become general, especially in districts without large markets in which milk can be sold. It appears paradoxical that despite increases in herd size, the sons of settled Fulani often have fewer rights to sell cattle than do their nomadic counterparts.

The inheritance of cattle among Fulani was touched upon earlier in connection with the new custom of owners' employing their sons to herd cattle and the declining practice of dividing herds among sons upon their maturity or marriage. Generally, however, the number of animals given by a father to his children is unaffected by ecological factors; rather, this depends on the size of his herd, his generosity, his desire to remain pastoral or to take up residence in town, the number of sons, and whether the sons show sufficiently good management of those animals for which they

---

[3] The first marriage (a betrothal marriage, according to Stenning [1959]) is often the least expensive in Mambila, unlike in Gwandu (Hopen 1958), since little bridewealth is transferred. In Yola, where Fulani marriages to non-Fulani are quite common, the bride payment is higher for a Batta woman and lower for a Verre or Chamba woman.

have been assigned responsibility. Estates of cattle generally continue to be transmitted agnatically, although Islamic norms of inheritance are sometimes followed. However, Muslim Fulani often settle their estates prior to death in order to prevent their herds from becoming more fragmented. Other reasons for disposing of one's herds prior to death are to take up residence in town, to study the Koran or make the pilgrimage to Mecca, or to engage in cattle trading or other occupations.

The different physical environments in the North Eastern State seem to have little effect on Fulani systems of regulating sex, marriage, and divorce. More important have been the influences of sedentarization and the spread of Islam. Premarital sexual relations remain relatively free, especially among nonsedentary groups. During naming and other ceremonial occasions sexual freedom is characteristic among young adults and older children. With the growth of towns, an increasing number of both unmarried and married females are deserting their natal homesteads to become courtesans, prostitutes, concubines, or wives of sedentary Fulani and non-Fulani. Others retain their marital residences but embark on extramarital sexual relations with townsmen whom they meet in the course of selling dairy products.

Fulani households are still generally composed of multiple dwellings occupied by an agnatic core, with spouses and children and sometimes other affines or unrelated Fulani or non-Fulani. Monogamous or independent polygynous families are common, the latter being associated more with wealth, sedentarization, and Islamic faith than with ecological variables. The necessary additional females obviously come from non-Fulani ethnic groups, although hypergamy occurs as well between nonsedentary Fulani women and sedentary Fulani men.[4] "Concubine wives" are also present in some households, particularly in Yola, reflecting the political extension of the nineteenth-century Sokoto Caliphate. Women who marry into Muslim households are often partially secluded from public activities in the community, although these restrictions are sometimes applied only with difficulty to wives from nonsedentary homes; they are applied even less frequently to concubines or to wives from ex-slave lineages. Postmarital residence remains chiefly patrilocal or virilocal, but the changes mentioned earlier regarding the ownership of stock have brought an increase in virilocality and neolocality.

Although the spread of Islam has brought a shift toward bilaterality, patrilineality remains the key to kinship organization among Fulani in all the districts studied. Filiation and collaterality are probably more important than lineality, since the normal patrilineal kin group (*sudu*) rarely exceeds two or three generations. The *sudu*, as well as the maximal lineage of clan (*lenyol*), is used mainly to establish one's identity rather than to

---

[4] The lack of potential wives among nonsedentary Fulani females may contribute to the town migration and the "irresponsible" herd management of young Fulani males.

determine patterns of behavior. However, the consciousness of descent seems to be greatest among those Fulani who are the most sedentarized and/or own the larger herds.

Actual or putative descent is still used to organize first marriages. Quadrilateral cousin marriages are common, and a strong (Islamic) preference that a boy marry his father's brother's daughter is exhibited among the more sedentary Fulani. In Yola, marriage to cross-cousins is proscribed among Muslim Fulani. Local endogamy is preferred in all districts but is not always followed, as indicated above. Young Fulani males of sedentary households sometimes also marry non-Fulani girls who have been fostered or "adopted" by their parents. In addition, a few politically inspired marriages are arranged between Fulani and non-Fulani families.

Frequent divorce and remarriage have been characteristic of Fulani populations. The growing acceptance of Islam has provided a new means for legitimate divorce, but the evidence is unclear as to whether this has affected the divorce rate. More obvious factors contributing to divorce have been the growth of markets and towns, bringing increased exposure to nonkinsmen and other ethnic groups as well as to Western ideas and female behavior patterns, plus an increase in polygyny, which is positively associated with income and political authority. Divorce or the death of a wife among Fulani is less disastrous to the viability of the household than it was earlier in the century, however, because non-Fulani are now more commonly employed to herd and milk cows. In Mambila, in fact, divorce may help to raise a man's prestige, since it is an indication of his wealth. In the same district, a man's daughters usually remain with him rather than go with their mother in the event of divorce. Both remarriage and the inheritance of widows by junior brothers seem to be as common as ever.

Formal age grades have been noticeably absent among Fulani peoples, although age-based cooperation occurs in herding, circumcision, and youthful dancing and sexual relations in all districts. The spread of Islam has encouraged the development of transethnic circumcision operations, and these have contributed to informal age grading. Similarly, as an increasing number of non-Fulani own or herd cattle, cooperation in work and play has generated age bonds among males of different ethnic groups. The *soro* (*sharo*, *shadi*) rituals, which test manhood and fortitude among pastoral Fulani, are found in all districts except Mambila. In the Yola area, Verre herdsmen are sometimes "adopted" for several years to help tend cattle, but they are excused from the *soro* test. In most areas, unlike in Bornu (Stenning 1959), elder males are not "socially dead" but generally retain control of their herds until death occurs. Among females, there is virtually no informal, adult, age-based cooperation outside multifamily households and market places. Sedentarization and Islamization have probably discouraged the development of such sex-based bonds. On the other hand, in some districts there are status-differentiated bonds between paired sedentary Fulani and non-Fulani housewives.

External political and religious factors have greatly modified whatever significance the natural environment once had on the development of adaptive political institutions. In Madagali and Yola, pastoral Fulani *ardo*s remain only camp leaders or heads of lineages and clans, while in Gombe and Mambila they are also officials in the local administrative structures. The responsibilities of *ardo*s in the latter two districts are limited to territorially demarcated areas (*ardoate*s).[5] In all areas except Madagali, these headmen help to collect cattle taxes (*jangali*) and allocate grazing lands for all Fulani irrespective of lineage or clan affiliations. In Gombe, a further officer (*sarkin Fulani*) has been appointed to coordinate relations between the *ardo*s and the government, although wealthy Fulani can escape his control by going directly to veterinary officials. In all districts *ardo*s are subordinate to district heads, but only in some are they responsible to village heads. Among semisedentary and sedentary Fulani, appointed headmen, often known as *jauro*s, are under the authority of district and village heads. In Dass, Yola, Mambila, and many other districts, sedentary Fulani occupy district headships as well.

Where *ardo*s are appointed, they may be dismissed or assigned to other *ardoate*s, although this is rarely done. Traditionally, headship among pastoral Fulani was based on patrilineality, knowledge, popularity, and, to some extent, wealth. As the conditions of stability and security have been modified, and as supra-Fulani political structures have developed during this century, considerations of wealth, popularity, and identification with Islam have become more important as qualifications for holding office. These criteria are of even greater relevance in the choice of village and district heads. None of these variations in political leadership, it seems, are significantly dependent upon features of the physico-biotic environment.

Fulani cattle raisers in Nigeria characteristically have not had separate consultative bodies. Elders (*maube*) of lineages and clans commonly advised their *ardo*s or decided jointly with them on seasonal movements and settled disputes together. In Yola, each *ardo* has a council, but whether it is informally or formally constituted is not clear. In none of the areas are there district-wide councils among cattle-owning populations. Rather, individual cattlemen may be elected or appointed to district councils and to higher councils and offices. If they are wealthy and identify with Islam, they frequently exert considerable political influence in district affairs.[6]

[5] In Mambila, *ardo*s also appoint assistants (*wakili*s) to help them with various duties.
[6] This works in two directions: wealthy or patronage-seeking Fulani council members may give gifts, tributes, or "bribes" of cattle or money to higher-ranking officials; alternatively, they may be persuaded to vote in certain ways by receiving the same considerations from farmers or graziers who are not council members. Non-Fulani

With respect to judicial matters, most of the authority formerly held by *ardo*s and *maube* has been transferred to civil and criminal courts. The autonomy and sovereignty of both sedentary and nonsedentary Fulani has declined as they have become increasingly integrated into wider political, economic, and religious systems. Meanwhile, wealth and status differences have noticeably widened in recent years (Frantz 1972a). In all the districts studied, prestige is associated with a combination of criteria: wealth (especially in cattle), polygyny, Islamic identification and Koranic learning, political office, employment of several men, and patronage or support of a large number of dependents (kinsmen and nonkinsmen, including Koranic teachers). These differences are manifested in clothing, housing, occupation, and informal interactions, and, preferably, by making a pilgrimage to Mecca. In Mambila, cattle owners actually boast of the number of animals in their herds, a quite atypical Fulani pattern of behavior! *Ardo*s and other important officeholders may receive income from salaries, commissions, gifts, or tributes, in addition to the sale of cattle. Unless this wealth is visibly applied toward supporting followers and helping others, however, it has little significance in determining prestige.

With the continued spread of Islam in the North Eastern State, where it receives governmental support, and with the diffusion of knowledge about soils, grasses, animal husbandry techniques, and human and cattle diseases, traditional Fulani religious beliefs and rituals have noticeably declined. These changes have obviously been greater among the sedentary Fulani, where both Islamic and Western ideas and practices are stronger. Pastoral Fulani in all districts still depend in varying degree on traditional healers of human and cattle ailments. Charms, which are thought to offer humans or cattle protection against knives, swords, arrows, sticks, diseases, and climatic catastrophes, are worn in Gombe and other districts, and not only by migratory Fulani. In Yola some transhumant Fulani participate in rain dances held by the Verre. Generally, however, interethnic religious coparticipation is found among individuals who embrace the Islamic faith. Islamic rites concerned with birth and naming are followed in almost all situations, and Islamic forms of marriage, divorce, and burial are becoming more common among Fulani regardless of their degree of dependence on horticulture or animal husbandry.

Let us now return to the cultural ecologist's postulate that the social organization of cattle-raising peoples basically depends upon features of the physical-biotic environment and the techniques used to exploit natural resources. The first way in which the validity of this postulate may be tested is by comparing the organization of two Fulani groups living in the

---

farmers and townsmen who are councillors often display the same patterns of behavior as their Fulani comembers.

same or equivalent environments. In the districts studied, the settings north-east of Gombe City and in the vicinity of Yola are almost identical. The pastoral Fulani have virtually the same social organization in both areas. There is, however, a significant difference between Fulani who live some twenty or thirty miles apart on opposite sides of the city of Yola. Those west of Yola spend the dry season herding cattle in the bush and along the Benue River and its tributaries, while those east of the city can use only the bush near their homes because of dry-season crops grown along the rivers. In the wet season, those west of the city go to the hills and plant crops, which are harvested and brought back with them as the dry season begins; in consequence, their settlements are relatively small in population all year around. In contrast, Fulani east of the city spend the wet season near rivers, where they grow various crops; therefore their residences are both larger and occupied throughout most of the year. In the former case, herds are split during the wet season, and in the latter case during the dry season. Lineage-based cooperation in herding is more common west of the city, whereas the employment of distant kinsmen and non-Fulani is more general east of Yola. Also, east of the city, polygyny, clan exogamy, and interethnic marriage are more common; the *soro* is not practiced; and headmen are significant in terms of territoriality rather than of descent groups.

These differences can be partly attributed to the cultivation of different crop varieties and to the different seasons in which they are harvested. However, the main causes for the differences in social organization relate to political and religious events over the course of more than a century. The Muslim Fulani who settled east of Yola did not displace most of the non-Fulani inhabitants, although they controlled them politically. Pastoral activities therefore developed differently there than west of the city, where either conquest was incomplete or Fulani herding groups did not develop such strong symbiotic ties with non-Fulani ethnic groups. Thus we conclude in this case that sedentarization, Islam, and government control under a Fulani regime resulted in different social organizations within an essentially identical physical environment.

The second way to examine the significance of the physical environment is to compare the social organization of Fulani groups who live in dissimilar natural settings. The previous example indicated the scope of change that accompanied the sedentarization of migratory Fulani east of Yola following their conquest of local horticulturalists. Similar changes can be seen in many parts of Nigeria (de St. Croix 1945) and bordering nations. In the districts covered in this study, the most contrasting physical environments lie in the Madagali and Mambila districts. In the former, a more "typical" sedentary pastoral organization exists. However, in the dry season some Fulani migrate to the Chad Basin or to the highlands lying to the east, while many others stay at or close to their wet-season residences. Earlier, I mentioned that in Madagali three types of land-use agreement are found between graziers and farmers. On the Mambila Plateau, which lies some 1,000 to 1,500 meters higher and has twice as much annual precipitation, only one of these types of agreement is found. In fact, access to land is highly regulated by the government during both the wet and the dry seasons. The more verdant grass, however, enables the Fulani to remain in their rainy-season pastures for a longer portion of each year and consequently to build more permanent camps or hamlets. Dry-season locations are usually only a few miles away in nearby river valleys. However, the growth of the cattle population has been so rapid that dry-season grazing areas are under great pressure, particularly since the non-Fulani farmers have begun to use their land throughout the year either to intercrop or to raise nitrogenous fallowing plants.

With Mambila's greater potential for grazing, the size of wet-season settlements has increased. The division of labor has also broadened to include more non-Fulani herdsmen, and there is less cooperation within lineages and clans. With the expanding number of cattle, polygyny has increased and marital residence has more frequently become virilocal and neolocal. The *soro* ceremony is no longer performed, and Islamic influence has spread considerably. Ownership of herds is more individualized than in Madagali and other districts. In both Madagali and Mambila, fathers retain their herds until death rather than giving them to their sons at marriage, and sons are often paid in cash instead of cattle for their labor contribution. In Mambila, however, where the market for milk is smaller, cattle owners sell more of their livestock in order to buy food and other necessities; but lately, as more Fulani have become sedentarized, they have been growing a higher proportion of their own foodstuffs. In Madagali, Fulani *ardo*s remain heads of lineages or clans and do not collect cattle taxes, whereas in Mambila they are now associated with territorial units (*ardoate*s) and play a crucial role in collecting *jangali*. The Fulani headmen in Mambila have much more autonomy and power in district affairs than do their counterparts in Madagali. In addition, a greater sense of corporate identity has been emerging among Mambila Fulani of all lineage and clan affiliations.

These differences between Madagali and Mambila are clearly associated with environmental variations. The presence of abundant and unused verdant grasslands has obviously contributed to the efflorescence of cattle raising on the Mambila Plateau, not only for Fulani, but increasingly for non-Fulani as well. The attractive climate, in fact, encouraged so many lowland Fulani to migrate with their cattle that the government began to impose restrictions two decades ago. However, it can be argued that the present social organization of Mambila Fulani is *not* basically due to the physical environment, if one examines Fulani life in the area immediately to the east, across the boundary with the Republic of Cameroun. There, in a virtually identical physical environment, Fulani social organization is quite unlike that in Mambila. On the contrary, Fulani social organization in the Adamawa highlands of Cameroun is more like that found in the lowlands east of Yola. This suggests, therefore, that political conquest and Islamic influence are of greater causal importance than natural environment (see Pfeffer 1936; Froelich 1954a, 1954b; Hurault 1964; Dupire 1970).

The third way to analyze the effect of natural environment upon social organization is by studying changes in organization that occur when one group moves permanently from one ecological zone to another. Again, the Mambila Plateau is a significant locus because it is the most atypical natural area of the North Eastern State. Since there are no studies of Fulani on the plateau before and after their migration from the lowlands, we must depend primarily upon comparing the present social organization of Fulani groups in different natural habitats. Some evidence of changes in social organization, obtained in the course of field inquiry, indicates a movement away from the norms found among nonsedentary Fulani in various districts. The changes in social organization on the plateau were outlined in the last three paragraphs; the contrasting system of social organization in Mambila and the adjoining (i.e. continuing) highlands of Cameroun was cited. These data suggest, then, that migration to quite different physical environments does not of itself produce any substantial change in social organization. More important factors are the presence or absence of conquest, prior occupation by and density of horticultural peoples, opportunities and techniques for expanding cattle or crop production and marketing, and government control of those natural resources important to both farmers and graziers.

The final way in which the importance of the effect of natural environment upon social organization may be examined is to study a particular group before and after it moves permanently from one location to another ecologically similar or identical. Here again, there are no extant longitudinal studies which can facilitate an adequate analysis. The best cases in the districts studied involve Fulani groups that formerly lived outside the North Eastern State. One of these involves a group of Aku clans that moved from the Jos Plateau to Mambila about forty years ago as the result of the development of an extractive mining industry and an accompanying expansion of towns and horticulture on the Jos Plateau. There the Aku'en had raised a particular variety of cattle, practiced horticulture, had some slaves as laborers, and were moderately Islamicized. Although they reorganized their descent groups[7] in Mambila, they have otherwise apparently maintained their traditional forms of organization. The known

---

[7] Many Aku'en now identify themselves as Rahaji, a term used for an emergent cluster of clans or lineages that lived in diverse localities during the nineteenth century.

changes in their social organization are those which also occur among other cattle-raising Fulani on the Mambila Plateau, described earlier.

Many other pastoral Fulani groups have moved from the drier and more densely populated northwestern part of Nigeria to the relatively more verdant grasslands and valleys in the southern part of the savanna. Some of these migrations have been prompted more by religious than by economic motives, however, for the Bima Hills east of Gombe City have been a pilgrimage center since the turn of the century (Tiffen 1972: 57, 302). In many cases the environmental conditions of former and present settlements are almost identical. Upon their arrival near the Bima Hills, however, many Fulani established semisedentary (and some eventually fully sedentary) communities, and they often became intermingled with other Fulani and non-Fulani peoples. Most of these newcomers had previously been in more intimate contact with Hausa farming communities and trading centers, and they spoke Hausa more often than Fulfulḋe. Their residence in the North Eastern State has been accompanied by increasing sedentarization, farming (often including cash cropping for the first time), polygyny, and the raising of cattle for sale or plowing rather than solely for milk production. The division of labor changed as modifications were made in the production and distribution of food. With the expansion of the agricultural population and government-sponsored cash cropping, grazing regulations have also been introduced in some localities. Thus in several ways their new forms of social organization are similar to those which have emerged among sedentarized Fulani in various districts, including the Mambila Plateau.

The data from this preliminary study in the North Eastern State of Nigeria favor the conclusion that physical environment has only a limited causal effect upon the organization of cattle-raising Fulani groups. It is, in fact, difficult to demonstrate any necessary or essential relationship between the two. Several reservations may be raised about this conclusion, to which I would respond as follows:

1. *The physical environments within the state are not contrastive enough.* The evidence, however, indicates there is as great a variation in altitude, rainfall, temperature, vegetation, etc., as in East Africa (see Porter 1965) or in other parts of the continent where cattle provide the main basis of subsistence.

2. *The physical environment is atypical, since most pastoral societies live in marginal environments* (Goldschmidt 1965: 403; Berque 1959: 483). The evidence suggests that pastoralism or cattle raising has erroneously been identified with semiarid environments, not only in Nigeria but in other parts of Africa as well.

3. *Cattle do not occupy a sufficiently central role in Fulani economy and life* (i.e. they are seldom used to transport goods, their blood is not drunk,

they are not as ritually or symbolically important as in other parts of the continent, and they are not usable for offensive and defensive purposes in the way camels or horses are). This objection has some merit, but I believe it illustrates the methodological difficulty arising with the use for cattle-raising societies of models that are based either upon such groups as the Masai or the Nuer or upon societies whose main subsistence comes from camels, sheep, or goats.

4. *In cases of groups moving from one physical environment to another, there has been insufficient time for their social organization to adapt to the new setting.* The Nigerian data indicate, first, that forms of social organization may continue relatively unchanged for a century or more, and second, that sudden changes in social organization may occur as the result of social and cultural factors (e.g. holy war, religious conversion, heavy taxation, or the cessation of raiding) without concomitant changes in location or physical environment.

These considerations suggest strongly that ecological limitations or determinants may be quite limited, perhaps even incidental, in their influence upon the structure of cattle-raising societies. Gray (1964: 6) has cogently criticized early structural-functionalist methodology for undertaking the analysis of social relationships as if they were suspended in thin air, so to speak, unrelated to basic ecological and economic variables. The perspective of cultural ecology has sought to bring analysis back to the ground, as Steward (1955), Forde (1971), Gulliver (1955), and others have recommended. However, this approach frequently overemphasizes adaptation to the natural environment and asserts or implies that human responses are essentially passive, accommodative, or adjustive.[8]

In my view, advancement in theory can occur if, on the contrary, emphasis is placed on the creative or rational choice behavior displayed in human societies. All the districts studied in the North Eastern State contain many unused resources and unfilled opportunities for expanding the absolute quantity or widening the variety of foods that may be consumed by cattle-raising communities, a situation similar to that found among the !Kung of Botswana (Lee 1968). Furthermore, cattle herding imposes no inherent limitations on the use of other techniques of animal husbandry such as storing fodder and distributing it to penned animals, consuming the blood of cows, raising proportionately more cattle for sale, eating fish, goats, or pigs, and growing and storing plant foods. The reasons these potential food resources are not used must be discovered empirically, of course. As the results of other investigations indicate, however, it is likely that such reasons will include the inertia of customary systems of production, local settlement, and social organization, as well as value systems,

---

[8] Ecological analysis in anthropology has sometimes been as guilty of teleological thinking as were the early structural-functionalists, whom many anthropologists have criticized.

attitudes, and competition and/or control by members of ethnic groups that have different types of subsistence systems.

The creative and selective use of natural resources should be studied with caution, e.g. the common assumption that herding communities seek to maximize the ownership of cows or the utilization of resources must be questioned. Our study indicates that forms of food production and consumption may persist in dissimilar natural environments and that they are not necessarily oriented toward providing more than optimal caloric requirements. It is also improper to assume that some "more natural" or "adaptive" form of social organization prevailed among the Fulani before the colonial and independent governments introduced taxation, grazing regulations, and many other factors described earlier. The available history of the territory included in the present North Eastern State indicates that fluctuating intensities of trade, slavery, warfare, bureaucratic administration, and Islamic practices have existed for several centuries (Abubakar 1970; Stenning 1959; Dupire 1970; Low 1972; Smith 1966). This constellation of events suggests that at least some varieties of pasture utilization, settlement, and social organization found among various Fulani populations may directly or indirectly be due more to political than to physico-biotic features of the environment.[9]

Most anthropologists abandoned environmental determinism several decades ago in preference for some type of "possibilist" orientation. I suggest that possibilism may be too vague to be of much use and, furthermore, that it focuses unnecessarily upon the causal role of the natural environment. If, as in the North Eastern State, virtually identical social systems can arise or persist in different environments, and, alternatively, different kinds of social organization can coexist in the same environment, then possibilism becomes virtually a vacuous concept.

A strong case has recently been made by Forde (1971) for considering the causal significance of external (ecological or environmental) factors upon social organization. In my view, anthropological theory can be more productive if prior consideration is given to a different set of external factors, i.e. to political, economic, and religious relations *between* cattle-rearing peoples and neighboring societies. Analysis should then proceed to identify *internal* constants and variables, such as levels of taxation, tribute, or forced labor, protection, clientage, cattle raiding and theft, warfare, marriage preferences, and restrictions upon women doing certain kinds of labor. Once these tasks have been accomplished, the causal significance of physico-biotic factors upon social organization may then be determined with greater certainty.

[9] Stenning (1959) describes how the conquest and pacification of non-Muslims in northern Nigeria enabled the nomadic Fulani to extend their pastoral orbits. See also Hopen (1958), Abubakar (1970), Smith (1954), Dupire (1962, 1970), Low (1972), and Tiffen (1972).

REFERENCES

ABUBAKAR, SA'AD
1970   "The Emirate of Fombina, 1809–1903: the attempts of a politically segmented people to establish and maintain a centralised form of government." Unpublished Ph.D. dissertation, Department of History, Ahmadu Bello University, Zaria.

BERQUE, J.
1959   The nomads and nomadism in the arid zone. *International Social Science Journal* 11: 481–510.

DE ST. CROIX, F. W.
1945   *The Fulani of Northern Nigeria.* Lagos: Government Printer.

DUPIRE, M.
1962   *Peuples nomades: étude descriptive des Wodaabe du Sahel nigérien.* Travaux et Mémoires 64. Paris: Institut d'Ethnologie.
1970   *Organisation sociale des Peul: étude d'ethnographie comparée.* Paris: Plon.

FORDE, D.
1945   "The rural economies," in *The native economies of Nigeria.* Edited by D. Forde and R. Scott, 29–215. London: Faber and Faber.
1971   Ecology and social structure. *Royal Anthropological Institute of Great Britain and Ireland Proceedings for 1970*, 15–41.

FRANTZ, C.
1972a   "Stratification and ecology on the Mambila Plateau, Nigeria." Paper read at the 71st Annual Meeting of the American Anthropological Association, Toronto.
1972b   "Contraction and expansion in Nigerian bovine pastoralism." Paper read at the 13th International African Seminar, "Pastoralism in tropical Africa: traditional societies and their development," Niamey.
i.p.   Shades of Fulani. *Nigerian Journal of Anthropology and Sociology* 1.

FRICKE, W.
1964   "Cattle husbandry in Northern Nigeria: natural and social environments, characteristics and seasonal movements," in *The cattle and meat industry in Northern Nigeria*, volume one. Edited by Werner Werhahn et al., 1–150. Frankfurt on the Main.

FROELICH, J.-C.
1954a   Ngaoundéré: la vie économique d'une cité peule. *Études Camerounaises* 43/44: 3–65.
1954b   La commandement et l'organisation sociale chez les Foulbé de l'Adamaoua. *Études Camerounaises* 45/46: 3–91.

GOLDSCHMIDT, W.
1965   Theory and strategy in the study of cultural adaptability. *American Anthropologist* 67: 402–408.

GRAY, R. F.
1964   "Introduction," in *The family estate in Africa.* Edited by Robert F. Gray and P. H. Gulliver, 1–33. London: Routledge and Kegan Paul.

GULLIVER, P. H.
1955   *The family herds: a study of two pastoral tribes in East Africa, the Jie and the Turkana.* London: Routledge and Kegan Paul.

HOPEN, C. E.
1958   *The pastoral Fulbe family in Gwandu.* London: Oxford University Press.

HURAULT, J.
  1964   Antagonisme de l'agriculture et de l'élevage sur les hauts plateaux de l'Adamawa (Cameroun). *Études Rurales* 15: 22–71.
JACOBS, A. H.
  1965   African pastoralists: some general remarks. *Anthropological Quarterly* 38: 144–154.
KRADER, L.
  1968   Pastoralism. *International Encyclopedia of the Social Sciences* 11: 453–461.
LEE, R. B.
  1968   "What hunters do for a living, or how to make out on scarce resources," in *Man the hunter*. Edited by R. B. Lee and I. DeVore, 30–48. Chicago: Aldine.
LOW, V. N.
  1972   *Three Nigerian emirates: a study in oral history*. Evanston, Ill.: Northwestern University Press.
MALUMFASHI, AHMED TIJJANI
  1969   "Problems involved in settling the Fulani," in *Livestock development in the dry and intermediate savanna zones*, 49–54. Zaria: Institute of Agricultural Research, Ahmadu Bello University.
MONOD, T., *editor*
  i.p.   *Pastoralism in tropical Africa: traditional societies and their development*. London: Oxford University Press.
MURDOCK, G. P.
  1967   Ethnographic atlas: a summary. *Ethnology* 6: 109–236.
NETTING, R. M.
  1971   *The ecological approach in cultural study*. Modular Publication 6: 1–30. Reading, Mass.: Addison-Wesley.
PAINE, R.
  1964   Herding and husbandry: two basic concepts in the analysis of reindeer management. *Folk* 6: 83–88.
PFEFFER, G.
  1936   Die Djafun-Bororo: ihre Gesellschaft und Wirtschaft auf dem Hochland von Ngaundere. *Zeitschrift für Ethnologie* 68: 150–196.
PORTER, P. W.
  1965   Environmental potentials and economic opportunities – a background for cultural adaptation. *American Anthropologist* 67: 409–420.
SALZMAN, P. C.
  1971   Comparative studies of nomadism and pastoralism. *Anthropological Quarterly* 44: 104–108.
SMITH, M. G.
  1954   Slavery and emancipation in two societies. *Social and Economic Studies* 3: 239–280.
  1966   "Pre-industrial stratification systems," in *Social stratification and mobility in economic development*. Edited by N. J. Smelser and S. M. Lipset, 141–176. Chicago: Aldine.
STENNING, D. J.
  1957   Transhumance, migratory drift, migration: patterns of pastoral Fulani nomadism. *Journal of the Royal Anthropological Institute of Great Britain and Ireland* 87: 57–73.

1959   *Savannah nomads: a study of the Wodaabe pastoral Fulani of western Bornu Province, Northern Region, Nigeria.* London: Oxford University Press.

STEWARD, J. H.
1955   *The theory of culture change.* Urbana: University of Illinois Press.

TIFFEN, MARY
1972   "The enterprising peasant: a study of the agents of, and constraints on, agricultural development in Gombe Emirate, North Eastern State, Nigeria." Mimeographed manuscript. London: Overseas Development Administration.

VAN RAAY, J. G. T.
1970   "Animal husbandry," in *Zaria and its regions.* Edited by M. G. Mortimore, 149–156. Occasional Paper 4. Zaria: Department of Geography, Ahmadu Bello University.

VAN RAAY, J. G. T., P. N. DE LEEUW
1970   The importance of crop residues as fodder: a resource analysis in Katsina Province, Nigeria. *Tijdschrift voor Economische en Sociale Geografie* 61: 137–147.

Characteristic Features of Nomadic Communities in the Eurasian Steppes

A. M. KHAZANOV

Nomadic cattle breeding sprang up in the Eurasian steppes as a result of the adaptation of the communities with a producing economy to specific ecological niches created by the simultaneous effects of various natural geographic, socioeconomic, and historical factors.

Nomadic cattle breeding as an economic, cultural, and social phenomenon can only arise on the basis of certain prerequisites, such as an appropriate geographical environment (an arid zone where nonirrigated agriculture is difficult and unprofitable); a species structure of the livestock best adapted to the conditions of a given region; availability of saddle animals and wheeled draft vehicles; a certain degree of property differentiation involving private familial ownership of cattle; and, finally, an opportunity for the division of labor between the cattle breeders and the farmers.

Although in certain regions of the Eurasian steppes cattle breeding became more important than agriculture as far back as the Neolithic period, and in spite of the fact that even in the fourth millennium B.C. the livestock in the steppes north of the Black Sea included all the main species except the camel, many scholars, including this author, believe that nomadic cattle breeding emerged at the beginning of the first millennium B.C. From the Neolithic period to the end of the Bronze Age this territory had been dominated by mixed cattle breeding and agricultural cultures. Osteological evidence indicates, however, that for several thousand years there had been no marked traces of evolution of the species composition of the livestock nor any change in its relative importance that would mark a shift toward a nomadic economy (Tsalkin 1970: 253).

The horse was saddled not later than the first half of the second millennium B.C., and wheeled draft transport seems to have made inroads into the steppes from the Near East still earlier. Archaeological evidence suggests that already in the second millennium B.C., and more probably far earlier than that, the population of the steppe zone had experienced a period of disintegration of primitive relations. By the first millennium B.C. immediately south of the steppes there had emerged civilizations which brought some economic, and possibly political, pressure to bear on their northerly neighbors (Lattimore 1951). All these factors made possible a transition to a new form of economy, which became indispensable at the turn of the first millennium B.C. when the drying of the steppe due to a gradual change of climate, which had gone on for over a thousand years, reached its climax (Shnitnikov 1957). Since then and up to modern and contemporary times, nomadic cattle breeding has become a predominant branch of the economy of the Eurasian steppes.

The following chief types of cattle-breeding economy can be singled out on the territory of Eurasian steppes, semideserts, and deserts:[1]

1. The whole population moves from place to place, having no fixed routes and staying nowhere for long. This is an extraordinary type observed only during mass resettlements, conquests, and the subsequent development of the new territories. The cases in point are the Scythians of the eighth and seventh centuries B.C., the Huns of the fourth and fifth centuries A.D., the Avars of the sixth century, the Hungarians of the eighth and ninth centuries, the Turks (Oghuz in southern Russia) of the tenth century, and the like. It is not a coincidence that there are exceptionally few archaeological finds related to such cultures in these times, and it is very difficult to identify them.

2. The whole population roams all the year round using relatively unstable meridional or radially circumferential routes and having no stable winter centers. In the modern period such a mode of nomadism has been noted in the most drought-ridden and snowless areas of Kazakhstan, Turkmenistan, and Mongolia.

3. The whole population roams using stable routes and having winter centers. This kind of economy is based on keeping the livestock at grass all the year round. Agriculture is lacking. The cases in point are the ancient Sarmats, the Kalmyks, and some of the Kazakhs in the modern period.

4. The whole population roams during the spring, summer, and autumn in meridional or vertical directions, spending the winter in permanent settlements. Agriculture is practiced alongside nomadic cattle breeding, but only as a subsidiary branch.

5. Part of the population roams during this or that part of the year in meridional or vertical directions, while the remaining part leads a sedentary life, being engaged mostly in agriculture.

The last two types are in fact characteristic of a seminomadic, rather

[1] Here I mostly follow Rudenko (1961) adding some supplementary and clarifying material.

than purely nomadic, economy. Yet precisely these modes were most widespread in the Eurasian steppes. Thus most peoples traditionally called nomads were in fact seminomads in the strictly scientific sense, although in most cases cattle breeding was more important than agriculture.

Two contrary trends, sedentarization and nomadization, are observed during almost the entire history of the nomadic societies in the steppes. Initially these processes occurred simultaneously, within the framework of one and the same community. Thus, among the Turkmen and southern Kazakhs in the nineteenth century it was a common thing for a nomad who had lost his livestock to settle down on land or for a rich farmer to buy a herd and to shift again to nomadism. Second, these processes depended for their development on specific historical conditions. Thus, in the areas north of the Black Sea, the trend toward sedentarization which dominated the end of the Scythian epoch was cut off by the advance of the Sarmats and particularly the Huns; in the eighth to tenth centuries A.D. the nomads of the Khazar Khaganat started to settle down, but in the tenth century, after the Pecheneg invasion, they once more reverted to nomadism; in the twelfth century the economy of the Polovtsy (Kipchaks) started acquiring features of an agricultural cattle-breeding complex with their attendant traits of a semisedentary way of life, but the Mongol invasion in the thirteenth century brought an end to this process.

On the whole, the trend toward sedentarization is promoted by the internal socioeconomic development of nomadic societies (impoverishment of some of the nomads, the policies of the upper social stratum interested in agricultural products and handicraft wares, as well as some other factors, such as an unfavorable political situation, a reduction in the number of pastures, influences of agricultural neighbors, etc.). The opposite trend more often than not springs up in the wake of political events (resettlements, invasions of new masses of nomads) and also as a result of internal reasons (for instance, attempts to solve internal contradictions through external expansion, or the urge of the ruling stratum to preserve the nomadic way of life). It is possible that changes of climate had a role to play in these processes, but this is still an open question.

The social specificity of nomadic societies stemmed from the prevalent production conditions as well as, though to a smaller extent, from their relations with sedentary agricultural societies. The limited economic potential of extensive nomadic cattle breeding set a limit to its social growth. Among the limiting factors which contributed to the stifling of growth of the nomadic cattle-breeding economy, mention should be made, above all, of its instability and the constantly present menace of mass loss of cattle through jute,* droughts, epidemics, enemy forays, etc. By way of an example, at the end of 1892 and the beginning of 1893, the Kalmyks

* A severe frost following a thaw, which freezes pastures.

of what used to be the Stavropol government lost 1,201,187 head of cattle in a mere twenty-five days (Dubrova, 1898: 231). In the nineteenth century in Kazakhstan, large jutes which killed from one-half to three-fourths of the entire livestock struck once in every six to eleven years, whereas local jutes occurred almost yearly (Tolybekov 1959: 55). In Mongolia, up to half of the total livestock and more was periodically lost in epidemics (Vjatkina 1960: 161).

Another no less serious factor was the economic need to roam in small groups because of the impossibility of feeding and watering all the cattle on a limited territory. Numerically larger groups could band together for only a fraction of the year, except in times of natural calamities, wars, and mass resettlements. So, as a general rule, the roaming unit usually consisted of a small community or just one rich family.

One should also remember that a nomadic economy is comparatively labor-unintensive. Thus, in Inner Mongolia, an unmounted shepherd could tend 150 to 200 sheep, while a mounted one could look after 500 sheep or 150 horses. And two mounted shepherds could be entrusted with 2,000 sheep (Goto 1968: 95). A Turkmenian shepherd, assisted by one herdsboy, would tend 400 to 800 head of small cattle (Orazov 1964: 4–5). With the Kalmyks, two shepherds would tend 1,500 sheep or 300 horses (Zhitetskij 1892: 95). True, additional labor was needed to dig and maintain wells and cattle watering places, to work up cattle-breeding products, and to do some other jobs, but still on the whole labor consumption in cattle breeding was far smaller than in plow or irrigation farming, which was one of the reasons why the nomads were reluctant to give up their traditional way of life and settle down on the land.

The specific feature of livestock as a quickly accumulated and easily disposable kind of property provided at first for the rapid development of property and social differentiation in the nomadic community, as noted long ago by Ferguson and Smith. None of the nomadic societies of the Eurasian steppes known to science has ever been found to be developmentally lower than the epoch of class formation. But this very peculiarity of livestock is also one of the reasons why the subsequent social stratification in nomadic societies becomes severely stunted after a period of initial rapid development. In addition, sparse pasture under conditions of extensive cattle breeding limits the possible growth of the product.

The unstable economy and the lack of a need for large amounts of labor, as well as regular wars for cattle and pastures and the specific relations with agricultural communities on the one hand hampered class crystallization in nomadic societies and made it necessary to preserve some forms of mutual aid and cooperation; on the other hand, all these factors tend to encourage social institutions capable of coping with economic and military-political tasks.

A multilayer tribal structure proved to be the most suitable form of

organization, a prerequisite for the normal functioning of nomadic societies. On the lower rungs of the hierarchy, the social structure was based
on actual consanguineous relations; at the top, the structure was supported by a purely fictitious belief in common ancestors, which facilitated
social integration. This kind of structure is labeled a genealogical clan by
Abramzon (1951); Bacon calls it an "Obok" (1958). It shows features of
similarity with Kirchhoff's conical clan (1955), though the principle of
genealogical seniority is rarely consistently upheld by the nomads.

The family has always been the central production institution in any
nomadic society. The question as to which form of family is to be considered the most widespread is still open, but we can hardly agree with
Krader, who maintains that it is an extended family in all steppe societies
(1963: 338). There are reasons to believe that small family units were
predominant even among the ancient nomads (the Scythians and the
Huns). Apparently both forms of family often coexist, yet I am inclined
to regard the nuclear family as more typical of the nomads.

But along with separate families there have always existed groups of
kindred families related by blood and closely knit socially and economically. They often roam together and, being the lowest subdivision of the
tribal structure, constitute the backbone of a nomadic community.

The higher rungs of the nomads' social structure (subtribe, tribe, tribal
association) are amorphous and flexible; they show a capacity for restructuring on short notice, depending on the circumstances, in order to
incorporate and assimilate foreign tribal groups.

It is at this level that the traits of military-political organization are
most evident. Nevertheless, decentralization was the most common state
of nomadic societies, with central authority appearing only when there
was an opportunity for regular military exploitation of other communities.

The dominant socioeconomic relations within nomadic societies are
far from egalitarian. On the contrary, these groups exhibit a definite,
sometimes very considerable, social stratification. Thus, the royal Scythian
tribe regarded all the other Scythians as their slaves. From among the
bulk of the rank and file Kazakh nomads who constituted the common
people, the "black bone," there separated out a "patrician estate," the
"white bone," that traced their origin to the House of Genghis Khan.

The members of the upper strata exploited the impoverished community
members, often using them as shepherds and farmhands. Another widespread form of exploitation was the allotment by big cattle breeders of
dairy, draft, or other animals as payment for work or sharecropping.
The ordinary nomads were victimized through a system of various extor-
tions and outwardly voluntary donations, which can by and large be
regarded as an unfixed rent. And yet, in nomadic societies, exploitation
of the bulk of the population often took rather mild forms.

The forms of exploitation which were shaped by the economic and social structure of nomadic communities changed little with time. Thus, as far back as the Scythian time, there already existed a layer of impoverished population. Furthermore, exploitation had always been of a restricted and latent nature, disguised by traditions of tribal solidarity. It was also severely curbed by the need to preserve a military-political organization rooted in the tribal structure and to have the majority of the fit population able to take part in battle.

Slavery had never had a chance of becoming an essential economic element, both for purely economic reasons and because of the nomadic way of life.[2] That is why the aspirations of nomadic aristocracy were spearheaded toward the conquest and exploitation of other societies, above all agricultural ones. External expansion, in its turn, was a means of smoothing or even settling internal conflicts by taking them outside the society, thereby temporarily consolidating the latter.

Apart from the social factor connected with the internal processes in nomadic societies, their relations with the outside world were largely shaped by economic factors. The economy of seminomads, let alone pure nomads, is of a far less autarchic character than the combination of agriculture and cattle breeding, which is the vastly predominant form of economy in sedentary farm communities. The nomads cannot do without farming products and handicraft wares, whereas the farmers generally can. In many regions of the world they actually managed to do without the products traditionally offered for exchange by the nomads.

The Eurasian nomads had always been much more eager to trade with the farmers than vice versa, and when the farmers, for this or that reason, restricted or stopped their trade with the nomads, the latter would often assert what they saw as their right to trade by force. Such was the attitude toward China of the Central Asian nomads from the Huns to the Mongols. One of the Chinese chronicles frankly admits that the markets to trade with the nomads had been organized early in the Ming Dynasty "in order to consolidate the borders and with a view to cutting down defence expenditures" (Martynov 1970: 235). And when the nomads felt strong enough, they would attempt to conquer and subjugate agricultural societies, regarding conquest as the most efficient way of securing an uninterrupted supply of agricultural products and handicraft wares.

All these reasons are at the bottom of the sometimes patent aggressiveness of nomadic societies. As for their independent development, they never go beyond early class relations, the latter emerging under the impact of sedentarization of some of the nomads. As a general rule, nomads evolve their state formations only on the eve of raids into agricultural areas, in the process of such conquests, or immediately following them. In such cases, the habitually decentralized structure is superseded by a strong and centralized organization. It is precisely in this manner that

[2] For more detail, see Khazanov (1972).

nomadic "empires" were created. But while owing their emergence to the nomads, such empires owed their predominant socioeconomic relations to the level of development of agricultural territories which had fallen under their sway. This was the case with the states of the Karakhanides, Genghisides and Sheibanides in Central Asia; such was the case in other places. The nomadic areas of these states, as often as not politically dominant, had always been the most backward socioeconomically.

However, having formed a single state with farmers, the nomads would receive an impetus to their development. Characteristically one of Genghis Khan's advisers said, "Though we have won an empire on horseback, it is impossible to rule it on horseback." Townships sprang up in the steppe – centers of handicrafts, trade, and political power. Not infrequently, the ruling nomadic stratum would rapidly turn into a ruling sedentary class. A trend toward sedentarization would also sweep the ordinary nomads (Zhdanko 1961: 57).

The specific features of extensive cattle breeding and its lack of potential for internal development account for the stagnant nature of nomadic society, for the virtual economic impasse it would invariably reach. Hence, the reversibility of social processes in nomadic societies. The same ethnic groups enter the period of class formation, reach the early class stage of development, conquer agricultural areas and evolve a state formation, and then, that state having disintegrated, find themselves thrown back to the early class or even some lower stage of development. Over the past three thousand years in the nomadic world of the Eurasian steppes, movement in a circle has definitely overshadowed progressive development, and whatever elements of the latter did take place, they were mostly caused by the stimuli which emanated from agricultural areas. Even in the sphere of material culture, tradition dominated innovation. For these reasons, I thought it possible to group all nomads together in spite of the considerable differences of a spatial and temporal character.

REFERENCES

ABRAMZON, S. M.
1951 Formy rodoplemennoj organizatsii u Kochevnikov Srednej Azii [Forms of tribal organization among nomads of Central Asia]. *Trudy Instituta Etnografii AN SSSR*, novaja serija 14. Moscow.
BACON, E. E.
1951 *Obok. A study of social structure in Eurasia*. New York.
DUBROVA, JA. P.
1898 *Byt Kalmykov Stavropol'skoj aubernii do izdaniia zakona 15 marta 1892 goda* [Life of the Kalmyks of the Stavropol province before the promulgation of the law of March 15, 1892]. Kazan.
KHAZANOV, A. M.
1972 O kharaktere rabovladenija u skifov [On the character of slave ownership among the Scythians]. *Vestnit Drevnej Istorii* 1.

KIRCHOFF, P.
1955 The principles of clanship in human society. *Davidson Anthropologica Journal.*
KRADER, L.
1963 *Social organization of the Mongol-Turkic pastoral nomads.*
LATTIMORE, O.
1951 *Inner Asian frontiers of China.*
MARTYNOV, A. S.
1970 O nekotorykh osobennost'jakh torgovli chaem i losnad'mi v epokhu Min [On some peculiarities of tea and horse trading in the Ming period]. *Kitaj i sosedi.* Moscow.
ORAZOV, A.
1964 *Khozjajstvo i osnovnye cherty obshchest vennoj organizatsii u skotovodov zapadnoj Turkmanii v Kontse XIX – nachale XX V.* [The economy and basic features of social organization among the cattle breeders of western Turkmenistan at the end of the nineteenth and beginning of the twentieth century]. Moscow.
RUDENKO, S. I.
1961 K voprosu o formakh skotovodcheskogo khozjajstva i o kochevni-kakh [On the question of the kinds of cattle-breeding economy and of nomads]. *Geograficheskoe Obshchestvo SSSR, Materialy po Otdeleniju Etnografii* 1. Leningrad.
SHNITNIKOV, A. V.
1957 Izmenenie obshchej uviazhennosti materikov Severnogo polusharija [The changes in the overall precipitation in the continents of the northern hemisphere]. *Zapiski Geograficheskogo Obshchestva SSSR,* novaja serija 16. Moscow, Leningrad.
TOLYBEKOV, S. E.
1959 *Obshchestvenno-ekonomicheskij stroj kazakhov v XVII–XIX vekakh* [Socioeconomic order of the Kazakhs in the seventeenth to nineteenth centuries]. Alma-Ata.
TSALKIN, V. I.
1970 Drevnejshie domashnie zhivotnye Vostochnoj Evropy [The oldest domestic animals of Eastern Europe]. *Materialy i Issledovanija po Arkheologii SSR* 161. Moscow.
VJATKINA, K. V.
1960 Mongoly Mongol'skoj Narodnoj Respubliki [Mongols of the Mongolian Peoples' Republic]. *Trudy Instituta Etnografii AN SSSR,* novaja serija 9. Moscow, Leningrad.
ZHDANKO, T. A.
1961 Problema poluosedlogo naselenija v istorii Srednej Azii i kazakhstana [The problem of the semisedentary population in the history of Central Asia and Kazakhstan]. *Sovetskaja Etnografija* 2.
ZHITETSKIJ, I. A.
1892 *Astrakhanskie kalmyki (nabljudenija i zametki)* [The Astrakhan Kalmyks (observations and notes)]. Astrakhan.

The Problem of Origin and Formation of the Economic-Cultural Type of Pastoral Nomads in the Moderate Belt of Eurasia

S. I. VAJNSHTEJN

Soviet ethnographic science has scored great achievements in creating and developing the theory of economic-cultural types. There are, for instance, the works by Tolstov, Levin, Cheboksarov, and Andrianov. Yet a number of problems connected with this theory cannot yet be considered solved. These include the problems of the origin and formation of the economic-cultural types of pastoral nomadism.

Several economic-cultural types evolved from pastoral nomadism. Two of the largest are in the steppes and arid zones of the Old World. The first in Asia Minor and North Africa, for the most part in the arid zone of the subtropical belt, is to be found mostly among the Arabs. The other is predominantly in the arid zone of Eurasia's moderate belt, mainly among the Turkic-Mongolian peoples. The attempts by certain researchers to combine the two economic-cultural types can hardly be regarded as successful, since these types emerged and exist currently in different natural geographical conditions and are characterized by economic and cultural complexes that differ considerably.

Yet the origin of pastoral nomadism in the steppes and arid zones of the Old World and, indeed, in other regions is apparently characterized by a number of general laws. For a long period of time the dominant concept in literature, dating back to ancient times, was that hoofed animals were first tamed by hunter peoples and that these peoples became pastoral nomads.

The theory that animal husbandry emerged out of hunting was countered by Gai at the end of the nineteenth century. He considered that animal husbandry was preceded by land cultivation and that the domestication of animals was possible only under the conditions of a sedentary way of life (Hahn 1892). However, until recently, many prominent researchers dealing with the history of culture did not share his views. Back in the late 1920's, for instance, Bogoraz-Tan wrote

The taming of big-sized herbivorous animals thus occurs in the plains, even in the deserts, and from hunting it leads us to animal husbandry. The herd, expanding, gives rise to cattle-breeding or the so-called nomadism. Animal-husbandry on the plains, nomadism, is a special form of culture, parallel to land cultivation (Bogoraz-Tan 1928: 84).

In recent decades the view that pastoral nomadism originated among the hunter peoples has lost support to the spreading concept that, under conditions of neopolitical revolution, in a number of steppe and foothill areas of Eurasia a complex kind of farming emerged involving sedentary and productive land cultivation and animal husbandry on the basis of which, in certain mountainous and steppe areas, a transition occurred in some of the tribes to pastoral nomadism (Grjaznov 1957; Sal'nikov 1967; Markov 1967). Most of the researchers contend that this transition occurred between the Bronze and early Iron Ages, i.e. at the end of the second and the beginning of the first millennium B.C. The main reasons for the transition to nomadism were, some researchers feel, the increasing numbers of livestock and the accumulating experience of a more progressive, mobile, pastoral animal husbandry (Grjaznov 1957). Other researchers hold that changes in the landscape and climate led to a forced limitation of grazing grounds and their destruction, as a result of which the formerly sedentary land cultivators and cattle breeders were obliged to become nomads (Sal'nikov 1967). Finally, a view is expressed that the transition to a nomadic way of life was the result of overpopulation, as a consequence of which certain groups with a complex economy emphasizing animal husbandry turned to a nomadic way of life, in which they were joined by some of the neighboring hunter tribes (Khlopin 1970).

A number of researchers consider that the process of transition to pastoral nomadism was a lengthy one, extending over thousands of years. Others, on the contrary, think it was short and had been accomplished within one or two generations. However, all these researchers contend that nomadism emerged from a stationary complex economy. The supporters of this view reason mainly from the fact that, first, a mobile way of life ruled out the possibility of domesticating animals, and, second, in many areas of Eurasia's steppe belt the nomadic cultures were preceded by the cultures of sedentary land cultivators and animal breeders.

However, it may be asked whether these circumstances can be regarded as sufficient grounds for claiming that there was only one way for pastoral nomadism to originate in the steppe belt of Eurasia and thus ruling out the possibility of the independent transition of roaming hunters to pastoral nomads.

There are clearly not enough archaeological facts to back the assertion since science still lacks the evidence to prove indisputably the genetic heredity of the nomadic and sedentary land-cultivating and animal-husbandry cultures, the main ancient cultures that we now know. As to ruling out the immediate transition to pastoral nomadism by the hunter tribes of the steppe zone because the domestication of animals in their medium is impossible, this conclusion is hardly grounded sufficiently. One cannot agree with the researchers who claim that the most ancient domestication of animals (apart from the dog), including animals used for transportation purposes, took place among the sedentary tribes. This does not, however, rule out the possibility that such domestic animals could have been borrowed from sedentary tribes by the neighboring hunter tribes, such as the Tunguses of northern Asia or the North American Indians.

In northern Asia nomadic reindeer breeding was first pursued almost solely by the taiga and tundra tribes traditionally engaged in hunting and food gathering. Thus, for instance, the ancient Tungus tribes of pedestrian hunters and food gatherers, having borrowed reindeer from their neighbors, resorted to nomadic reindeer breeding, preserving the basic ancient forms of material culture but to a considerable degree adapting them to a mobile way of life (Vajnshtejn 1970, 1971; Vasil'evich 1969). Certain earlier sedentary and semisedentary peoples engaged in complex farming also began to engage in nomadic reindeer breeding after being forced from the more southern districts to the north. They adopted to a considerable degree the material culture of the taiga aborigines, who were adapted to a mobile way of life.

A largely similar picture can be seen among the North American Indians. Prior to the coming of the Europeans they had no domestic livestock. Only at the turn of the sixteenth century did the Indians begin to acquire horses, and gradually there emerged on the plains tribes with characteristic features of the way of life of nomadic herders. Before the Indians had horses the plains were relatively sparsely inhabited. The population clung to the southern fringe of the plains. These were roaming buffalo hunters and food gatherers and also cultivators in the Missouri river basin. The culture of the food gatherers was well adapted to a mobile way of life. The collapsible and transportable tepee served as their home. The horse introduced by the Europeans was at first used mainly by the sedentary land-cultivating population to the south of the plains and then borrowed from them by the hunters. By the eighteenth century the plains of North America were inhabited by numerous tribes of nomadic horse breeders. Some of them, such as the Comanches, had earlier been roaming hunters and food gatherers, others had been sedentary land cultivators. Some tribes were forced into the plains by the European settlers; others, who used to live on the fringe of the plains, after receiving the horse then moved into the plains and quickly developed. It is noteworthy that some sedentary land-cultivating tribes were forced to resort to a new form of farming. These tribes had been pushed out into the plains by the colonists. Thus, for instance, the Dakota tribes, once sedentary land cultivators and wild-rice gatherers in the Great Lakes area, when moving westward gradually lost their old farming habits and instead adapted themselves to nomadic horse breeding and horseback buffalo and fur hunting (Averkieva 1970).

Thus, both in northern Asia and in North America the hunters who moved about on foot borrowed the animals already domesticated and took to a nomadic way of life, preserving to a considerable degree the material culture adapted to a mobile way of life.

There is less information on the origin of pastoral nomadism in the steppe and arid zones of the Old World. However, in ancient literature and written documents from the archives of the Mari settlement in Mesopotamia, grounds are found for supposing that pastoral nomadism spread there on the basis of the economy and culture of roaming hunters who borrowed domestic animals from their sedentary neighbors. The most ancient documents on the nomadic elements of the population refer to the beginning of the second millennium B.C. (Klengel' 1967: 61). At first the nomads of Mesopotamia introduced chiefly sheep and donkeys, using the latter to transport their tents and other belongings as well as for riding. Only in the first millennium B.C. did the nomads of Mesopotamia begin to use camels, though camels had been domesticated in the second millennium B.C. by the settled population of the area. The camel enabled the nomads to develop animal husbandry in desert areas that were particularly poor in water. In Asia Minor the horse was already known at the beginning of the second millennium B.C., but written sources indicate that the nomads began to use it extensively only in the first millennium B.C. (Klengel' 1967:64).

The sources shed less light on the origin of pastoral nomadism in another major area where it developed – the central part of Asia. It has been established as a result of archaeological probing that in the steppes of that part of Asia, particularly in Tuva, Mongolia, and the trans-Baikal area, the wild horses (*kulans*) and wild oxen were in Neolithic times major targets for mobile pedestrian hunters who specialized in killing them. The way of life of the pedestrian hunters, judging from archaeological finds, was extremely mobile and adapted in essence to the nomadic way of life. Okladnikov discovered and described the traces of their ephemeral habitations, which bore the imprint of a nomadic life (Okladnikov 1970: 179). It may be supposed that in the Bronze Age these tribes of ancient hunters in the trans-Baikal and Mongolian steppes borrowed domestic animals from their settled neighbors and gradually developed cattle raising, while preserving to a considerable extent their old way of life, including the material culture adapted to mobility, with the skin tent as home. It should be noted here that the new type of mobile home for the nomads, the yurt, was basically patterned after the hunter's skin tent. Incidentally, the latter was until recently retained by the cattle breeders in the central part of Asia, parallel to the yurt. Certain tribes engaged in forest hunting apparently also pushed into the steppes after they began to use the horse. This possibility is also indicated by certain archaeological and paleo-anthropological materials. It is most probable that this pattern of development explains the formation of at least some of the pastoral nomadic tribes of the Huns. One can suppose that analogical phenomena also occurred in Central Asia, where traces have been discovered of mobile hunter tribes who lived alongside sedentary land cultivators and cattle breeders. Such were, for instance, the tribes of the early Kelteminars, who, possibly, in a later stage of development, borrowed domestic animals from their neighbors. At the same time one must, however, take into consideration that a major proportion of the nomads who appeared in Central Asia had originated outside the area.

In conclusion I should like to note that the frequent instances of nomad tribes or parts of tribes becoming sedentary or semisedentary in no way means that in the past those tribes were shaped on the basis of a sedentary economy. This transition was usually conditioned by social and economic factors, rather than by ancient traditions.

In literature one can frequently come across the assertion that the economic and cultural types of nomadic livestock raisers of the moderate belt were formed at the end of the second and beginning of the first millennium B.C. But this assertion hardly holds water. Though the study of the economy and culture of the pastoral nomads of the steppe indicated that many economic and cultural elements, characteristic for them in the late nineteenth and early twentieth centuries, indeed closely resembled those of the nomads in the first millennium B.C., this does not provide sufficient grounds for backing the assertion. If one turns to the archaeological materials and written sources characterizing the economy, the composition of the flocks, and the culture of the early nomads of the first millennium B.C., a number of specific features emerge which distinguish their economic and cultural complex from that of later nomads. Only by the middle of the first millennium B.C., in ancient Turkic times, was the formation of the basic features characterizing the economic and cultural type of nomad livestock raisers in the moderate belt of Eurasia completed – in particular, there was a spread of the collapsible dwelling with a latticed frame, the hard saddle with stirrups, and different types of utensils made of leather, wood, metal, and thick felt, which almost completely replaced ceramics. Forms of mobile life emerged which, without any significant changes, have existed up to the present ethnographical period (Vajnshtejn 1966, 1969). We shall note, however, that according to certain researchers the formation of the pastoral nomads of Arabia, the Bedouin, which began at the turn of the second millennium B.C., was completed only in the first half of the first millennium A.D. (Gaskel 1957: 7; Dostal 1958: 10).

In the history of the formation of the economic-cultural types of pastoral nomads of the moderate belt it is possible to distinguish two stages: the first is the early stage, or the stage of the formation of the economic-cultural type we are examining; the second is the later stage, or the stage of the economic-cultural type already formed. The early stage extended until the middle of the first millennium A.D., while the later stage covered the period from the middle of the first millennium A.D. up to the present ethnographic period.

In the early stages of development there was a changing character of interaction between the economic, cultural, and ethnic processes, traditions, and innovations. When an economic and cultural type was being formed, new achievements in the nomadic culture of one people rapidly spread, not only among their neighbors but also among remote groups of nomads interested in taking over these achievements. This, as we see it, explains the seemingly paradoxical phenomenon of the extremely rapid spread over the vast areas of the steppe belt of Eurasia of similar forms of harness, tools, homes, clothing, etc., a development that took place in the first millennium B.C. and the first centuries A.D. After the formation of the economic and cultural type, when the process of adapting the basic cultural elements to the conditions of the economy had been largely completed, achievements embracing mostly secondary elements of culture spread more slowly, and, significantly, the nomads became noted for their marked ethnic distinctions. The general nomad economic-cultural type for different ethnic groups created favorable conditions for assimilation. Thus, on this basis there emerged large but insufficiently close-knit ethnic communities. In the early stage the economic-cultural type of pastoral nomads in the moderate belt of Eurasia was to a considerable degree represented among the Iranian-speaking tribes of the steppe zone and in the later stage among the Turkic-Mongolian peoples of the zone. For the Mongolians the later stage of the economic-cultural type became characteristic only in the early part of the second millennium A.D. Significantly, the spread of Turkic animal breeders resulted in the relatively quick assimilation of their predecessors – the Iranian-speaking and other tribes of the steppe.

REFERENCES

AVERKIEVA, JU. P.
1970   *Indejskoe kochevoe obshchestvo XVIII–XIX vv.* [Indian nomadic society of the eighteenth and nineteenth centuries]. Moscow.

BOGORAZ-TAN, V. G.
1928   *Rasprostranenie kul'tury na zemle* [The spreading of culture on earth]. Moscow.

DOSTAL, W.
1958   *Archiv für Völkerkunde* 13.

GASKEL, W.
1967   Die Bedeutung der Beduinen in der Geschichte der Araber. *Arbeitsgemeinschaft für Forschung des Landes Nordrhein-Westfalen* 8.

GRJAZNOV, M. P.
1957   Etapy razvitija skotovodcheskikh plemen Kazakhstana i Juzhnoj Sibiri v epokhu bronzy [Stages in the development of cattle-breeding tribes of Kazakhstan and southern Siberia in the Bronze Age]. *K.S.I.E.*, vyp. 26.

HAHN, E.
1892   *Die Wirtschaftsformen der Erde.* Gotha.

KHLOPIN, J. N.
1970   Vozniknovenie skotovodstva i obshchestvennoe razdelenie truda v pervobytnom obshchestve [The emergence of cattle raising and social division of labor in primitive society]. *Leninskie idei v izuchenii istorii pervobytnogo obshchestva, rabovladenija i feodalizma.* Moscow.

KLENGEL', K. H.
1967   Ekonomicheskie osnovy kochevnichestva v drevnej Messopotamii [Economic bases of nomadism in ancient Mesopotamia]. *V.D.I.* 4.

MARKOV, G. E.
1967   "Kochevniki Azii" [Nomads of Asia]. Unpublished doctoral dissertation. Moscow.

OKLADNIKOV, A. P.
1970   Neolit Sibiri i Dal'nego Vostoka [The Neolithic in Siberia and the Far East]. *Kamennyj vek na territorii SSSR.* Moscow.

SAL'NIKOV, K. V.
1967   *Ocherki drevnej istorii Juzhnogo Urala* [Essays on the ancient history of the southern Urals]. Moscow.

VAJNSHTEJN, S. I.
1966   Nekotorye voprosy istorii drevnetjurkskoj kul'tury [Some questions on the history of the ancient Turkic culture]. *Sovetskaja Etnografija* 3.
1969   *Proiskhozhdenie i istoricheskaja etnografija tuvinskogo naroda* [Origin and historical ethnography of the Tuvinian people]. Moscow.
1970, 1971   Problema proiskhozhdenija denevodstva v Evrazii [Problems of the origin of reindeer breeding in Eurasia]. *Sovetskaja Etnografija* 1970 (6); 1971 (5).

VASIL'EVICH, G. M.
1969   *Evenki* [The Evenki]. Leningrad.

SECTION TWO

Ethnogenesis, Evolution,
and Continuity

Ethnic Communities with Survivals of Clan and Tribal Structure in Central Asia and Kazakhstan in the Nineteenth and Early Twentieth Centuries

T. A. ZHDANKO

The present stage of development of ethnographic studies in the Soviet Union is characterized by an interest in the theory of ethnos. A number of special articles have been published on the study of such categories as ethnos and ethnic community (Bromlei 1970a, 1970b, 1971; Kozlov 1967, 1969; Cheboksarov and Cheboksarova 1971: 8–37). The elaboration of the classification of ethnic communities in their various aspects has been accompanied by lively discussions.

According to this classification, three principal types of ethnic community have become generally accepted in Soviet ethnography: the tribe or group of kindred tribes (affinity of tribes), for the primitive communal system; the nationality, for the precapitalist stages of class society; and the nation, for the period of capitalism and socialism (Cheboksarov 1967). However, the use of this classification for systematizing the ethnic diversities of different periods and regions demands further elaboration. Researchers are coming to the conclusion that there are transitional forms of ethnic communities at "the intermediate stages of the process at the start of which there were primitive tribes, or an alliance of these tribes, and at the end, the nationality of the early class period" (Tret'jakov 1966: 3).

Another specific feature of ethnic development has been revealed in the course of investigations: the existence (not only during transitional historical periods but also during the flourishing of new socioeconomic structures) of relics of earlier types of ethnic communities; for example, tribes in the feudal epoch and nationalities that did not develop into nations or become parts of nations under capitalism and socialism. Such "relic" tribes and nationalities do not remain immutable under new historical conditions. While they retain the general ethnic traditional makeup of earlier epochs, their social structure, as well as certain ethnic features, undergo profound qualitative changes; for example, the loss of tribal dialects by relic tribes. To this transformation of ethnic communities can be applied Marx's apt characterization of primitive communities whose vestigial forms have persisted at all stages of historical development. Marx said that, just like geological formations, such historical formations went through a number of primary, secondary, tertiary, etc., stages.

The need for differentiating the concept of nationality in its ethnic aspect and introducing scientific terminology to emphasize its essential distinctions in different historical epochs has repeatedly been stressed in literature devoted to the subject (Cheboksarov 1967; Tokarev 1964; Cheboksarov and Cheboksarova 1971). In one of the latest works on ethnic theory, Arutjunov and Cheboksarov suggest that a special terminology be introduced to reflect the various phases of nationalities on the grounds that:

Modern nationalities cannot be fully identified with the nationalities of ancient times and the Middle Ages. This is impossible even because the latter nationalities were the principal, highest taxonomic units in the classification of ethnoses of the period. For the modern age, however, the nation is the highest taxonomic unit, whereas the nationality is its hierarchically subordinate taxonomic unit (Arutjunov and Cheboksarov 1972: 26–27).

The authors therefore argue that these essentially different concepts should not be covered by one term, and that the term "primary nationalities" should be introduced for the nationalities of ancient times and the Middle Ages. Modern nationalities which failed to consolidate into independent nations should be called "secondary nationalities" (Arutjunov and Cheboksarov 1972: 27).

The premises advanced by these authors should make for a more profound historical classification of ethnic communities, and they seem rather promising, particularly for the study of the questions connected with the subject being considered here. Just as in near-modern times considerably modified (socioeconomically and ethnically) "secondary nationalities" coexist with nations under feudalism, relic "secondary tribes" existed (not only in the early states but later as well) along with the nationality – the ethnic community typical of that structure. These tribes, however, were thoroughly transformed and had lost the basic features typical of the ethnic communities of the primitive communal system. They were usually organic elements in the distinctive ethnic structure of certain nationalities.

A wide range of nationalities in the nineteenth and early twentieth centuries incorporated tribal groups instead of the territorial ethnographic groups common for this type of ethnic community. This is a typical feature of the social and ethnic structures of many peoples whose economies were always dominated by nomadic cattle breeding, irrespective of their ethnic affiliation (Turkic-speaking, Iranian-speaking, Arabic-speaking, and others). The archaic features of such ethnic structures are stipulated by the tenacity of survival of the primitive communal system peculiar to nomadic cattle breeders of desert and arid steppe regions, who in modern times are characterized by a backward socioeconomic structure and way of life.

In prerevolutionary Russia the Turkic-speaking peoples of Central Asia – Kazakhs, Kirghiz, Turkmen, and Karakalpaks – had an ethnic structure with remnants of tribal division. The same structure continued to exist among some of the Uzbeks (the so-called seminomadic or Desht-i-Kipchak Uzbeks) who were descendants of tribes that had merged with the Uzbeks at a later stage of their ethnic formation. This ethnic structure was also typical of many Turkic-speaking peoples living in the Volga and Ural regions (Bashkirs), in the Caucasus (Nogai), in Siberia (Altaic, Shortsi, and others), and also of some peoples belonging to other ethnolinguistic communities (Circassians and other mountain nationalities). Thus, certain peoples in the far north and the far east – gatherers, hunters, and fishermen of the taiga and the tundra, who represented economic and cultural types still more ancient in their origin than the nomadic cattle breeders of the steppes and deserts of Central Asia and Kazakhstan – retained the tribes and affinities of tribes in modern times in a still more archaic form with more pronounced features of the ethnic community of the primitive communal system (Dolgikh 1967; Gurvich 1966). Crop raising, along with nomadic and distant-pasture cattle breeding, had deep-seated historical traditions among some of the above-mentioned Central Asian peoples, especially the Turkmen and the Karakalpaks (Zhdanko 1961; *Ocherki istorii zemledelija* 1971). Stability of clan and tribal divisions was as typical of many peoples who from ancient times combined these two branches of economy as it was of the nomads (Vinnikov 1954; Zhdanko 1950).

By the early twentieth century the Turkmen numbered about nineteen large tribes; the Karakalpaks, twelve; the Kirghiz, thirty-nine; the Kazakhs, over forty. The clan and tribal structures were cumbersome and multistepped. The tribes formed two *kanat* [wings] among the Kirghiz, two *arys* among the Karakalpaks and three *shuz* among the Kazakhs. Each tribe was divided into a multitude of clan groups and smaller units (on the patterns of clan and tribal structure, see *Narody Srednei Azii* 1962: vol. 1, pp. 412–413; 1963: vol. 2, pp. 17, 19). As a rule, tribes and big clans had their own intricate *shezhire* [genealogies]. At first sight the outward ethnic structure seems profoundly archaic, but the impression changes if one takes into account the distinctive features of the transformation of secondary tribes.

The essence of the later-period tribe is examined by researchers today mainly in its social context. Special works devoted to the typology of ethnic communities of nomadic peoples are so far very rare (Lashuk 1968).

It is not possible to dwell on the voluminous literature dealing with the controversial problem of the social system of nomadic cattle-breeding peoples (Lashuk 1967a, 1967b; Khazanov 1968; Abramzon 1970; Markov 1970), but mention should be made that it contains a profound treatment of the question of the social structure of the later-period tribe under feudalism and in modern times. Despite the lively discussions (on class formation, early class relations, patriarchal-feudal relations) that have been going on for decades and the wide gap between the points of view of scholars participating in them, no one today adheres to the prerevolutionary conception of the allegedly classless nature of nomadic societies and the absolute predominance of the patriarchal-tribal system in them. Today researchers consider the internal social contradictions within the later-period tribe to be the most important feature distinguishing it from its classical primitive form. Despite a great variety of conceptions, contemporary researchers are unanimous in admitting a far-reaching social differentiation among the nomadic peoples in the nineteenth and early twentieth centuries, the period analyzed here. The second feature of the later-period tribe is the obliteration of consanguineous ties and the gradual transformation of tribes into political or territorial and administrative communities. Historical and ethnographic investigations invariably confirm that survivals of consanguineous ties are revealed only in the lowest units of clan and tribal structures, in their smallest groupings, with family and relatives' groups comprising the nomadic village communities (Abramzon 1951).

The makeup of the later-period tribe, with its new social functions, in the Central Asian Uzbek khanates of the nineteenth century is aptly characterized by Ivanov, a specialist in Oriental history. According to him the clan and tribal communities of that time in Central Asia were:

Originally economic, political and administrative units...the assessment of duties and taxes, distribution of land and water, recruitment into the army, and so forth, proceeded on the tribe basis. Each tribe occupied its strictly delimited territory which usually had pastures and plots of arable land, as well as strong points which often were the residence of the tribal chief (Ivanov 1952: 128–129).

The loss by the tribes of the basic features of ethnic communities of the primitive communal type (consanguineous ties and social equality) and their transformation into secondary-type tribes is an important factor explaining why, despite the usually stable character of these traditional communities, processes of consolidating nationalities were in evidence even in the early Middle Ages.

The specific features of the ethnic history of the Central Asian peoples were many: a great variety of components taking part in their ethnic formation; the prominence of migrations stemming from military conquests and other events of political history; and the permanent ethnic contacts of the settled population of farming regions with the cattle-breeding tribes that roamed the nearby steppes and were constantly moving to oases and settling there among the farming population, with whom they gradually mixed and merged.

Comprehensive investigations of the problem of the ethnic origin of the peoples of Central Asia and Kazakhstan, based on historical, archaeological, linguistic, ethnographic, and anthropological data, warrant the conclusion that the initial elements of ethnic community among them appeared as early as the Middle Ages, between the ninth and twelfth centuries. In that period the fundamentals of their languages, their ethnic territories, and the ethnographic specificity of their economies and way of life evolved (*Narody Srednei Azii* 1962–1963:38–103). The process of consolidation was facilitated by the fact that components of future nationalities became incorporated into powerful feudal states (the Samanid state, ninth to tenth centuries; the Karakhanid state, eleventh to twelfth centuries; the state of the Khorezm-Shahs, twelfth to thirteenth centuries) and that large tribal alliances were formed in the steppe regions around the Aral Sea (the Pecheneg and West Oguz in the ninth to eleventh centuries, the Kipchak in the eleventh to twelfth centuries).

The thirteenth and fourteenth centuries were marked by mass invasions by the alien Turkic-Mongol steppe tribes following the Mongol conquest of Central Asia and Kazakhstan. In the fifteenth and early sixteenth centuries Desht-i-Kipchak tribes were moving into the farming regions of Central Asia conquered by the Uzbek khan, Sheibani. Both these waves of invading tribes exerted a great influence on the composition of the Turkic-speaking nationalities that were emerging in Central Asia; therefore, the concluding stage in their ethnic formation, in the opinion of researchers, was the sixteenth century.

In the sixteenth to eighteenth centuries the peoples of Central Asia lived in the territory of three big feudal despotic states headed by khans of Uzbek dynasties: Bukhara, Khiva, and Kokand. In each of these khanates numerous tribes of seminomadic Uzbeks made up a considerable part of the population. The remaining peoples were also divided between the khanates: the Turkmen between Bukhara and Khiva, and the Kazakhs in all three khanates. The middle of the last century marked a new stage in the history of Central Asia and Kazakhstan: they were joined to Russia.

Despite the unfavorable historical situation that had resulted in the division of the Central Asian peoples for four centuries between various state formations, the level of their ethnic consolidation was high enough even on the eve of their joining Russia. They were known in Russia and Europe as nationalities with definite names, each with a distinctive ethnographic makeup. On the very first ethnographic maps, their territories were specially marked, and detailed descriptions of them were contained in the first Russian ethnographic works of the eighteenth and early nineteenth centuries. Russian researchers knew that the nomadic Kazakhs, Kirghiz, and Turkmen were divided into numerous tribes, but that did not interfere with their conception of these peoples' ethnic integrity. Back in 1832, Levshin, author of a three-volume monograph about the Kazakhs, wrote that the Kazakh tribes "had merged into one people," proof of which was "their common language, religion, way of life and customs" (Levshin 1832: 5).

As mentioned, the spoken languages of the Turkic-speaking peoples of Central Asia were formed in the Middle Ages (*Jazyki narodov SSSR* 1966). An analysis of the dialects with a view to finding survivals of tribal languages produced very interesting results. Such survivals were found only in some languages (e.g. Turkmenian). The dialects of the Kirghiz, Kazakh, and Karakalpak languages have been found to belong to systems whose division had been mainly determined, not by the clan and tribal structure, but by the territorial principle (e.g. the northeastern, southern, and western groups of dialects in the Kazakh language; the northern and southern groups in the Kirghiz language) (Baskakov 1970: 682–688). The territorial division of dialects shows that survivals of the tribal division of nationalities had long ago ceased to affect the development of languages.

The stable character of self-appellations of nationalities should be noted despite the wide spread of the names of regional local groups among them (Tashkentslik, Khivalik, Bukharalik, Farghantalik, and so forth). The incorrect use of the ethnonyms (names of ethnic groups, tribes, etc.) "Kazakh" and "Kirghiz" before the 1917 October Revolution was due not to their instability or vagueness but exclusively to mistakes by incompetent authors and administrators (Levshin 1827: 432–433).

The development of ethnic self-awareness and the identification with one nationality is attested to by a multitude of legends about the origin of the names of nationalities (e.g. "Kazakh," "Kirghiz") in historical folklore, as well as by the popularity of genealogies of entire peoples (Turkmen, Karakalpaks, and others), along with genealogies of tribes and clans (Kononov 1958; Davkaraev 1959: 192–195). These common genealogies, compiled in the traditional form, demonstrating the imaginary kinship of all the components of a nationality (which had allegedly sprung from one ancestor), were a specific indication of the ethnic self-awareness of the peoples under examination. Of great interest in this connection is the story told by Abu-l-Gazi, the seventeenth-century khan who was a historian, about the reasons which induced him to write his famous *Genealogy of the Turkmen*. In the preface to his work he narrates that he was approached by Turkmenian mullahs and sheikhs; having learned that he was an authority on history, they asked him to replace the multitude of various genealogies of the Turkmen with "one correct and trustworthy history" (Kononov 1958: 36–37).

Joining Russia, despite the policy of colonial oppression under tsarism, resulted in a number of progressive developments in Central Asia's economic, social, and cultural life. Certain shifts also took place in ethnic development. The process of formation of bourgeois nations started among the largest nationalities: Uzbeks, Tajiks, and Kazakhs (Zhdanko 1972).

CONCLUSIONS

Despite a distinctive ethnic structure with survivals of clan and tribal divisions, the Turkic-speaking peoples of Central Asia and Kazakhstan constituted ethnic communities of the category typical of the feudal period, habitually called "nationality." These were fully shaped ethnosocial entities with ethnic territories and languages of their own, with ethnonyms, specific ways of life, material and spiritual culture, and ethnic self-awareness distinguishing them in their own eyes from other Turkic-speaking peoples.

The tribal groups within this range of nationalities were the relic secondary tribes which had long lost the determinative features of ethnic communities of the primitive communal system (consanguineous ties and absence of class differentiation). At the same time, survivals of tribal ethnic communities indicated the incomplete national consolidation which, according to the historical classification, distinguishes nationalities from the nation: their structure, a multitude of small, isolated ethnic groups and local variants of culture and ways of life; their dialectal distinctions in language; and the duality of their ethnic self-awareness.

In the process of further ethnic consolidation, some of these nationalities began forming nations as early as the beginning of the twentieth century; this process, however, was not completed by the time of the October Revolution.

The integration of tribal groups among the Turkic-speaking nationalities of Central Asia and Kazakhstan that had been going on for many centuries (e.g. seminomadic Uzbeks undergoing sedentarization) resulted in their erosion and disappearance. The remaining tribal groups, when regarded from the point of view of classification of ethnic communities, changed into internal units common to all nationalities: ethnic groups of the genetic type (Cheboksarov and Cheboksarova 1971). They retained tribal names, sometimes very ancient, in addition to the name of their nationality, and they sometimes had specific features in language (dialects), in material culture (appointments of dwellings, headgear), and in applied art (carpet and rug patterns, embroidery). At the same time they formed an organic part of their nationality, just as the local ethnic groups did.

During the Soviet period, the integration of the former tribal groups entered its final stage as part of the process whereby the socialist nations were consolidated and national cultures formed.

REFERENCES

ABRAMZON, S. M.

1951   "Formy rodo-plemennoi organizatsii u kochevnikov Srednei Azii"
[Forms of clan and tribal organization among the nomads of Central
Asia], in *Rodovoe obshchestvo*. Moscow: *Trudy Instituta Etnografii
AN SSSR* 14.

1970   Nekotorye voprosy sotsial'nogo stroja kochevykh obshchestv [Some
questions on the social structure of nomad societies]. *Sovetskaja
Etnografija* 6.

ARUTJUNOV, S. A., N. N. CHEBOKSAROV

1972   Peredacha informatsii kak mekhanism sushchestvovanija etnosotsial'-
nykh i biologicheskikh grupp chelovechestva [The transfer of information as a mechanism of the existence of ethnosocial and biological
groups of mankind]. Moscow: *Rasy i Narody* 2.

BASKAKOV, N. A.

1970   Etnolingvisticheskaja klassifikatsija dialektnykh sistem sovremennykh
tjurkskikh jazykov [The ethnolinguistic classification of the dialect
systems of modern Turkic languages]. Moscow: *Trudy VII Mezh-
dunarodnogo Kongressa Antropologicheskikh i Etnograficheskikh
nauk 5*.

BROMLEI, JU. V.

1970a   K voprosu o sushchnosti etnosa [On the question of the nature of
ethnos]. *Priroda* 3.

1970b   Etnos i etnosotsial'nyi organizm [Ethnos and the ethnosocial organ-
ism]. *Vestnik AN SSSR* 8.

1971   K kharakteristike ponjatija etnos [Toward a characterization of the
concept of ethnos]. Moscow: *Rasy i Narody* 1.

CHEBOKSAROV, N. N.

1967   Problema tipologii etnicheskikh obshchnostei v rabotakh sovetskikh
etnografov [The problem of typology of ethnic communities in the
works of Soviet ethnographers]. *Sovetskaja Etnografija* 4.

CHEBOKSAROV, N. N., I. A. CHEBOKSAROVA

1971   *Narody, rasy, kul'tury* [Peoples, races, cultures]. Moscow.

DAVKARAEV, N.

1959   *Ocherki po istorii dorevoljutsionnoi karakalpakskoi literatury* [Essays
in the history of prerevolutionary Karakalpak literature]. Tashkent.

DOLGIKH, B. O.

1967   Obrazovanie sovremennykh narodnostei Severa SSSR [The formation
of the contemporary nationalities of North U.S.S.R.]. *Sovetskaja
Etnografija* 3.

GURVICH, I. S.

1966   *Etnicheskaja istorija Severo-Vostoka Sibiri* [Ethnic history of the
Siberian Northeast]. Moscow.

Jazyki narodov SSSR

1966   *Jazyki narodov SSSR, II. Tjurkskie jazyki* [Languages of the peoples
of the U.S.S.R., volume 2: Turkic languages]. Moscow.

IVANOV, P. P.

1952   *Ocherki po istorii Srednei Azii* [Essays in the history of Central Asia].
Moscow.

KHAZANOV, A. M.

1968   *Voennaja demokratija i epokha klassoobrazovanija* ["Military democracy" and the period of class formation]. *Voprosy Istorii* 12.

KONONOV, A. N.
1958 *Rodoslovnaja turkmen. Sochinenie Abul-gazi khana Khivinskogo* [Gene-alogy of the Turkmen. A work of the Khiva khan Abul-gazi]. Moscow.

KOZLOV, V. I.
1967 O ponjatii etnicheskoi obshchnosti [On the concept of ethnic com-munity]. *Sovetskaja Etnografija* 2.
1969 *Dinamika chislennosti narodov* [The dynamics of population]. Moscow.

LASHUK, L. P.
1967a O formakh donatsional'nykh etnicheskikh svjazei [On the forms of pre-national ethnic ties]. *Voprosy Istorii* 4.
1967b O kharaktere klassoobrazovanija v obshchestvakh rannikh kochev-nikov [On the character of class formation in early nomad societies]. *Voprosy Istorii* 7.
1968 Opyt tipologii etnicheskikh obshchnostei srednevekovykh tjurok i mongolov [An attempted typology of the ethnic communities of medieval Turks and Mongols]. *Sovetskaja Etnografija* 1.

LEVSHIN, A.
1827 Ob imeni kirgiz-kazach'ego naroda i otlichii ego ot podlinnykh ili dikikh kirgizov [On the name of the Kirghiz-Kazak people and its distinction from the genuine or wild Kirghiz]. *Moskovskii Vestnik* 4 (14).
1832 *Opisanie kirgiz-kazach'ikh ili kirgiz-kaisatskikh ord i stepei* [A descrip-tion of the Kirghiz-Kazak or Kirghiz-Kaisak hordes and steppes], part 3. St. Petersburg.

MARKOV, G. E.
1970 Nekotorye problemy obshchestvennoi organizatsii kochevnikov Azii [Some problems of social organization of Asian nomads]. *Sovetskaja Etnografija* 6.

Narody Srednei Azii
1962–1963 *Narody Srednei Azii i Kazakhstana* [Peoples of Central Asia and Kazakhstan], volumes one and two. Moscow.

Ocherki istorii zemledelija
1971 *Ocherki istorii zemledelija i agrarnykh otnoshenii v Turkmenistane* [Essays in the history of agriculture and agrarian relations in Turk-menistan]. Ashkhabad.

TOKAREV, S. A.
1964 Problema tipov etnicheskikh obshchnostei [The problem of types of ethnic communities]. *Voprosy Filosofii* 11.

TRET'JAKOV, P. N.
1966 *Finno-ugry, balty i slavjane na Dnepre i na Volge* [Finno-Ugrians, Balts, and Slavs on the Dnieper and the Volga]. Moscow, Leningrad.

VINNIKOV, IA. R.
1954 Sotsialisticheskoe pereustroistvo khozjaistva i byta daikhan Maryiskoi oblasti Turkmenskoi SSR [The socialist transformation of the eco-nomy and everyday life of the Daikhs in the Mary Region of the Turkmenian SSR]. Moscow: *Sredneaziatskii Etnograficheskii Sbornik* 1.

ZHDANKO, T. A.
1950 *Ocherki istoricheskoi etnografii karakalpakov* [Essays in the historical ethnography of the Karakalpaks]. Moscow, Leningrad.
1961 Problema poluosedlogo naselenija v istorii Srednei Azii i Kazakhstana [The problem of the semisedentary population in the history of Central Asia and Kazakhstan]. *Sovetskaja Etnografija* 2.
1972 Natsional'no-gosudarstvennoe razmezhevanie i protsessy etnicheskogo razvitija u narodov Srednei Azii [National and state demarcation and the processes of ethnic development among the peoples of Central Asia]. *Sovetskaja Etnografija* 5.

Early Elements in the Ethnogenesis of the Uzbeks

K. SHANIJAZOV

The Uzbek people have come into existence as the result of prolonged and complicated ethnic processes. Their ethnic base was formed by the ancient inhabitants of the western Central Asian interfluvial region and of Khorezm (the Saks, the Massagets, the Sogdians, the Khorezmians, etc.). Components originating in other regions of Central Asia, the Syr Darya River area, and the Aral Sea area also had a share in forming the Uzbek people. Certain Turki ethnic components which helped form the Uzbek people in early medieval times came originally from various other ethno-cultural environments: the Pecheneg-Kangly group (Kangly); the Oguz (Oguz, Turman); the West Turki (Arghyn Türgesh, Uz); and from other ancient tribal confederations: the Usun (Uishun); the Tele (Telengut or Telengit, Uighur, Az); the Karluk; the Kipchak. In the ethnic composition of the Uzbeks there is also a very small Ugrian element, i.e. Mazhar (Majar). The above ethnonyms (names of ethnic groups, tribes, etc.) were still in use up to the late nineteenth and early twentieth centuries as the self-designation of certain Uzbek groups. It should be noted that the ethnic base of these population groups had undergone great changes in the course of their long history: ethnic elements of different origins came together under the same ethnonym.

The ancient components differed as to their share in the formation of the Uzbek people. The most important components in the past were the Karluks, the Kipchaks, and, presumably, the Oguz, who not only played an important part in the ethnic composition of the Uzbeks but also strongly influenced the formation of the Uzbek language. In modern Uzbek there are three dialects: Karluk, Kipchak, and Oguz.

The Kangly and the Uishun (Usun) both belonged to the earliest tribal confederacies in Central Asia and Kazakhstan. Some researchers identify the Kangly with the "Kangüy" (Kljashtornyi, 1964: 171–179) mentioned

in Chinese dynastic chronicles from the late third to the first centuries
B.C. and the seventh century A.D. It is presumably the Kangly who are
mentioned under the name "Kengeres" in the Orkhon inscriptions
(eighth century); are given the name "Kangary" in the works of Constantine the Porphyrogene (tenth century); and are the "Khankakishi"
of Al-Idrisi (twelfth century) (Kljashtornyi 1964). It should, however, be
noted that the "Kangüy" of the Chinese chronicles was the name of a
state, while in the Orkhon inscriptions, in the works of Constantine the
Porphyrogene, in Al-Idrisi, and in later authors, "Kangly" is the designation of a tribe or a tribal confederation. In the seventh and eighth centuries most of the Kangly were settled along the middle reaches of the
Syr Darya and in the Aral Sea areas, i.e. in the areas inhabited by their
historical ancestors. In the mid-eighth century the steppes in the Syr
Darya and Aral areas were occupied by the Oguz. The Kangly were
ejected from their territory; many of them moved west and settled down
in a region to the north of the Caspian Sea along the Yaik [Ural] River;
the area to the west of this river was at that time inhabited by the Pechenegs. Another group of the Kangly settled in the upper reaches of the
Talasa and the Chu Rivers (Abu-l-Gazi, 1906: 34).

It should be pointed out that in the early medieval period or possibly
even earlier, part of the Kangly tribe had already turned to a sedentary
way of life and had become mixed with the surrounding population; other
groups, those that had retained their ethnic self-designations and carried
on a nomadic and seminomadic livestock-breeding economy, were in the
medieval period involved in various political groupings which had arisen
in Desht-i-Kipchak. A substantial group of them joined the Kipchak confederation in the tenth to twelfth centuries. The Kangly played an important part in the formation of a number of Central Asian peoples: the
Uzbeks, the Karakalpaks, the Kazakhs, and the Kirghiz. Within Uzbekistan, the Kangly Uzbeks lived, in the eleventh century, in separate groups
in Khorezm, in the Jizakh, Samarkand and Tashkent *uyezd*s [districts],
and in the Fergana Valley. Most of them adopted a sedentary way of life,
while about twenty thousand others continued to carry on a seminomadic
mixed cultivating-and-herding economy up to the beginning of the twentieth century, retaining their self-designations and their clan divisions.

The Uishun (or Usun) were already living in Semirechye close to the
Kangly in the first centuries A.D. (Bichurin 1950: vol. 1, p. 55; vol. 2,
pp. 155–157, 159–161). They participated in public and political life in the
West Turki Khaganate and in subsequent early feudal states of Central
Asia. Later, the Uishun took part in the formation of many Turkic-
speaking peoples: Kazakhs, Kirghiz, and Karakalpaks. A fairly numerous
group became part of the Uzbeks. Those Uishuns who had earlier
migrated to Maverannahr had, however, long since settled down and
mixed with sedentary Uzbeks.

At the beginning of the sixteenth century, new Uishun groups migrated to Maverannahr from Desht-i-Kipchak. In subsequent centuries they too made the transition to a sedentary way of life. Only a few of them retained their ethnic self-designation up to the beginning of the twentieth century. They lived in the central part of the Zerafshan Valley. In the past, the Uishun formed a part of a number of Uzbek clan and tribal divisions: the Kipchak, the Naiman, the Kurama. At present, there are no more groups calling themselves Uishun.

The Karluks and related tribes (Chigils, Khalaj), who had played an important role in the ethnogenesis of the Uzbek people, have a history going back to very early times (Shanijazov 1964). Their first appearance in Central Asia dates from the early medieval period. In the eighth to tenth centuries the Karluk tribal confederacy occupied a wide area: Semirechye, the Fergana Valley, the Tashkent Oasis, and the Zerafshan Valley. Certain groups dwelt in Tokharistan and in Tibet. In the tenth to twelfth centuries the Karluks took a direct part in founding the Kara-khanid state and developing the Uzbek nationality within it. This process went on in later periods, and the majority of the Karluks gradually joined the sedentary Uzbeks. However, a remaining group bearing the ancient tribal name still retained some features of their traditional way of life up to the beginning of the twentieth century. These, numbering about twenty thousand, were dispersed in individual villages in the area at present embracing the Samarkand, Bukhara, Kashka Darya, and Surkhan Darya regions of Uzbekistan and the southern districts of Tajikistan. As for the Chigils and the Khalaj, they had long since merged into the settled Uzbek population; early in the twentieth century only a small group in the Bukhara Oasis still remembered that it belonged to the Khalaj. In the past, a considerable group of Khalaj seems to have dwelt here, as evidenced by the names of six villages in the Oasis. Besides the above sedentary population groups, groups calling themselves *Karakhani* also lived in the Middle Zerafshan drainage area, in the Bukhara Oasis, and in the upper reaches of the Kashka Darya. They appear to be the remainder of the multitribal population of the Karakhanid period (tenth to twelfth centuries).

In the late nineteenth and early twentieth centuries the ethnic composition of the Uzbeks also included a group called *Nuratin Turkmen*, as well as a group (in one of the clan subdivisions of the Kungar Uzbeks) called *Oguz*. Both these groups testify to the part played by the Oguz component in the ethnogenesis of the Uzbeks.

The Nuratin Turkmen were formed in the course of the last thousand years. Like the Oguz, they are in the main descendants of the ancient Oguz who lived along the Syr Darya in the eighth to early eleventh centuries. After moving to the Maverannahr region, the Turkmen lived along the right bank of the Middle Zerafshan and in the Nuratin mountains.

They remained in this territory up to the present century, and in the 1920's they numbered over thirty-five thousand. According to folk tradition, the Turkmen broke away from the main stream of the Oguz-Turkmen tribes when the latter migrated westward in the time of the Seljuk migrations (tenth and eleventh centuries). They also absorbed fragments of Turkmenian tribes which had, at various times, come to Maverannahr from the left bank of the Amu Darya. Subsequently both the local Uzbek tribes and the tribes of Desht-i-Kipchak origin grouped themselves around the original nucleus, i.e. the part of the Oguz-Turkmen tribes that had remained in the Nuratin mountains (Moshkova 1950). This is substantiated by the fact that the names of many clan subdivisions of the Nuratin Turkmen (such as Kazayakly, Bagajily, Kanzigaly, and Aitamgaly) are encountered within a number of Uzbek tribes that migrated to present-day Uzbekistan in the fifteenth and sixteenth centuries. Having merged with the above group, the local Uzbek tribes furthered their cultural ties with the population of the Central Asian interfluvial area.

The Kipchaks are related in origin to the ancient and medieval tribes of the Kipchaks of southwestern Altai and the steppes of north Kazakhstan. In the tenth to thirteenth centuries they formed a number of independent tribal confederations and began to play an appreciable role in the political life of Central Asia and Kazakhstan as well as of Eastern Europe. The Mongol invasion had an adverse effect upon the fortunes of the Kipchaks. The former Kipchak confederation broke up. Many of the nomads fleeing from the Mongol persecution moved westward into Turkey, Hungary, Bulgaria, and even Egypt (Golubovskii 1884: 127–130). The remaining Kipchaks formed a few comparatively small tribal groups and continued to wander, mainly in eastern Desht-i-Kipchak. After the downfall of the Golden Horde and of the state of nomad Uzbeks, the nomads of Desht-i-Kipchak underwent a new regrouping: the old tribal confederations and alliances fell apart and new ones sprang up. Some of them were formed under the same names: Kipchak, Kangly, Karakalpak, etc.; others under new ones: Nogai, the Eldest, Middle, and Youngest Kazakh Zhuz, etc. Kipchak elements were included in most of the confederations. It should be observed that the Kipchaks of the late medieval period were extremely heterogeneous in ethnic composition: they had become mixed both with pre-Mongol Turkic-speaking tribes (Kimak, Pecheneg, Kangly, Uz, etc.) and with the Turkicized Mongol tribes.

Two Kipchak groups took part in the ethnogenesis of the Uzbeks in the tenth to sixteenth centuries: the eastern or Syr Darya group, which had been in contact with the population of Maverannahr and Khorezm since the tenth and eleventh centuries; and the western (or east European) group, one part of which fell into the Uzbek ethnic sphere at the close of the fourteenth century (owing to their transplantation to Maverannahr by Timur) and the other in the fifteenth and sixteenth centuries.

The Kipchaks who had migrated to Maverannahr and Khorezm turned to a sedentary way of life during the tenth to sixteenth centuries. They gradually lost their clan and tribal names and finally merged with the local agricultural population.

The Kipchak groups whose descendants retained their ethnonym up to the beginning of the present century had migrated into the oases of Central Asia from the southern Kazakh steppes in the late seventeenth and early eighteenth centuries. In the process of their further merging with sedentary Uzbeks, the numerical strength of the Kipchaks gradually decreased. By the beginning of the twentieth century they numbered about 120,000. They were distributed in two compact groups: one in the Fergana Valley (42,500), the other in the Middle Zerafshan drainage area (52,000) (*Statisticheskii ezhegodnik* 1924, vol. 1). Individual groups were also encountered in territories now including the Bukhara, Kashka Darya, and Khorezm regions. Together with the Kipchaks, who had migrated there in the fourteenth to sixteenth centuries, came clan groups named *Kumak* (Kimak) and *Kuba* (Kuman, Kuban). These ancient ethnonyms survived as Kipchak clan names up to the beginning of the twentieth century. They also occur in toponymy in some localities in the south of the Uzbek S.S.R.

The ethnonym *Telengit* (Telengut) is mentioned in the past as a clan name within the Uzbek tribe of Kungrat; it apparently goes back to the ancient ethnonym *Tele* (Potapov 1969: 147). In the middle of the first millennium A.D., Tele tribes roamed in the area now constituting Mongolia, Tuva, and Altai. In the period of the ancient Turki Khaganate (sixth to eighth centuries), Tele tribal groups lived between the Aral and the Caspian seas (Potapov 1969: 151). In subsequent ages, individual Tele groups appear to have joined a number of tribal confederacies in Desht-i-Kipchak. It is possible that fragments of this ancient Turki confederation had already joined the Kungrat tribe at the time they dwelt in Desht-i-Kipchak (thirteenth to fifteenth centuries); the Tele afterwards wandered (in the late fifteenth and early sixteenth centuries) into the territory of present-day Uzbekistan; here they became part of the ethnic components of the Uzbek people while retaining their ethnonym.

The Uighurs and the Az also formed part of the Tele or Teguz-Oguz confederation in early medieval times. In Uzbekistan there were in the past two groups of Uighurs. One of them, numerically very small, appears to have retained the name of an ancient people and to have taken part, in the dim past, in the ethnogenesis of the Uzbeks. This is testified to by the presence of the ethnonym *Uighur* among Uzbek clan and tribal subdivisions. Uighur groups dwelt in Khorezm and in the territory of the former Bukhara Khanate; some of them became amalgamated with the Karakalpaks (Zhdanko 1950). Another group, at present regarded as an ethnographic group of Uzbeks, is settled in the Fergana Valley. The ancestors of this last group originated in eastern Turkestan, from which they migrated during the eighteenth and nineteenth centuries. This part of the Uighurs had no common name prior to the Revolution: individual groups were named according to their former habitation: Kashgars, Yargindians, Taranches, etc. The name "Uighur" was reassumed as recently as 1921.

In the eighth century the Az dwelt in northwestern Mongolia and in present-day Tuva. In the middle of that century some of them moved to Semirechye; there they lived in the Chu River drainage area. In the year 766, Semirechye was overrun by the Karluks. The Az who did not want to submit to the conquerors moved to the steppes northeast of the Aral Sea and to the lower reaches of the Syr Darya (*Materialy po istorii* 1939: vol. 1, pp. 144-145). Some groups moved to the Fergana Valley and to other regions of Maverannahr. These Az groups participated in the formation of the Uzbek people as far back as the early medieval period. Small fragments of them were amalgamated with the Kirghiz (Abramzon 1971: 39). Substantial Az groups from the Aral and Syr Darya areas later merged with the Saray and Naiman tribes; in the fifteenth and sixteenth centuries they migrated, together with these tribes, to the territory of present-day Uzbekistan. "Az" survived as the name of large clans within the Uzbek tribes of Saray and Naiman (Az-Naiman, Az-Saray, Zhaman-Az) up to the beginning of the twentieth century. They lived in the western districts of the Samarkand region and in the upper reaches of the Kashka Darya.

The Saray tribe mentioned above also had among its clan divisions the ethnonym *Mazhar* (Majar). The origin of this ethnonym is probably historically linked with the ancient Ugrian tribe of Majar (Madyar), a part of which was still living in the Syr Darya steppes in the eighth century. It is within the bounds of possibility that Turkicized groups of ancient Majars later merged with the Uzbek Sarays.

The Arghyn (Argu) lived in eastern Tarbagatay in the eleventh and twelfth centuries; they were included in the West Turki Khaganate. After its downfall many of them remained in Semirechye and afterwards became involved in the ethnogenesis of the Kazakh people. A small group of the Arghyn, having sided with the Seljukid movement in the eleventh century, emigrated to Khorasan (*Materialy po istorii* 1939: vol. 1, p. 381). A large part of the Arghyn migrated to Maverannahr and took a direct part in the formation of the Uzbek people under the Karakhanid state (tenth to twelfth centuries). Under Timur and his heirs they took an active part in the political life of the country and were one of the privileged tribes. Many chiefs belonging to the Arghyn feudal ruling circles served as governors of regions in Timurid territories. After the country was conquered by Sheibani-Khan and ruled by the Sheibanids, the Arghyns lost all their privileges and their political influence, turned to agriculture, and gradually merged with the sedentary Uzbeks. Only a small part of them still retained their ethnonym up to the close of the nineteenth century;

these were settled in the Tashkent Oasis and the Zerafshan drainage area; at present there are no groups calling themselves Arghyn among the Uzbeks.

The Tyrkash (Turkash) and the Uz were also among the western Turki ethnic elements that had survived among the Uzbeks up to the close of the nineteenth and beginning of the twentieth centuries. The name *Turkash* appears to go back to the ancient Turki ethnonym *Türgesh*. In the seventh to eighth centuries the Türgesh occupied the area between the Chu and Ili rivers (Gumilev 1967:259). They played a leading role in the political life of the Western Turki Khaganate. In the 760's a part of the Türgesh retreated to Maverannahr under the attacks of the Karluks. Here, together with other Turkic-speaking tribes (Karluks, Chigil, Khalaj, Yagma, Tukhsy, Argu, etc.), they constituted one of the earliest components that had gone into the forming of the Uzbek people. The majority of Türgesh were already turning to a sedentary way of life in early medieval times. However, a small group of them, though mixed among half-sedentary Uzbeks (particularly the Kungrat Uzbeks of Khorezm), retained their self-designation up to the close of the nineteenth and beginning of the twentieth centuries. In the Tashkent Oasis there are two small villages called "Turkesh." This fact is convincing evidence that members of the groups described – Türgesh or Tyrkash – dwelt here in the not-so-distant past.

After the Western Turki Khaganate broke up, some tribes that had been its component parts emigrated to the lower reaches of the Syr Darya and to regions lying in the north of the Aral Sea area. Among these were, presumably, the Uz. In the middle of the ninth century they moved still further westward and settled down between the Emba and the Wil rivers. The Uz appeared on the political scene at the close of the ninth and beginning of the tenth centuries, when they carried on an active struggle against the Pechenegs (Bagrjanorodnyi 1934: 10, 15, 16). A large group of them, having become involved in the political events taking place in Eastern Europe in the eleventh century, migrated westward into Byzantium (Vasil'evskii 1872: 36–37). The eastern branch of the Uz migrated to the regions of high culture in Maverannahr at various times, beginning in the eleventh century; they gradually merged with the sedentary Uzbeks. A small group of them (about 12,000) (Shanijazov 1970: 73), retaining the self-designation of their ancestors, lives in the present-day Bukhara and Kashka Darya regions of the Uzbek S.S.R. In addition to these, there is a substantial Kara-Uz group included in the Kipchak Uzbeks of Middle Zerafshan. It is interesting to note that the ethnonym *Kara-Uz* is mentioned in archive documents of the Ottoman Empire from the sixteenth to eighteenth centuries (Eremeev 1971: 67). The Kara-Uz mentioned there are probably historically linked with the Uz and Kara-Uz that had merged with the Uzbeks.

Among the ethnic components of the Uzbeks there is a small group known under the generalized name of *Turki*. They are historical descendants of various Turki and Mongol tribes that moved into Uzbekistan in the period between the sixth and the sixteenth centuries (Karmysheva 1960). The Turki (numbering over 60,000 in the early twentieth century) lived in the former Bukhara Khanate, in the Samarkand region, and in the Fergana Valley. A certain number of them had also been noted in the districts of Ura-Tübe and Jizakh and in the Tashkent Oasis. Before the beginning of the twentieth century the Turki made a distinction between themselves and other half-sedentary Uzbeks originating in Desht-i-Kipchak and regarded themselves as an independent ethnographic group. However, in their everyday life and culture, they were very close to the surrounding sedentary Uzbeks, because of the fact that the Turki were one of the early components of the Turkic-speaking population of Central Asia and had taken an active part in the formation of the Uzbek people. Their dialect had exerted an appreciable influence on the Uzbek literary language.

Here we have dealt mainly with the Turki components that contributed to the formation of the Uzbek people in the early medieval period. The formation of the main nucleus of the Uzbek people was completed between the eleventh and the first half of the twelfth centuries. The Turki elements that took part in Uzbek ethnogenesis later, in the twelfth to fifteenth centuries, were mainly of local origin (from the western Central Asian and Syr Darya regions) and only a few stemmed from other regions of Central Asia.

In the sixteenth century a new wave of nomads migrated to Uzbekistan territory from Desht-i-Kipchak. They formed the last component in the ethnogenesis of the Uzbek people. Most of them have turned to a sedentary way of life, but some clan and tribal Uzbek groups originating in Desht-i-Kipchak, such as the Kungrat, the Manghyt, the Saray, the Naiman, etc., were still engaged in a half-sedentary economy and retained a clan and tribal structure and certain peculiarities in their way of life up to the close of the nineteenth and beginning of the twentieth centuries.

The tribes and peoples that have come to be included in the present-day Uzbek people underwent a long and complicated process of evolution. In this process the consolidation of the Uzbek people took place: a common language, territory, economic life, mental makeup, and other elements of the future nation were formed. However, up to the beginning of the twentieth century the Uzbeks had not, in the course of their ethnic development, become a completely formed nation. Only as a result of the Great October Socialist Revolution did the Uzbek people attain a territorial, economic, and cultural unity; they became a socialist nation and now form their own sovereign state within the Union of Soviet Socialist Republics.

REFERENCES

ABRAMZON, S. M.
1971   *Kirgizi i ikh etnogeneticheskie i istoriko-kul'turnye sujazi* [The Kirghiz and their ethnogenetic and historical-cultural ties]. Leningrad.
ABU-L-GAZI
1906   *Rodoslovnoe drevo tjurkov* [Genealogical tree of the Turks]. Kazan.
BAGRJANORODNYI, KONSTANTIN
1934   Ob upravlenii gosudarstvom [On state administration]. *Izvestija Gosudarstvennoi akademii istorii material'noi kul'tury*. Moscow, Leningrad.
BICHURIN, I. JA.
1950   *Sobranie svedenii o narodakh, obitavshikh v Srednei Azii v drevnie vremena* [Collection of information on the peoples inhabiting Central Asia in ancient times], volumes 1 and 2. Moscow, Leningrad.
EREMEEV, D. E.
1971   *Etnogenez turok* [Ethnogenesis of the Turks]. Moscow.
GOLUBOVSKII, P.
1884   *Pechenegi, torki i polovtsy do nashestvija tatar* [Pechenegs, Torks and Polovtsians before the Tatar invasion]. Kiev.
GUMILEV, L. N.
1967   *Drevnie tjurki* [The ancient Turks]. Moscow.
Istorija Tuvy
1967   *Istorija Tuvy* [History of Tuva], volume 1. Moscow.
KARMYSHEVA, B. KH.
1960   Etnograficheskaja gruppa "tjurk" v sostave uzbekov [The ethnographic group "Turks" in the composition of the Uzbeks]. *Sovetskaja Etnografija* 1.
KLJASHTORNYI, S. G.
1964   *Drevnetjurkskie runicheskie pamjatniki kak istochnik po istorii Srednei Azii* [Ancient Turkic runic monuments as a source for Central Asian history]. Moscow.
Materialy po istorii
1939   *Materialy po istorii turkmen i Turkmenii* [Materials on the history of the Turkmen and Turkmenistan], volume 1. Moscow, Leningrad.
MOSHKOVA, V. G.
1950   Nekotorye obshchie elementy v rodoplemennom sostave uzbekov, karakalpakov i turkmen [Some common elements in the clan-tribal composition of the Uzbeks, Karakalpaks, and Turkmen]. *Trudy Instituta istorii i arkheologii AN UzSSR*, volume 2. Tashkent.
POTAPOV, L. P.
1969   *Etnicheskii sostav i proiskhozhdenie altaitsev* [Ethnic composition and origin of the Altaic]. Leningrad.
SHANIJAZOV, K.
1964   *Uzbeki-karluki* [The Uzbek-Karluks]. Tashkent.
1970   Uzy [The Uz]. *Obshchestvennye nauki v Uzbekistane* 2.
Statisticheskii ezhegodnik
1924   *Statisticheskii ezhegodnik 1917–1923* [Statistical yearbook 1917–1923], volume 1. Tashkent.
VASIL'EVSKII, V. G.
1872   Vizantija i pechenegi [Byzantium and the Pechenegs]. *Zhurnal ministerstva narodnogo prosveshchenija* 11.
ZHDANKO, T. A.
1950   Ocherki istoricheskoi etnografii karakalpakov [Essays on the historical ethnography of the Karakalpaks]. Moscow, Leningrad.

Historical Stratification of Generic and Tribal Names and Their Role in the Ethnogenetic Study of Turkic Peoples of Eastern Europe, Kazakhstan, and Central Asia

R. G. KUZEEV

The period from the first centuries A.D. to the middle of the second millennium is known in the history of the Turkic, Ugrian, and Mongolian peoples as the period of mass migrations, covering most of the Eurasian continent. Numerous tribes covered immense distances, making contact with one another and with the indigenous population. The ethnohistorical processes of this period had many important consequences; one of them was the wide distribution of Turkic languages in the vast area west of Central Asia and the Altai.

The appearance of Turkic languages in these areas was the result of a very complex integration of Turkic-speaking immigrants with local ethnic groups speaking different languages. In considering the relative contributions of different ethnic elements to the ethnogenetic process, both substratum and superstratum are of great importance.

The fifteenth and sixteenth centuries saw the final stages of mass Turkic migrations. The dynamic combinations of tribes of different origins which had developed during the previous centuries gradually became stabilized because the nomads now migrated shorter distances. This stabilization also resulted in social and economic changes leading to the emergence of feudal states and political organizations. It was mainly in the fifteenth century that such khanates as the Kazan, the Nogai, the Uzbek, the Siberian, the Kazakh, the Kirghiz, and others came into being in Eastern Europe, Central Asia, and Kazakhstan. At the same time there appeared vassal principalities of Turkic-speaking peoples in the territory of the Ruse; among these were the "kingdom of Kassimov" on the Oka River and a small "principality of Jagoldai" in the Kursk region, which was a tributary of Lithuania (Grekov and Jakubovskii 1950: 416–418). These khanates succeeded the collapsed Mongolian states of the previous period such as the Golden Horde, the White Horde, and the Chagatai Ulus.

Ethnically, the population of these khanates to a large extent succeeds the tribes of Desht-i-Kipchak.

The interaction of several factors – ethnic, territorial, geographical, and political – was terminated in the fifteenth and sixteenth centuries by the consolidation of many Turkic-speaking groups which were ethnically quite distinct. The Turkic peoples who have until recently largely preserved their ethnic unity in this region are divided into four territorial groups: (1) the Gagauz and the Karaim in the western regions of the Turkic migration; (2) Nogais, Kumyks, and Karachai-Balkars in the northern Caucasus; (3) the Tatars (Kazan, Kassim, West Siberian, Misharian), Bashkirs, and the Chuvash in the Povolzhie and Preuralie; (4) Uzbeks, Karakalpaks, Turkmen, Kazakhs, and the Kirghiz in Central Asia and Kazakhstan.

The origin of the Turkic-speaking peoples was found by synthesizing research data on their language, physical type, and cultural complex (both material and intellectual). These conclusions were correlated with material on archaeology and general history. However, the linguistic, anthropological, and ethnographic indexes frequently do not coincide. This may be attributed to the complex processes whereby these groups evolved, as well as to the various combinations of substratal and superstratal elements (Alekseev and Bromlei 1968: 36). All these factors necessarily resulted in the differences in development of the individual languages, anthropology, and culture. Sometimes these indexes differed even within the same ethnic group (for instance, Kazan Tatars and Misharis). On the other hand, the fact that these indexes could be made also shows the progress of science and the extent of possible generalization. Therefore, the reliability of the conclusions reached in different scientific areas about the ethnogenesis of a people will be greater when all these sciences are equally well developed and when their methods of research and generalization are identical or similar.

The broadest and most systematic generalizations in modern Turkic studies are made in the field of linguistics. There are several classifications of Turkic languages based upon the correlated differences in phonetics, grammar, and lexicology. These classifications generally take into account the fact that, in the course of the historical integration and differentiation of the Turkic peoples, different linguistic traits developed (Baskakov 1962; Samoilovich 1922; Menges 1968). Ethnologically, these different linguistic classifications bring together all the various language traits of the peoples under study.

To reconstruct the ethnogenesis of the Turkic-speaking peoples, it is necessary to improve the analytical methods of anthropology and ethnography. In this connection, some new historico-ethnographic interpretations of the Turkic ethnonymia (names of ethnic groups, tribes, etc.) seem quite possible today.

Ethnogenetics has used Turkic generic and tribal ethnonyms for about a hundred years. The research at the end of the nineteenth century by N. A. Aristov has become almost classic. During recent decades, scientists' interest in the generic and tribal ethnonymia of the Turkic peoples has increased tremendously (Zhdanko 1950; Abramzon 1960; Vostrov and Mukanov 1968; Kuzeev 1957).

Two basic trends have developed in the historical interpretation of generic and tribal ethnonyms: the first is linguistic, the second ethnographic. Both kinds of research have yielded valuable results. However, the material on generic and tribal ethnonyms can offer much more information. The results already obtained could have been more fruitful had there been sufficient correlation between the historico-ethnographic and historico-linguistic analyses. Furthermore, there is not enough representative material on many Turkic peoples, and methods of collecting and systematizing generic and tribal names are often not sufficiently developed or standardized.

We believe that our experience in collection, systematization, and analysis, gained during our ethnographic study of the Bashkirs, indicates that the above difficulties may be overcome. Our investigations aimed at studying all aspects of the ethnogenesis of the Bashkirs over a considerable period of time. We should emphasize that (1) the study was very detailed, embracing the entire ethnic condition and various sources of the ethnic composition of the Turkic peoples; (2) we traced the origin of the ethnonyms and their subsequent evolution in different linguistic environments; (3) we fixed the time and historical conditions in which the ethnonyms and their carriers appeared in a particular ethnos.

At present, masses of ethnonymic material are being accumulated. The generic and tribal composition of Kirghiz (about 2,000 names), Karakalpaks (over 350 names), Kazakhs, and Uzbeks has been studied most thoroughly. Some hundreds of ethnonyms are presented in different publications; 2,200 names are cited in the summary list of genera and tribes of the Bashkirs.

This mass of ethnonymic material has the advantage of lending itself to both historical and stratigraphic analysis. Such analysis reveals ethnonymic layers embracing names of different origin as well as groups of their carriers. If we can determine the sequence and chronology in which the carriers of these names entered the layers of ethnic evolution, we may be able to explain the history of the ethnic composition of the people under study. Any etymological or semantic investigations which reveal at least relative dating for the particular ethnos naturally become of higher historical value and thus add to the significance of ethnonymic materials as sources of ethnogenic information. Let us illustrate all of this with the material on the generic and tribal ethnonyms of the Bashkirs.

Bashkir generic and tribal ethnonyms can be separated into seven historico-stratigraphic layers. Each layer has been given a conditional name, since this name reflects only the ethnic characteristics of the leading components, while the formations are on the whole mixed.

1. The Finno-Ugric-Samodiian layer includes three groups of names related to the ancient Samodiian ethnonyms (such as *syzgy: sysky, kelser, kul-il-mets, shad*;) to the ancient Ugric or Turkic-Ugric names (such as *terhek, setspen, epei, bekatin*;) and to the local east Finnish names (such as *ynanysh, veresh*, etc.).

The suggested grouping is based upon historico-ethnographic materials (mainly ethnogenetic legends) and also upon language parellels between the Bashkir, Samodiian-Ugrian, and east Finnish peoples; compare, for example, the Bashkir *sysky* and the Samodiian *syski* [boat]; the Bashkir *kul* and the Samodiian *kule* [raven]; the Bashkir *ter-hep*, the Mancian *tar(i)*, and the Hungarian *dar(u)* [crane] (Potapov 1957; Lytkin 1953: 55).

The most difficult task remaining is to prove linguistically that the ancient Samodiian and Ugric as well as the local east Finnish components do exist in the ethnic substrata of the Bashkir culture. At the same time, this research trend opens new vistas, because it is based upon reliably established archaeological data which prove that the Ugrian-Samodiian migration from Siberia to the Volga-Ural region played quite an important role in the third to seventh centuries (Gening 1971). The fact that ancient Samodiian-Ugrian and, to a lesser extent, local Finno-Ugrian components were present in the ethnic composition of the Bashkirs can be illustrated in the historical comparative analysis of their material culture, the depths of which have revealed vast complexes analogous to those discovered in the culture of the peoples of Siberia, Altai, and the Volga-Kama regions.

2. The Bulgaro-Magyarian layer of the eighth to tenth centuries includes such names as *yurmaty, yurmi, yenei, geinetarkhan, kese, suler, tanyp, yomran, negmen, yulaman, imes, misher*. Seven of these ethnonyms have analogues in ancient Hungarian ethnonyms: *yurmaty/Gyarmat, yenei/Jeno, geine/tarkhan/Taryan, kese/Keszi, yulaman/Gjula, misher/ Megyer, negmen/Nyek* (Németh 1966). The first five are "of Turkic origin and have Bulgarian traits" (Németh 1966: 17). According to Németh, the ethnonyms *negmen* and *misher* are of Ugric origin. Two names, *yurmi* and *suler*, have parallels in the ethnonyms of Great and Volgan Bulgars (Kunik 1878: 128). Finally, two more names, *tarkhan* and *imes*, also originate in the Bulgarian period and find analogues in Chuvash ethnonyms (Ashmarin 1878: 128).

3. The ancient Bashkir layer of the ninth to tenth centuries includes such names as *usergen, meiten, boerien, tamian, tungener, bailar, un, bishul, uran, surash, yagalbai*, etc. All the names in this third layer have been traced to eastern sources, to the ethnonyms of medieval Turkic peoples (Pechenegs, Uighurs) or to the generic and tribal grouping made up of

Uzbeks, Karakalpaks, Kazakhs, Kirghiz, Altaians, Tuvinians, and Mongols. Some of the tribes mentioned, such as *berien* (*burdjan* or *bordjan* at their eastern sources), *usergen*, and *tungeuer*, before they migrated from the regions of Preuralie and Precaspie to the Volgo-Urals, had been united and known by the common name *bashkort* (*badjgard*, *bashgard*, *bashkard*, at their eastern sources) (Garkavi 1870:148).

4. The Oguzo-Kipchak layer (tenth to twelfth centuries) includes such names as *ei*, *tyrnakly*, *hart*, *komly*, *kyzylbash*, *etimgen*, *koesock*, *ishtek*, and so on. These names have their parallels chiefly in Turkmenian ethnonyms, and to some extent in those of the Uzbeks and Kirghiz. This can be attributed to the Oguz origin of most medieval bearers of the aforementioned ethnonyms or to their appearance in the eighth to tenth centuries in the Oguz ethnic environment on the banks of the Syr Darya River.

5. The Kipchak layer of the thirteenth to fourteenth centuries is divided into four ethnonymic groups: (1) the Kipchak proper: *kypsak*, *kauly*, *gere*, *hary*, *koshsy*, *iylan*, *biauly*, etc.; (2) the Katai group: *katai*, *haliot*, *balyksy*, *naiman*, *maskara*, etc.; (3) the Tabyn group: *tabyn*, *dyuan*, *kyuakan*, *syrzy*, *bezrek*, *taz*, *uishin*, *soeioendek*, *kuu-kshi*, *teleu*, *baryn*, etc.; and (4) the Min group: *mets*, *kyrk*, *kyrk-uzek*, *subi-merket*, etc.

All of these ethnonyms have been traced to medieval eastern sources and are Turkic or Mongolian formations. Most of the ethnonyms of the Kipchak layer have their parallels in the generic and tribal names of Kazakhs, Karakalpaks, Uzbeks, Kirghiz, Turkmen, Altaians, Khakas, Crimean Tatars, Tuvinians, and Mongols.

6. The Nogai layer of the fifteenth to sixteenth centuries includes numerous names such as *nugai-yurmaty*, *nugai-kypsak*, *nugai-boerien*, *nygaizar*, and *kyzyl-nugai*. They are established everywhere throughout south and southeast Bashkiria.

7. The Povolzhie and Central Asian layer (sixteenth to eighteenth centuries) mainly incorporates names of small generic subdivisions: *kazakh*, *kalmak*, *karakalpak*, *uzbek*, *toerockmen*, *tatar*, *tipter*, *misher*, *sirmesh*, *synash*, *mykshy*, *ar*, *kazanlar*. This layer characterizes the ethnic interaction which had already taken place between the peoples of the Volga-Urals and Central Asia. On the one hand, it shows that the previously established ethnic contacts were rather inert. On the other hand, it also shows that new ethnic groups of neighboring peoples had infiltrated the group of Bashkirs.

Some new aspects in the study of ethnogenesis emerge from a study of the historical stratification of generic and tribal ethnonyms and a linguistic analysis of characteristic names.

This approach widens the possibilities for studying the ethnic history of particular peoples. Thus, such historical-stratigraphic layering of Bashkir generic and tribal ethnonyms permits the following conclusions:

1. The chronological sequence of the described ethnonymic layers corresponds to the scientifically proven picture of historical events in the Volga-Urals region.

2. The ethnic substratum of the Bashkir ethnos quite obviously reveals the alien Samodiian and Ugrian (perhaps Turkic-Ugrian) components from Siberia. Quite unexpectedly, the ancient local Finnish substratum in the Bashkir ethnonyms is not apparent, although some of its traits have been identified (Kazakov 1970: 260).

3. The ethnonymic material testifies to the presence of a Bulgarian or, more exactly, Bulgarian-Madyar component in the earlier stages of the Bashkir ethnogenesis. At the same time, this material does not support the widely held opinion that the Volga Bulgars (who themselves were a complex ethnic formation) had been genetic ancestors to only one of the Turkic peoples of the Povolzhie (Tatars or Chuvash).

4. The stages of the Turkic migration played a decisive role in the history of the Bashkir ethnos: the migration of the ancient Bashkir in the eighth and ninth centuries, and the Kipchak migration in the thirteenth to fourteenth centuries. The crucial stage in the formation of the Bashkir language and culture occurred during the Kipchak migration of the thirteenth to fourteenth centuries, although the Bashkirs completed their formation into a people at a later period.

5. This significant role of the Bulgarian and especially of the Kipchak components in the formation of the Bashkir people led Baskakov (1962) in his historical and linguistic classification to include the Bashkir language in the Kipchak-Bulgarian subgroup of the Kipchak group. He also believed that the Bashkir language developed during the Middle Turkic period, the tenth to sixteenth centuries.

The next and higher level of ethnogenetic generalizations based upon the historically interpreted ethnonymic material may be valid for all Turkic peoples. Correlative ethnic tables of closely related peoples show the greatest number of ethnic parallels for Bashkirs, Uzbeks, Karakalpaks, Kazakhs, and Kirghiz. About one hundred coinciding names of races and tribes have been discovered in the ethnonyms of these peoples. Thirty of them were Bashkir-Uzbek (*kipchak, kangly, kushchi, ktai, sarysh, balgaly, uishun, badragly, ming, taz, bailar, bishul,* etc.). Over twenty were Bashkir-Kazakh (*tabyn, telyau, tama, yagalbai, kereit, maskar, zheti-uru, kypchak, naiman, dulat, usun, tastar,* etc.). Fifteen ethnonymic Bashkir-Karakalpak parallels were found (*muiten, bishul, istek, kypchak, ktai, uishun, kyrk,* etc.); about twenty-five of them are parallel to the territorially rather distant Turkmen (*aiy, dagly, kumly, kyzylbash, itemen, kushchi, balyksy, kyrkuili,* etc.). There are also some parallels with Kirghiz (eighteen), Nogai (ten), Osman Turks (one), Azerbaijani (one), Altais (eight), Khasis (three), and Tuvinians (two). The fact that generic and tribal names of the Kipchak period prevail in the ethnonymic parallels of Bashkirs, Uzbeks,

Karakalpaks, and Kazakhs show that the late medieval ethnic superstratum of these peoples was common to all of them. The ethnonymic parallels of Bashkirs with Turkmen, and especially with Altais, Khasis, and Tuvinians, also relate partially to the Kipchak period, but they originate mainly from the history of the Asian nomadic tribes before the tenth century A.D.

Correlative ethnonymic analysis shows that the distribution of ethnonymic groups of Turkic origin does not correspond to the conventionally accepted linguistic classifications of their languages. The generic and tribal ethnonyms of the Bashkirs, for instance, show that they are most closely related to similar indexes of the peoples whose languages (according to Baskakov's classification) belong to the Karluk group (Uzbeks), and to the Kipchak-Nogai subgroup of the Kipchak group (Kazakh, Karkalpak) of Turkic languages. Evidently, under the approximately equal influence of later ethnic layers, the underlying layers played different roles.

This genetic comparison of Turkic ethnonyms with the generic and tribal names of non-Turkic peoples (with extensive material available on all the compared peoples) makes it possible to establish the external ethnic and cultural links of the studied peoples at different stages of ethnic evolution. The Bashkir-Samodiian and Bashkir-Ugric parallels relate to the earlier stages of the Bashkir ethnogenesis. Of greater importance are the later-developed Bashkir-Mongolian ethnonymic parallels, such as *tangor*, *tuma*, *kidan*, *naiman*, *maskar*, *salchzhot*, *baaryn*, *mingat*, *merkit*, etc.

This kind of historical and stratigraphic division of the mass of ethnonymic material is currently one possible scientific approach, and we believe that its reliability can already be sufficiently illustrated. We should all strive to synthesize available ethnographic and linguistic information to correctly interpret the entire bulk of the Turkic ethnonyms. This is an enormous task. To accomplish it, we suggest the following sequence of research: (1) a historical and stratigraphic division of the mass of ethnonymic material relating to individual peoples; (2) a composition and analysis of correlative tables on the ethnonyms of Turkic peoples; (3) a historical and genetic study of ethnonymic groups in a wider region including different peoples, for instance, Turkic, Mongolian, and Finno-Ugrian. The conclusions thus developed should be further correlated with linguistic, anthropological, archaeological, and other scientific data. It will then be possible to elaborate a scheme of ethnic evolution which will be valid for a vast region.

REFERENCES

ABRAMZON, S. M.
1960   Etnicheskii sostav kirgizskogo naselenija Severnoi Kirgizii [Ethnic composition of the Kirghiz population of northern Kirghizstan]. *T.K.A.E.E.* 4. Moscow.

ALEKSEEV, V. P., JU. V. BROMLEI
1968   K izucheniju roli pereselenii narodov v formirovanii novykh etnicheskikh obshchnostei [Toward the study of the role of peoples' migrations in the formation of new ethnic communities]. *Sovetskaja Etnografija* 2.

ARISTOV, N. A.
1894   Opyt vyiasneniia etnicheskogo sostava kirgiz-kazakov Bol'shoy ordy i karakirgizov na osnovanii rodoslovnykh skazanii i svedenii o sushchestvuiushchikh rodovykh deleniiakh i o rodovykh tamgakh, a takzhe istoricheskikh dannykh i nachinaiushchikhsia antropologicheskikh issledovanii [An attempt to explain the ethnic structure of the Kirghiz-Cossacks of the Great Horde and of the Karakighiz on the basis of the genealogical legends and data on the existing clan divisions and clan symbols as well as of historical data and early anthropological investigations]. *Zhivaya starina* 3, 4. (Separate issue St. Petersburg 1895.)

1896   Zametki ob ètnicheskom sostave tjurkskikh plemën i narodnostei i svedeniia ob ikh chislennosti [Remarks concerning the ethnic structure of the Turkic tribes and ethnic groups and data concerning their number]. *Zhivaya starina* 3, 4. (Separate issue St. Petersburg 1897.)

ASHMARIN, N. I.
1902   *Bolgary i chuvashi* [The Bulgars and the Chuvash]. Kazan.

BASKAKOV, N. A.
1962   *Vvedenie v izuchenie tjurkskikh jazykov* [Introduction to the study of Turkic languages]. Moscow.

GARKAVI, A. JA.
1870   *Skazanija musul'manskikh pisatelei o slavjanakh i rusakh (s poloviny VII v. do X v. po P. Kh.)* [Stories of Muslim writers about the Slavs and the Rus (from the mid-seventh to the tenth century A.D.)]. St. Petersburg.

GENING, V. F.
1971   Etnicheskii substrat v sostave Bashkir i ego proiskhozhdenie [The ethnic substratum among the Bashkirs and its origin]. *A.E.B.* 4. Ufa.

GREKOV, B. D., A. JU. JAKUBOVSKII
1950   *Zolotaja Orda i ee padenie* [The Golden Horde and its decline]. Moscow, Leningrad.

KAZAKOV, E. P.
1970   O kharaktere sviazei povolzhskikh finno-ugrov s naseleniem Volzhskoi Bolgarii [On the character of the ties between the Volga Finno-Ugrians and the population of Volga Bulgaria]. *Voprosy finno-ugrovedenija*, vyp. 5. Ioshkar-Ola.

KUNIK, A.
1878   O rodstve khagano-bolgar s chuvashami po slavjano-bolgarskomu "Imenniku" [On the relationship of the Khagan-Bulgars and the Chuvash according to the Slavic-Bulgarian "Imennik"]. *Zapiski Imperatorskoi Akademii Nauk* 32, bk. 2. St. Petersburg.

KUZEEV, R. G.
1957   *Ocherki istoricheskoi etnografii bashkir* [Essays on the historical ethnography of the Bashkirs]. Ufa.
LYTKIN, V. I.
1953   Iz istorii slovar'nogo sostava permskikh jazikov [From the history of the lexical structure of Permian languages]. *V.Ja.*, no. 5.
MENGES, K.
1968   The Turkic languages and peoples. An introduction to Turkic studies. *Ural-Althaische Bibliothek* 15. Wiesbaden.
NÉMETH, G.
1966   Ungarische Stammesnamen bei den Baschkiren. *Acta Linguistica* 16: 1–2. Budapest.
POTAPOV, L. P.
1957   Zum Problem der Herkunft und Etnogenese der Koibalen und Motoren. *Journal de la Société Finno-Ougrienne* 59. Helsinki.
SAMOILOVICH, A. N.
1922   *Nekotorye dopolnenija k klassifikatsii turetskikh jazykov* [Some supplements to the classification of Turkish languages]. Prague.
VOSTROV, V. V., M. S. MUKANOV
1968   *Rodoplemennoi sostav i rasselenie kazakhov* [Trival composition and distribution of the Kazakhs]. Alma-Ata.
ZHDANKO, T. A.
1950   *Ocherki istoricheskoi etnografii karakalpakov* [Essays on the historical ethnography of the Karakalpaks]. Moscow, Leningrad.

Some Basic Problems of the Ethnogenesis of the Turkmen

S. G. AGADZHANOV and A. KARRYEV

The problems of the ethnic history of the Turkmen have repeatedly been central for Soviet and foreign scholars. Not only historians and anthropologists but also ethnographers, archaeologists, philologists, and linguists have taken part in their elaboration. The first attempts to establish the origin of the Turkmen date back to the seventeenth and eighteenth centuries. The French historian D'Herbelot was one of the first to acquaint Western scholars with the data collected by a number of Eastern authors on the genealogy of the Turkmen, connecting their origin with the Oguz (D'Herbelot 1789: 545).

Certain questions concerning the ethnic history of the Oguz and the Turkmen were also dealt with in a work by Jean Deguignes (1756). Essentially, his concept states the historical continuity between the Huns and the medieval Turkic nomadic tribal unions. Deguignes considered the Oguz and other Turkic tribes to be the descendants of the ancient Huns. At the same time, he points out that in the Middle Ages the Oguz were divided into two large groups: western and eastern. The western Oguz tribes, which had reached Greece and Macedonia in the eleventh century, were known to Byzantine historians as the Uz. The eastern group of Oguz, which inhabited the steppes along the border and a number of the settled regions of Iran, was called "Turkmen" (Deguignes 1756: 225).

Among early works by western European authors was Malcolm's history of Persia (1830). This compilation also deals with the history of the medieval Oguz and the Turkmen. Speaking of the origin of the Oguz, Malcolm tries to prove that they are one of the most ancient tribes of western Asia. He believes that their ethnogenesis goes back to the Outians mentioned by Herodotus (1830: 229).

In Russia, the first attempts to study some questions pertaining to the origin of the Turkmen date back to the early nineteenth century. Tatishchev expressed the view that the Oguz were agkin to the Massagets, but he regarded the Turks and the Turkmen as close relatives of the Mongols. Karamzin (1833, vol. 1, nn. 87, 396; vol. 2, n. 106) identified the Oguz with the Turks of ancient Russian chronicles. This suggestion, put forward by the "father of Russian historical science," was the basis for further studies carried out by Pogodin (1857), Ilovaiskii (1876), and other historians.

In 1836 the eastern coast of the Caspian Sea was explored by an expedition headed by G. Karelin. It collected a great deal of valuable material about the Turkmen and their country. Karelin suggested that the "Turkmen were probably the ancient Massagets."

Galkin also collected interesting information about Turkmenian tribes. He notes that the ancestor of the Turkmen was Uzkhan, who had two sons, Essen-khan and Sain-khan. Essen-khan's descendants are the Goklens and Essen-ili; the remaining Turkmen tribes descend from Sain-khan (Galkin 1869:5).

Raverty, an English Oriental scholar, also dwelt on the question of the origin of Oguz and Turkmen. On the basis of data obtained from medieval Oriental authors, he claimed that the term "Turkmen" in Iranian means "Turklike" (1881: 128). Raverty made an attempt to revive D'Herbelot's view.

In the early 1860's, the well-known Hungarian traveler Vambery visited Central Asia. During his trip he made a number of valuable ethnographic observations of the Turkmenian way of life. Vambery was one of the first European scholars to describe the tribal division of the Choghdurs, the Salyrs, the Goklens, the Tekins, and other Turkmenian tribes. He also made an attempt to find the etymology of the term "Turkmen." In his view, it consists of the word "Turk" and the collective suffix "men." Vambery believed that the word "Turkmen" means "Turks," "people belonging to the Turks" (1885).

Works by Golubovskii (1884) are especially worthy of note among the investigations by Russian scholars of the latter half of the last century. There was a rather vague notion about the Turkic nomads of Eastern Europe in the Middle Ages in Russian and foreign historiography. Suffice it to say that Golubovskii's predecessors held conflicting views regarding the origin of the Oguz, the Pechenegs, and the Polovtsy-Komans. A number of contemporary historians considered the Oguz and the Polovtsy one and the same. Others identified the Oguz with Khazars, Hungarians, Uighurs, or Pechenegs. Golubovskii, on the basis of an analysis of sources, showed how close ethnically the Turks were to the Oguz. He also pointed to their connections with the tribes of the Seljuk group (Agadzhanov 1970).

Among nineteenth-century western European works on the subject, special mention should be made of an article by Houtsma (1888). On the basis of the data provided by Rashid-ad-din and other medieval authors, he wrote that in olden times the name "Turkmen" was given to the tribes "resembling the Turks." Proceeding from this, he advanced a hypothesis that the Turkmen were "Turks Iranised to a certain degree." About the origin of the ethnonym (name of ethnic groups, tribes, etc.) he wrote, "With regard to the etymology of the word Turkmen given by Rashid-ad-din as Turk plus man, one can argue until it is established that this name comes from the Turks or as he, Rashid-ad-din, asserts from the Iranians" (Houtsma 1888: 228).

The problem of the ethnogenesis of the Oguz and the Turkmen became more topical at the end of the last century in connection with the discovery of the Orkhon inscriptions. The deciphering of the ancient Turkic runic written language on monuments in Mongolia brought forward the question of the Central Asian origin of the Oguz. The study of the Tonyukuk and Kultegin inscriptions and other texts showed that the Oguz were one of the ethnic components of the ancient Turkic Khaghanate. Scholars were faced with the problem of the formation of the Oguz tribal confederation and its ethnic ties with other Turkic-speaking peoples of Central Asia and Russian Central Asia.

Tomsen (1896) was one of the first to study the Orkhon inscriptions; he believed that the Oguz of the early Middle Ages were identical with the Uighurs. He was of the opinion that the name "Oguz" was more ancient, and that "Oguz" was an ethnic term and "Uighur" a political term. Tomsen considered that the Oguz were a group of tribes ruled by an Uighur dynasty.

Radloff, a Russian Oriental scholar, also contributed to the study of the medieval Turks, and among them the Oguz. Classifying the Turkic peoples in the same way as the Persian historian of the thirteenth and fourteenth centuries, Rashid-ad-din, Radloff includes the Oguz in a group of "purely Turkic" tribes:

According to his [Rashid-ad-din's] informers, who, naturally, could have added some inventions of a legendary character, all Turkic tribes originated from the clan of Oguz-Khan, the son of Kara-Khan the son of Dib-Bakui, the son of Abulja-Khan who was one of Noah's sons (Radloff 1891).

Radloff dwelt on this problem in other works too, the most important of which is his analysis of ancient Turkic manuscripts. His studies of the runic texts of Mongolia showed that the Oguz lived in Central Asia at the time of the Turkic Khaghanate. Radloff believed that their main place of residence was once the region between In-Shan and Khangai. The discovery of the Orkhon inscriptions in the nineteenth century stimulated interest in the Turks and dictated the necessity of writing a comprehensive work about their ethnogenesis. In 1896, the Russian scholar Aristov made the first attempt to compile such a work, in which he also covered the Oguz and the Turkmen. Aristov considered the Oguz and the Uighurs of Central Asia one people (Aristov 1896: 401).

In his monograph Aristov also wrote that "the Oguz, or Polovtsy, or Komans (Kumans) were, probably, like the Pechenegs, a union of the Kangly and Kipchak clans." As for the Turkic tribes in Eastern Europe, Aristov opposed Golubovskii's view (1884) that the Turks were identical with the Oguz. According to Aristov, the word "Oguz" is of totemic origin and means "ox." In the eighth and ninth centuries, he claims, the Kangly and Kipchak tribes living along the Syr Darya River began to be called "Oguz" due to the cult of the ox, widespread among them. He also held the view that the Turkmen came from the Kangly tribes (Aristov 1894: 415).

Aristov's work immediately drew the attention of orientalists. Reviewing it in 1897, Bartol'd criticized many of Aristov's views, notably that the Turkmen and the Oguz were of Kangly origin (Bartol'd 1921).

In the late nineteenth and early twentieth centuries questions of the genesis of the Oguz tribes were dealt with in works by the German scholar Markwart. In his paper on the Polovtsy-Kumans, he made a special point of the origin of the Oguz, the Turks and the Berendeis. He defended the view that the Polovtsy-Kumans were identical with the Oguz. The very word "oguz," Markwart believed, means "bowman" (1914: 22, 38).

Among later works dealing with the range of problems under discussion, mention should be made of works by Deny (1921), Ligeti (1925), Németh (1930), Pelliot (1930), Bazin (1953), and other scholars. The majority of these articles and papers center on a historical, philological, and linguistic analysis of the terms "Oguz" and "Turkmen." Deny, for instance, attempts to discover the meaning of the word "Turkmen." He holds the view that "man" or "men" in this word is an augmentative suffix. In general, he explains the meaning of the term as "pure-blooded Turks" (1921: 226).

An original etymology of the term "Oguz" has been suggested by the Polish scholar Kotwicz. In his view, the Turkmen are the direct descendants of the Türgesh. Kotwicz notes that the word "Turkmen" appears in medieval sources from the time when western Turks came into close contact with Iranians, and he considers that the word "Turkmen" is a synonym of the word "Türgesh" (1948).

Deny's theory is most popular in modern historiography in other countries. Quite recently, the Türkish historian Kafesoglu made an attempt to bolster Deny's theory with new linguistic material. In his work Kafesoglu tries to find the time and circumstances of the appearance of the term "Turkmen." He comes to the conclusion that it is connected with the formation of the Karluk state in the Semirechye [of the Seven Rivers] area in the eighth century. The tribes that were included in the Karluk grouping got the name "Turkmen," meaning "pure-blooded, genuine, great, etc., Turks" (Kafesoglu 1958).

However, this view conflicts with the data contained in medieval sources and paleontological materials about the Turkmen. It does not fall into line, above all, with the evidence of Abu Reikhan Biruni (1937: 84), Makhmud ibn Khusain (1335), Rashid-ad-din (n.d.), and other medieval authors. Historical and anthropological materials show that the Turkmen were formed from the descendants of the Indo-European population merged with Mongoloid Turkic-speaking peoples (Agadzhanov 1963).

Bartol'd was the first Soviet historiographer to begin the study of the ethnogenesis of the Oguz and Turkmen. His works laid the foundation for the scientific investigation of the Turkmen's past. He noted that the first mention of the name "Turkmen" was made in Arab geographical literature in the latter half of the tenth century. He also stated that this name in the form "To-ku-mong" had been mentioned in a Chinese encyclopedia in the eighth century.

Bartol'd believed that "Oguz" was the name of Central Asian Turkic tribes, some of whom moved to what is now Soviet Central Asia in the early Middle Ages. In the tenth and eleventh centuries the Oguz and the Karluks were named "Turkmen" but later only the Oguz retained this name (Bartol'd 1963).

Jakubovskii, a member of the Soviet Academy of Sciences, made a great contribution to the study of the problems bearing on the genesis of the Oguz and the Turkmen. In his view, the Turkmenian nationality was formed of three ethnic components: the ancient Iranian-speaking nomadic population of the Central Asian steppes, medieval Ephthalite-Turkic tribes, and medieval Oguz tribes. Jakubovskii thinks that the penetration of the majority of Turkic-speaking peoples into the territory of modern Turkmenistan that took place in the sixth to eleventh centuries was of great importance for the ethnogenesis of the Turkmen:

The process of "turkicization," as far as the language was concerned, of the non-Turkic element on Turkmen territory began before the appearance of the first wave of the Oguz, that is before the 9th century and the Turks themselves that lived in the region of Merv, Balkh and Dikhistan, as well as their kindred tribes in the Balkhans and elsewhere, were active participants in that process. The process of "turkicization" especially intensified after a great number of the Oguz had concentrated on the territory of Turkmenistan in the 9th and 10th centuries. The Alans and the Arses lost their language and "turkicized" as far as their language was concerned. The Turkic language prevailed in all contacts or mixing. However, the ethnic, or rather anthropological, specific features of the physical type of the local Iranian-language tribes did not vanish without a trace. They gave the people who had ultimately been formed there and received the name Turkmen, their dolichocephalia, or long-headedness (Jakubovskii 1947: 48–54).

Works by Tolstov, also a member of the Soviet Academy of Sciences, occupy a prominent place in the study of the ethnogenesis of the Oguz and the Turkmen. Contrary to the majority of historians, Tolstov believes that the Oguz are one of the ancient Massaget tribes. According to his concept, their formation took place in Central Asia, and the initial area of their ethnogenesis was the Aral Sea region and the lower reaches of the Syr Darya River. He is of the opinion that the name "Oguz," which was given to Turkmen by medieval sources, is a version of "Oks," the ancient name of the River Amu Darya. Tolstov's investigations showed that the Oguz tribes were rather heterogeneous in their composition and included the most varied ethnic elements. He expresses the view that the Oguz were the descendants of the Ephthalites turkicized in the sixth and seventh centuries (*Narody Srednei* 1962; Karpov 1928). Historians in Turkmenistan joined the study of the ethnogenesis of the Turkmen in the late twenties. Among their works on the subject, mention should be made of those of Karpov. For more than twenty years, from the mid-twenties to the mid-forties, he studied the historico-ethnographic background of various Turkmenian tribes. The late scholar did a great deal of work comparing the medieval and modern Turkmenian clan and tribal division. His results showed that the majority of the Oguz tribes already extant in the eleventh to fourteenth centuries were subsequently incorporated into the Turkmen. He wrote that "the Oguz of ancient times were the Turkmen whose remnants formed, to a great degree, the foundation of the Turkmen clan and tribal unions that appeared during the period of the Mongol invasion" (Karpov 1945).

A number of works on the ethnogenesis of the Turkmen were published in the Turkmen Republic in the fifties and sixties (Rosljakov 1955; Agadzhanov 1963; etc.).

The majority of historians in Turkmenistan shared the view current in Soviet historiography that the ethnogenesis of the Turkmen was connected with the long Turkicization of Central Asian, mainly Iranian-speaking, nomadic and seminomadic tribes (first the Dakhs and the Massagets, and later the Alans and the Ephthalites). At the same time they made certain corrections and additions, as follows:

1. The Oguz played an outstanding role in the ethnogenesis of the Turkmen, but their identification as Turkmen would not be correct; for, on the one hand, only the southern branch of the Oguz took part in the ethnogenesis of the Turkmen, and, on the other, numerous non-Oguz elements were also included in the Central Asian Turkmen.

2. The agricultural peoples in Central Asia in the tenth and eleventh centuries began to call "Turkmen" that part of the Turkic-speaking population which settled along the border of agricultural regions and was closer culturally to the Tajiks, the Khorezm and Khorasan peoples.

3. Apart from the Oguz and the Alans, the settled population of western Khorezm and northern Khorasan played a great role in the ethnogenesis of the Turkmen, who also merged with large groups of Mongol-Tatars, Kipchaks, and other steppe tribes and nationalities of Central

Asia and Kazakhstan, as well as separate groups of Arabs, Kurds, and other nationalities that lived in the territory of modern Turkmenistan.

4. The formation of the Turkmenian nationality in Central Asia proceeded especially actively in the eleventh and twelfth centuries, in the so-called Seljuk period, but was completed only in the fourteenth to fifteenth centuries, during the post-Mongolian period, and after a considerable number of Turkmen had left Central Asia for India, Azerbaijan, Asia Minor, and Iraq.

5. The Oguz played a definite role in the ethnogenesis of the Azerbaijanian, Karakalpak, and Turkish peoples; the majority of the Khorasan people merged into the Iranian people; and the majority of the Khorezm people became part of the Uzbek people. Therefore the Turkmen, in their origin and ethnic composition, are closely connected with a number of peoples of Central Asia and Kazakhstan, as well as some in the east outside the Soviet Union.

Soviet anthropologists have made a great contribution to the elaboration of the ethnogenesis of the Turkmen. Investigations by Oshanin (1959); Trofimova (1962), Ginzburg (1959), Zezenkova (1964), and Kijatkina (1964) revealed a close connection between the ancient autochthonous and the modern anthropological types of the population in Turkmenistan. On the basis of a craniological investigation of Turkmen conducted by Oshanin, the theory of a Scythian-Sarmat origin for the Turkmen was advanced in 1926. One of Oshanin's basic arguments is the fact that the dolichocephalous European racial type prevails among the Turkmen.

A distinguishing feature of the studies of the ethnogenesis of the Turkmen in Soviet historiography is their comprehensive character. Soviet scholars do not reduce this problem simply to attempts to etymologize the term "Turkmen." The problems of ethnic history and of the origin of the Turkmen are studied by anthropologists, archaeologists, and ethnographers, as well as by medieval historians.

Soviet ethnographers study various aspects of the ethnic history of the Turkmen: the old clan and tribal structure of the Oguz and the Turkmen, their material culture, literature and art, and their ethnic ties with other peoples. Vasil'eva (1964) and Vinnikov (1962) are successfully working in this field, while in Turkmenistan it is being tackled by Ovezov (1959), Dzhikiev (1964), and other young Turkmenian ethnographers.

Works by Soviet archaeologists are a help in studying the ethnogenesis of the Turkmen. Of special importance are the results of archaeological investigations of ancient monuments of the Dakho-Massaget and other tribes that lived in the territory of modern Turkmenistan. The lengthy field investigations carried out by the Khorezm expedition, the South-Turkmenistan archaeological expedition, and the department of archaeology at the Institute of History under the Academy of Sciences of the

Turkmen Republic yielded valuable materials, making it possible to learn something about the life and culture of the peoples that lived in our republic's territory in ancient times and in the Middle Ages, and about their role in the ethnogenesis of the Turkmen.

Despite almost three hundred years of study, the problem of the ethnogenesis of the Turkmen cannot yet be considered solved. Many questions on the ethnic history and genesis of the Turkmen remain unanswered. The historical stages of the development of the Turkmenian language and the specific features, material culture, literature, and art of the Turkmen have been investigated rather poorly. The question of the manner and time of formation of the Turkmenian nationality remains especially controversial.

A solution to these problems is an urgent task facing historical science. Complex work by historians, philologists, ethnographers, anthropologists, and other scholars is needed to complete the studies of the ethnogenesis of the Turkmen.

REFERENCES

ABU REIKHAN BIRUNI
   1937   *Biruni's picture of the world*. Memoirs of the Archaeological Survey of India 53. Delhi.
AGADZHANOV, S. G.
   1963   Novye materialy o prois-khozhdenii turkmen [New material on the origin of the Turkmen]. *Izvestija AN Turkmenskoi SSR. Serija Obshchestvennykh Nauk* 2.
   1970   Nekotorye problemy istorii oguzskikh plemën Srednei Azii [Some problems of the history of the Oguz tribes of Central Asia]. *Tjurkologicheskii Sbornik*. Moscow, Leningrad.
ARISTOV, N. A.
   1894   Opyt vyjavlenija etnicheskogo sostava kirgiz-kazakhov Bol'shoi Ordy [An attempt to uncover the ethnic composition of the Kirghiz-Kazakhs of the Great Horde]. *Zhivaja Starina*, vyp. 3–4, 415.
   1896   Zametki ob etnicheskom sostave tjurkskikh plemën i narodnostei i svedenija ob ikh chislennosti [Notes on the ethnic composition of Turkish tribes and nationalities and information on their number]. *Zhivaja Starina*, vyp. 6, 401.
BARTOL'D, V. V.
   1921   Novyi trud o polovtsakh [New work on the Polovtsy]. *Russkii Istoricheskii Zhurnal* 17.
   1963   "Ocherk istorii turkmenskogo naroda" [An essay on the history of the Turkmen people], in *Sochinenija* by V. V. Bartol'd, volume two, part 1. Moscow.
BAZIN, L.
   1953   Notes sur les mots "Oguz" et "Türk." *Oriens* 6 (2): 315–318.
DEGUIGNES, JEAN
   1756   *Histoire générale des Huns, des Turcs, des Mongols et des autres Tartares occidentaux*. Paris.

DENY, J.
1921   *Grammaire de la langue turque* (*dialect Osmanli*). Paris.
D'HERBELOT DE MOLANVILLE, BARTHLÉMY
1789   *Bibliothèque orientale ou dictionnaire universel.* The Hague.
DZHIKIEV, A.
1964   *Etnograficheskie dannye po etnogenezu turkmensalyrov* [Ethnographic data on the ethnogenesis of the Turkmen-Salyrs]. Moscow.
GALKIN, M. N.
1869   *Etnograficheskie i istoricheskie materialy po Srednei Azii i Orenburg-skomu kraju* [Ethnographic and historical material on Central Asia and the Orenburg territory]. St. Petersburg.
GINZBURG, V. V.
1959   Materialy k antropologii naselenija Juzhnoi Turkmenii v epokhu pozdnei bronzy [Material for the anthropological study of the population of southern Turkmenistan in the late Bronze Age]. *Trudy Jutake* 9.
GOLUBOVSKII, P. I.
1884   Ob uzakh i polovtsakh [On the Uzy and Polovtsians]. *Zhurnal Ministerstva Narodnogo Prosveshchenija* [Journal of the Ministry of Popular Education] 224.
HOUTSMA, M. T.
1888   *Die Ghuzenstämme.* WZKM 2.
JAKUBOVSKII, A. JU.
1947   Voprosy etnogeneza turkmen v VIII–X vv. [Questions of the ethnogenesis of Turkmen in the eighth to tenth centuries]. *Sovetskaja Etnografija* 3: 48–54.
ILOVAISKII, D. I.
1876   *Istorija Rossii* [The history of Russia]: 23. Moscow.
KAFESOGLU, I.
1958   À propos du nom Turkmen. *Oriens* 11.
KARAMZIN, M. N.
1833   *Istorija gosudarstva Rossiiskogo* [The history of the Russian State], volumes one and two.
KARELIN, G.
n.d.   O vostochnom berege Kaspiiskogo morja [About the eastern shore of the Caspian Sea]. *Tsgada*, f. 21, d. 6, ch. 2, l. 218.
KARPOV, G. U.
1928   Rodoslovnaja turkmen [The genealogy of the Turkmen]. *Turkmen ovedenie* 12.
1945   Turkmeny – oguzy [Turkmen – Oguz]. *Izvestija Turkmenskogo Filiala Akademii Nauk SSSR* 1.
KIJATKINA, T. P.
1964   Kraniologicheskii material iz katakombnykh zakhorenii antichnogo vremeni v Juzhnoi Turkmenii [Craniological material from catacomb burials of antiquity in southern Turkmenistan]. *Problemy Etnicheskoi Antropologii.* Tashkent.
KOTWICZ, W.
1948   Contributions à l'histoire de l'Asie Centrale. *Rocznik Orientalistyczny*: 15.
LIGETI, L.
1925   *Die Herkunft des Volksnamens Kirgis.* Közösi Csoma Arkhivum. Bd. 1, N. 5, 120–131. Budapest.

MAKHMUD IBN KHUSAIN AL-KASHGARI
1335   *Divan lugat at-tjurk* 10 (3): 304–307. Istanbul.

MALCOLM, J.
1830   *Geschichte von Persien von den frühesten Zeiten bis zu den neuesten nach morgenländischen Quellen.* Stuttgart and Tübingen.

MARKWART, J.
1914   *Über das Volkstum der Komanen.* Berlin.

Narody Srednei
1962   *Narody Srednei Azii i Kazakhstana* [The peoples of Central Asia and Kazakhstan], volume one. Moscow.

NÉMETH, G.
1930   *A honfoglaló magyarság kialakulása.* Budapest.

OSHANIN, L. V.
1926   Tysjacheletnjaja davnost' dolikhotsefalii u turkmen i vozmozhnye puti eë proiskhozhdenija [The millennial antiquity of dolichocephalism among the Turkmen and the possible modes of its origin]. *Izvestija Sredazkomstarisa*, vyp. 1.
1959   Antropologicheskii sostav turkmenskikh plemën i etnogenez turkmenskogo naroda [The anthropological composition of the Turkmen tribes and the ethnogenesis of the Turkmen people]. *Trudy Jutake* 9.

OVEZOV, D.
1959   Turkmeny murchali [The Murchali Turkmen]. *Trudy Jutake* 9.

PELLIOT, P.
1930   Sur la légende d'Urguz-Khan en écriture oulghoure. *T'oung Pao* 27: 247–358.

POGODIN, M. I.
1857   *Issledovanija, zamechanija i lektsii* [Research, remarks, and lectures], volume five, page 136. Moscow.

RADLOFF, W.
1891   *Das Kudatku Bilik des Chass-Haclschib aus Balasagun.* St. Petersburg.

RASHID AD-DIN FAZLALLAKH
n.d.   "Dzamu' at-tavarikh." Manuscript belonging to the collection of the M. E. Saltykov-Shchedrin Library, PNS 46, sheet 49a. Leningrad.

RAVERTY, H. G., *translator*
1881   *The Tabaqati-i Nasiri: a general history of the Muhammadan dynasties of Asia.* London.

ROSLJAKOV, A. A.
1955   Turkmeny i oguzy [The Turkmen and the Oguz]. *Uchënye zapiski Turkmenskogo gosudarstvennogo universiteta*, vyp. 3. Ashkhabad.

TATISHCHEV, V. N.
1962   *Istorija rossiiskaja* [History of Russia], vol. 1. Moscow, Leningrad.

TOMSEN, W.
1896   *Inscriptions de l'Orkhon.* MSFO. Helsinki.

TOLSTOV, S. P.
1935   Perezhitki totemizma i dual'noi organizatsii u turkmen [Survivals of totemism and dual organization among the Turkmen]. *Problemy Istorii Dokapitalisticheskikh Obshchestv* 9–10.

TROFIMOVA, T. A.
1962   *Drevnee naselenie Khorezma i sopredel'nykh oblastei po dannym paleoantropologii* [The ancient population of Khorezm and adjacent regions according to paleoanthropological data]. Moscow.

VAMBERY, H.
1885 *Das Türkenvolk in seinen ethnologischen und ethnographischen Beziehungen.* Leipzig.

VASIL'EVA, G. P.
1964 *Etnograficheskie dannye o proiskhozhdenii turkmenskogo naroda* [Ethnographic data on the origins of the Turkmen people]. Moscow.

VINNIKOV, IA. R.
1962 Rodoplemennoi i etnicheskii sostav naselenija Chardzhouskoi oblasti Turkmenskoi SSR i ego rasselenie [The clan-tribal and ethnic composition of the population of the Chardzhou region of the Turkmen SSR and its distribution]. *Trudy Instituta Istorii, Arkheologii i Etnografii AN TSSR.* Ashkhabad.

ZEZENKOVA, V. JA.
1964 K voprosu o proiskhozhdenii turkmenskogo naroda [On the question of the origin of the Turkmen people]. *Problemy etnicheskoi antropologii Srednei Azii.* Tashkent.

Family-group, Family, and Individual Property Categories Among Nomads

S. M. ABRAMZON

The problems of property in general, and those of nomads in particular, have been thoroughly investigated in their sociological, historical, and economic aspects. Soviet economists, historians, and ethnographers widely discussed the problem of property among nomads in the mid-fifties (*Materialy ob"edinënnoi* 1955; Potapov 1954).

It is a known fact that private ownership of livestock arises at a very early stage; its emergence marks the advent of cattle breeding as an economic system and a switchover to the monogamous family. As Lenin wrote, both private property and inherited property represent categories of a social order which features well-defined, small, monogamous families with barter and exchange already extant (Lenin n.d.: 152).

Until recently, the problems related to the private ownership of livestock in nomadic communities have been considered primarily in a general form. And yet ethnographic sources allow a more specific approach to the concept of private-family ownership of livestock among herding peoples. The available ethnographic data can be used (1) to trace certain stages in the development of this form of ownership, and (2) to determine the existence of such a category of ownership of livestock and of other property of nomads which in its original form may be regarded as characterizing patriarchal, large-family communities.

Before characterizing this category of community ownership, which will be referred to as *family-group ownership*, it should be noted that it is never encountered in a "pure" form but rather coexists, and sometimes intertwines, with other kinds of ownership, particularly with the private ownership by individual families that crystallized somewhat later.

Family-clan groups, which are in fact small communities in their own right, constituted a real form of social organization among nomads, conducive to the preservation of vestiges of collective ownership. Studies of a community made up of kindred families indicate that it resulted from the disintegration of the patriarchal family community, at the same time remaining the smallest subunit of a clan[1] in which relations of consanguinity were still viable (Abramzon 1971:180–197; Kisljakov 1969:29–32; Potapov 1969:114–146).

Bride money and the dowry should be included in the category of family-group property which was simultaneously a private-family form of property. Many scholars still hold the view that bride money was paid primarily or exclusively by the groom's family and was administered solely by the bride's father. Hence the widely accepted definition of the type of marriage based on bride money payment as "marriage by purchase." Close scrutiny reveals, however, that the persons who took part in the collection of wealth to pay for the bride and in the "appropriation" of that wealth were far from confined to the groom's and bride's parents.

Here are several lines of evidence. Among the southern Altaic tribes, the groom was helped to pay the bride money by his relatives, particularly his next of kin on the father's side; in some cases the groom's father's relatives pooled to pay the bride money (Dyrenkova 1926: 251; Efimova 1926: 229; Potapov 1953: 262). According to an oral report by Potapov, among the Touvinians the relatives likewise took part in the collection of bride money. And here is what an archive source says about the Kirghiz: "...custom dictates that the bridegroom's relatives are bound to help him in the payment of the bride money." This is borne out both by literary sources and by our own field observation (*Obychai karakirgizov* n.d.; Starynkevich 1930: 233; Dzhumagulov 1960: 18–19; Abramzon 1959: 32–33). The physician Pojarkov vividly wrote:

> If a young woman is widowed childless, she is taken as wife by one of the deceased husband's brothers or other relatives with all her possessions and livestock, *and the livestock is divided among the relatives...for all the relatives had taken part in the payment of the bride money for the widow...* (Pojarkov n.d.: 367: 2. Emphasis added.)

Characteristically, all close relatives by blood or marriage got together to discuss their contributions to the bride money.

Similarly, among the Kazakhs contributions from the relatives were also customary. Thus, Makovetskii notes:

> However, the groom's father is not solely responsible for the payment of the bride money, for the groom's relatives also make contributions which are the

---

[1] Many nomadic and seminomadic Turkic tribes preserved a late patriarchal "genealogical" clan with its inherent "generationwise" exogamy. It consisted of persons tied together not only by the consciousness of a common origin, but also by strong political and economic common interests, the latter being decisive under feudal conditions. As a rule, a clan was governed feudally. A clan would sometimes include groups of alien origin, too; their adoption was not accompanied by any rites.

greater, the more valuable the gift made by the bride's father (*Materialy po Kazakhskomu* 1948: 251).

A number of other authors testify to the same effect.

One should add that the members of the small Turkmenian clan subunit (*garyndash*) helped the groom pay the bride money; the Karakalpak groom was helped not only by his close relatives but also by his distant relatives, particularly on his mother's side (Vasil'eva 1954: 177–178; Bekmuratova 1970: 69).

Such situations have been characterized by Kisljakov in his fundamental work

... bride-money payment among all peoples who practiced this custom, concerned not only the narrow circle of the groom's next of kin and close relatives, but involved a great number of persons who assisted in its payment... (Kisljakov 1969: 67).

As follows from the above sources as well as from special investigations, it is precisely the members of the family-clan group to which the groom's family belonged who were bound to pay, in varying amounts, the bride money. Thus, the very method of collecting bride money reflected the collective nature of this category of ownership.

No less indicative is the subsequent lot of the bride money. A considerable body of evidence indicates that a large, not small, portion of it was spent to prepare the bride's dowry, on the one hand; and that, on the other, it became the property of those kindred families which had taken part in the collection of the dowry and in other wedding expenses. Anichkov, writing in the nineteenth century, gave convincing evidence as to the right, among the Kazakhs, of the bride's relatives to part of the bride money (1899: 3, 4). This is also borne out by our field material collected among the Kirghiz, and by the observations of other authors.

In this respect, of special interest are the customs practiced by the Touvinians. The livestock presented by the groom's family to the bride's parents was regarded as common property by all the bride's relatives, and the bride's parents were required to share the gift livestock with their closest relatives, giving them *up to two-thirds* of the total number, according to material collected in the Alash Valley. Hence, anyone receiving livestock was in turn obliged to participate in supplying the bride's trousseau, which, upon her marriage, became her personal property for life in her husband's home (Potapov 1969: 248–249).

The Kirghiz had a very revealing custom: the bride's father's relatives ambushed and seized part of the livestock which the groom's father was sending as payment for the bride. This act was not deemed reprehensible, not was it called robbery, and the seized livestock remained in the possession of the relatives who had taken part in the seizure. This goes to prove again that the bride's relatives had a real right to part of the groom's payment for her.

Hence, the bride money became the property not only of the bride's father, but of all his closest relatives, members of the family-clan group. The dowry, just like the bride money, seems a private or private-family form of property only to a very casual observer. Actually, the dowry had also evolved all the way from family-group to family to individual (personal) property. But to tackle this problem in depth, it is necessary first to analyze the concept of "dowry." It is called *indye* by the Altaic, *inji* by the Khakases, *inzh* by the Mongols, and *inji* by the Turkmen. Yet the very same Altaic and Kirghiz use another term for dowry – *sep*, meaning trousseau, ornaments, or utensils, *but not livestock*. A similar term standing for dowry (*ouyer*) is present in a fourteenth-century list of Turkic words. In the Mongolian *inzh, mal* denotes the livestock that are part of the dowry. The Touvinians (Kirghiz group) used the word *onch* to denote property which the bride received from her parents as her personal possession and which included various species of livestock, various clothes, utensils, etc.

It is obvious that the dowry should be distinguished from that property given to the bride by her parents which represented her share of the common-family possessions. This share was called *enchi* by the Kirghiz (the same term was used to denote a share of inheritance or the share apportioned to a son). But this share consisted primarily of *livestock*, whereas the dowry brought to the husband's home included everything needed to form a separate economic unit (including a tent), *except livestock* – save for the horse which brought the bride to her groom and the camel which transported the dowry, in Kazakh practice.

According to Kazakh and Kirghiz custom, the daughter received her share (denoted by the Kazakh word *yenshi*) as late as one to three years after her marriage, when she visited her parents or relatives as a mother. Some sources indicate that the Kazakhs, too, apportioned the bride's share in cattle and not in things.

A student of the genesis and nature of both the dowry and the *enchi* will appreciate the value of the Touvinian material collected by Potapov (1969: 237, 245, 248–251, 261–262, 264–266). The Touvinian bride brought to her husband's home her property (*önchoo*) which included a tent with complete furnishings, her personal trousseau, and a certain number of head of livestock of various species. It is here, among the Touvinians, that we find an early *undivided* form of property brought by the bride to her husband's home, whereas other nomadic peoples differentiated this property into the dowry proper and the part apportioned by the father from his property. The same Touvinian material provides a full answer to the question as to how this undivided bride's property, and hence the dowry, was formed. The bride's relatives were obliged to take part in the preparation of her dowry along with her parents. The relatives prepared a new tent for the newlyweds, provided all the required furnishings and utensils, and allotted to the bride a small quantity of livestock.

In the Chohodoo group, certain relatives of the bride were bound by custom to make quite substantial gifts: the bride's elder sister's husband, for instance, presented the bride with a saddled and bridled horse. Thus, the assembly of a dowry (*önchoo* or *onch*) was a collective process among the Touvinians. The Kirghiz also practiced a custom whereby the bride's father was helped by his relatives in livestock, utensils, gowns, carpets, and sometimes money: this help was termed *koshoomcha*.

In their turn, the groom's relatives claimed part of the dowry, as evidenced by field ethnographic materials on the Kirghiz and some sources on the Kazakhs. Thus the groom's male sponsor at the wedding (his relative) was entitled to any item of the dowry; Levshin wrote (1832) on the basis of his personal observations that "the greedy relatives [of the groom] hasten to grab [from the dowry] whatever is to their liking..."

And what about the bride's own rights to her dowry and *enchi*? Practically all sources assert that among the Kazakhs and the Kirghiz the dowry became the husband's full and inalienable property (though used by the whole family) if it had been apportioned to him, or the property of the bride's father-in-law, if it had not been apportioned to the married son. If the woman tried to leave her husband, she could not reclaim her dowry. Only on rare occasions would a Kazakh husband after a divorce provide his ex-wife with a saddled horse, bedding, and part of the dowry; yet sometimes she would be given her entire dowry.

There are several lines of indirect evidence, however, indicating that at one time a woman had enjoyed broader rights to her dowry. Thus, the Kazakhs treated certain items of the dowry as unquestionably belonging to the woman: upon the death of a childless wife the husband was to return to her relatives the tent, her headgear (*sahukele*), the bedding, the saddle horse, and one of the draft camels of the deceased. The newlywed made gifts to the sponsor at the wedding *from her dowry*. When the dowry was apportioned to her husband, she presented her father-in-law with one of the best items of *her* dowry.

A Kirghiz girl at the age of ten started "to embroider her trousseau and horse outfit including the saddle" (Pojarkov n.d., 364: 10). Exactly these items of the dowry constituted the woman's personal possessions, a fact that is attested to in the following archive document:

In a divorce, provided the guilt was the husband's, from the part of the bride money returned to him a sum was withheld required to provide his ex-wife with an outfit of clothes and "a saddle set" (Pojarkov n.d.).

But the Kirghiz did not extend the rules of the dowry to the *enchi*. The *enchi* was regarded as the wife's property, and she had the right to it if she was left a childless widow and desired to return to her parents' family. The Touvinian woman, too, in case of divorce, had a right to take the *önchoo* brought to her husband's home and return with it to the *aal* [nomadic settlement] of her parents.

The woman's right to this kind of property was recognized by custom in various divisions and redivisions of property. The livestock forming part of the *önchoo* was added to the husband's herd, and the whole herd was common and indivisible, though for a long time after the marriage each spouse knew his or her livestock. Practically, this "differentiation" of livestock was important only in cases of controversy over the property rights of one of the spouses. It should be noted that with the Toubalars (a northern Altaic tribe) the property brought by the woman to her husband's household – rootdigger, clothes, bedding, and kitchen utensils (the *kystyn yenchizi*) – was used by the whole family; but in case of divorce all this property was returned to the woman, and in case of her death it was claimed by her next of kin – brothers, father, etc. (Potapov 1953: 129).

The question as to how the personal (or individual) property of both the girl and the boy was formed is of particular interest. According to Ch. Ch. Valikhanov (1964: 41), the Kazakhs had a custom whereby his parents allotted a certain quantity of livestock to a boy during the ceremony of circumcision; this livestock constituted his *inchoo* (or *yenshi*). This gift notwithstanding, during the division of a deceased father's property, this son was entitled to claim his part of the inheritance, on a par with the other heirs. Rich Kazakhs, notes S. E. Tolybekov (1971: 530), branded with special marks the ears of a foal, a baby camel, or lambs and kids intended as presents, in this case *yenshi*, to the *children of poor relatives*. According to A. T. Tagirjanov's verbal report, the Povolzhie Tatars also had the custom of *inchi* as a gift to infants in the form of livestock.

The Touvinians have also been found to practice a similar custom. If a newborn was presented by some relative with a ewe or a foal, this was considered the infant's *onch*. The children's livestock grazed and grew in their parents' herd, but everybody knew the animals which constituted each child's *onch* and recognized their right of ownership of these animals.

Among the Touvinians of the Erzinsky district, each boy and each girl acquired an *önchoo* (or *onch*) at the moment of birth, when the newborn was presented by relatives with domestic animals (this was also done at the naming ceremony, at the first hair cutting rite, etc.). By the time of marriage the livestock accumulated through presents, together with all breeding stock, formed an *önchoo*.

The above data not only disclose one of the main methods of personal property accumulation among nomads but also irrefutably testify to the *role of relatives* in the formation of this kind of property, as exemplified by the Touvinians.

Bypassing the problem of inherited property, one more social institution merits attention. This institution, called by the Kazakhs and the Kirghiz *yenshi* and *enchi*, respectively, is the custom of apportionment to the son by his father at the time of his marriage and formation of an independent household, whereby he was allotted a part of the common-family property, primarily in the form of livestock. The property left *after the father's death*, and subject to division (that is to say, inherited property proper) was denoted by special terms of an obviously Arabic origin (*muras, muraz, myras*, and *murapy* in Kirghiz; and *ata murassy* in Kazakh).

The process of apportionment to a son from his father's, or rather from the common family, property was conducted by the Kazakhs and the Kirghiz as a solemn ceremony. The Kazakh ceremony was attended by relatives, who in their turn presented the protagonist with domestic animals and various other items. This custom of assistance was termed *nemeourin*. The Altaic had a custom according to which, after the son's marriage, his father, *assisted* by all relatives, erected a new tent for the newlyweds.

The livestock allotted to the bride by her relatives was added by the Touvinians to the herd allotted to the groom by his relatives. In the Erzin-sky district a newly married Touvinian boy soon after the wedding visited his parents' tent and received his *khuuv* (in Mongolian *khuvj* [part, share]; in ancient Mongolian *khubi* [appanage, share]). Rather than giving a voluntary wedding present, it was custom-sanctified to allot a certain portion of property, including livestock, to a relative about to get married and start a new, independent life. This property formed the husband's personal possession. The medieval Mongols had a custom whereby "fathers while still living allotted a share of their estate to their apparently married sons (*omchi, yonchi*)" (Vladimirtsov 1934: 171). So this category of private-family property was also formed with the help of relatives, above all on the father's side.

It remains to be said that the Kirghiz term *enchi* also had other connotations: the territory of a tribe or of its subunits was called *enchi*; vassal tribes, like groups of subjects of large feudal lords, could also turn into *enchi*; summer pastures were likewise sometimes considered *enchi*. These "living" pieces of evidence of a not-too-distant past have a direct correlation with some of the social institutions of medieval nomads reported in written sources: *inju* or *inji* which had a dual meaning: (1) persons allotted by the sovereign as part of the dowry, and (2) appanage apportioned to the members of a khan family (Rashid-ad-din 1952: 280; Vladimirtsov 1952: 68).

Thus, Genghis Khan, while still living, apportioned to each of his three oldest sons an appanage (*inju*), i.e. a certain number of nomadic hordes (*ulus*) and a sufficient space for their upkeep (*yurts*). Similarly, Ughedei gave Maverannahr to his brother Jagatai as an appanage (Bartol'd 1963: vol. 1, pp. 535–577, 585).

In the same way Tagai, one of the legendary forefathers of the Kirghiz, allotted as *enchi*s to his sons – the subsequent forefathers of the large Kirghiz tribes Bogorston, Koilon, and Jidiger – large territories within the boundaries of present-day Kirghizstan, which one cannot help regarding as appanages of a sort. Of course, medieval institutions represent a very late stage in the development of these categories of private-family property.

In the light of these data one can see how the nomads switched from a collective form of ownership by patriarchal family communities, referred to later as family-clan groups, to the principle of private ownership by individual families. Such a form of private property evolved in several ways: allotment of livestock to newborns and children, and later to adolescent boys and girls; apportioning to sons from the common-family estate; and, finally, division of inherited property.

One social institution particularly specific to the nomads was apportioning to sons by their fathers; the emergence of this institution marked a changeover from the principle of family-community ownership to ownership by the separate small family. Characteristically, the process of formation of private-family property involved not only males but also girls and women, which argues in favor of this being *the earliest stage* in the development of private property.

Nevertheless, in the subsequent period, too, nomadic private-family property had its specific features. In this respect, the evidence of sources related to the Kazakhs and the Kirghiz merits special attention. Among poor and middle-status Kazakh cattle breeders, the common-family property would often include the share of a brother who lived far away and visited his native settlement only occasionally. The needy father, too, retained a broad right to the property apportioned to his son; he could take whatever he liked of his son's possessions and use it as long as he liked. Another instance of a similar nature is the right of the grandsons (*zhiyen*) to theft and even appropriation of any animal or possession from their maternal grandfather (*nagashi*). A similar custom of appropriation by the nephew (*zhehen*) of any item, however valuable, of the maternal uncle's property (*tayake*) also existed among the Kirghiz and the Altai.

A source related to the Kirghiz asserts that apportionment to a family member is not governed by any strictly delineated and exclusive rights of the owner to his property, as was the case with the Russian peasants; the recipient is "governed by the clan principle of indivisibility of property and mutual aid." If the clan lived in harmony, though newly formed families lived in their separate tents, the livestock of the clan was common for one, two, or three years after marriage, before children appeared and for the same period after their birth. The father did not need permission to take a ewe or a horse from his son's herd during this period, or sometimes even afterward; he could even sell it and the son would have no objections.

It follows then that for all the preponderance of private-family ownership among the nomads, this principle not only coexisted with viable vestiges of the family-group ownership principle but even, to an extent, bore a conventional character.

REFERENCES

ABRAMZON, S. M.
1959 Svadebnye obychai kirgizov Pamira [Wedding customs of the Pamir Kirghiz]. *Trudy Akad. Nauk Tadzhikskoi SSR* 120: 32–33.
1971 *Kirgizi i ikh etnogeneticheskie i istoriko-kul'turnye svjazi* [The Kirghiz and their ethnogenic and historico-cultural ties]. Leningrad.
ANICHKOV, I.
1899 "K voprosu o kalyme" [The problem of kalym], in *Ocherki narodnoi zhizni Severnogo* [Essays on folk life in northern Turkestan]. Tashkent.
BARTOL'D, V. V.
1963 *Sochineniia* [Works], volumes one and two. Moscow.
BEKMURATOVA, A. T.
1970 *Byt i sem'ja karakalpakov v proshlom i nastojashchem* [Customs and family of the Karakalpaks in the past and present]. Nukus.
DYRENKOVA, N. P.
1926 *Rod, klassifikatsionnaja sistema rodstva i brachnye normy u altaitsev i teleut* [Kin, the classification system of kinship and marital norms among the Altaic and Teleuts] (first edition). *Materialy po svad'be i semeino-rodovomu stroju narodoy SSSR.* Leningrad.
DZHUMAGULOV, A.
1960 *Sem'ja i brak u kirgizov Chuiskoi doliny* [Family and marriage among the Kirghiz of the Chuya Valley]. Frunze.
EFIMOVA, A.
1926 *Teleutskaja svad'ba* [The Teleut wedding] (first edition). *Materialy po svad'be i semeino-rodovomu stroju narodov SSSR.* Leningrad.
ENGELS, F.
n.d. "Proiskhozhdenie sem'i, chastnoi sobstvennosti i gosudarstva" [The origin of the family, private property, and the state], in *Sochineniia* [Works] by K. Marx and F. Engels, volume twenty-one.
KISLJAKOV, N. A.
1969 *Ocherki po istorii sem'i i braka u narodov Srednei Azii i Kazakhstana* [Essays on the history of the family and marriage among the peoples of Central Asia and Kazakhstan]. Leningrad.
LENIN, V. I.
n.d. *Polnoe sobranie sochinenii* [Complete collected works], volume one.
LEVSHIN, A.
1832 "Opisanie kirgis-kazach'ikh ili kirgiz-kaysatskikh ord i stepei" Chast III. [Description of Kirgiz-Kazakh or Kirgiz-Kaisakh hordes and steppes], Chast 3. *Etnograficheskie Izvestiya* [Ethnographic Papers]. St. Petersburg.
Materialy ob"edinënnoi
1955 *Materialy ob"edinënnoi nauchnoi sessii, posvjashchennoi istorii Srednei Azii i Kazakhstana v dooktjabr'skii period* [Proceedings of the general scientific session devoted to the history of Central Asia and Kazakhstan in the pre-October period]. Tashkent.

Materialy po kazakhskomu
1948   *Materialy po kazakhskomu obychnomu pravu* [Materials on Kazakh customary law], collection one. Alma-Ata.
Obychai karakirgizov
n.d.   *Obychai karakirgizov Tokmakskogo uezda* [Customs of the Kara-Kirghiz of the Tokmak district]. Central Government Archive of the Kazakh SSR, stock 64, inventory 1, work 5089, division 5: "The Family," § 43.

POJARKOV, F.
n.d.   O kara-kirgizakh [On the Kara-Kirghiz]. Kazakh government public library, numbers 364 and 367.

POTAPOV, L. P.
1953   *Ocherki po istorii altaitsev* [Essays on the history of the Altaic]. Moscow, Leningrad.
1954   O sushchnosti patriarkhal'no-feodal'nykh otnoshenii u kochevykh narodov Srednei Azii i Kazakhstana [On the essence of patriarchal-feudal relationships among the nomadic peoples of Central Asia and Kazakhstan]. *Voprosy Istorii* 6.
1969   *Ocherki narodnogo byta tuvintsev* [Essays on the national customs of the Tuvinians]. Moscow.

RASHID-AD-DIN
1952   *Sbornik letopisei* [Collection of chronicles], volume one, book two. Moscow, Leningrad.

STARYNKEVICH, I. D.
1930   Formy zakljuchenija braka u turetskikh plemem Sibiri i u kochevnikov Srednei Azii [Forms of marriage arrangements among the Turkic tribes of Siberia and among the nomads of Central Asia]. *Sbornik Muzeja Antropologii i Etnografii* 9: 233. Leningrad.

TOLYBEKOV, S. E.
1971   *Kochevoe obshchestvo kazakhov v 17- nachale 20 veka. Politiko-èkonomicheskii analiz* [Nomadic society of the Kazakhs from the 17th to the beginning of the 20th century. A political and economic analysis]. Alma-Ata.

VAINSHTEIN, S. I.
1961   Tuvintsy-todzhintsy [Tuvinians-Todzhinians]. Moscow.

VALIKHANOV, CH. CH.
1964   *Sobranie sochinenii y piati tomakh* [Collected works in five volumes], volume 3. Alma-Ata.

VASIL'EVA, G. P.
1954   Turkmeny-nokhurli [Turkmen-Nokhurlians] Sredneaziatskii ètnograficheskii sbornik 1. *Trudy Instituta Etnografii* 21: 177–178. Moscow.

VLADIMIRTSOV, B. JA.
1934   *Obshchestvennyi stroi mongolov* [Social system of the Mongols]. Moscow.
1952   *Sbornik letopisei* [Collection of chronicles], volume two. Moscow, Leningrad.

The Formation of National Cadres of Industrial Workers in Cattle-Breeding Districts of Soviet Eastern Republics: The Turkmen Soviet Socialist Republic

SH. ANNAKLYCHEV

Prior to the Revolution, the Turkmen were mainly employed in agriculture – cultivation and livestock herding. As in other regions of Central Asia and Kazakhstan, the indigenous population of the area was almost totally concentrated in *auls*.

By the beginning of World War I in 1914, there were 296 so-called industrial plants in the Transcaspian region (Artykov 1950: 33); actually they were mere handicraft industries. Consequently, it was very difficult to decide where handicraft production ended and industrial manufacturing began, and vice versa (Massal'skii 1913: 536). Despite being part of Tsarist Russia for over thirty years, Turkmenistan remained one of its most backward regions.

As is well known, only large-scale industry can serve as the material base of socialism. Without industrialization it was impossible to build the material technical base of socialism in Turkmenistan or in the other Central Asian republics and Kazakhstan. Industrialization became the decisive factor in overcoming Turkmenistan's backwardness, the heritage of its prerevolutionary past. Hence, the Soviet government proceeded to nationalize existing industry and transportation, to carry out the confiscation of land from the rich *bais* [the upper strata of clans, clergy, etc.], and to do away with the domination by foreign capital. The nationalized industries, lands, etc., became the basis of the socialist economy. These revolutionary measures resulted in the establishment of the necessary political and economic preconditions for the transition to socialism of Turkmenistan, as well as of the other Central Asian republics and Kazakhstan.

The industrialization of Turkmenistan was carried out in accordance with the following plan: inseparably linked to the development of the country's national economy, Turkmenistan received constant fraternal aid from other, more developed Union republics. In this process the socialist principles of spatial distribution of productive forces (the need for bringing industry nearer to sources of raw materials) were taken into account.

In the Soviet years, the Turkmenian people, aided fraternally by other Union republics, transformed their formerly semifeudal, extremely backward region into one of the advanced republics of the Soviet Union. One need only remember that fifty years ago Turkmenistan was totally dependent on imported industrial products, while at present the products of many of its industrial enterprises enjoy wide demand, not only within the Soviet Union but in over fifty foreign countries of Europe, Asia, Africa, and America. High-quality iodine, bromide, sulfur, and sulphanol, large-sized ventilators, centrifugal petroleum pumps, window panes, and many other commodities are exported from Turkmenistan. Socialist construction has completely shattered the pseudoscientific anti-Soviet theories which circulated in the early years of industrialization: that feudalism in Turkmenistan was inviolable, and that the development of industry there would for that reason be impossible.

Parallel with the development of the republic's industry was the process of forming from a rural population – former nomadic herdsmen, cultivators, and fishermen – a young, indigenous, national working class, necessary in order that Turkmenistan, along with other Central Asian republics and Kazakhstan, might make the change to socialism, bypassing the stage of capitalism. This change was based on the industrialization and reconstruction of the republic's national economy.

It should be borne in mind that, prior to the first Five-Year Plan, there were very few Turkmenian industrial workers. At that time few Turkmen dwelt in cities; in 1926 there were in all 719,792 Turkmen in the republic, of whom only 9,790, little more than one percent, were living in urban areas. At the same time, in the central Kara Kum Desert alone, there were about 100,000 nomads (*Vsesojuznaja perepis' naselenija* 1928: 73).

The formation of an indigenous national working class in Turkmenistan was greatly furthered not only by industrialization, but also by collectivization in agriculture. True, the transformation of a cattle-breeding economy began later than it did in agricultural regions. In the mid-1920's, animal husbandry still remained the most backward branch of the national economy of Turkmenistan; it was based on primitive methods and retained vestiges of former feudal and clan relations. Grazing lands were regarded as common property, but wells belonged to individuals or to families of well-to-do livestock owners. Disagreements arose whenever strange cattle appeared near the water. The development of cattle herding was greatly hampered by the activities of the *basmatche*s [counter-revolutionary terrorist bands].

The transformation of a nomadic and seminomadic economy required that administrative centers be set up in cattle-breeding regions. The economic unification of such regions was a hoped-for result of these measures.

At the Second Plenary Session of the Central Committee of the Communist (Bolshevik) Party of Turkmenistan (March, 1926), special decisions were taken to improve the condition of the nomads and seminomads. Among other measures, an administrative division specially designed to delimit nomadic pastoral areas was envisaged. Schools and boarding schools for children of nomads were to be built more rapidly; animal products were to be purchased from the herdsmen by the state; trade was to be extensively developed, credits granted, zootechnical measures expanded, etc. These developments subsequently played an important part in transforming the economy and the everyday life and culture of the Turkmenian herdsmen.

A generous amount of aid was granted the Turkmenian cattle breeders by the Soviet government. In the years 1925 to 1928, 4.7 million rubles were assigned from public funds for zootechnical measures and collective-farm building in the Kara Kum alone (*Tsentral'nyi gosudarstvennyi arkiv TSSR* n.d. 544: 175). This and many other measures made possible the transition, beginning in the second half of the 1930's, from a nomadic to a sedentary way of life. The transition was carried out in an organized manner, based on Lenin's cooperation plan: the nomads were enlisted into consumers' and producers' cooperatives and drawn into wide participation in socialist construction in the republic. By 1928, thirty-eight *aul* soviets and dozens of schools had been set up in the remotest parts of the Kara Kum (*Istorija Turkmenskoi SSR* 1957: vol. 2, p. 301).

Nomads who settled down were granted free aid in the form of money, livestock, necessary tools, building materials, agronomical aid in land delimitation and organization, etc. The settlement of nomads was promoted by the successful reorganization of their small-scale commodity economy to large-scale collective farming. The settlement of livestock breeders upon new land tracts led to a breakdown in the exclusiveness of their clans and tribes. The old territorial community was losing its clannish character as it became infiltrated by members of other clans and tribes. The breakdown of traditional clan and tribal divisions contributed to the emergence of the Turkmenian socialist nation.

There were developments in technology paralleling those taking place in agriculture. With the transition of nomads and seminomads to a sedentary way of life, and with the construction of industrial plants, every year saw an increase in the national working class.

Before the 1930's, methods for securing indigenous industrial cadres in Turkmenistan were still only being devised. In that period, it was mainly the *aul* poor, rural laborers, and some of the *daikhan*s of moderate means who came to work in industry, transportation, construction, etc. Since trainee workers were mainly drawn from a rural population, accustomed to working and living conditions far different from those existing in urban industrial centers, it was not easy for them to adjust to their new life. Turkmen who had only just begun work in industry were still closely linked with their former occupations. Thus, as many as 34 percent of the workers in the main workshops of Kizil-Arvat had a plot of land in one of the nearby *auls*, and 20 percent also owned livestock. In other districts of the republic, 30 to 60 percent of Turkmenian workers retained households in *auls* (Karpych 1927: 6). This explains those individual cases in which Turkmen who had just started work in a factory would leave industry and return to their former occupations.

The formation of local workers' cadres for all branches of the national economy took place (as happens in every country where power passes into the hands of the laboring masses) under conditions of fierce class struggle, accompanied by the struggle of the old, dying ideology against socialist ideology.

However, drawing the local population into industrial production was one of the most important political and economic aims of socialist construction in a formerly backward region such as Turkmenistan. Failing this, it would have been impossible to proceed with the industrialization upon which socialist construction in backward or partially developed countries is based. Consequently, it was first of all necessary to create a proletarian backbone of Turkmenian workers who would later be able to act as managers and directors and hold other responsible positions. That is why the party, the trade union, and the public organizations in the republic gave their ceaseless attention to the formation of national cadres. Special commissions were formed, whose members made the rounds of rural districts in order to enlighten the working people on the purposes of industrialization and explain to them the nature of working conditions in factories. In industrial centers, special dwellings were built for Turkmenian workers arriving from the *auls*; good living conditions were arranged for them; they were surrounded with care and attention and granted various privileges.

The Soviet State implemented a number of measures which played an important role in the formation of indigenous national cadres. Those Turkmen who studied outside the republic received allowances larger than those usually granted to students and were provided with free clothing, while members of their families received monetary aid. Those students at courses for textile workers who were sent to Moscow and other cities received a guaranteed wage at the fifth level. Each man was given a warm coat, boots, two changes of underclothing, winter trousers, and shirts; each woman, warm dresses and shawls. The state paid for transportation to the place of study and back (*Tsentral'nyi gosudarstvennyi arkhiv TSSR* 48: 77). On their return from their studies, workers were immediately provided with living quarters, while the state helped them build individual houses, supplied them with building materials at reduced prices, and granted long-term loans.

These and other measures attracted increasing numbers of rural Turkmen, especially young people, to industrial work. At that time it was almost impossible to draw adult *daikhkan*s [nomads] into industrial production or train them for highly skilled work. The complexity of the equipment made it difficult for them to adjust to the conditions in a factory or other industrial enterprise. Therefore, large sums were expended on the education of teenagers, to train them to become highly skilled industrial workers. At the same time, there existed another method: the supplementary training of adult workers. In this way the number of Turkmenian industrial personnel grew. Thus, whereas early in 1929 there were only forty-six Turkmen in the sulfur mines of the central Kara Kum (56 percent), in 1934 there were about 300 and in 1943, 644 – 463 of them Turkmen who had previously been employed in livestock breeding. In the ozokerite works there were 181 workers in 1929, 97 percent of them Turkmen. In 1933, there were 313 workers, most of them formerly Turkmenian herdsmen and fishermen (*Tsentral'nyi gosudarstvennyi arkhiv TSSR* n.d. 6: 11–14). At the beginning of 1929, 193 people were working in the oil industry of the republic, only 30 percent of them Turkmen; in 1933 there were 2,080 workers including 1,210 Turkmen (*Tsentral'nyi gosudarstvennyi arkhiv TSSR* n.d. 28: 8). In the 1932–1933 school year, the number of schools for training factory workers ("FZO" schools) reached ten and the number of pupils 1,073. In 1931 alone, 370 worker/pupils were being trained at courses organized in industrial plants of the republic, 166 of them Turkmen (Atemasov 1964: 19).

The increase in the number of Turkmenian industrial personnel beginning in the 1930's is due not only to the substantial development of industry but also to the settlement of nomads and seminomads and to the positive results of measures taken to attract rural Turkmen to industrial production.

At the beginning of the second Five-Year Plan, the influx of Turkmen from rural districts grew with particular intensity. Inhabitants of Turkmenian *aul*s in the vicinity of industrial centers, of oil works and ozokerite works, and of sulfur mines in the Kara Kum and Guardak arrived in groups to join up for work. Most of them had in the past been poor herdsmen who had had to work for local *bai*s. In industry their working conditions were much improved; they had stable wages and good living quarters. At the same time, they were still closely tied to their relatives in the *aul*s. These ties played an important part in accustoming former herdsmen, fishermen, and land cultivators to a new culture. Workers living in industrial settlements and cities became accustomed to new ways of life and exerted a strong influence on the world outlook, way of life, and culture of rural inhabitants.

The rise of new industries in the years of the second Five-Year Plan led to continued growth in the number of indigenous workers. The number of factory courses ("FZO" schools), technical schools, and various educational and training institutions where people could learn a specialty – either on or off the job – was on the increase.

As a result, by 1937 Turkmen already constituted a majority in certain branches of industry. Thus, whereas in 1934 the total number of workers was 3,525 including 2,050 Turkmen (58 percent), in 1937 there were 3,810 Turkmen out of a total of 6,202 workers (61 percent). Whereas, in 1934, 1,845 people were employed in the sulfur mines, including 1,350 Turkmen (73.3 percent), in 1937 the total number employed was 4,625, of whom 3,560 (77 percent) were Turkmen (*Tsentral'nyi gosudarstvennyi arkhiv TSSR* n.d. 28: 8). It should be noted that most of the Turkmenian workers in the above branches of industry had quite recently been fishermen and herdsmen (those in the ozokerite works and the oil fields of Creleken), herdsmen (those in the oil fields of Nebit-Dagh and the sulfur mines of the Kara Kum), or herdsmen and cultivators (workmen in the Guardak sulfur factory). A similar pattern was to be observed among groups of workers in many other branches of industry.

These data show that in spite of great difficulties in drawing Turkmen into industry, the number of indigenous national industrial workers has been increasing year by year. Positive steps were taken to attract a labor force from the inner regions of the republic, specialists were invited from other republics, and various courses for training personnel were organized. The Turkmenian *aul*s were connected with industrial centers through related families by a thousand links; this also made for greater ease in the transition of rural Turkmen to industrial labor.

In 1937 the Sixth Extraordinary Congress of Soviets of the Republic approved the new constitution of Turkmenistan. Its text rightly notes that the course of socialist construction had solved not only problems of industrialization and collectivization but also political problems of such primary importance as the formation of an indigenous national working class.

In this way, by the beginning of the Great Patriotic War [World War II], a working class numbering many thousands had been formed in the republic. The average number of workers and employees in 1940 had reached 172,900 (*Sovetskii Turkmenistan* 1964: 98). By that time hundreds of Turkmenian workers who had begun work in the industrialization years had mastered specialties in the oil industry, the ozokerite industry, and sulfur mining, with the help of workers of other nationalities, and could themselves teach their skills to beginners.

Further growth of industry and of the indigenous working class has been observed in the postwar years and especially in the last two decades. By the beginning of the fourth Five-Year Plan many demobilized soldiers had returned to their former pursuits. Thus, in 1946, 1,440 exservicemen were assigned to work in Chardzhou region and 493 to industrial plants in Kizil-Arvat (*Partarkhiv Turkmenskogo* n.d. 384: 48). This number of workers was, however, insufficient to cope with the demands facing the republic's industry. Consequently, it became necessary to return to the well-tested method of securing cadres of workers by attracting rural inhabitants into industry. Many cultivators, cattle breeders, and fishermen started to move into industrial centers. In the fourth quarter of 1946 alone, about 400 Turkmen arrived to work in the oil fields from the Hassan-Kuli, Krasnovodsk, Kizil-Atrek, Kazandjik, Kaakhkin, Tedzen, Kirov, and Geok-Tepe districts (*Tsentral'nyi arkhiv* n.d.: 25). Between December 27, 1948, and January 11, 1949, 158 persons joined up for work in enterprises affiliated with the "Turkmenneft" firm (*Tsentral'nyi arkhiv* n.d.: 92).

Beginning in 1950, the influx of rural Turkmen into industry became still greater. In 1951 alone, over 1,990 workers were newly employed in the oil fields, most of them Turkmen (*Tsentral'nyi arkhiv* n.d.: 92). In 1952, over 350 people were working in the Bezmein cement factory, 25 percent of them Turkmen who, before entering the factory, had worked in collective farms in the vicinity of present day Bezmein (*Materialy Bezmeinskogo* 1961).

In recent years, the republic's industries have become much better provided with highly skilled personnel. In 1966, the number of specialists employed in the national economy who had completed secondary or post-secondary education was 78,700, of whom 31,200 were Turkmen (*Turkmenistan za gody Sovetskoi vlasti* 1967: 104). In 1971, there were over 100,000 such specialists (Klychev 1972: 14). In the course of industrialization in Turkmenistan the ethnic national composition of the population underwent changes, and its ethnic heterogeneity became more pronounced. Besides Turkmen and Russians (the earliest nonindigenous population of the republic), Turkmenistan's cities are at present inhabited by Azerbaijanis, Georgians, Armenians, Tatars, Ukrainians, Uzbeks, Kazakhs, and many other national groups. Joint labor in one factory by members of different nationalities, living conditions prevailing in large apartment houses, etc., have radically altered Turkmenian attitudes toward non-Turkmen.

Everyday contacts at work and at home as well as common interests and aspirations lead to firmer friendship between Turkmen and people of other nationalities. All these factors promote rapprochement between different peoples, help overcome vestiges of the former Turkmenian isolation, eliminate harmful traditional customs and rituals, and enrich the people's national culture.

Among the republic's industrial workers there are some Turkmenian families from which whole working-class dynasties have arisen. At present, the working class is being increased mainly by local young people. The place of experienced Turkmenian workers retiring on a pension is taken by their sons and daughters, representatives of the younger generation. It is gratifying that the republic's industry has raised hundreds of excellent masters of production. Among them are the Heroes of Socialist Labor A. Ashirov, Kh. Ashirov, N. Derakuliyev, E. Ovezova, S. Udayev, R. Khudainazarov, the Lenin Laureate B. Alaberdyiev, and many others. Scores of scientists, public men, cultural workers, etc., have originated in the indigenous working class. A. Klychev, president of the Supreme Soviet of the Turkmen Soviet Socialist Republic, comes from a family of oil-field workers in Cheleken. O. Orazmukhammedov, president of the Soviet of Ministers of the Turkmen SSR; D. Karayev, president of the Turkmen Trade Union Organization; B. Geldyiev, secretary of the Turkmenistan Communist Party's Central Committee; M. Shabasanov, secretary of the Ashkhabad City Committee of the Turkmenistan Communist Party; and many others formerly worked in industrial plants.

The formation of indigenous national working-class cadres was of great importance for Turkmenistan, as it had been for other Central Asian republics and Kazakhstan. The change in the social structure of the Turkmenian people was one of the main prerequisites for their con-solidation into a socialist nation. The young working class, in its path toward unity of national interests, eliminated former tribal isolation due in large part to its position of opposition to artificial divisions between peoples and states and its stand in favor of proletarian internationalism.

Thus, one of the many important achievements of the Turkmenian people during the Soviet years is the rise of the army, many thousand strong, of cadres of the national working classes and technological intelli-gentsia, whose numbers are increasing from year to year.

REFERENCES

ARTYKOV, A.
   1950   *Promyshlennost' Turkmenskoi SSR za 25 let* [Industry of the Turkmen S.S.R. over twenty-five years]. Ashkhabad.
ATEMASOV, K. V.
   1964   *Rozhdenie novogo klassa* [Birth of a new class]. Ashkhabad.
Istorija Turkmenskoi SSR
   1957   *Istorija Turkmenskoi SSR* [History of the Turkmen S.S.R.], volume two. Ashkhabad.
KARPYCH, F. F.
   1927   Turkmenija k X-letiju Oktjabrja [Turkmenistan on the tenth anniver-sary of October]. *Turkmenovedenie* 2–3. Ashkhabad.
KLYCHEV, A.
   1972   V bratskoi sem'e narodov Sovetskogo Sojuza [In the brotherly family of peoples of the Soviet Union]. *Slovo lektora* 2.

MASSAL'SKII, V. I.
1913   Turkestanskii krai [The region of Turkestan]. *Rossija, Polnoe geo-graficheskoe opisanie nashego otechestva.* St. Petersburg.
Materialy Bezmeinskogo
1961   *Materialy Bezmeinskogo tsementnogo zavoda 1961 g.* [Reports of the Bezmein cement factory, 1961].
Partarkhiv Turkmenskogo
n.d.   *Partarkhiv Turkmenskogo filiala Instituta marksizma-leninizma pri TS K KPSS* [Party archive of the Turkmen division of the Institute of Marxism–Leninism of the Central Committee of the C.P.S.U.], f. 1, op. 23.
Sovetskii Turkmenistan
1964   *Sovetskii Turkmenistan za 40 let* [Soviet Turkmenistan over 40 years]. Ashkhabad.
Tsentral'nyi arkhiv
n.d.   *Tsentral'nyi arkhiv ob"edinenija "Turkmenneft"* [Central archive of the firm "Turkmenneft"], f. 1, op. 2, op. 18.
Tsentral'nyi gosudarstvennyi arkhiv TSSR
n.d.   *Tsentral'nyi gosudarstvennyi arkhiv TSSR* [Central state archive of the T.S.S.R.], f. 1, op. 1; f. 54, op. 9; f. 259, op. 2.
Turkmenistan za gody Sovetskoi vlasti
1967   *Turkmenistan za gody Sovetskoi vlasti* [Turkmenistan in the years of Soviet power]. Ashkhabad.
Vsesojuznaja perepis' naselenija 1926
1928   *Vsesojuznaja perepis' naselenija 1926* [All-Union population census for 1926], volume sixteen. Turkmenskaja SSR. Moscow.

SECTION THREE

Stratification, Authority, and Power

The History of Sovereignty Among the Kel Ahaggar

MARCEAU GAST

We should first of all note that the Kel Ahaggar, like most Berber peoples, seem to be rather uninterested in their own history.[1] They have retained in its entirety a legend that explains everything for them: a female ancestor from Tafilalet gave birth to a family, from among whom the *aménoûkals* [supreme chiefs] of all the tribes are chosen. The famous Tine Hinane, whose tomb near Abalessa has provided a rich and important source of data on funerary objects (Camps 1965: 65–83), has for some time interested Westerners. This interest is due to the small amount of historical material that can be found in the writings of Arab travelers, in those of religious cults,[2] in the oral reports about the last century, or in oral literature in the form of poetry (de Foucauld 1925–1930).

We have no texts at all of Berber origin on the Kel Ahaggar. All of the written material has come from foreign observers of the Imoûhar, and from Arab speakers. Among these written sources of information, there are some that are suspect insofar as their bias is considerable. We cannot, however, entirely disregard them, for they give a good notion of the state

---

[1] This is often due less to lack of interest than to fear of the kingdom of the dead. Old men do not like to mention the names of their dead relatives, nor do they very often recount stories of these people to their descendants. This history is sometimes transmitted by others, but, in general, no one likes to stir up the past, for old disagreements may be aroused and "the spirits of the dead demand vengeance."

[2] The religious groups of Touat and Tidikelt possessed some documents on the history of the Tuareg. A. G. P. Martin, a military interpreter, and M. Benhazera had the opportunity to examine a large number of these manuscripts dating from 1905. Before them, H. Duveyrier had access to other documents. Unfortunately, what now remains of these documents is jealously guarded by a few people or a small number of families, and it has been extremely difficult for me to approach them. It would take long months of discreet and patient work to gain the confidence of the owners of these texts, before they would allow them to be microfilmed (cf. Gast 1973).

of mind of those people living close to the Imoûhar, more or less subject to them.[3]

The Berbers seem to have formed an immense population of tribes characterized by a common language and by certain customs that are rather different from those of the eastern Arabs in particular. Very early in their history, they frequented the countries inhabited by blacks (who must have occupied the Sahara well before them) and fought battles from Tripoli to Tangier, from the Atlantic Ocean to Niger and Senegal. The veiled Sanhadja then gave rise to the Almoravides, who reached Spain at the height of their power. With their faces veiled, these lords, mounted on great dromedaries, traveled extensively throughout all of western Africa, sometimes exercising authority over neighboring black kingdoms. This was true except during the period of the Melli (Mali) Empire in the fourteenth century, when Mença-Mouça seems to have reigned without any fear of the Imoûhar. The veiled ones had a great commercial center which siphoned off a large portion of trans-Saharan trade from Ouargla and Morocco and which was also in competition with the capital of Melli. This is the famous Tadmekket, also called Es-Souk, whose extensive ruins are visible from forty-five kilometers to the northwest of Kidal in Mali.

After the complete abandonment of Es-Souk in the seventeenth century, it seems that there was an important redistribution of many tribes, on the one hand southward toward the Niger area, and on the other hand toward Ahaggar in the north and Ajjer in the northeast. The destruction of Es-Souk appears to have been accompanied by a change in the caravan stations of the region (which resulted in the growth of In Salah, among others). At this time as well, we learn that the Imenanes (a tribe claiming Muslim origin) were reigning as masters over the Ajjer and Ahaggar, from the Adrar of the Iforas to Ghadamès. The Imenanes, also called *sultan*s in Arabic, were driven from power in the second half of the seventeenth century by a tribe of Tuareg nobles, a portion of whom were from Aïr; these were the Ouraghen. The latter did not feel unduly concerned about Ahaggar, a region that was vast, sparsely populated, and poor. After about a century of anarchy, the Kel Ahaggar agreed to select a chief from among themselves, Salah, whose precise origins are not known. After Salah, his son, Mokhammed el Kheir, succeeded him; and then the son of the latter, Sidi ag Mokhammed el Kheir, took command. He

---

[3] The first Arab traveler to speak of the Tuareg (whom he called Kel Tamasheq) was Ibn Haukal (tenth century); after him came El Bekri (eleventh century), Edrissi (twelfth century), Ibn Said, Ibn Fatima, Aboudelfa; then Ibn Batoutah gave some rather careful descriptions in the fourteenth century. Ibn Khaldoun, in his monumental work on the history of the Berbers, synthesizes what was known in his time (fourteenth century). The Genoese researcher Antonio Malfante went to Touat in 1447 and saw Tuareg people, whom he called Philistines; and Léon l'Africain (sixteenth century) leaves us spicy stories but rather little information on the Tuareg. Finally, the *Tarikh el Fatah* of Mahmoud Kati (sixteenth century) and the *Tarikh es-Sudan* of Sadi, written around 1650, both of which are travel diaries, provide a great deal of information.

married Kella, whom all of the traditions agree in recognizing as a descendant of Tine Hinane.

When the Kel Ahaggar sovereigns are asked about their origins, they all respond that Tine Hinane is their ancestor and that Kella gave birth to the Kel Relas.

At the time of Sidi's reign (at the end of the eighteenth century), several tribes of noblemen were arguing about power, and they set up a *tobol*, a form of self-government.[4] In other words, they demanded the right to have vassals of their own, the creation of a line of chiefs, and the sharing of land.

All of the tribes of noblemen formerly called Kel Ehan Mellen or Kel Ahamellen [people with white tents], who thickly populated Touat, Tidikelt, and Ahaggar,[5] were opposed to the Issetafenen. (The latter were "the people with dark tents," i.e. all the Tuareg groups stationed in the sub-Saharan and tropical zones of Africa that were more or less mixed with black groups. It might be asked whether these "people with white tents" really did exist earlier, or if this expression only alludes to the color of their skin, signifying the purity of their race. This expression can also be related to that used by Tine Hinane in designating the ancestor of the sovereigns of Ahaggar: "to be different from the colored people" and "to have white skin," which must have signified in earlier times the same thing as "to be noble," "to be of noble race," "of pure race." In French, an equivalent expression is sometimes used: "c'est un fils de grande tente," which means, "he is the son of a great family," indicating a sovereign, or one of noble rank.[6])

Therefore, Sidi, in order to retain peace, and most certainly also because he was the husband of Kella and wanted to preserve his interests as best he could, found himself obliged to cede two fractions of Isseqqamarenes to the Tedjehe Mellet in the east; these were the Kel Ohet and Kel Terourit, as well as a fraction of the Aït Loaienes. To the west, too, he had to give the Kel Ahnet (a part of the Imessiliten), the Tedjehe n Efis (part of the Tedjehe n Elimen, which became Agouh n Tahlé among the central Kel Rela), and the Kel In Tounine (a clan of the Isseqqamarenès) to the Taïtoq.

---

[4] The *tobol* is a drum of skin stretched over a flat circular piece of wood that is made and beaten as a call to war by the artisan-metalworkers of the *aménoûkal*. This drum, which only the *aménoûkal* may possess, is the symbol of his authority. "To have the *tobol*" is either to be in possession of sovereignty or to be a possible inheritor of sovereignty by matrilineal lines (for more on the *tobol*, see Benhazera 1908; Lhote 1955: 191; Regnier 1961).
[5] Prior to, it seems, the increase in strength and in numbers of the tribes that populate Ahaggar today. On this topic, see Benhazera 1908: 90–91, 109ff.; de Foucauld 1951–1952: 536; Lhote 1955: 214.
[6] It is probable that all of these expressions, despite their Berber character, in fact come from Arabs who, with regard to tents, seem to have greatly influenced the Maghreb people.

Sidi ag Mokhammed el Kheir retained under his control the Dag Rali, the Agouh n Tahlé, and the central Isseqqamarenès, i.e. the most numerous troops, and the impregnable territory of the Atakor. But after the death of Sidi, the Tedjehe Mellet, cut off on their eastern side from the markets of Touat controlled by the Kel Rela, attempted to destroy the Kel Rela by making an alliance with the Chaâmba. But the opposite situation developed: some of the Tedjehe Mellet fled into Touat and made an alliance with the "Arabs"; then their numbers diminished, which earned them the name of Ouled Messaoud from the Chaâmba, to whom they have been related since. They lost their *imrad* and *tobol* under the reign of Moussa ag Amestane, who was supported by the French.

The Taïtoq also tried to destroy the Kel Rela, but were beaten despite some assistance from the Kel Aïr. "In order to seal the reconciliation, the two sons of Sidi, Younès and Ag Mama, would marry the daughters of the Taïtoq" (Benhazera 1908: 110). Thus, the descendants of Younès and Ag Mama would give birth to inheritors of the *tobol* of the Taïtoq, as we shall see.

In the accession to power of El Hadj Akhmed (the sixth *aménoûkal*), who was chosen as the successor of Ag Mama after much discussion (Duveyrier 1864: 368–369), we can see the precise operation of a rule for the transmission of sovereignty. This rule has only failed to operate in the reign of the current *aménoûkal*, the twelfth inheritor of the *tobol*.

The male descendants in the matrilineal line, issue of Tine Hinane by Kella, are the inheritors of the right to sovereignty. It is from among them that the *aménoûkal*, the supreme chief of the Kel Ahaggar, is chosen.

Given the separation of the Taïtoq from the Tedjehe Mellet and the elimination of the Kel Ahamellen as a force representing a sovereign power, this rule granted total authority to the Kel Rela, the only recognized descendants of Tine Hinane and Kella (in spite of the claim of the Taïtoq through a cousin of Kella).

In the time of Ibn Khaldoun, Arab and Berber genealogists already agreed in designating the Hoouara tribe "children of Tiski." Tiski was a Berber woman (Ibn Khaldoun 1925: vol. 1, pp. 275–276) whom the Berbers still call "Tiski the lame" (*el ardja*). Now, it is recognized that the name of Hoouara has been transformed into Ahaggar (de Foucauld 1951–1952: 533). This tribe, called the Haččar by Ibn Batoutah, was already occupying the central Sahara by the fourteenth century (Ibn Batoutah: 1853–1858).

The kingdom of Melli around 1350 shone with an international renown, thanks to the magnificence of its sovereign, Mença-Mouça. The father of the latter, Abou-Bekr, was chosen "to be king according to the principle of barbarian nations that placed the sister [of the deceased monarch] or son of his sister in possession [of the throne]" (Ibn Khaldoun 1925: vol. 2, p. 111).

The inheritance of sovereignty by matrilineal relationships was therefore a characteristic feature of some Berber peoples of western Africa and even some groups of black peoples (perhaps influenced by the Berbers). Could this rule also have existed among the Berber tribes in the north? No text or researcher has yet been able to give an argument permitting the validation of such a hypothesis.

This rule of transmission of power through the maternal line appears to have safeguarded the tribal or confederal patrimony (lands, herds of animals) against absorption by foreigners, while still permitting quite extensive exogamy.[7]

In the Appendix each of the *aménoûkals* beginning with Salah is examined individually.

Upon the death of Aïtarel in 1900, certain problems regarding his succession arose anew. The French were entering In Salah, and their political and economic pressure was greatly upsetting to the Kel Ahaggar, who were cut off from their principal market. Mokhammed, the son of Ourzig and elder son of the elder sister of Aïtarel, was the first pretender by law, but he was old and without any great influence.

Attici, son of Amellal and Khaouila, the younger sister of Aïtarel, was the second pretender. But he was younger than Mokhammed son of Ourzig; along with his brother Anaba, he distinguished himself by his merciless treatment of the last survivors of the Flatters mission,[8] and he represented the party hostile to the French. The majority of the noblemen and all of the vassals preferred him to Mokhammed.

There then intervened, as is often the case in disagreements among the Berbers, two Muslims who represented the religious authorities of this period: Rabidine and Beketa/Brahim, both quite hostile to Westerners.

Rabidine, "in order to bring peace to the discord, put both hands in his chaplet and cried out: you will both be sultans of the same kind! then he divided his turban into two pieces and placed one half upon the head of Attici and one upon the head of Mokhammed ag Ourzig" (Benhazera 1908: 368–369).[9]

---

[7] We shall explain this observation in detail in a subsequent study treating inheritance among the Kel Ahaggar.

[8] In 1880 the French Minister of Public Works entrusted Colonel Flatters with an exploratory mission. His mission came under the auspices of the "Projet du Trans-saharien (Méditerranée-Niger)," established in 1862 by the agreement which Henri Duveyrier signed with the Touareg Ajjer at Ghadamès. The Kel Ahaggar, however, set a trap for Col. Flatters' second mission and massacred all the members of his party (about a hundred men) with the exception of a few Algerian survivors (see Brosselard 1896; Valette 1973).

[9] "Moussa ag Amastane had also been, from the vote for Attici, the candidate supported by the Imrad and Isseqqamarenès, who recognized him as one who could revitalize them in the south by reestablishing peace between the Kel Ahaggar, the Ioullimiden, and the Kel Aïr. It is also said that Aïtarel had designated him, after Attici, as his successor. Another candidate, Mohammed ag Othmane, was also in evidence" (Michel Vallet, personal communication, October 1972).

From then on, there was general discord. The two chiefs levied taxes concurrently in the tribes in a *tiuse* or *tioussé* fashion. The Muslims Rabidine and Beketa prohibited the consumption of In Salah dates rendered "impure" by the presence of the *roumi*s [non-Muslims] in the town. Beketa also had bundles of sugarcane and cloth burned in Tazrouk, and wanted to declare a holy war. In order to survive, the Kel Ahaggar launched raids, and they were raided in return. The vassals, tired of abuse and exactions, then turned their hopes towards Moussa ag Amastane, whose personality began to dominate the Kel Ahaggar. Some tribes (one family of Taïtoq and the Kel Ahnet) came to solicit peace from the French at In Salah in 1901 and 1902. The Kel Rela continued to pressure the tribes which had made peace with the French, leading Commandant Cauvet of In Salah to order a counter-razzia or counter-offensive by Lieutenant Cottonest in 1902. After having crossed the entire Ahaggar area, the hundred men commanded by Cottenest brought about a resounding defeat of the Kel Ahaggar at Tit, in May 1902.[10]

After 1902, Attici left for Ajjer, where he was to ask for *aman* [grace] from the French in 1911. Then he fled and died in Libya. Because of the defeat at Tit in 1902, there was total demoralization among the noblemen and all the Ahaggar warriors. Everyone fled and awaited even stronger reprisals. There was practically no more leadership in Ahaggar. In fact, power had become "vacant." For the second time, the problem of succession had arisen during the lifetime of an *aménoûkal* (in this case, there were two *aménoûkal*s in title, but neither had authority any longer).

After the fall of Attici and Mokhammed son of Ourzig, sovereignty could be attributed to Anaba son of Amellal, younger brother of Attici, but the latter had already died; Guekha son of Ourzig, younger brother of Mokhammed; Kyar son of Heguier; Amastane son of Heguier; Bouhane and Amayas, sons of Khebbi; Othmane son of Amastane, older brother of Moussa; Amechaoui son of Amastane, older brother of Moussa; and to other younger pretenders, among whom was Moussa ag Amastane.

From all of these possible pretenders, it was Moussa son of Amastane who was chosen, against the rules governing the succession, which gave precedence to the brothers of the dead *aménoûkal* over the nephews, and to the older before the younger.

The reasons for this choice were the following, in order of their importance:

1. The physical and moral personality of Moussa: he was noble and magnanimous in combat and just in dividing the spoils; he had the con-

---

[10] The Kel Ahaggar achieved a total of about a hundred dead among the Dag Rali and the Kel Rela (cf. Cauvet 1945). This raid was followed immediately by that of Lieutenant Guilho-Lohan, and then in 1903 by a police tour into Ajjer, led by Lieutenant Basset.

fidence, esteem, and admiration of all who approached him, as well as their gratitude (see n. 9).

2. He was a new man, free of any sort of political intrigue. He had had a difficult youth in the Adrar of the Iforas, guarding the flocks of his uncle Amder, and he had fought successfully against the Ioullimiden of Niger.

3. The political skill of his uncle, Khyar son of Heguier, who all his life had ambitions for supreme power and who preached reconciliation with the French (Benhazera 1908: 124–125). It was he who convinced Moussa to go to In Salah to make peace in 1904. Upon his return, Moussa, by the rulership of In Salah (Métois 1906) already recognized as "chief of the Tuareg," who had dressed him in the red burnoose of the *qaid*s, was unanimously proclaimed supreme chief by his peers, and this before Moussa had been formally invested by the French authorities.

4. Finally, Moussa was known to be the *providential man*, who could give back to the Kel Ahaggar their unity and honor.

His reign is seen as the high point of the power and wealth of the Kel Rela. They defeated both their eastern adversaries, the Kel Ajjer, and their western enemies, the Taïtoq, whom they caused to flee from Ahaggar completely, and from whom they took over the territories of Abalessa and Silet. The greater part of the pasturelands of the Adrar of the Iforas was still left to the Taïtoq, after the establishment of the border at Timiaouine. The Kel Ahaggar set up their camel reserves, augmented by the booty they had taken from the Kaocen people in battle, in an area that had previously been infested with bandits. But the region also contained good pastureland, notably Tamesna, in the northern part of present-day Niger.

They resumed peaceful trade relations with the Touat, and their salt-millet caravans continued to run to the Zinder region (in Niger) of the Damergou.

Thus, Ahaggar represents a geographical and administrative unity that is completely unique in the Saharan territories under the military control of the French, based in the Oasis Territory (Ouargla Prefecture).

The election of the three chiefs who followed Moussa seems not to have posed any important problems.

Bey son of Akhamouk had at this time ambitions, violently manifested, to succeed his father. Some say that the French military commandant who was in power at that time, Captain Florimond, might have rigged the election in favor of Meslagh. It is certain that Meslagh was a far more approachable chief than Bey son of Akhamouk. He prevented Meslagh's being accorded the high esteem of the Kel Ahaggar.

A committed Muslim and a rather rigorous leader, steeped in notions about his role and his authority, Bey was able to surround himself with clever and intelligent counselors. These people aided him throughout his career as supreme chief, as well as during that difficult period of history ending in the independence of Algeria. The Kel Ahaggar, such great fighters throughout history, remained uninvolved in the Algerian war, which affected the northern territories in particular.

It is true that since around 1930 the Kel Ahaggar have continually wasted their energies, and they cannot be said to believe in their own culture any longer.

Bey son of Akhamouk, elected deputy and vice-president of the Algerian National Assembly in 1963, represents his country as a deputy and no longer as a traditional chief, for the latter is a title and a job no longer recognized by the Republic of Algeria. The *aménoûkal* has been practically stripped of all the functions that he traditionally exercised; he receives a deputy's salary in return. He remains a living symbol of the past. Aged and resigned, he is content to provide for his family (relatives and servants) in his residence at Tioulaoualenès, by means of his salary.

When we study the short but often violent history of the twelve chiefs who have been the highest dignitaries of the Kel Ahaggar from around 1750 until the present time, we might be amazed by the political power of the groups that they were supposed to be leading. We might also be amazed at the sort of renown attributed to these chiefs, in spite of their unified leadership being more symbolic than real. They underwent very frequent periods of anarchy, worsened by economic problems resulting in endemic misery; but they never lost their pride.

In the final analysis, we can see that the Imoûhar have not ceased fighting among themselves for survival, over a geographical area that is both vast and economically valuable but which has seen constant battles throughout the centuries: groups of Kel Ahamellen being destroyed by the Touat and the Ahaggar, battles between western Taïtoq (Abalessa, Silet, Oualen) and central Kel Rela, fights between Kel Rela and Kel Ajjer over the final liquidation of the Ajjer Imenanes (Gardel 1961), and, lastly, the final eviction of the Taïtoq from Ahaggar (they had already aided in the revolt of Mohammed ben Abdallah around 1860) after their participation in the revolt of 1917 and the fall of Kaocen in Aïr. Because of these successive fragmentations of Tuareg power over the Adrar of the Iforas by the Touat and the Ajjer, the reduced geographical area of the Ahaggar permitted the Kel Rela to take power definitively. They were able to do this by means of Moussa ag Amastane's appearance in the area as well as of the arrival of the French in the political arena of the Saharan countries. But the latter could not put in an appearance until after El Hadj Akhmed, after the massacre by Attici and Anaba of the Flatters mission, and after the badly executed double election of Attici and Mokhammed ag Ourzig as *aménoûkal* to succeed Aitarel.

From the examination of such genealogies as traditions permit us to observe, we can claim that the first three chiefs succeeded one another from father to son, therefore in an apparently patrilineal manner, though we do not know the origin or status of their mothers or wives;[11] and that these three men all had Arabic names, which might lead us to believe that they were all members of one of those privileged groups among the Tuareg of the eighteenth century, the only ones, in that period of discord, who could reestablish some degree of cohesion among the turbulent and anarchical Imoûhar.

It might also be noted that the socially privileged group that, in the east (Ajjer) as well as in the west and the south, was always selected as the arbiter of conflicts, was related to the *chorfa*. And the latter are the ones to whom the sacred power of the *baraka* has always been attributed through their descent from the prophet.

However, since oral tradition still tells of the union of Kella (the female descendant of Tine Hinane), we note that there has followed a line of inheritors who carry specifically Berber names for the most part. In other words, as soon as close ties with foreign mediators came into play (as seems to have been the case with Salah and his two descendants) with regard to the sovereign Berbers, the system of patrilineal transmission of sovereignty gave way to a new system of matrilineal transmission. From then on, everything would derive from Tine Hinane and not from Salah. Since Sidi and Kella had two sons, it would be Younès and Ag Mama who would apparently reign in the normal patrilineal system, but in fact the system was already changed to the succession of the lineage of Tine Hinane and Kella.

The preceding remarks are confirmed in the work of Duveyrier (1864) regarding the election of El Hadj Akhmed. The latter was "elected in transition" between the two different systems of transmission of sovereignty. He embodied three important conditions:

1. the title of *marabout*, which was accorded respect;
2. a "foreign quality," which was to diminish all the local rivalries;
3. the fact of his being the son of a sister of Guemâma (i.e. Ag Mama).

In order to make this solution acceptable, "the Marabout, Sidi-el-Bakkay, from Timbuktu, was to send one of his brothers into the places" (Duveyrier 1864: 369).

Here again, we find the mediation of *marabout*s, arbitration that is always carried out among the Berbers after the introduction of Islam. By safeguarding a sense of harmony in the sovereignty of these turbulent Berber tribes, the *marabout*s were not only defending their prestige, their lineage, and sometimes even their economic interests, but they were also above all defending Islam as a source of civilization.

---

[11] We mean here that it is possible that these men were married to Berber women who were also transmitting the power of sovereignty to their sons. But we strongly doubt that this was so, given that all the oral traditions available seem to derive sovereignty from Tine Hinane and not from anyone else.

The theoretical rule for the attribution of sovereignty is the following:
1. eldest son of the eldest daughter of Tine Hinane or of Kella;[12]
2. younger sons of the eldest daughter of Tine Hinane, until the male line has been exhausted;
3. eldest son of the second daughter of Tine Hinane or of Kella, then younger sons until the male line is exhausted;
4. after the children of the last daughter of Kella, inheritance again derives from the male line: the sons of the eldest daughter of the first daughter of Kella, etc. (see Figure 1).

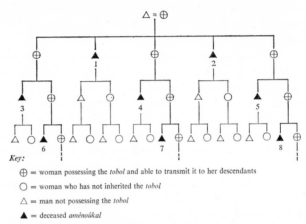

Key:

⊕ = woman possessing the *tobol* and able to transmit it to her descendants

○ = woman who has not inherited the *tobol*

△ = man not possessing the *tobol*

▲ = deceased *aménoûkal*

Figure 1. Theoretical schema expressing the mode of transmission of sovereignty among the Kel Ahaggar. (Key applies to all figures in this article.)

There is a vertical transmission of power through the females and a horizontal succession by age, from the oldest to the youngest, among the male members within a single generation. This being the rule, the real choice is far from simple.

In the light of the history of the last seven chiefs, it can be established that the person elected must first have the esteem and the confidence of the people and the *amghar* [a representative of a single tribe or clan]. He must also be judged capable of assuming his role both morally and physically. These qualities are even more important in times of political or economic crisis. Finally, it is the best man or the most capable one who takes power, from among the group of possible inheritors.

[12] From the historical documents at our disposal, we can confirm that the rules of matrilineal succession appear in the progeny of Kella. Was there a line of chiefs between Tine Hinane and Kella? History does not provide an answer to this question, but it could be possible, given the hiatus separating Tine Hinane and Kella. Kella was living at the end of the eighteenth century, while the death of Tine Hinane is dated by archaeologists at around the end of the fourteenth century, Carbon-14 dating of wood from the funeral chamber of Tine Hinane was carried out in Algiers in 1969 by the Institut d'Études Nucléaires; the date thus obtained was 1370 A.D.

Appendix: Succession of the *aménoûkal*s

I. SALAH *ibn*? (toward the middle of the eighteenth century)
   a. Name of spouse unknown.
   b. One descendant and successor known: his son.
   c. He rises to power as a result of the accord of the Touat *chorfa* and that of the Sheik of the Kounta.

II. MOKHAMMED EL KHEIR *ibn* Salah
   a. Spouse's name unknown.
   b. One descendant known: his son and successor.

III. SIDI *ibn* Mokhammed el Kheir *ibn* Salah
   a. Husband of Kella, descendant of Tine Hinane.

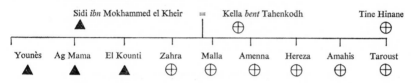

IV. YOUNÈS *ibn* Sidi (around 1795–1820)

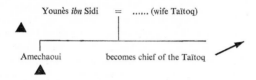

V. AG MAMA *ibn* Sidi 1820–1850 (?)

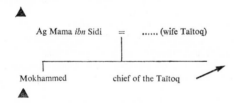

COMMENTS on I to V:
1. Four chiefs succeeded each other from father to son.
2. The fifth succeeded his brother.
3. The descendants of this family, married to Taïtoq wives, furnished the chieftainship of the Taïtoq and no longer that of the Kel Rela.
4. The younger brother of Ag Mama, El Kounti, died before Ag Mama.

VI. EL HADJ AKHMED *ibn* el Hadj el Bekri (1850–1877)
   a. Succeeds his maternal uncle, still living, since the latter has become impotent; is, however, recognized and definitely accepted after the death of Ag Mama, since he is competent and the principal holder of the title.[a]

[a] If El Hadj Akhmed had not satisfied the Kel Ahaggar, his title would certainly have been questioned upon the death of Ag Mama, in which case other more competent pretenders would have wanted to exercise their rights.

b. Oldest son of the elder sister of Ag Mama (i.e. Zahra); in other words, the nephew of the last *aménoûkal.*
c. Iforas Muslim by his father.[b]
d. Succeeded to the *tobol* through his mother Zahra, first daughter of Kella.

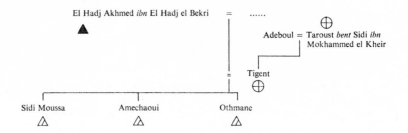

e. Children dead before any possibility of succession.
COMMENTS:
1. During the reign of El Hadj Akhmed (1850–1877), the four possible pretenders to the throne were the following:
Bassa, son of Zahra/Kella and of Sheik/Amma;
Ourzig, son of Malla/Kella and of Akhrou/Hamidou;
Keradji, son of a Taïtoq woman and of Mohammed/Biska;
Aitaral, son of Amenna/Kella and of Mohammed/Biska.
2. Oral history does not disclose any difficulties connected with the succession of El Hadj Akhmed. It seems that Bassa and Ourzig were either deceased or too elderly at the time of the *aménoûkal's* death. Keradji would certainly have been chosen as successor, but he died before El Hadj Akhmed. Therefore, there remained only Aïtarel, who was elected.
VII. AïTAREL *ibn* Mohammed Biska (1877–1900)
a. He was the parallel cousin of El Hadj Akhmed (*ana* [brother]), i.e. the son of the maternal aunt of the latter.
b. He was the son of Amenna, the third daughter of Kella, while El Hadj Akhmed was the son of Zahra, the first daughter of Kella.

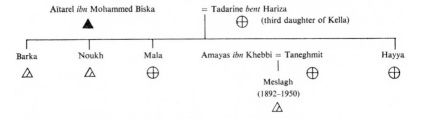

VIII. ATTICI *ibn* Amellal (1900–1904)
a. Elder son of the younger sister of Aïtarel.
b. Preferred to Mokhammed, son of Ourzig and elder son of the elder sister of Aïtarel, who was old and without any influence.
[b] See the political reasons and the circumstances surrounding the election of El Hadj Akhmed, in Duveyrier (1864: 368–369).

IX. MOUSSA *ibn* Amastane (1904–1921)
   a. Great-grandson of Sidi son of Mokhammed el Kheir by Tar'oust, the last daughter of the latter and Kella.
   b. In the seventh generation of descent from Salah, the first *aménoûkal*.
X. AKHAMOUK *ibn* Ihemma (1921–1941)
   a. Descendant in the matrilineal line of Tar'oust, the sixth and last daughter of Kella and Sidi.
   b. Father of Bey, the present *aménoûkal*.
XI. MESLAGH *ibn* Amayas (1941–1950)
   a. Descendant of Hariza, the fourth daughter of Kella and Sidi.
   b. Younger than Akhamouk but from the same generation.
XII. BEY *ibn* Akhamouk (1950–1962)

REFERENCES

BENHAZERA, M.
  1908   *Six mois chez les Touareg du Ahaggar*. Algiers: A. Jourdan.
BROSSELARD, HENRI
  1896   *La deuxième mission Flatters au pays des Touareg Azdjer et Hoggar*. Paris: Jouvet.
CAMPS, G.
  1965   Le tombeau de Tin Hinan. *Travaux de l'Institut de Recherches Sahariennes* 24: 65–83.
CAUVET, CDT.
  1945   *Le raid du lieutenant Cottenest au Hoggar, combat de Tit, 7 mai 1902*. Marseilles: Raoul et Jean Brunon.
DE FOUCAULD, P
  1925–1930   *Poésies touarègues*, two volumes. Paris: Leroux.
  1951–1952   *Dictionnaire touareg-français*. Paris: Imprimerie Nationale.
DUVEYRIER, H.
  1864   *Les Touareg du nord*. Paris: Challamel.
GARDEL, G.
  1961   *Les Touareg Ajjer*. Institute of Saharan research. Algiers: Baconnier.
GAST, MARCEAU
  1973   Témoignages nouveaux sur Tine Hinane, ancêtre légendaire des Touareg Ahaggar. *Revue de l'Occident Musulman et de la Mediterranée* 23 (14): 395–400. Aix-en-Provence.
IBN BATOUTAH
  1853–1858   *Voyages*, five volumes. Translated from the Arabic. Paris: Defrémery et Sanguinetti.
IBN KHALDOUN
  1925   *Histoire des Berbères et des dynasties musulmanes de l'Afrique septentrionale*, two volumes. Translated from the Arabic. Paris: Geuthner.
LHOTE, H.
  1955   *Les Touareg du Hoggar*. Paris: Payot.
MÉTOIS, CAP.
  1906   *La soumission des Touareg du nord*. Paris: Challamel.
REGNIER, J.
  1961   À propos du droit au commandement chez les Kel Ahaggar. *Bulletin de Liaison Saharienne* 41: 55–65.
VALETTE, J.
  1973   Quelques aspects nouveaux de l'expédition Flatters. *Revue de l'Occident Musulman et de la Méditerranée* 15 (16): 375–390.

The Traditional Power of the Mósì Nānámsè of Upper Volta

JEAN BIGTARMA ZOANGA

POLITICAL POWER

The history of the Mósì[1] centers around their traditional political organization. This, according to folklore, began around the twelfth century. The state founded in Gambaga in the northern part of present-day Ghana was, and still is, centralized. The chiefs (nábà, plural nānámsè)[2] are part of a dualist hierarchy that is reflected, although imperfectly, in the separation between political and religious spheres.

The nobles (nākómsè) stand at the source of this history and govern the land they have conquered. The circumstances which brought them to power (marriages, wars) are, according to legend, religious. Consequently, worship of the earth, which in principle should be reserved for the socio-professional class known as the tĕng-sóbĕ-dámbà [possessors of the earth], was already part of the rights of territorial authority.

It is necessary to isolate the traditional political power of the Mósì nā-nám-sè as it existed before colonial influence manifested itself, in order to deal with it under the three following headings: abstract power (ná-ām); individual power, the chief (ná-bà); and collective power, the chiefs (nā-nám-sè). The Mósì language, Mõrē, is made up of tones and classes. The three terms cited above all contain the same root: nā. This, depending on the circumstances, is followed by an appropriate class suffix. The plural suffix -se does not simply replace the singular suffix -ba; it follows on repetition of this root syllable and changes its significance.

---

[1] Mósì is the plural of Mõágà, the population of the central part of Upper Volta. Two spellings of the name are permissible: Mósì or Mossi. The two traditional kingdoms with which this study is especially concerned are Ouagadougou and Ouahigouia.
[2] Mõrè, the Mósì language, has twelve genders and thirteen classes, including a singular ending in -a, with corresponding plural, -se; e.g. nábà, less commonly nānámgà [chief]; plural, nānámsè [chiefs].

Power (ná-ām)

Three words are involved in the semantic composition of the terms designating authority: *ná-ām* [power]; *só-bà* [possessor]; and *kåsmà* [elder].
However, political authority consists mainly of prestige (*ziírì*) and
strength (*pångà*).

It is possible to ascertain the degree of a chief's personal authority by
observing the respect paid him by his subjects (*tál-sè*, singular *tál-gà*).
When a person is not nobly born, his age has no importance. A commoner
is not just a poor man, he is a man unworthy of consideration: "Even
though the commoner is older than the chief, his superiority still counts
for nothing" (*tálg kêm nábà, ā kêm zálèm*) [literally, "the commoner is
older than the chief, he is older than nought"].[3]

Respect is shown mainly in the way in which greetings are given.

> The Mosi observe a ritual in greeting the naba. The Mosi lays down everything,
> his burden, his hat, his sabre; he removes his sandals, sits on the ground, his
> legs slightly bent, his chest leaning forward, he keeps his elbows on the ground,
> as wide apart as possible; the fore-arms are turned in towards the chest; both
> hands half-closed, with the thumbs pointing into the air, strike the ground to-
> gether three or four times; then, the individual rises, rubbing the palms of his
> hands together. Throughout this ritual he never once looks into the face of the
> person he is greeting, but keeps his eyes slightly lowered (Mangin 1916: 15).

It is interesting to take a closer look at the gestures of deference involving the eyes (*ní-nì*) and the elbows (*kā̃-tísè*). These gestures represent
the distance separating the *nábà* from the *tálgà*. "If the elbows were of
any importance, the praying mantis would be chief" (*kā̃-tís sā̃ n bè yồdō,
gómbèg yā nábà*). In other words, if the act of resting the elbows on the
ground and turning the forearms upward preparatory to rubbing the hands
on the earth in greeting had anything to do with noble bearing, then the
praying mantis, which behaves in exactly that manner, would be king of
kings.

In the sacrifice of the goat killed by the *têng-sóbà* [priest], possessor of
têngà [divinity], the word "eye" (*nífù*) means "fear." This is fully expressed in the priest's initiation: "If the possessor of divine power (*têngà*)
has been ordained by the sacred object (*tē̃-kúgrì* [altar stone]), then he
does not fear the eye of the he-goat [that is to be sacrificed]" (*têg-sòb sā̃ n
tar tē̃-kúgrì nồrè, ā pā zóet bwég níf yè*). The explanation of the above
proverb is as follows: "When the sacred altar stone has ordained, through
divine intervention, that a goat be sacrificed, the *têg-sóbà* kills the goat
without paying any attention to its attempts at resistance" (Tiendrebéogo
1964: 177).

---

[3] *Zálèm* [literally, "nothing"] means "total absence, complete lack, zero." The proverb should be taken as dealing with effectiveness: there is no point in citing age where
power and influence are concerned.

High position is surrounded with dignity and pride. It is the commoner's duty to wait upon the chief (*tálg n̄ guùd nábà* [the commoner waits upon the chief]); this is regarded as normal, customary behavior. Once he has experienced this, the chief would rather die than lose his prestige:

Because the French administrator, Carrier, had threatened the chiefs that he would strip them of their authority if they misbehaved in any way, the Chief of Nobere[4] said, in December, 1906, that death was preferable to this calamity. The day they decide I should no longer be chief, I order you to take a gun and kill me (Baudu 1956: 73).

Prestige is expressed by two onomatopoeias, *kílīlīlì* and *dím-dim-dìm*. The first of these is a cry uttered during funeral dances in honor of ancestors, on the day a woman is given, and at the election and enthronement of a chief. The second is reminiscent of the deep rumbling of thunder. When uttered in a very low register, it is weighted with gravity and applies to the measured, majestic stride of the sovereign. The chief is advised to walk softly, as his prestige takes on its fullest meaning in the slow repetition of his paces. "Place your footsteps softly" (*tábg-y zém-zèm* [literally, "tread with measured pace"]).

According to the fable of the man and woman living in heaven, the first of the three *dim*s is male, while the other two are female. The Mósì say that whenever there is a storm the first clap of thunder corresponds to the first *dim*. This is the loudest of them all. It is violent because it is uttered by an angry husband determined to instill fear. The other *dim*s are progressively quieter and are those of a woman. We may interpret them as meaning "Be careful, be careful, violent male thunder, don't be too brutal, there are sons of man on earth, save them, I beg you." Thunder, therefore, represents a family scene. In addition, lightning is given a divine character because of its ability to kill; men's lives are in its power.

Ná-ām [leadership or the art of being chief] includes power (*pãngà*),[5] which is associated with energy. In the expression, "this remedy has strength" (*tí-kãngà bè pãngà*), the reference is to healing strength, but it also refers to the strength in the remedy itself. Physical violence sometimes predominates over the law: "When strength follows a track, law

---

[4] Nobere is situated about seventy kilometers south of Ouagadougou.
[5] The term is widespread and has the same meaning through a great part of West Africa. The following is a list given by Professor M. Houis of the Institute of Oriental Languages, Sorbonne, Paris:

Dagara (Upper Volta):	*fang*
Bobo (Upper Volta):	*fana*
Kono (Guinea):	(Ala) *tangana*
Serer (Senegal):	*pangol*
Malinke (Mali):	*fâka*
Dogon (Niger):	*pagna*
Susu (Guinea):	*tâge*
Koniagi	*fanka*

strays into the bush" (*pång tûd sòrē, bùm bútā môgò*). While it is true that the commoner is supposed to stand aside for the passage of the chief, it is equally true that strength of any kind overcomes weakness, quite apart from considerations of law and right, by the mere fact that it enforces power.

Strength and weakness cannot exist side by side; they cannot share the same path. It is obvious that they are dualistic and opposed, for there is another expression where the words "truth" and "falsehood" replace "strength" and "law" in the proverb quoted above: "When truth follows a track, falsehood flees into the bush" (*sîd tûd sòrē, zírī bútā môgō*). The first proverb implies abuse of power; the second does not.

Physical strength is transferred into the realm of moral power. "Strength" attains the meaning of "ability to act on all planes," and this is what authority is about. Thus strength is personified and comes to designate supreme authority, the sovereign, the king of kings, whose individual name may no longer be uttered once he has been crowned, so great is his prestige and such is his might. The sovereign resides in a place where there is only power, expressed by the locative *pångê* [residence of power]. The mere presence of the chief is enough to found a settlement; the other inhabitants can be counted on to follow.

To be the personification of *pångà* is eminently appropriate for God, in whom rest royalty and power (*ná-ām nê pångà*) and strength and knowledge (*tôog nê mínèm*). These qualities live in God (*wêndê*) just as the chief lives in the settlement (*pångê*). God is known as "the possessor of prestige" (*ziīr-sóbà*), while God the sovereign is called *nábà wêndê*.

The phrase, "it isn't easy" is rendered in *Môrē* as "it's not chief's beer" (*kà náb râm yè*). The beer in question is especially brewed for the chief and is stronger than the usual. The difficulty alluded to in this expression is the alcoholic content. This difficulty is expressed elsewhere by the problem of gaining direct access to the chief; in fact, it is impossible to approach him. An intermediary is needed: there are no good chiefs, the saying goes, only good intermediaries (*nā sông kà yè, nā-yír-dē sông n̄ bè*).

A dead chief has two kinds of representative: a wife, who replaces him, and a man who incarnates him. It is customary to temper the severity of the chief by the goodness of a woman-chief, the *kúrītà*. She remains remote from the chief, whom she is not supposed to see. She "eats" (*rítà*) the power of the dead chief whose funeral rites (*kúrè*) have just been celebrated. She has her own little territory, with her own subjects and servants.

In times of famine or prolonged drought, a man (never a woman) is appointed to incarnate the spirit of the chief to be invoked. This man, known as *sólēn̄gò*, takes his place at the head of a group and runs, dances, shakes, and calls for sacrifices of tamarind or sorrel seeds stirred in water (*zōm-kóom bī bí-koòm*). Properly speaking, this is a form of shamanism.

The hair of the chief's servants is arranged like the women's hair, plaited in triangles on the head. They also greet him the way women do: when they pass near the chief they bow without stopping; alternatively, they rub their hands on their thighs, only ceasing once they are in front of the chief or out of sight.

Going into a private house is a delicate business. Excuses are offered on entering someone else's home, and the visitor announces himself by saying *nā*. The head of the household will almost certainly reply to this form of address, since he is a man (*vir*). There is no doubt that the house, too, is a representation of the universe, a microcosm of the world commanded by the chief. *Ná-ām* is an abstract noun; the suffix *-m*, denoting power and strength, distinguishes this term from a series of expressions containing the root *nā*.

The word *nā* is also the masculine response to a call, and it signifies "present." The feminine response is *ǐ'mà*. A subject acquiesces in all that the *nábà* [chief] says, interrupting his flow of speech with *nā*s; thereby all the chief's desires are received as orders; the subject bows to his chief's will like the chicken that cannot flee before the master's knife which is raised to slaughter it. "The chicken does not fear the knife of its master" (*nōág pā zwét ā sòb súug yè*). Because its master (*sóbà* [possessor]) has fed it, and because it belongs to him by right, the chicken does not even attempt to resist its fate; it submits totally, blindly obedient and passive.

Nevertheless, the Mósì are aware of the fact that mere surface submission is prejudicial to relations. If one always says yes to the chief without ever thinking for oneself or daring to disagree, public affairs degenerate and the country is ruined through the lack of initiative shown by the subjects.

The personal power of the chief rubs off onto those close to him, his relatives and friends. When the chief sends discordant parties away without passing judgment and suggests a reconciliation, it is because the litigant who is in the wrong is his friend. When the chief does not have the courage to settle a question to the disadvantage of his friend, he tells the two suitors, both of whom are his subjects, "Go away, go away, depart and settle matters between yourselves" (*kúlī yâ n̄ tī tál-ȳ tábà* [literally, "depart and go and 'have' yourselves between yourselves"]). Fear of partiality is so great that a person is wary of bringing an accusation against anybody belonging to the chief's entourage. No one, for example, would dare suggest that the chief's mother is a witch (*swêyâ*)[6].

Fear of the chief's partiality is also such that the person in whose favor

---

[6] Women who live in isolation are often accused of being witches. Their sorcery is supposed to be harmful to society; they cast a spell on people and turn them into chickens, which they kill, cook, and eat. At night they walk abroad in the form of sparks. The healing magician has a different role, concerned with the source of life, the propounding of cures for illness and remedies against sterility and drought. This type of witch is nearly always a man.

the verdict has been passed does not let it happen twice, for fear that the chief may go back on his word. He whom the chief has declared to be in the right does not linger in the *nábà*'s house: *pàm búum pā zì nā-yír yè* [literally, "to be in the right...not remaining in the chief's palace"]. Prevention is better than cure, even with the *nábà* at law. It is better, they say, to look after one's affairs well oneself than it is to have them inquired into by the chief; the slowness of the legal process is likewise here alluded to, but also included is fear of facing up to the chief, although he is not always of bad faith or unjust.

The chief, as administrator of justice, has alternative ways out of difficult situations. An authorized person can question the chief. Even when the chief has pronounced a death sentence, it is possible for the condemned person to be exempted. Those whose duty it is to carry out the task use veiled words to make the *nábà* understand that he has been unjust in his decision. The executioners do not say, "You were in the wrong, we have given reprieve," but "We did not tie the prisoner up securely enough, and he escaped." Although the chief is aware of his power to have the man brought in again, he understands that he does not condemn a man without there being the possibility of an appeal. The chief's discretionary power, while absolute in principle, is, in practice, held in check. Whether his motivation is to seek justice or he has some other objective, a subject always presents himself to the chief with a gift. It is his greeting (*púusèm*), but it also has a more utilitarian purpose. The subject wants to see the chief in person and to give the gift, if not into the chief's own hands, at least directly to him without anyone's coming between them. He considers it a waste of time and money if the chief does not come out of the palace into the courtyard to receive him.

Marcel Mauss gives hierarchical instability as the reason for the *potlatch*,[7] which he divides into three categories of presenting, receiving, and reciprocating a gift (Mauss 1960: 155). What is the role of various types of gifts in Mósì *nâām*? Modesty demands that the gift be presented as a thing (*búmbù*). This term seems to indicate that the object (*búmbù* or *bóndò*) is not passive. The gift, the giver, and the recipient are all connected in some way (*a bóndo* [so-and-so]). Three words distinguish services and gifts: salary (*yáodò, yáō* [to pay]); gift (*dóà*); and tip (*léngà* [literally, surplus gratis]). Marcel Mauss reports that Malinowski also divides gifts into three categories: the large, open-handed obligatory offering or "opening gift," committing its recipient to giving in return; the gift which ties up a transaction, the "clinching gift"; and finally the salary, the "solicitory gift."

At market every Mósì asks to taste the *dolo* [millet beer] and cooked meat before buying them. The vendor is obliged to supply it though admittedly in small quantities; and if he is not well disposed, he will

---

[7] A Chinook word from North America, meaning "to nourish."

choose poor-quality goods for the *léngà*. To call it a "tip" is incorrect, if by that one understands a supplement; the *léngà* is not an extra or an addition, it is free and is provided before the sale as a sort of sample.

The Chief's Person (nábà)

Since the time of the *mõog-nábà* called Wárgà [weeds], twenty-second in the Ouagadougou dynasty, the chiefs have adopted mottoes at their enthronement: the first of these expresses recognition, the second the program of action, and the third a trait in the character of the newly chosen chief. The name Wárgà is taken from the saying "Rock does not permit weeds, the weeds damage their roots there" (*píig tôt wárgà, wárdēb nã sâm ēb wâgsè*). The rock represents the newly-elect on whom enemies (weeds) stub their roots. The failure of the weeds to take root refers to the defeat of those people who have tried to prevent the ruler's taking power. Even though the majority of chiefs have adopted this custom of changing their names, they are, however, a great deal more concerned about the existence of the figure three[8] and the conquest of power than about any ideas of recognition, character, or program. The system of rules for interpreting these sayings is not made up of three well-defined ideas. One motto can contain three key words, as is the case here: rock, weeds, injure.

The characteristics of the conqueror, his courage and sternness, and above all his warlike ability and power in battle are involved. It is not surprising that all the mottoes depict and try to describe the vanquisher, rarely however, they concern his physical appearance, being more often concerned with his moral features, his noble origin, his determination, the misadventures attending his struggle, his desire for vengeance. It is only during a second period that the program of action is apparent, promising abundance and peace to the population.

Among the natural elements in these mottoes, rock and rain are especially stressed. The stability of power signified by the rock is a cultural truism. Power is almost never relinquished. Occasionally a chief is poisoned, but as he is always on his guard, it is a difficult business. "When the stone of blessing has settled into place, it is hard to remove it" (*yélsòmd kúgrí pàm zígà, t'ã víkrí lébēg tóogò*). This has less to do with the stability of power than with the difficulty any enemy would encounter in opposing the newly elected ruler.

"When rain falls, the alluvial deposits (*bégdò*) bring rejoicing to the blind and the lepers" (*sáag níd bégdò, nã mànēg zwes lã wâobà*). The least-favored social categories wait for benefits from the newly elected chief,

---

[8] In certain ethnic groups, the figure three, ascribed to men, and the figure four, ascribed to women, enumerate sexual features. This is the case among the Dogon.

who promises to be magnanimous toward them. The metaphor is not directly concerned with fertile soil, a source of abundance for all, nor with the freshness of the water, nor with fruitfulness. "The waters join together to form a torrent and the rivers laugh aloud" (*kóom sùd tâpò, tí kũl-kẽmēs làd moágnà*). It is rather a question of small streamlets making large rivers, and neither more nor less than this. The union of the waters explains the spread of the torrent and the great uproar it makes.

The names of animals are by far the most infrequently used. The example of *nábà* Wobgo [elephant] is relatively recent. This ruler was removed from the throne by Lieutenant Voulet in 1897 and replaced by his uncle. When the explorer Crozat asked the meaning of this chief's name, he was told, "He's an elephant, the king of kings, as the elephant is king of animals. Furthermore, he is a king elephant; he rules over 333 chiefs as their uncontested master, and when he speaks to them it is as though God himself spoke to them in person" (Skinner 1964: 32).

Tauxier affirms that the elephant is the king of animals (1917: 412), although it is almost never so called. It is the lion which carries the title "king of beasts." In fables, the lion is almost never called by its real name (*gígemdè*). When people speak of the lion, they use euphemisms: *bõ̀-yêegà* [the clawed one], *wé-nĩ-kẽmā* [the old man of the bush] (Canu 1969: 328). The lion, master of the bush, should never be attacked first; the hunter attacks only if the lion is known to have killed a human being, thus only for vengeance. (Mention should be made here of the mythical ancestor, Gigma, of Tougouri, 170 kilometers from Ouagadougou. This emperor is said to have held an important position under the Nakomse rule in the eastern part of present Mósì territory [Izard 1970: 136]. Gígemdè and Gigma, which have the same meaning, exist as family names.)

A motto of *nábà* Sânèm [gold] unites the lion and the elephant. *Nábà* Sânèm (1871–1889) is represented in it as a lion and the throne as an elephant: "When a young lion is mounted on the back of an elephant, all the buffalo can do is look for a place to hide" (*gígèm põl zóm wóbgò, tí wē-niìg nã̀ n̄ báo zìg n̄ wúndì*). Were modern political chiefs thinking of that when, in 1960, they took the lion and the elephant as emblems? Their antagonism was embodied in a picture of an elephant (the Rassemblement Démocratique Africain, RDA) crushing a lion (the Parti du Régroupement Africain, PRA) who was groaning, crying out "*pra, pra, pra.*" The humor, if it were humor, was folkloric.

The characteristics of power are symbolized in the enormous size of the elephant and the authority of the lion. The elephant is so large it can be considered "a meat reserve; it can be cut into at will." This analogy is illustrated by a fable: the lion, the hyena, and the elephant are playing checkers (*wárè*).[9] The lion and the hyena allow the elephant to win,

[9] *Wárè*, a type of checkers. The game consists of fifty-four small holes dug in the ground. Each player has twelve pieces. Three pieces must be lined up vertically before

whereupon he shows his joy over the victory by bursting into laughter. The two other players enter his wide-open mouth several times to remove choice morsels without his being aware of it. Fables depicting the lion as king of beasts are more numerous. The idea of the lion commanding, judging, and waging war like a human chief is more common.

The chief called emperor or king, the *môog-nábà* [chief of the world], has been designated by several authors as the first among his peers, a superior chief. He is more than that, for once he is chosen and enthroned, his former peers are no longer his equals; all other chiefs are merely his subjects. As proof of this, they offer salutations in the same way as ordinary subjects do, and they are nothing more than executors of his orders.

Two sorts of chiefs can be distinguished according to the nature of their power: the titular chief does not hold full rights for the use of force, he watches over the maintenance of customs without legislating, his characteristics are persuasiveness and generosity; the strong chief has authority and full sovereignty. The king is differentiated from the chief by the extent and intensity of his power (Balandier 1967: 24).

By these criteria, the *môog-nábà*, titular head of the Mósì empire (both of the territory and the culture), is a strong chief and a king.

The Mósì chiefs (and above all the *môog-nábà*) have sometimes been compared to the sovereign lords of the Middle Ages (Kabore 1962: 609–623) but opinions on the subject are divided: "The European feudal system, where land was conceded to the protected by the protector, whatever fine distinctions are drawn about it, is not met with among the Mosi" (Pageard 1969: 103). There is an element of this relationship between the king of Ouagadougou and the king of Ouahigouia: "The relationship has been thought of in feudal terms, whereas, in fact, it was based on kinship" (Zahan 1967: 103). In reality, historical-mythological kinship as handed down by tradition is the origin and sole explanation for the authority exercised by a higher chief over an inferior one and by a chief over his subjects. All chiefs, all subjects, all classes are seen by the Mósì from this point of view.

Some explanations about the *môógò* are necessary. The root is *mo*. The suffix *-go* indicates the locality. The inhabitant is indicated by the suffix *-ga*. *Môógò*, territory inhabited by the *Môágà*, plural *Môosè*. Mósì or Mossi is the French corruption of *Môosè*. According to certain traditions, the Mósì very early on had contact with the Malinke; if this theory is accepted, one can say that the meaning of *mogo*, "man" in Malinke, Bambara, and Diula, is not unimportant in the Mósì legend. However, the term *môrē*: *môógò* should not be taken for a linguistic borrowing. This would be a major error. Gaston Canu (1968), quite correctly, does

---

a player can take one from his opponent. The winner is the player who takes all his opponent's men.

not give the term *môógò* in his lexical work on 1,296 words borrowed by the Môrè language.

In theory, every village which has a chief of some importance residing there should have at least two distinct sociological districts, as is the case in Ouahigouia. "In Ouahigouia there are the Mossi and Bingo areas. Mossin [Mósê] is the district for royal servants of local origin (*nayirdemba*), and Bingo that for royal servants of captive origin" (Izard 1967: 119).

The Mósì identified the royal servants' quarter with the whole village, then the country they inhabited with the whole world. "Mósê" is a locative,[10] but "Mósì" means an ethnic group which is very difficult to define. This same principle of identifying one concept with another causes them to identify the *môós-nábà* [chief of the Mósì] with the larger idea of the *môog-nábà* [chief of the world as they know it, head of their collective universe]. Even today this linguistic ambiguity can be observed when emigrant Mósì ask for *môòg-kíbārè* [news], which can be news of their home or news in general.

The Mósì are a bush people (Izard 1967: 116) according to the Dagomba, from whom they say they are descended. If that is so, history separated the two. The territorial wars of conquest waged by the Mósì to establish themselves in the territories north of the Dagomba have been interpreted as the cutting of an umbilical cord.

Bingo, the Ouahigouia town quarter assigned to royal servants of captive origin, is reminiscent of the Fada N'Gourma region, which the Mósì call Bingo. Tradition juxtaposes groups of strangers and natives, creating the coexistence of two distinct geographical districts. This is an attempt at salvaging a part of the culture, since, in fact, the Bingo district is not inhabited by foreign Gourmantche from Fada but by native Mósì. The relationships between Fada, Ouahigouia, and Ouagadougou, and between Gourmantche, Yadse, and Mósì can be explained in terms of kinship and slavery, in the strict sense of the words.

Folklore, passed down by word of mouth, presents the Mósì cultural background in a jumbled fashion, incorporating historical origins. Literal translation attempts to untangle the various elements by bringing attention to bear on sound similarity (homophony) and tone similarity (homotony). This issue is of limited significance. Arguing over problems of terminology is usually unprofitable. "There are enough similarities [between African and European political systems] to permit the use of the term, feudal, but at the same time the terms communistic and democratic could be equally well applied" (Herskovitz 1965: 231). The main point is that the very first *môog-nábà* "simply needed to display great authority; he had to be extremely imperious and positive" (Marshal 1966: 25).

---

[10] Mósê: district inhabited by Mósì. The term is not precise, for in a village containing only Mósì, the word Mósê can denote the district inhabited by the uncircumcised. Then it takes on a disparaging connotation.

The Hierarchy of Chiefs (nãnámsè)

Just as there is a connection between chief and subject, there is one between chiefs. It has a real, dynamic meaning and is not merely a legal bond. "When a snake's head is cut off, a stick is left," says a proverb (*sã n̄ kúug wáaf zúgù, sē kétā yà dā-sárè*), meaning anything can be done to a tail which lacks a head or to subjects who have no chief; the literal meaning is that, when an animal is killed, the tail, deprived of life, dries out and becomes like dead wood (*dāsárè*).

Proof that a person has killed a venomous snake is given by exhibiting the head. "When a person kills a snake he cuts off the head" (*f sã n̄ kú wáafò, f̄ kúugda ā zúgù*). This was the request addressed to *nábà* Kâongò [doubled] by a soothsayer. Before becoming *môog-nábà* of Ouahigouia, Kâongò, pursued by his enemies, presented himself to the soothsayer and asked for something to drink. The exhausted fugitive gave the following reason for his thirst: "I followed and killed the counterpart Kâongò, he said; I killed the *kínkírgā*-Kâongò" (E. Ouedraogo 1968: 30). Kâongò was known by name and reputation among claimants to the throne, so well known that the people of Yatênga bore him a grudge. Kâongò's speaking of Sosia Kâongò (*kínkírgā* Kâongò) was a roundabout way of introducing himself without revealing his identity. The soothsayer, who desired nothing more than Kâongò's death, was unaware that he was, in fact, dealing with him, and asked the unknown visitor to prove what he had said by showing the head of the victim Kâongò claimed to have killed.

At the top level of chiefs (*nãnámsè*), six rulers bear the title emperor (*môog-nábà*). The emperor of Tenkodogo is the paternal uncle (*sámbà*) of them all, the emperor of Ouargaye is their grandfather (*yábà*), and the four others call themselves cousins or "brothers" (*saṁbísi*). These are the emperors of Boussouma, Fada N'Gourma, Ouahigouia, and Ouagadougou. The *môog-nábà* of Boussouma pays a personal visit to the emperor of Ouagadougou; and when he is there he is the guest of the *wìd-nábà* [head of the stables].

Hierarchy of emperors

	Ouargaye-*nábà* (*yábà* [grandfather])		
	Tenkodogo-*nábà* (*sámbà* [paternal uncle])		
Ouagadougou-*nábà*	Ouahigouia-*nábà*	Boussouma-*nábà*	Fada(Bingo)-*nábà*
twin brothers		half brothers	
	brothers (cousins)		

Kinship is bound up with Tenkodogo (Tēn-kúdgò [the old country]), theoretically the country of origin upon which Ouargaye depends politically, and with Ouagadougou, which has established predominance over the six and upon which Boussouma depends (Ouahigouia is, however, detached from it). Tenkodogo and Ouargaye border the traditional Gambaga.

When any Ouagadougou mogo naba dies, the naba of Gambaga is informed. The deceased's shoes, headgear and rod of office are sent as presents. These objects are placed on the ancestor's tomb. Gifts are also sent to the naba of Fada, known to the Mosi as Bingo. The chief of Fada receives the deceased's bow and quiver, his two best saddled horses and his youngest two wives, as well as 12 bullocks, one slave and three bars of salt. When the naba of Fada dies nothing is sent to the mogho naba of Ouagadougou, whilst to the chief of Gambaga is given his finest horse (Mangin 1916: 4).

No mention is made of any relations between Ouagadougou and Ouahigouia involving visits or gifts because of their conflicts over conquest and influence. The Ouagadougou dynasty pushed toward the west (Samo, Bobo, Dagari), while the Ouahigouia dynasty extended its conquests toward the north (Timbuktu, Malinka, and the Arab countries). The former is in contact with largely agricultural peoples and the latter, through commerce and animal farming (Arabs, Peuls), with Islam. The twin brothers (Ougadougou-*nábà* and Ouahigouia-*nábà*) could hardly avoid being at variance because of these differing influences. However strong the basic ties binding them, the least that can be said about the conflicts themselves is that they were cultural shocks.

The present region of Koudougou contains two sensitive spots, Lallé and Yako, both stopping-off places on the Ouagadougou–Ouahigouia route. The crucial nature of their location explains the rebellions of Lallé chiefs during the last century, as well as the *môog-nábà*'s false departure ritual every morning, when he pretends to leave for La-Toden (in the region of Yako). This custom is explicable not for personal reasons, such as wanting to rejoin an absent wife, but for state reasons: it represents an attempt by the *môog-nábà* of Ouagadougou to regain regalia stolen by his elder brother, the *môog-nábà* of Ouahigouia.

Here, at the very heart of the subject, where Mósì political authority is most controversial, we should summarize the tradition about Gourcy, first capital of the Yatênga, a tradition which is connected with the two brothers' separation. Yadega, elder brothsr of Koundoumie (both were princes of the blood), was adopted by *tǎpsóbà* Suida. The latter concealed the death of Yadega's father from the prince and heir, but it was revealed to him by a woman at a well. The younger brother was already on the throne. Yadega, knowing he had been dispossessed, went to Ouagadougou. With the help of his sister Pabré, he stole the regalia: the *tíbò* [literally "remedy," but here meaning "religious object"], the *wúbrì* [a religious object with the same name as the founder king of the Mósì empire], and the *gâóngò* [skin]. In a village north of Gourcy, in the Bulli [wells] quarter, he had a well dug, and there he assassinated Suida. He had the body removed from the well and dressed it in sheep and bullock hides before giving it to his supporters.

A strong hypothesis exists which maintains that legendary events end up having a more important carry-over into folklore than historical events. The striking point in this story is the belief in the king of Ouahi-gouia's superiority simply because he was the elder brother (*kásmà*). Here, in fact, are found elements which add to the original myth. Stress is no longer placed on the exogamous marriage between a girl of noble birth, Princess Yênnêga, and a young hunter called Riare, and on their only son, Wēdráogò [male horse]. Those concerned are two brothers and their sisters. It is curious to note that religious symbols are numerous: the regalia, the well in the shape of a chief's tomb, and the sacrifice of the sheep and bullock which are stripped of their skin (*gáóngò*). Why exactly is it Suida who is killed and not Koundoumié, the brother who had be-come an adversary, if not an enemy? Was it because Suida was part of the religious group of the *têng-sóabē-dámbà*?

The attitude of Pabré appears in contrast to Yênnêga's behavior as far as marriage and kinship are concerned, but it is not without cultural analo-gies if the fable is to be believed: a brother and sister, orphans, inherit a horse. A robber tries to steal the horse. The brother is killed trying to defend the family possession. The sister, who decides to revenge her brother's death, succeeds in marrying the thief, kills her husband, and manages to escape on the horse after promising her favors to the best horseman, the one who can follow and catch up with her.

Similarities to the Yênnêga fable are found in this story of a girl who rides the horse and uses a trick to get married in order to end the marriage by homicide. The analogy to the Pabré story is found in the same girl's taking over her brother's duty of carrying on the family and in the double theft of the horse. Pabré helps Yadega in the acquisition of power.

The meaning of the place-names "Ouagadougou" and "Ouahigouia" is the same: "come and honor us" (*wá-ȳ-yúgī-yâ* and *wá-ȳ-wáogī-yâ*). It would seem to be an invitation by a *mŏog-nábà* to the people in conquered territories. Nevertheless, it is reasonable to ask whether they could not have addressed the same invitation to each other in unknown circum-stances.

Beneath these six rulers, subordinate only to God (*kí-yī-wêndê*: *ki* [to be related to], *yít* [to be issue of, descend from], *wêndê* [God]), are six other petty kings (*dímdámbà*),[11] who could name the lower chiefs under their dominion (*sólèm*). These are the *nãnãmsè* of Mane, Risiam, Téma, Yako, Konkistênga, and Kayao, descended from Koundoumié, eighth emperor of Ouagadougou. Folkloric tradition, it would seem, attempts to explain the country's division into small kingdoms as it explains the division of the two large kingdoms.

Below these minor kings are 333 regional leaders. Three categories of persons are represented within this symbolic number. Descendants of emperors other than Koundoumié are called "king's sons" (*dím-bīsì*) and

---

[11] *Dímdámbà* is the regular plural of *dímà*, and *dímbīsì* that of *dímbīlà*. In the Yadre dialect of Ouahigouia, *dímbīlà* or *dímà* is used in place of *dímbīlò* or *dímbìo*.

positioned two degrees lower than the emperor in a strict vertical hierarchy. At this level are ranked eleven chiefs, including those of Koupèla, Boulsa, and Poa, who are representatives of deceased emperors (*kurítbà*). For example, the chief of Boulsa should not see the emperor of Ouagadougou, for he represents a member of the emperor's ancestry. Also among the symbolic 333 are three great officials of the emperor and eleven ministers and court dignitaries. The figure 333 is symbolic because three is the "affair of the man" (*búmbù*) (the figure four is the female number; see n. 8) and because the Mósì include all the many district chiefs (*kōmbémbà*, singular *kómbère*) and village chiefs (*ĩê kwêk nānámsè*).

At the imperial court, the ministers (known as "chiefs of provinces") have a special place reserved, marked by a stone. The name given them comes from this: "those who sit on the stone" (*kūg-zít-bà*, singular *kūgzítà*: *kúgrì* [stone], *zíndì* [to sit]). Every morning they take part in two levee ceremonies for the emperor, the *wénd púsēg yâ* [the sun comes out] and the *lébgā sâorè* [it is the dawn]. They participate in his election and drink a sacred draft (*tíbò*) at his enthronement.

Philology opens up interesting avenues for research. Reigning is "eating the power" (*rī-nàm*). At the beginning of this study, mention was made of the term denoting "order and authority" (*nẽrè*), which also denotes "mouth" and "door." In the expression "when the priest receives the word (command) of the altar stone he does not fear the eye (threat) of the he-goat," the eye referred to is taken to be a vindictive look and a means of exerting influence. To be bold and impudent is "to make the eye" (*màan nífù*). There are other figures of speech relating authority to parts of the body. "It is in his hand" (*bé ā núgê*) means, according to context, either "it is in his power" or "it is subordinate to him." Something permitted by the chief is what "comes out from his hand" (*sẽ yít nàb núgê*) or what he gives in the form of either a gift or a command. The chief, of course, has jurisdiction over life and death, and life is breath. The person whose responsibility it is performs an execution by "cutting the nose" (*kúrēg yẽrè*). The condemned man would have begged mercy from the chief (*yẽk náb sègà*: *yókè* [to catch hold of] and *ségà* [the loins]): the man would have fallen to his knees and acted like a child pleading with a father who was beating him.

Comparison should be made between the four ministers of the emperor of Ouagadougou and of the emperor of Ouahigouia. Those attached to Ouagadougou are the *wìd-nábà*, the *lárl-nábà*, the *gúng-nábà*, and the *báloūm-nábà*. Mention has already been made of the second term in these complementary constructions, *nábà* [chief], the subject of this whole study. The meanings of the terms preceding it are as follows: *wéfò*, plural *wídì*, "horses." *Larle* comes from the expression *lāg-lágè*, an onomatopoeic word imitating the sound of wind shaking the leaves of a tree. *Gúngà* means "cheese-maker." *Báloùm* comes from the verb *bálèm* or *bálmê*, "to honor." It is in fairly general use in West Africa: the word exists in Bambara, Malinke, and Susu and means "to honor by singing the praises."[12]

Apart from the head of the keepers of horses (*wìd-nábà*) and the head of the official servants (*bálōum-nábà*), the two kingdoms each have a master of war (*tắp-sóbà*). The *tắpsóbà* or *tắsóbà*[13] is head of all the ministers in time of war; he is placed last here, subject to this proviso.

The order given below for Ouahigouia ministers differs from that attributed to them by some others. P. B. Hammond sets them in the following order: *bálòum*, *wídì*, *rásèm*, *tógò* (Hammond 1966: 154). *Rásèm* comes from *rāsémbà*, plural *rāsángà*, "handsome young people." The *rásèm-nábà* is the head of the youth. The *tōg-nábà* of the adults is spokesman for the emperor of Ouahigouia. Izard, writing in 1967, placed the *tógò* at the head, then the *bálòum*, the *wídì*, and finally the *rásèm* (1967: 119). He changed this order in 1969, putting the *bálòum* at the head. For him, the ministers are *nēsómbà* [men of property]. Ouédraogo (1969: 123) reverses *tógò* and *rásèm* in the order given by Hammond.

These various authors do not give any more precise criteria for their classifications. The apparent meaning of the words and the offices filled are described in general, rather than specific, terms. We retain the points on which the majority of them are in agreement:

Rank:	1	2	3	4	5
Ouahigouia:	*bálòum*	*rásèm*	*wídì*	*tógò*	*tắpsóbà*
Ouagadougou:	*wídì*	*larle*	*gounga*	*bálòum*	*tắpsóbà*

There is no *rásèm* or *tógò* at the Ouagadougou court and no *larle* or *gounga* at the Ouahigouia court. The *tắpsóbà* at Ouagadougou was accompanied to war by a *sórē-nábà* [drummer], who led the warriors, and by a *kãmsắogò-nábà* [eunuch], whose responsibility it was to put prisoners immediately into slavery (Cornevin 1960: 293, 300). In peacetime there was a commander-in-chief at Ouahigouia, created by *nábà* Kângo.

To the south-east of Ouahigouia Naba Kângo established the small settlement of Oula, at the head of which he placed a man from his retinue whom he judged capable in warfare, and to whom he gave authority over all the *tẽsóbẽdámbà* [chiefs of colonies] and even, from the military standpoint, over his ministers. Then he specified that this high ranking ta-soaba should, at his death, be replaced, not by his brothers or his son, but by some person that he or his successors would again choose from all ranks, even including royal slaves, as being especially capable. Even now the chief of Oula is named by the Mogho-naba of Yatênga, and his duties are not handed on by right of birth. This position immediately became one of the most important in the country (Izard 1969: 13).

---

[12] One method of winnowing consists of shaking a small gourd to separate the grain from tiny pebbles. This action (*bálè* or *bàlm*) gives rise to a particular sound, which can be easily imitated. Among musical instruments are gourd rattles which are shaken during dancing and accompany the music that goes with songs of praise.

[13] *Tắp-sóbà* is made up of *tắpò* [bow] and *sóbà* [possessor]; whereas *tắ-sóbà* is made up of *tắo* [to draw the bow] and *sóbà*.

The title *tǎ-sóbà* warrants attention to the second part, *sóbà* or *sóabà*. This term shows its complete meaning in another composite noun, *zū-sóbà* [head-owner]. The two parts here have equal importance by and for each other. *Zū* is the root in *zúgù* [head]. In many African languages a person is referred to by the head. In Peul, "I have hurt myself" is rendered by "I have hurt head of me" (*mi nyani hoore am*). In Dogon, "he has committed suicide" is "he has killed his head" (*ku wo mo dêi*). Among the Mósì, all responsibility is assumed by the master (*zū-sóbà*). It is, as it were, carried "on" him rather than "by" him, for the word *zúgù* [head] is the same as the preposition "on," "having contact with." Thus authority is a burden, but also, like the head which thinks, authority is the place of centralization and organization. The *môog-nábà*, the *tǎp-sóbà*, and the *yír-sóbà* (*yírì* [house]) are wholly responsible and direct society as *zū-sóbê-dámbà* [respective masters]. *Zū-sóbà* also denotes the chief of the king's eunuchs. He is master of the body of his servants, whose fidelity he thus represents.

Sóbà is a noun agent derived from the verb *soógè* [to possess]. The following are a few examples of usage in which it retains the same function in complementary syntagms. The expression "cunning as a francolin" (*yám sóbà kóadēgà* [possessor of intelligence like the francolin]) means that the bird in question must have a great deal of wit to steal the seeds sown in the fields, as much wit as the hare in the fables. The expression *tūb-sóbà* [the long-eared] refers to the hare because his ears seem out of proportion to his body. During the temporary association arising from preparing the soil for planting, *sō-sóagà* (singular *sōsó-soábà*) denotes the farmer who takes the initiative of asking others to help him hoe and till, whereas the *zíig-sóbà* (*zíigà* [place, area, spot]) cultivates the field and causes it to be cultivated, as beneficiary and owner (*púug-sóbà*).

The *wìd-nábà* is as important as the *tǎ-sóbà* in the Ouagadougou kingdom. There he is called *môs bà* [father of the Mósì] and *sīd sóbà* [holder of truth]. In him the voices of the *môog-nábà*'s electors are united; he plays the principal part in announcing the emperor's death.

Among court dignitaries, it is the Ouid-naba who represents the sovereign's power. That is why there is a Ouid-naba, just as there is a tansoba among the Dimbi and Dimbisi, who are descendants of a mogho-naba. He is head of the cavalry, but does not, himself, go to war. He remains beside the mogho-naba during battle, and organizes the remounting. Two high functionaries are under his command, the *wédrang-naba*, head of stables, and the *wedkim-naba*, head of horsemen (Tiendrebéogo 1964: 95, 122).

In Ouagadougou and Ouahigouia, the *wìd-nábà*'s and *tǎsóbà*'s standing is related to the importance of the horse in the *nàm*. The *môog-nábà*'s favorite horse stands ready each morning in the *sámāndè* [courtyard]. This same horse is sacrificed by the head butcher (*némd-nábà* [chief of meat]) on the emperor's death. The expression "too many stable-hands, the horse dies of thirst" (*wēd-kíim kuúngò, weèf kídà kō-yúdù*) means only that when many people are responsible for the same work, it does not get done. Mósì horses are so well treated, especially the king's horses, that there is no risk of their dying of thirst.

The horse was important to all the Mósì in general before it became important to the *nábà*. "Each horse has its groom, the horses are fed on millet, chiefs confiscate the stallions and leave the mares for the common Mosi people" (Canu 1968: 25–34). The color of the horse's coat and the positioning of white patches (*kámbālè*) are closely studied and interpreted as omens. The omen is directed first of all to the head of the family, the horse's owner. Horse excrement is important: a horse which eats its own droppings will not fall ill and will be hard to sell. If an animal urinates on leaving the stable, it will die or be sold. If it urinates on entering the stable, it will live and remain the property of its master. To be sold and to die are almost synonymous as far as omens go, since both are concerned with the horse's departing from its owner. If a horse paws the soil with its hoof, it is burying its master there. If, when the animal is recumbent, the hind legs curve around so that the back hooves and front hooves are almost touching, thus forming a circle about the stake to which the animal is tethered, its position shows the shape of its master's tomb. The stake represents the head of the family. The horse which lies with its back to the stake will die, because it is turning its back on its master, showing that it wishes to leave him and is therefore doomed.

In wartime, the ass assumes the horse's role to some extent and is used by certain heads of infantry. Otherwise, it is primarily used in trade. Among the Mósì, trade is the prerogative of the *yadse* or *yarcé*. Hence the expression "the donkey knows the *yárgà*" [the person who controls it with a stick] (*bǒag mī yárgà*). It is a warning and a threat. The Mósì also point out that each person should be self-sufficient with a saying referring to the *yádgà* and his donkey: "A *yádgà* does not lose his trousers looking after someone's else's donkey" (*yádēg pā rígdà tō bǒag tī bénd kédèg yè*). The horse, along with the ass and the dog, is supposed to have superhuman foresight. If a person wishes to see spirits, he should go in the early morning, fasting and without speaking to anyone, and rub his eyelids with the rheum that runs from horses' eyes (*wéf nī-púudù*: *nínì* [eyes] and *púudù* [flowers]) (Maurier 1967).

To understand the full meaning of *wìd-nábà*, it is not enough to know that he is chief of the horses (*wídì*), for this is only concerned with the word *wéfò*, plural *wídì*. It is necessary to isolate the root, *wēd*, in the composite nouns *wēd-ráogò* [male horse] and *wēd-kímà* [guardian of horses]. In these two composites, "the meaning implied is horse in general, the generic, equidae; whereas in the term *wìd-nábà* it has to do with individual horses, the specific concern of the *nábà* in question" (Houis 1970).

Taking into account the distinction between literature and linguistics and between history and mythology, all power symbols are crystallized in the role held by the Mósì horse. It is a chiefly emblem. It exists for the purpose of warfare. When on parade, it symbolizes honor. It is not harnessed for agricultural work. Finally it, along with money, represents riches. This latter characteristic provides a significant end for this section. According to legend, the horse is the source of money, which it invented and introduced to man by teaching him commerce. The story tells of a husband and wife who have no children but own a horse on which they lavish as much care as, if not more than, they would bestow on a real son. The animal is fed on millet, the Mósì's main foodstuff, and receives three meals a day, although the people themselves, in actual practice, have only one full meal a day. Conscious of this fine treatment, the horse tells the wife how to set about making the local beer (dåm, also called dolo) out of millet. Next he advises her to sell the beverage to make money, in the form of cowrie shells. The sale of beer brings about interethnic trade. Family authority runs as an undercurrent through this story.

The Mósì not only own horses but care for them themselves, whereas they confide their bullocks into Peul hands. The cowrie shells kept as money by the Mósì are worn as jewelry by Peul women.

The horse obviously occupies the place belonging to the ancestor, Wēdráogò. Wēdráogò, as a result of conquest, founded authority on interethnic relations. It is remarkable that his name is no longer bestowed on individuals but kept as a clan name. Wéfò [horse] is occasionally given as an individual name, when, for example, the child's father has had a fall from a horse (Houis 1963: 48). This, however, is rare, and there is a strong tendency to avoid using a clan name as a personal name.

It was logical that this section should conclude with considerations on the special custody of the royal horses and the importance of the wìd-nábà.

FAMILY POWER

Up to now we have stressed the importance of kinship in political authority. Now we turn our attention to traditional authority, by commenting on the following text, a written record of the spoken style, translated into English, which throws light on the nuclear family. The Mõrè version was recently broadcast over Upper Volta radio.[14]

This poetic song fits the definition of spoken style:

A text which is to be spoken is characterized by a scheme affecting both the mnemotechnic structure and the attention aroused, moreover this style concentrates the listeners' willingness to listen and retain certain semantic elements (Houis 1970b: 232; cf. p. 60).

[14] The reader is referred to the R.T.V. Service at Ouagadougou for inquiries concerning the tape. To the best of our knowledge the text has not yet been transcribed or published.

When heard, the text falls into two distinct parts. Having made the announcement, "Listen to the story of this woman," the singer introduces himself to his audience. He does not do so by immediately giving his name, but by indicating his clan and specifying his function; in this way his identity and role are defined. The first part of the song is not accompanied by any music.

The remainder of the song makes up the second part. We have chosen to divide up this second part in continuous fashion, for the first section seems to us an introduction which cannot be separated from what follows; subdivisions in the second part result in passages of about the same length as the introduction. The second section has two characteristics: rhythm is provided by a percussion instrument and by repetition of the title. This double rhythm is supplied by a second singer-musician, who intervenes from line 16 to the end. The verse is given shape by these repetitions in all sections after the introduction.

Because the theme is ethnological, we give a fairly broad translation here, bringing out significant wording. The family concerned is the nuclear family; a boy does exactly as his mother asks him; she prefers her daughter. A brief commentary and concise notes follow, justifying the division of the text and clarifying our observations on the Mõágà nuclear family.

Before Listening

The singer-musician asks listeners to pardon him, for he is going to fulfill a formal duty. He explains his position in Mõágà society with respect to the chief and other clans. He introduces himself to his audience.

1. May the chief excuse me
2. May those on my left hand excuse me
3. And those on my right hand also
4. For whatever my height may be
5. I am no taller than the crown of my head
6. It is the *bénd-nábà*'s concern
7. The concern of the *lund-nábà*
8. That of the chief of the *gâgâdo*
9. That of the chief of the *rudsi*
10. I myself (if I do it) am only looking for my tip
11. I am not a *yumde*, and you know it
12. A *yôyôga yumde*?
13. I am a profiteering parasite
14. It is the *Pag-yelwênde* song I am about to strike up
15. Understand who can
16. Believe who wishes

The Three Protagonists

A woman, Paga, her daughter, Poko, and a boy, Raogo, her son and Poko's brother, enter. This is a large proportion of the members of the nuclear family.

17. May the chief excuse me
18. For I begin my teaching
19. Listen rather to the story
20. Which I shall tell
21. Judge yourself of the wickedness
22. Of her who brought two children into the world
23. Naming the girl, Poko, as first
24. Relegating to last the boy, Raogo
25. Poko the favorite, and not Raogo
26. . . . . .

The Chickens

THE DISTRIBUTION. Paga, mother of Poko and Raogo, acquires some chicks which she distributes to her children. Her intentions will become clear when the chickens are grown.

27. Raogo, my son, I am leaving for the field, says she
28. At once she went out
29. She went to pick *zâmnê*
30. She picked, and went and sold it for ten francs
31. With this she bought some chickens
32. It was the time for low, low-priced chickens
33. One of them she gave to Raogo
34. The other to Poko
35. Prudent Raogo marked the toe of his with a cut

THE CHICKENS START TO LAY. The chickens have grown. The biological function of each becomes economically important. The hen seeks to lay and sit.

36. By God, do you know what had come to pass?
37. *M ba* Raogo had a hen
38. Poko's bird was a cockerel
39. Then Poko spoke to *m ba* Raogo
40. Truly, my son, you love me not
41. See, by God
42. *M ba* Raogo's bird seeks to lay
43. My cockerel cannot do as much
44. Now then, the woman was not motherly
45. Not at all. She to her Poko:
46. She to her Poko: Patience, I will have your brother

SALE OF THE BIRD

1. The mother advises Raogo to sell the bird. Since she regrets having given her son a hen and her daughter a cockerel, she tries to get rid of her son by disposing of the chicken.

47. She causes Raogo to come to her, the ill-natured woman
48. My son, you will rise up tomorrow
49. Catch, kill, and sell your hen
50. It will sell well, I advise you to do it
51. For Poko to say: oh, come now, Mother
52. Admit that a hen should not be killed like a goat
53. Don't hold to that, *m ba* Raogo does as he is told
54. He rises up the next day, seizes his hen
55. Buys salt at the market for "ten-five"
56. Buys pimento there also for "ten-five"
57. Rubs, seasons with salt and *kaolgo*
58. Begins plucking the chicken in hot water

2. A buyer tastes the poultry before buying. The customer, Yarga, takes the hen from Raogo, but the child gains by it. In the economic exchange the hen's value appreciates.

59. And you, do you know what happened?
60. That's right, a *yárgà* arrived and begs Raogo
61. My dear, some chicken to sample, I beg you
62. And Poko intervenes: Yarga
63. Chicken is never sampled like beer
64. Never in the slightest does *m ba* Raogo contest it
65. He takes of a leg and gives some to Yarga

3. The buyer takes the bird on credit, asking Raogo to trust him until the following day. He assumes that such a good chicken must be very dear. He had not made provision for buying it, so he buys it on credit.

66. Yarga renews his request
67. Let me have the whole chicken on credit
68. Dear friend, thanks, go in peace, I will pay tomorrow
69. And Poko, jealous: Yarga
70. How much does a chicken on credit weigh?
71. But Raogo never disputes
72. His fowl, there it is, completely given over to Yarga
73. Empty-handed, he lies down in the evening till the next day
74. The next day, he goes to claim his money

The Horse

THE RIDER. Instead of money, Yarga gives Raogo a horse, which he rides back home. His mother and sister are displeased.

75. You, guess what happened next
76. Generous Yarga hoists Raogo onto a horse

77. *M ba* Raogo returns home on horseback
78. But Poko was waiting for him firm-footed at the door
79. And her mother within the hut hid herself away, away
80. Poko calls out: Oh, Mother
81. Quickly, come and see the miracle
82. My brother's hen, a horse
83. Maternal ill-will is not turned aside
84. Not at all, and she reassures her daughter
85. Stay patient, my daughter, I will have your brother

THE STABLE (*wúbrì*). How are they to get rid of Raogo's horse? By imprisoning it, shutting it up in a shelter resembling a stable, where it will die of hunger and thirst. The three work on the building together, but not, of course, with the same intentions.

86. Raogo does not allow himself to be turned aside either
87. You, then, judge
88. When you wake up tomorrow
89. Choose good brick-making ground and hollow it out
90. While she and her daughter go and fetch water
91. Then trace a circle, build a tightly-sealed round cabin for your horse
92. Yet again *m ba* Raogo does as he is told
93. Begins at daybreak to make mortar
94. His mother and sister being at the stream
95. The three together trace the circle, using a cord for a compass
96. The three together build the shelter, tomb of their horse
97. Take care to cap it with a roof
98. To the roof they give thought; of the door no question
99. It was Mother Earth who nourished it with hay
100. The god-chief Zidwênde gave it water
101. To water it, the Spirits of the Rivers, the Lands,
        and the Ancestors set to work
102. Acknowledge how great was its protection
103. Horse corpse, nine days old, burst the cabin with its bulk
104. But Poko to her mother: alas
105. You do not want to love my brother
106. Whom Earth and Sky cherish
107. Whom all the gods cherish
108. Whom all the spirits cherish
109. What can you do, great God, behold
110. His horse has become so large it has burst open the cabin

The Universe Represented by Straw

STRAW. The roof of the shelter is made of straw. The hay given the horse is, once again, dry straw. The mother has not been able to kill the horse with hunger or thirst; she tells Raogo to exchange it for a bundle of straw.

111. The woman only wishes more harm to her son
112. And calls out to her favorite Poko
113. Patience, I will use your brother ill

114. Then she calls Raogo
115. Raogo, my son, at daybreak
116. Mount your horse, watch well at the crossroads
117. And when you see the children with their bundles of straw
118. Exchange your horse for a bundle
119. Which you will bring me to cover my roof
120. For the rainy season is near
121. And Poko it is who responds: Mother
122. Tell him to exchange his horse for a cow
123. Like that we will have milk to draw
124. And you tell him to bring a bundle?
125. This exchange must not be made
126. Never in the least does Raogo oppose anything
127. At the directed hour he mounts on horseback
128. From the children going past with their bundles
129. He takes a bundle, and leaves his horse

THE BUSH. Straw is not only the roof, the hay, and the bundle, but also and especially the bush, which it covers. Gâmbaga, traditionally the country from which the Mósì come, can be reached only by crossing the bush.

130. Arrives back home to give to his mother
131. Finds Poko still at the door, standing
132. And his mother within the hut hides away, away
133. It is Poko who says: Mother, oh Mother
134. Did you not say to take the bundle to Gâmbaga?
135. Great God
136. It was *m ba* Raogo's turn to say: *M ma wèè*
137. Were you not mocking me, exchanging my horse
138. On the pretext of making a roof of it?

PILGRIMAGE TO THE SOURCES. The road to Gâmbaga is beaten through the bush, across the "straw." It leads there inevitably. The bush and the track develop into mystic themes, although Gâmbaga, country of origins, actually exists to the north of present-day Ghana.

139. It is for you yet to take it to the "Old Country"
140. No protest from Raogo, for sure
141. Early in the morning, the bundle on his head
142. Clop, clop: *zuga-zuga*
143. His steps as heavy as the deep voice of Mankudgu
144. He arrives in Gâmbaga
145. My God, what next?
146. Autumn rain will have floated off the bundle
147. Who is it! asks the king of Gâmbaga
148. King, it is raining outside, murmurs Raogo-son
149. Then come into the house, don't get wet
150. Raogo does not have to be begged
151. Misfortune, Gâmbaga in person, blind
152. His first wife, blind

153. The king's eldest son, blind
154. Raogo has the honor of being questioned
155. Raogo, my son, you doubtless have straw
156. Pity, a handful to make fire
157. Raogo is known for his obedience
158. He sacrifices the whole bundle to Gâmbaga
159. As soon as the king puts the straw on the fire
160. Miracle, his eyes open: unclouded
161. The handful meant for the wife
162. Same effect, her eyes open: unclouded
163. Third handful intended for the boy
164. Same effect, his eyes open: unclouded
165. What gratitude: to Raogo are given a hundred wives
166. To him also, a gift of a hundred children
167. Furthermore he profits by a hundred horses

THE ORIGINAL PARADISE. Raogo's obedience led him right to Gâmbaga, country of origins. The pilgrimage to his ancestral sources turns his fortune. The kind deeds of its king transform Gâmbaga into an original paradise for him, whence he departs, comforted.

168. The women in single file, he returns
169. Poko was still waiting at the door
170. And his mother in the hut hid away
171. Poko, astounded: Mother, oh Mother
172. You still do not love your son Raogo
173. I assure you that Divine White Dust cherishes him
174. Ancestor Wubri and his Mountain cherish him
175. God Sky and Goddess Earth cherish him
176. Let us lament, both of us
177. *M ba* Raogo's straw? Multitudes of wives
178. His bundle? Innumerable sons
179. The cursed bundle? A hundred horses
180. His mother remains unnatural
181. Even though the hundred daughters are hers
182. Spoilt by a hundred grandchildren
183. Enriched by her son's hundred horses
184. What does being queen matter to her? Her name is *Kaod yaogo*
185. There is her son on the horse's back, hearken to his
            royal uproar, one would say

Grinding the Millet

GRINDING THE MILLET. It was Paga's responsibility to see to Raogo's marriage. Gâmbaga did it in her place. Raogo's wives begin to prepare the food, first grinding the millet.

186. The mother takes no heed of all that
187. Only her Poko matters
188. In her eyes, Raogo is without charm

189. Patience, darling, I am plotting his unhappiness
190. She calls out to Raogo
191. Tomorrow, see to it, my son
192. That you fill a basket up with millet
193. A basketful that will be winnowed close by the grinding stones
194. The hundred beautiful women go there in single file
195. Mother-in-law, return and put the sauce on the fire
196. What is a basketful for a hundred women?

THE VIPER. While Raogo's wives grind the millet, Paga finds a viper in the bush. It is beneficent towards Raogo, whom she calls with the intention of having him killed by the snake. A snake is sometimes euphemistically referred to as *môogo* [straw].

197. Behold, the woman keeps plotting evil
198. Instead of going and beginning the sauce
199. She, on the contrary, goes off into the bush
200. Into the bush, under pretext of relieving herself
201. In the grass she finds a viper gliding
202. With all her strength she calls Raogo
203. Run, come quickly, don't bring a stick
204. She takes care he doesn't bring one to kill the creature
205. The wicked woman: bring nothing, she says
206. *M ba* Raogo is wholly submissive
207. He runs, with nothing in his hand
208. The viper turns, goes back into its hole
209. Plunge in your hand and pull out what I want from that hole
210. Raogo, utter submissiveness
211. Hastens to push in his left hand
212. Up to the shoulder, draws out a necklet of pearls
213. Hastening to plunge in his right hand
214. Up to the shoulder, a hundred silver bracelets
215. Changed into good, his mother observes

DEATH OF POKO. The same viper is maleficent toward Poko. While fortune has laden Raogo with gifts, Poko is poisoned by the snake. Poko's death forces the mother to relent and give up her bias.

216. Come quickly, my daughter, my love
217. Come quickly, bring nothing in your hand, my daughter
218. Well, our sacred Earth does not approve of that
219. His sacred Majesty and his queen take offense
220. Wubri, our founder, takes offense
221. At her preference for Poko over Raogo
222. Poko came before her, panting
223. Pity, plunge in your hand and pull out my object
224. Poko takes her hand to put it in
225. Her hand scarcely passes the edge, the viper stings sharply
226. There was no time for Poko to be treated with sugar poultice
227. Poko responded at once to the call of the ancestors

Raogo's Magnanimity

Poko's death resolves a family conflict. The mother had been supported
by Poko in her evil conduct. Raogo triumphs. However, he refuses revenge
and remains magnanimous toward his mother, whom he pardons.

228. Everybody advising Raogo
229. To send his ill-natured mother to the devil
230. *Sala la la la, ra sudê la*, Raogo says
231. If evil is done to you
232. Refrain from returning this evil in like manner
233. For only the Divinity settles all debts
234. The spirits of the Earth and of Goama will render justice
235. The spirits of the Rivers, the Lands, and the Shades
         of the Departed will pay back your debts
236. Wisely, he builds two houses
237. With piety, six houses
238. There he places ten women at the service of his mother, within
239. There he places ten servants for his mother, within
240. And all in common at the service of Raogo, within
241. Thus ends the story of this woman...

What does the text teach us about authority in the nuclear family?
That, in the absence of the father, authority belongs to the mother. She
exercises it by giving advice, but she knows how to give orders; her wishes
are commands for Raogo. The mother will take care to remain impartial,
sex identity being only a pretext for giving in to favoritism.

Family in the broad sense, the extended family, is not neglected. In the
introduction, the whole Mõágà people is spoken of as a family with the
chief at its head. The king of Gâmbaga not only replaces Raogo's living
mother and absent father, he also confirms the idea of the Mósì as one
single family, culturally and historically.

Into what groups do the various characters in the poem fall? In replying
to this question we elucidate certain aspects of authority: orders or advice
given or received, various influences extended, the birth and resolution of
conflicts and tensions. We will start by giving our attention to the first
part (the introduction), then to the second (the narrative); in both cases
we will observe the relations of authority in the extended family, then in
the restricted family.

Because Mankudgu addresses himself first to the chief who is listening,
in order to excuse himself before giving a public lesson in morality, the
superiority–inferiority relationship between the two can be seen. In the
extended Mósì family, Mankudgu establishes relations of equality between what he himself is (*yôyôga*) and what the other musicians are
(*yuma*). He establishes this, not by making comparisons or by drawing
parallels, but by a negation which specifies his identity. "I am not a
yumde, I am a *yôyôga*."

No authoritative relationship to do with the nuclear family is stated in the first part. The first sixteen lines aim at introducing an analysis of authority relationships concerning the nuclear family. The simple announcement of the title, *Pagyelwênde*, is sufficient.

In the second part, where the extended family is concerned, authority relationships exist on two planes, horizontal and vertical. On the one hand, Raogo's relationship to Yarga is one of ethnic equality; on the other, the relationship involves inequality because of their age difference. The same Raogo is at the bottom of a vertical ladder which starts with the divinities and passes through the ancestors and the king of Gâmbaga before it reaches him.

In the nuclear family, absence is as significant as presence. The absence of the father progenitor allows the mother's educative ideas to be seen. These ideas are in opposition to customs confirmed by the conduct of the king of Gâmbaga. The daughter's absence, when she is removed by death, resolves the family conflict.

The relationship mother/Raogo is one of superior/inferior, adult/child, parent/son. The mother maintains another kind of relationship with her daughter, Poko: one of equality of sex and feelings. Raogo and Poko's equality through consanguinity is disrupted by favoritism, which gives Poko a superiority complex.

It can be seen that the text throws considerable light on the understanding of political authority. It acts as a reminder of the historical bases and political divisions of the past: the girl, Yênnêga, who marries the hunter, Riare, on her own initiative, in order to have her son, Wédráogò, recognized by the father, Nedega.

Grandfathers transmit power to maternal uncles, twin brothers divide up inherited territory, brothers contrive to govern with the help of their cousins. Chiefs are chiefs by blood only; commoners remain fixed in their hereditary positions. A more detailed analysis would show how the political alliance chief/subjects, is bound up with the religious alliance state/families through the exchange of women. The chief's authority and that of the head of the nuclear family open these perspectives to us.

Commentary on the Text

LINE

1. The singer "excuses himself," that is, he asks permission to speak in public, before an official audience.
4–5. The whole of lines 4 and 5 make up a proverb which means "I don't have to perform social duties which are beyond my professional capabilities as a musician specializing in moral tales."

6. *Bénd-nábà*: complementary syntagm made up of *bend-ro* [large round drum] and *nábà* [chief].
   "It is the concern...": according to the singer, the role of teacher is better suited to the musicians mentioned.

7. *Lund-nábà*: from *Lung-a* [small, tapered drum of about average length by comparison to the *gâgâogo*].

8. *Gâgâogo*, plural *gâgâdo*: large, filiform drum.

9. *Rudga*, plural *rudsi*: type of small violoncello strung with roughened horsehair.

10. "If I do it...": if I play the role of teacher by singing the story of the woman.

11. *Yumde*, plural *yuma*: group of musicians including all those previously mentioned.

12. *Yôyôga*, plural *yôyôse*: a group which is sociological and religious rather than professional. In the poem, *yôyôaga* is a direct opposite of *yumde*, whereas it is traditionally the opposite of *na-kombga* [descendant of the royal family].

14. "Strike up the song...": begin the real performance.
    Pag-yelwênde: complementary syntagm made up of *pag-* (*paga* [woman]) and *yel-wênde* (*yel-le* [affair, story], *wêndê* [God]); "a bad business concerning God," fault, error, sin; the moral error of this woman.

23. "Poko" is a feminine proper noun from *pug-go*, where *pug-* is the root of *paga* [woman].

24. "Raogo" is a masculine proper noun, in direct opposition to the preceding. Like *poko*, *raogo* can be used adjectivally: *no-raogo* (*no-*, root of *noaga*, depicts genus without specifying sex; *raogo*, from *raw-go* [male]) means cockerel; *no-poko* means hen. The reversal in the way in which the birds were given out is thus emphasized.

23-24. The order (Poko before Raogo) would suggest that the girl is the elder, whereas it is actually the mother's preference which determines the priority.

29. *Zâmnê*: a type of lentil prepared with butter and mixed with tender leaves.

30. "Sold for ten francs": *koos piiga* [literally, "to sell (for) ten"]. At the present exchange rate among the Môsì, the monetary unit is worth five C.F.A. francs (*Francs de la Coopération Financière en Afrique Centrale*).

33-34. The giving of the chickens will be followed by economic exchange: sale, barter, etc.

37. "*M ba* Raogo": literally, "my father Raogo." *Ba* is a title of respect and means "master."

39. The singer's mistake is obvious. Poko could not address Raogo as "my son," because they are brother and sister.

46 & 85. Advice, encouragement, and admonitions addressed to Poko by her mother.

52. "A hen should not be killed like a goat": a hen is killed by cutting its throat, a goat is slaughtered. The Mósì do not sell chicken at market, only beef, mutton, and goat-meat.

55. "Buys for 'ten-five'": "ten-five" is the translation for *pis-nu* (*pis*, plural affix of *piiga* [ten], *nu* [five]). In fact it is $10 \times 5 = 50$; more precisely, $50 \times 5 = 250$, or 250 C.F.A. francs.

57. "Rubs the chicken": that is, rolls it vigorously with salt and pimento, or crushes salt and pimento into it. *Kaolgo* is made like cheese and used to season sauces; it is widely known as *soumbala*.

60. *Yárgà* or *yadga*, plural *yad-se* or *yarcé*: inhabitant of *Yad-tènga*, the Yadega area. The capital today is Ouahigouia. During the remainder of the poem "Yarga" is used as a proper noun.

75. The teller of moral tales often invites his listeners' opinion; here he is asking them to judge and condemn the mother and to uphold his own disapproval of her actions.

76. "Hoists Raogo onto a horse": the horse is very important in *môógò* areas. Every chief and each man with the slightest claim to riches have one or more. Mósì warriors used the horse a great deal in armed warfare.

89. "Choose good brick-making ground and hollow it out": dig out the ground to moisten it, and knead it with the feet in order to make building mortar.

99. "Mother Earth" is a free translation of *têng-tê-pelem* [white dust of the earth]. It refers to the earth as the object of religious worship.

100. "God-chief Zidwênde" translates *nábà Zidwênde* [supreme chief Zidwênde]. The word *wêndê* [god] has already been encountered.

103. "Horse corpse, nine days old": the horse, deprived of food and water, is thought to be dead, but after nine days it is still alive.

134. Poko undergoes a transition in the successive exchanges from horse to bundle and from bundle to Gâmbaga.

136. This is the only time Raogo answers his mother. Every other time he obeys passively.

142. *Zuga-zuga*: onomatopoeia imitating the sound of rapid walking, heavy or light according to the speaker's interpretation.

146. "Autumn rain": a fairly free translation of *sigr-saaga* [rain at the beginning (of the rainy season)].

152. "His first wife": translation of *pug-kêema* [eldest wife, the oldest in the marriage gift (see commentary on line 165)].

156. "To make fire": in this context the warmth is to combat the coolness caused by the rain; the light is used to combat the royal family's blindness.

165. "Given a hundred women": there are three sorts of marriage: (1) marriage by giving a daughter, or *pug-kuuni* (from *kuuni* [gift]); (2) marriage by cooptation, with initiative mainly from the man, or *pug-rikre* (from *rikre* [grasp]); (3) marriage by chiefly intervention, or *pug-siure*. *Siure* is a juridic term indicating "the right (inaugurated by chiefly authority) over the first daughter of a girl given in marriage." The service which is the source of this right is one of persons, not one of common goods as in *pug-kuuni*.

166. "Gift of a hundred children": *kamba*, singular *biige*, meaning "children old enough to serve, servants."

167. "A hundred horses": the horse is a possession of economic value and at the same time one of honor (culture), just as are the children and women who are mentioned in parallel.

173. "Divine White Dust": literal translation of *têng-te-pelem*.

174. "Ancestor Wubri and his Mountain": Wubri was neither the first emperor nor the first known ancestor of the Mósì. If his name has entered into religion as the principal ancestral spirit, it is because of his prestige and possibly because of his first official contacts with the "possessors of the earth" (*têng-sóbê-dámbà*), which resulted in contracts which are considered sacred agreements. Wubri's mountain has not been identified.

181–182. What belongs to Raogo belongs to his mother, too, although this was not in fact so because of her attitude.

184. *Koad-yaogo*: complementary syntagm (*koada* [digger], *yaogo* [tomb]); literally, "tomb of the digger," site of Ouagadougou.

192. "Fill a basket up with millet": the man goes into the granary and takes a portion of the reserve grain to give to the woman. She winnows, crushes, and grinds it; he does not.

200. "Under pretext of relieving herself": translation of *fêeg yôore* [literally "clearing the nose," "blowing her nose"].

209. "What I want": translation of *bumbu* [thing].

223. "My object": translation of *bumbu* [thing].

224. "Poko takes her hand": literal translation of *Pok dik a nugu*. Poko makes the movement of plunging in her hand before doing so in fact, and this preliminary gesture is described.

236–237. "Two houses...six houses": two houses, because henceforth there are only the mother and the boy. We cannot see a reason for the six houses.

238–239. "Ten," because Raogo gives generously, a tenth of all he has: women to keep his mother company, servants to wait on her
240. Raogo finally ceases to obey in order to be served.

REFERENCES

BALANDIER, G.
1967 *Anthropologie politique.* Paris: Presses Universitaires de France.
BAUDU, P.
1956 *Vieil empire, jeune église.* Paris: La Savane.
CANU, G.
1968 De quelques emprunts lexicaux môre. *Journal of West African Language* 5.
1969 *Contes mosi actuels.* Dakar: Institut Français d'Afrique Noire.
CORNEVIN, R.
1960 *Histoire des peuples de l'Afrique de l'Ouest.* Paris: Berger-Levrault.
HAMMOND, P. B.
1966 *Yatenga.* New York: Free Press.
HERSKOVITS, M. J.
1965 *L'Afrique et les Africains.* Paris: Payot.
HOUIS, M.
1963 *Les noms individus chez les Mosi.* Dakar: Institut Français d'Afrique Noire.
1970a "Communication au Colloque de la Société d'Études des Langues d'Afrique de l'Ouest." Unpublished manuscript.
1970b *Anthropologie linguistique de l'Afrique noire.* Paris: Presses Universitaires de France.
IZARD, M.
1965 *Les traditions historiques des villages du Yatênga.* Ouagadougou: Cercle de Gourcy.
1967 *Colloque sur les cultures voltaïques.* Paris and Ouagadougou.
1969 Naba Kânga (1757–1787). *Notes et documents voltaïques* 2 (3): 13. Ouagadougou.
1970 *Introduction à l'histoire des royaumes mosi.* Paris and Ouagadougou: Centre National de Recherche Scientifique.
KABORE, G. V.
1962 Article in *Cahiers d'Études Africaines* 8 (11): 609–623. Paris.
MANGIN, E.
1916 *Les Mossi.* Vienna: Anthropos.
MAURIER, H.
1967 Christianisme et croyance mossi. *Ethnologie Religieuse* 14: 172–238. Rome.
MARSAL, M.
1966 *L'autorité.* Paris: Presses Universitaires de France.
MAUSS, M.
1960 *Sociologie et anthropologie.* Paris: Presses Universitaires de France.
OUÉDRAOGO, E.
1968 Comment Kângo devint roi. *Bulletin de Liaison de l'Institut Ethnologique et de Géographie Tropicale* 1. Abidjan.

OUÉDRAOGO, L. B.

1969   Une expérience d'animation rurale en Haute-Volta. *Archives Internationales de Sociologie et Coopération du Développement* 26. Paris.

PAGEARD, R.

1970   *Le droit privé des Mossi.* Paris and Ouagadougou: Centre National de Recherche Scientifique.

SKINNER, E. P.

1964   *The Mossi of Upper Volta.* Stanford, Calif.: Stanford University Press

TAUXIER, L.

1917   *Le noir du Yâtenga.* Paris: Larose.

TIENDREBÉOGO, Y.

1964   *Histoire et coutumes royales des Mossi de Ouagadougou.* Ouagadougou: Presses Africaines.

ZAHAN, D.

1967   *Colloque sur les cultures voltaïques.* Paris and Ouagadougou.

Conservatism and Change in a Desert Feudalism: The Case of Southern Baluchistan

STEPHEN PASTNER

In many instances the incorporation of an indigenous society into a wider polity signals the demise of traditional forms of social organization and a decline in the power of customary elites. In the Makran region of what is now southwestern Pakistani Baluchistan, just the opposite was the case until recently. The inclusion of Makran in the state systems of the Khanate of Kalat, and later in the British Raj, in fact strengthened traditional Makrani elites by granting them the additional status of "wardens of the march" and revenue collectors in a region which central governments habitually found difficult to control. Only in the recent decades of direct Pakistani rule have long-established Makrani patterns of political dominance begun to erode seriously. The present discussion outlines the ways in which the traditional Makrani system of social and political stratification has been influenced by the region's enmeshment in various state systems.

GENERAL BACKGROUND

Approximately 23,000 square miles in size, with an estimated population in excess of 150,000, Makran is one of the largest, least-populated districts in all of Pakistan. It is bounded on the north by the Siahan range, which separates it from the deserts of Kheran District; on the east by the mountains of Jhalawan and Las Bela districts; on the west by Iran; and on the south by the Arabian Sea.

Fieldwork in and around Panjgur oasis of Makran District was carried out between December, 1968, and May, 1969. Library research was conducted in London, at the British Museum, the India Office Library, and the School of Oriental and African Studies, University of London. Funds were provided by the National Institute of Mental Health and the Society of the Sigma Xi. I would like to thank Dr. Carroll McC. Pastner for her helpful comments and criticisms.

The terrain of Makran consists largely of a series of alternating barren mountains and valleys, running generally in a northeast to southwest direction. Three major massifs, from north to south the Siahan, the Central, and the Coastal (Talar-i-band) ranges, are divided by the major drainages of the Dasht in the south; the Ketch in central Makran; and the Rakshan in the north, which serves the oasis of Panjgur with its population of about 11,000.

The majority of the populace are Sunni Muslims, with a few Shi'ites and, particularly among the nomads (known locally as *pahwal*), a substantial number of Zikris, followers of a Mahdist (Islamic messianic) sect imported to the area in the late fifteenth or early sixteenth century (cf. Pastner and Pastner 1972a). Baluchi, an Iranian tongue, is the majority language and *lingua franca*, although there are also speakers of Brahui (a Dravidian language common in the mountainous areas to the east of Makran) and Jadgali, a Sindhi derivative.

Irrigation agriculture is practiced in the major river valleys, with an emphasis on date arboriculture, while the arid hinterland supports a scattered population relying on dry-crop cereal cultivation and pastoralism, separately or in combination (cf. Pastner 1971; Pastner and Pastner 1972b). Sheep and goats are the primary stock of Makrani herdsmen, both nomadic and sedentary. Pasni, Jiwani and Gwadur, the coastal towns of Makran, are trading ports and the home of the *med*s, who are fishermen.

Like the rest of Baluchistan, Makran has witnessed continuing encounters with foreign powers throughout its history. Alexander's Macedonians were mauled by the "hairy Gedrosians" in the passes of Makran; and Sassanid Persians, Sindhi Brahmins, Arabs, Ghorid Afghans, Mongols, and Portuguese all, at various times, laid nominal claim to the dubious treasures of Makran. Many a foreign ruler, confronted with Makran's sere landscape and unruly populace, must have echoed the sentiments contained in the lament of Sinan bin Salama, appointed to the governorship of Makran by the caliph Moawiya: "Thou showest me to the road of Makuran but what a difference is there between an order and its execution. I will never enter the country as its name terrifies me" (Baluch 1958: 62).

Actual power, in fact, appears to have resided until quite recently with local groups, the most notable being the Maliks, the Buledies, and the Gitchkis. The latter, variously tracing Sikh or Rajput ancestry, gained hegemony in the early 1700's and still represent a significant indigenous influence in Makran. They take their name from the Gitchk Valley, east of Panjgur, their original home in Makran.

After their eighteenth-century rise to power and a number of battles with the Gitchkis, the Ahmadzai Brahui khans of the Kalat region of northeast Baluchistan incorporated Makran into their confederacy, largely on a revenue-sharing basis. The late nineteenth-century pacification of

Baluchistan by the British, manifested in the so-called "forward policy" of indirect rule pioneered by Sir Robert Sandeman, drew Makran further into a wider society. After the partition of the subcontinent, a brief span of relative Baluch autonomy in the Baluchistan States Union was followed by the inclusion of the Baluch territories into the Pakistani nation. (For a good summary of Makrani history up to 1955, as well as an overview of land-use practices and population, see Field 1959.)

TRADITIONAL SOCIAL STRATIFICATION

There are three main social strata in Makran: the *hakim*, the Baluch, and the *hizmatkar*. The *hakim* are the traditional ruling elites of the area and include the Nausherwanis, the Bizanjau, and, most important, the Gitchkis. The Nausherwanis of Makran are few in number and are largely the descendants of mercenaries from the Kheran deserts, garrisoned in various parts of the country by the Gitchkis to support them in the traditional power politics of the area. Genealogically, the Bizanjaus of Kolwa in eastern Makran are Brahuis, but a long residence in Makran has Baluch-ized them in language and custom.

Although they claim a common ancestry from the Sikh or Rajput, Man Singh, the Gitchkis, like the other *hakim*, do not constitute a group with corporate or cooperative functions. Indeed, as will be seen, the Gitchkis have traditionally provided the main points of social cleavage in Makran, contending among themselves for political and economic power and the support of the other segments of society. There are two main branches of the Gitchkis: the Isazai, dominant in Panjgur, and the Dinarzai, rulers of Ketch and the Iranian borderland. However, there are a number of Gitchkis who, because of poverty or "bad blood" (hypergamy is per-mitted but not regarded too highly; hypogamy is forbidden and was punishable by death in the past) are called *tolag* [jackal] Gitchkis and are materially as wretched as many of the lower-status members of the population.

In other parts of Baluchistan the term "Baluch" is used to distinguish those so designated from other distinct ethnic and political communities, such as Pathans, Panjabis, or Brahuis. However, in Makran, although the Baluchi language is spoken by all strata and common kinship systems exist, the term "Baluch" has a specific social status reference within a stratified social and political system. It is reserved for the broad layer of society – nomads and independent agriculturalists – standing midway be-tween the minority of *hakim* elites and the large *hizmatkar* menial class. Among the Baluch are found a number of named tribes or *kom*, each of which can theoretically boast a distinctive agnatically phrased pedigree (*nasabi*). In fact, however, most Baluch seem to be unaware of their genealogies beyond three or four generations; and, in general, these "tribes" have little actual corporate role in Makrani social life. Instead, it is place of residence, economic interests, and allegiance to particular *hakim* or their local representatives (headmen, usually Baluch, known as *motaber* or *kauda*) which have traditionally determined the main political and economic demarcations in Makran and have crosscut, or even superseded, ties of kin, particularly in the case of Baluch villagers (cf. Pastner and Pastner 1972b).

Among the more notable Baluch tribal names in Makran are the Rais, traditionally village headmen in Ketch and close supporters of the Gitchkis; the Mullazai, who are prominent in Panjgur, particularly in the village of Tasp, where they are the hereditary *motaber*s; the Rinds of Makran's western borders, a well-known name elsewhere in Baluchistan, being the tribe of the greatest of Baluch epic heroes, Mir Chakar Rind, who established Baluch influence as far as the Panjab in the late fifteenth and early sixteenth centuries; the Mohammed Hassanis, a widespread group with representatives in Kheran and Jhalawan; and the Buledies, once the rulers of much of Makran but now influential mainly in the area of Buleda in western Makran.

At the bottom of the social ladder are the menial classes, generally known as *hizmatkar*. This category, which may comprise in excess of one-third of the total population, is composed mainly of a group known as *nakib*s in northern Makran and as *darzadag* in the south. It includes as well numbers of *loris*, the ubiquitous tinkers and metal workers of Southwest Asia, and the *med* fishermen of the coast. *Palawan*, epic singers and musicians, also come from this stratum.

Although nowadays all of the traditional menial classes are freemen, until the early decades of this century many were still legally slaves (*ghulam*), whose ancestors were imported from Africa via Arabia or were the descendants of Baluch war captives. Many of the *hizmatkar* are in fact quite negroid in appearance as contrasted to the "mediterranean" Baluch and *hakim*. Since this broad social category is the most economically depressed, it has traditionally provided the bulk of emigrants from Makran, notably to Karachi, which has led urban Pakistanis to stereotype all Makranis as Negroes, whom they disparagingly call *habshi*.

The *hizmatkar* class provides most of the laborers who work as sharecroppers (*sherik*) for wealthier landholders (*zimindar*), as servants, or as night-soil collectors or "sweepers" (*bangi*) – a job as little esteemed in Muslim Baluchistan as it is in Hindu India.

THE AGE OF WARRING CHIEFS

Before the establishment of the Brahui Kalet Khanate, Makran's history was that of warring groups and factions succeeding each other in dominance, the Gitchkis finally emerging as the dominant power in the early eighteenth century. Even after the rise of the Ahmadzai Brahui hegemony in northeastern Baluchistan and its extension to Makran during the reign of Nasir Khan, conditions were, if anything, exacerbated; for the khanate's sole concern with Makran was its capacity to provide revenues for the support of a lavish (by Baluchistani standards) court. After a number of battles in the mid-eighteenth century, the indigenous Gitchki overlords of Makran acceded to the khan and agreed to divide the revenues of the country with him in return for the right to continue, unmolested, their interminable internecine squabbles over *de facto* ruling power.

Delegates of the khan, known as *naib*, were posted to Makran, their main function being to oversee the collection of taxes, which came from a tithe levied on landholders, known as *dahak* [one tenth], and a further payment called *zar i shah* [ruler's price]. Beyond these obligations, the Gitchkis remained virtually sovereign rulers. From their ranks came the paramount chiefs, or *sardar*, of Makran, of which there were generally two major ones, based in Panjgur in northern Makran and the Ketch River valley to the south.

As already noted, it would be incorrect to call the Gitchkis a "group," even though they shared a common genealogical charter; for the main lines of social conflict in Makran were within the Gitchki lineage, each branch contending with the others for the right to rule and to act as revenue-takers for the khan. However, as a *category*, the Gitchkis were fairly secure in the seat of power. Marriage alliances, known as *shalwar* [trousers], linked the Isazai Gitchkis of Panjgur to the Ahmadzai Brahui ruling house, while the Dinarzai Gitchkis of Ketch had similar alliances with the Shahizai Mengals of Jhalawan, a powerful military arm of the Brahui Khanate (Bray 1913: 35). Hedging their political bets, Gitchkis established still other alliances with the powerful Nausherwani tribe of the deserts to the north, whose fighting prowess could be an incalculable aid in the arena of power politics which ruled the day.

Although grudging, the general willingness of the Gitchkis to accept revenue obligations to Kalat made it in the khan's best interest to maintain some sort of Gitchki rule in Makran; and he backed up this interest with the threat of military intervention on behalf of the feudal Gitchki lords, who, although periodically recalcitrant, were as firm an ally as could be reasonably expected in such an area. Major General Sir Charles Macgregor, visiting Panjgur in 1877, reported on Kalat's *laissez-faire* attitude *vis-à-vis* the Gitchkis:

The Khan's *Naib* is not the governor and does not pretend to govern the country or even to collect its revenue. He is, in fact, the receiver of such revenue as the actual governor may have agreed to pay the Khan. Consequently, the government of Panjgur has always been allowed to remain in the hands of the

Gitchkis, the actual individual exercising the functions of the governor being he who was strongest or he who agreed to pay the most. Thus, in trying to oust *Mir Gajian* [*the current Gitchi* sardar], *Mir Isa* [*his paternal cousin*] *does not necessarily throw off the authority of the Khan, but only wishes to make himself the actual governor of the district and the payer of the Khan's half of the revenue* (Macgregor 1882: 101; emphasis added).

The Gitchkis themselves often exercised only marginal control, particularly over areas removed from the irrigated tracts which were the seats of their power. As within the *hakim*, or predominantly Gitchki ruling class, a continual jockeying for authority also took place at the lower levels of Makrani society, among the Baluch headmen called *motaber*, *komash*, or *kauda*. Those headmen in closest proximity to the oases, and consequently to Gitchki authority, made themselves the delegates of the Gitchkis, thereby receiving tax exemptions and *jagirs* [land investitures] or *khillats* [miscellaneous financial rewards], while in more remote areas local chiefs were virtually autonomous.

Although administrative titles were nominally hereditary, it will be clear by now that *de facto* power was far more fluid, thereby creating the overall anarchic state of Makran.

The aspirant to power in Makran, whether he was a Gitchki at feud with his kinsmen, the headman of an oasis settlement attempting to ingratiate himself with the Gitchki *sardar*, or the fractious nomad chief of a hinterland region, sought to surround himself with a retinue of supporters known as *posht*, a word meaning "back," and applied as well to patrikin within a certain range of genealogical inclusion. The presence of these backers was the *sine qua non* of political power in Makran and was often a license for the arbitrary exercise of such power as the following adages imply:

Zurak-i ap sha jhala borza ro:t
["The water of the strong man can flow uphill"; i.e. if one is strong enough he may even defy natural law];
and

Ko:t o kalat sohn abit
posht o bras baz abit
taklif hich nabit
["When your fort and stronghold is secure and your supporters and brothers are many there will be no trouble"].

As a man rose in influence and esteem he attracted fortune seekers, eager for booty or for the chance to obtain land rights in the irrigated tracts. Those headmen directly beholden to a Gitchki *sardar* had the obligation to provide him with periodic *lashkars* [levies of fighting men] under a system known as *lank* or *suren bandi* [the girding of the loins]. The nonelite participants in a *lashkar* could receive land grants smaller than *jagirs*, known as *baratwar*.

For a commoner Baluch to attach himself to a rising political star or to join his *posht* was to enter into a patron-client relationship called *posht pannag* [watching out for one's support]. The social inferior in this dyad referred to his patron by the honorific *waja*, a general term of respect, prefixed with the first person possessive, *mani*. The latter regarded the client as *mani mard* [my man]. A commoner could not generally have more than one patron at a time, since the plethora of feuds, fights, and forays would have added to the already abundant crosscutting of alliances, as when a person's kinship ties and political ties were in different directions.

On the basis of available information, it seems that Makran's nomadic population, in particular, played an important part in the power politics which emanated from the settled tracts of Panjgur and Ketch. Rewards, in booty or land, to nomads for fighting services appear to have ranked with impoverishment as a major contributing factor in the overall historical trend toward sedentarization of the nomads in Makran. Even today there are old men in the oasis who remember a nomadic childhood which they or their fathers gave up to fight in the British levies, for cash and land payments, in the days when the old order of chiefly feuding was in the process of tapering off. During the pre-British days of the warring chiefs, the mobility of nomads enabled them either to align themselves with different headmen as the latter's power waxed and waned, or to flee out of the way of conflicts. Physical descriptions of Panjgur by early observers indicate that much of the population of the oasis was, if not fully nomadic, at least prepared for the possibility of physical movement to greener political pastures. The intrepid Pottinger, passing through the deserts north of Makran, wrote from hearsay that "'Punjgoor,' which lies nine days' journey north-northeast from 'Kedge,' is made up of twelve or thirteen villages composed '*mainly of tents*'" (Pottinger 1816: 304; emphasis added).

Similarly, the Makran *Gazetteer* notes that the pre-British village pattern of Makran consisted of nucleated settlements of tents, mud houses, and thatched huts surrounding the forts of local petty headmen, while after the British entrenchment brought some security to the area, a more haphazard settlement pattern developed (*Baluchistan District Gazetteer* 1907: 64).

Once established as landholders, many nomads appear to have lost the taste for further fighting, and power-seeking headmen were probably forced to look constantly to the pastoral sphere to replenish their forces. Thus Masson writes:

The nature and variety of the cultivated objects in Panjgur attest to the fertility of the soil...[while] the agricultural habits of the inhabitants have softened their manners, and they are as much distinguished from their turbulent neighbors for their peaceable demeanor, as for their superior acquirements in the arts and conveniences of life (Masson 1873: 291–292).

This overall process, whereby Makrani nomad fighters entered into the orbit of power politics in the settlements, thereafter losing contact with their pastoral cogeners in the hinterland, is similar, in microcosm, to macrohistorical processes detailed by Lattimore for medieval and ancient Central Asia under the rubric of "frontier feudalism" (1962: 514–541). In these situations, pastoral-nomad Turko-Mongols along the ecological and administrative frontier with China were drawn into the political sphere of the state, becoming incorporated into local settled communities via processes of ethnic superstratification. That is, the interests of the nomads, particularly the chiefs, became more closely entwined with those of the sedentary state than with those of their own nomadic kin of the steppes beyond the frontier. By assuming the privileged role of "wardens of the march," such people eventually wound up protecting the state against more distant pastoral raiders, ultimately losing their own sense of tribal identity.

The analogies between the Makran case and that of the Inner Asian Frontier should not of course be overdone. For instance, macroecological barriers separated the cultures and social economies of the assorted Chinese dynasties from those of the vast loess upland steppe of Central Asia. In Makran, the frontier between "steppe" and "sown," or, more accurately, between land used by cultivators and that exploited by nomads, can be measured in the feet or inches which separate a village's cultivations from the aridity surrounding it. The bridging of the gap between the community identity of *farmer* versus that of *nomad* was also easier in Makran than in Central Asia, facilitated by geographical proximity and by the shared culture of the two spheres. Also, the sedentarization processes along the Central Asian frontier were undergone by whole tribal groups *qua* groups, while in Makran it was individuals or, at most, families, that made the transition to a settled life in return for booty and/or security. (As I have indicated elsewhere [Pastner 1971], in Makrani nomadic camps, individuals and families are the basic social, economic, and decision-making units.) Nevertheless, the parallels between Makran and Lattimore's paradigm are useful up to a point.

THE COMING OF THE BRITISH

Prior to the coming of the British to Baluchistan, and for a considerable period after their influence was established, the Makran area was obviously extremely unsettled. British officers who had experienced the turbulent Pathan tribes of the Afghan border as well as such militant eastern Baluch tribes as the Marris, the Bugtis, and the Jakranis, were nonetheless struck by the chaotic state of Makrani affairs. Colonel Sir

T. H. Holdich, traveling through the area in the 1880's on a reconnais-sance of the Indo-Persian boundary, remarks that:

In no part of North-Western India from Persia to the Pamirs, have I heard expressed such a thirsty longing not only for the pax, but for the lex Brittanica; and such confidence in the power of the British Sirkar [Sir Robert Sandeman] to remove the yoke of misrule and anarchy from the necks of the people (Holdich 1901: 336).

With their rise to power on the subcontinent, the British saw in the sturdy hillmen of Baluchistan, including Makran, a safeguard against Russian ambitions in the "great game" for mastery of South Asia. Strategies, therefore, had to be developed to insure peace on the Baluch frontier. By buying the loyalties of the khans of Kalat and their con-federate chieftains, the British were able to create a buffer force of rela-tively dependable tribesmen between their Indian Empire and possible Russian invasion routes through Iran and Afghanistan. The British tactic of indirect rule reached its most progressive and least cynical form in the 1870's through the so-called "forward policy" of Sir Robert Sandeman (cf. Caroe 1965; Thornton 1895; Lee-Warner 1898). Sandeman managed by diplomatic and sympathetic means to quell the chiefly feuds which periodically disrupted the affairs of the khanate and to institute certain broad-based social reforms (notably in the *jirgah* [council system for settling disputes]), which, although based on customary practice, never-theless represented an improvement over the often high-handed and arbi-trary governance of the chieftains in the past. After his death in 1892, significantly while he was en route to arbitrate a feud in Makran, Sande-man's policy underwent a series of shifts, emphasis being placed now on increased British interference, then on greater Kalat responsibility (Lee-Warner 1898).

The coming of the British to Makran tended to "freeze" the various leadership statuses, whereas under the uninterested and usually ineffec-tive rule of Kalat, constant sparring for power and the right to share the khan's revenue took place among the dominant classes and their allies. By their military support of the khanate and their interest in leadership stability on the frontier, the British encouraged the establishment of what amounted to virtually statutory chiefs, thus arousing the anger and jealousy of numerous have-not aristocrats who felt thwarted in their polit-ical aspirations. In 1898 a revolt against the British-backed khan and his *naib* was instigated by one such disgruntled power-seeker, Mir Mehrab Khan, the brother of the British-Kalat-supported Gitchki *sardar* of Ketch.

The insurrection ended with a defeat of the rebels in the Gokprosh hills of southern Ketch by a force of native troops under British officers, and in the establishment of an even firmer and more rigid administration by the Kalat-British condominium. The title of *nazim* was conferred on the khan's agent in Makran, the first officeholder being a sagacious Brahui of the Raisani tribe, Mir Mehrullah Khan. He took wives from the Gitchki notables to strengthen his local power base, looked to the implementation of the newly established *jirgah* council system, and in general ruled with great firmness. He was ultimately given the title of *nawab*, an honorific status accompanied by substantial revenues, which reverted to the Gitchkis after his death.

It was typical of the British at this time to recognize that in a remote and physically difficult area like Makran, the use of force, either directly or through local intermediaries, was an impractical way of keeping the peace. So, as bribes for good behavior, assorted grants in land and money and in titles ranging from "sahib *bahadur*" to "Order of the British Empire" were awarded to those local headmen who were considered to have greatest trouble-making potential. Cases in point are "Sahib Bahadur" Mehrab Khan, the rebel of Gokprosh, and "Sir" Azad Khan, K.C.I.E., a freebooting chief of the Nausherwani tribe of the Kheran deserts to the north of Makran. (In the latter part of the nineteenth century he terrorized large areas of Makran with a band of desperados and a camel on which he had mounted a cannon.)

By 1904 a British commandant-*cum*-political officer was permanently posted to Panjgur as head of the Makran Levies, a Baluch-and-Brahui camel corps which kept the peace and patrolled the Iranian borderland. Although traditional elites continued to enjoy great influence, this direct British presence continued until the time of Partition in 1947.

PAKISTANI RULE

In March, 1948, Ahmad Yar Khan, khan of Kalat, acceded his dominions to the new state of Pakistan, but until 1955 the Baluch area enjoyed a semiautonomy which might have signaled the emergence of a distinct Baluch state in the twentieth century. This was the period of the Baluchistan States Union, composed of the traditional territories and chiefdoms of the Kalat Khanate, including Makran. Ultimately, however, an even more direct imposition of Pakistani rule prevailed. Since that time, Baluchistan has shared the Pakistani destiny, passing through the regime of Mirze and the basic democracy decade of Ayub Khan into the martial-rule era of President Yahya Khan, which began in March, 1969, ended with the debacle of Bangladesh, and led to the present regime of Zulfikar Ali Bhutto.

In 1968–1969, the time of the research on which this discussion is based, Baluchistan formed part of the Province of West Pakistan and comprised two administrative divisions, Kalat and Quetta, each in the charge of a commissioner. The divisions were composed of districts headed by a deputy commissioner. Lower administrative echelons included the *nazim*, *ex officio* magistrate for the various administrative areas within the district, below him a *tehsildar*, and still lower, *naib tehsildars*. As of 1969, Pakistan continued to use the British practice of applying special legal codes to the Baluch and Pathan peoples of the frontier. Popularly known as the *Quetta-Kalat ordinances*, they were modified versions of the customary laws contained in the older British *Frontier crimes regulations*, which grew out of Sandeman's "forward policy." Certain questions of customary law (e.g. those relating to bridewealth) could be settled by religious courts headed by *qazis* at the option of the litigants.

However, Pakistan officially ended the era of *de jure*, if not of *de facto*, Gitchki dominance. As of 1969, the nawab of Makran, Mir Baian Gitchki, resided in Karachi and received an allowance from the government large enough to persuade him to stay out of Makrani affairs. As in Baluchistan generally, civil service positions above the rank of *nazim* were staffed almost exclusively by non-Baluch, usually urbanite Panjabis, between whom and the local population little love was lost.

The introduction of universal suffrage under the basic democracy program of Ayub Khan theoretically opened the way to even more basic political changes. Under this system, elected representatives at various levels, from "wards" to "union councils," were to act as liaisons between the interests of their constituents and the appointees of the central government who actually determined local policy.

Since the advent of Pakistani rule, Makran is witnessing increasing but still negligible upward mobility among the traditionally depressed sectors of society. A small number have managed to achieve various degrees of prominence in local bureaucratic echelons, and among the more socially conscious of these an attempt is made to create formal traditions to enhance a traditionally low self-image. One such man, a *nakib* from Panjgur, identifies totally with an emerging spirit of Baluch nationalism and is one of its most eloquent spokesmen, being the author of a number of monographs on Baluchi language and custom and the elected president of a Quetta-based Baluchi Academy. While in no way denying his origins as a Makrani *nakib*, he believes that his particular group, admittedly servile in tradition, nonetheless had a noble origin as the warrior vanguard of the Arab hosts which invaded Makran in the seventh and eighth centuries.

But despite such changes and the existence of paper reforms for over a decade, the old feudal order has died hard. For their part, many members of the upper-status groups of Baluch and *hakim* seem to have shifted but little from conservative attitudes supportive of the traditional social hierarchy and to resent such changes as have occurred, minute though they are. With its history of local rulers acting more in self-seeking collusion with outside powers than for the local popular good, Makran has in fact seen the transformation of many traditional patterns of political organization into more contemporary idioms. The buying of votes and other forms of patronage have in many instances replaced military prowess as the foundation on which the still-vital political ambitions of the ruling families rest, but the prestige of traditional elites, once based on force of arms, has passed largely intact into an era of confirmation by ballot box. As to where the ultimate loyalties of such elites lie, all too often the sentiments expressed by a leader of the Marri Baluch of eastern Baluchistan apply equally well to the Makrani case: "I touch the political agent's boots and get a thousand to touch mine" (Pehrson 1966: 26).

However, an egalitarian spirit is emerging within a small but growing group of young, educated pan-Baluchistan nationalists; and certain attitude changes are manifested, superficially at least, by those traditional elites most concerned with maintaining their political viability in a period when universal suffrage makes it necessary for them to woo support from all levels of society. This was illustrated at a *diwan* [audience] which I attended at the home of an elderly Gitchki who was prominent in local politics. Also present were a number of *nakibs* of the *hizmatkar* class, who had some influence in nearby hamlets. When I questioned him about the traditional social order of Makran, on which he was an authority, the Gitchki replied that although the *hizmatkar* were at one time slaves and servants they were now as good as anyone else, since they too could become property owners and were especially entitled to honor because "they were once kings in their own lands."

In contrast, bazaar gossip had it that this same individual kept a number of his aging maiden daughters secluded in *purdah* for want of sufficiently high-status suitors. His public utterances, therefore, were generally regarded with some skepticism, and the egalitarian sentiments contained therein had to be evaluated on the situational bases of audience and political purpose.

THE FUTURE

I have no detailed information on the ways in which the martial law regime of Yahya Khan and the present regime of Zulfikar Ali Bhutto have affected the political situation which existed in Makran during my time in the region, in 1968–1969. However, it does appear that while fundamental changes are occurring in Baluch political organization and social identity, the seeds of which were evident several years ago, certain continuities also exist.

A pan-Baluch nationalism is becoming increasingly evident, marked by the emergence of a somewhat bewildering plethora of political movements. The *Baluch Mutaheda Mahaz* of Sind [United Baluch Front]; the *Azad Baluchistan* [Free Baluchistan] movement, directed primarily toward

Iranian Baluch; the Kabul-based *Pakhtunistan* propaganda campaign, which hopes to wean Pakistani Baluch and Pathans into the Afghan political sphere; and Ulfat Nazim's World Baluchi Organization, working out of Baghdad with Baathist backing, generally reflect Marxist ideological elements which are certainly foreign to the stratified parameters of traditional Baluch views of power and authority outlined above. It is not difficult, therefore, to envision the emergence of a new elite among the Baluch, whose leadership may indeed rest on criteria and ideologies alien to the traditional feudal ones described above.

However, like such predecessors as Azad Khan Nausherwani, K.C.I.E., with his cannon and camel, these new elites may well continue to serve wittingly or unwittingly as the new "march wardens" for more powerful polities, furthering such state interests even at the expense of their own people. For it seems clear that such potential insurrectionary movements are being covertly encouraged, if not actively fomented, by governments – notably India, Iraq, and Russia – which have an active interest in promoting discord among Iranian and Pakistani Baluch in order to further their own influence in the Baluch area, which controls strategic access to the Indian Ocean and the Persian Gulf.

In short, the age-old game for mastery of the South Asian frontier is expected to go on, with the majority of the Baluch continuing as pawns in the political intrigues of local and extralocal elites.

REFERENCES

BALUCH, M. S. KHAN
   1958   *History of the Baluch race and Baluchistan.* Quetta.
Baluchistan District Gazetteer
   1907   *Baluchistan District Gazetteer*, volume seven: *Makran.* Bombay.
BRAY, DENYS
   1913   *The life history of a Brahui.* London.
CAROE, OLAF
   1965   *The Pathans: 550 B.C.–A.D. 1957.* London.
FIELD, HENRY
   1959   *An anthropological reconnaissance in West Pakistan, 1955.* Cambridge.
HOLDICH, COL. SIR T. H.
   1901   *The Indian borderland.* London: Methuen.
LATTIMORE, OWEN
   1962   *Studies in frontier history.* The Hague: Mouton.
LEE-WARNER, SIR W.
   1898   "Memorandum on Makran" Letter from India 214 (Foreign), 17th November.
MACGREGOR, MAJ. GEN. SIR C. M.
   1882   *Wanderings in Baluchistan.* London: Allen.
MASSON, CHARLES
   1843   *Narrative of a journey to Kalat.* London.

OLIVER, EDWARD E.
1890   *Across the border: Baluch and Pathan.* London.
PASTNER, STEPHEN
1971   Ideological aspects of nomad/sedentary contact: a case from S. Baluchistan. *Anthropological Quarterly* 44 (3).
PASTNER, STEPHEN, CARROLL M. PASTNER
1972a Aspects of religion in southern Baluchistan. *Anthropologica* 14 (2).
1972b Agriculture, kinship, and politics in southern Baluchistan. *Man* 7 (1).
PEHRSON, ROBERT
1966   *The social organization of the Marri Baluch.* Chicago: Aldine.
POTTINGER, HENRY
1816   *Travels in Beloochistan and Sinde.* London: Longman, Hurst, Reese, Orme and Brown.
PROVINCIAL ASSEMBLY OF WEST PAKISTAN
1965   *The Quetta and Kalat civil and criminal law ordinance.* July 6, 1965 (revised version 1968). Lahore.
ROSS, E. C.
1868   *Memorandum of notes on Makran.* Transactions of the Bombay Geographical Society, volume 17. Bombay.
THORNTON, THOMAS HENRY
1895   *Col. Sir Robert Sandeman: his life and work on our Indian frontier.* London: Murray.

Kinship Terminology and Feudal Versus Tribal Orientations in Baluch Social Organization: A Comparative View

CARROLL McC. PASTNER

An attempt is made here to formulate several preliminary generalizations about the interplay between kinship, political organization, and cultural-ecological factors in Baluchistan. Situated in the easternmost corner of Southwest Asia, Baluchistan, both geographically and historically speaking, lies directly on the crossroads between the Near East, the Indian subcontinent, and Central Asia. However, ethnographically it is linked most closely to the Islamic Middle East and can be described partly in terms of social and cultural organizational features characteristic of that culture area.

The Middle East has been said to exhibit a "mosaic" quality, due not only to the presence of a number of ethnic groups but to the persistence of three major, mutually dependent types of communities: the city, the village, and the pastoral nomadic camp (cf. Coon 1951; Patai 1962). The metaphor of the mosaic should not imply stasis, however, since history has witnessed a continual flux between the three orientations at both the individual and the collective levels. Accompanying and insuring the flexibility of Middle Eastern social organization are features generally common to all three adaptations. These include patrilineality, patrilocality, kin endogamy, polygyny, and extended family structure. Kinship looms so large as an organizational feature that the Middle East has been labeled "a kinship culture" (Patai 1965: 347–348).

More specific than these often overly stressed generalizations are features of social organization relating to the difference between "tribal" and "feudal" orientations in the Middle East. A continuum of tribal

I would like to thank Philip Salzman and Stephen Pastner for their constructive criticisms, although the final responsibility for the contents of this paper remains my own.

Fieldwork was conducted on the oasis of Panjgur in Makran district in 1968–1969 and was supported by the National Institute of Mental Health.

structures would include groups which rely on segmentary lineage principles, with a minimal development of centralized authority as well as more tightly knit kin-based units led by autocratic chiefs. Integration in acephalous systems is largely achieved vertically through agnatic genealogies rather than horizontally through affinal links. Genealogies also play a significant integrating role in tribes with more centralized power structures. "Feudal" structures, on the other hand, witness the weakening of segmented lineage structures and the decay of tribal genealogical organization. The functions of the principle of descent are altered, since feudalism in the Middle East signifies the development of aristocratic family pedigrees based on "pure" descent, which includes the reckoning of the maternal line (cf. Bacon 1958). On the tribal level, the ideology of descent indicates strict patrilineality, even to the extent of subjecting matrilateral links to "amnesia" (Murphy and Kasden 1967: 10); while on the behavioral level, matrilateral links may actually be very significant (cf. Peters 1967).

The development of feudal power affects social organization at the village level by substituting a more classlike segmentation for lineage segmentation. Barth's comparative study of nine villages in southern Kurdistan (1953) illustrates this point clearly. "Tribal villages," inhabited by freehold farmers with lineage structure still intact, are distinguished from "tenant villages," dominated by absentee landlords and manifesting kinship organization which is essentially unstructured above the level of the household. In depicting the diversity found in Kurdish social organization, Barth indicates that the "tribal" and the "nontribal" poles are only "moderately stable," so that change between one and the other is "a fairly rapid process" (Barth 1953: 67).

A much vaster geographical region than Kurdistan, Baluchistan also manifests a good deal of diversity in terms of social organization. This diversity can be viewed as the result of historical factors, described below, and the differences between agricultural and pastoral nomadic adaptations.

BALUCHISTAN AND THE BALUCH

While the status of being Baluch is a recognizable identity, particularly vis-à-vis other ethnic and cultural groups, Baluchistan, meaning "the land of the Baluch," has never represented one unified political whole. At the present time, Baluchistan is divided between Pakistan and Iran, with a small northern strip in Afghanistan. The area as a whole represents the eastward extension of the Iranian plateau and is bordered on the north by the Helmand Basin in Afghanistan, on the east by Sind and the Punjab (i.e. the Indus River valley), on the south by the Arabian Sea and the Gulf of Oman, and on the west by Kerman Province in Iran. The vastness of the area (134,000 square miles for Pakistani Baluchistan alone) is matched by a low population density, testifying to the generally un-enviable ecological nature of its terrain. The traditional economy of Baluchistan is consistent with the largely arid nature of the environment, being based on various combinations of nomadic pastoralism, date palm cultivation, dry-crop agriculture, raiding, and fishing along the coast. The area has never supported cities. Substantiating its status as a crossroads, numerous groups in history have traversed Baluchistan en route to more ecologically luxuriant and politically alluring points, the Indus in par-ticular. Among the more prominent peoples passing through, and some-times maintaining a precarious hold on various regions within Balu-chistan, have been the Macedonians, the Sassanid Persians, the Sindhi Brahmins, the Arabs, the Seljuk Turks, several Afghan dynasties, the Mongols, and the Tartars. The effects of these early incursions have much to do with who the Baluch are and how they came to be where they are.

The origins of the Baluch are certainly diverse, but speculations as to their ultimate origin generally postulate that they were initially inhabi-tants of areas west of their present location. Linguistic and other evidence suggests a western Persian origin (Dames 1904; Field 1959). By the eleventh century, the Baluch were to be found in Kerman, until the Seljuk Turks forced them eastward into Seistan (Persia) and Makran (southwest Pakistan). A further eastward movement was precipitated by the Mongols, and by the fifteenth century they had reached the furthest limits of their expansion in the provinces of Sind and Punjab. It was at this period that the Baluch came closest to being one political entity, under the aegis of their major culture hero, Mir Chakar Rind. Political organization during this epic period revolved around a flexible segmentary organization capable of massive processes of fission and fusion. Segmentary capa-bilities are still evident among the easternmost Baluch; while to the west, where the effects of the Baluch migrations passed off earlier, different forms of organization developed, including feudal orders and ethnic stratification.

Given Baluchistan's complex history, its geographical vastness, and the more recent complicating factors of colonialism and modern political boundaries, is there any sense in speaking of the Baluch as "a people"? As will be shown, the social identity of the Baluch has regional variations which correlate with differences in ecological adaptation and political organization. Nonetheless, there is a significant and shared cultural com-ponent to the status of the Baluch, based on certain social customs, dress, oral traditions, religious affiliation (Sunni Islam), etc. Linguistically, the Baluch are united as well, Baluchi being placed, like Persian and Kurdish, in the western branch of the Iranian language family. There is a significant dialect difference between "eastern" and "western" Baluchi, this being just one of the manifestations of a traditional separation of eastern and western Baluch by a corridor dominated by the Brahuis, speakers of a Dravidian tongue.

A comparative discussion of Baluch social organization can proceed with this briefly stated background in mind. Three recent documented cases will be outlined, with supplementary data from a fourth, also recent, account. More specific emphasis will be placed on a description of the differences between bilateral and agnatic emphases in kinship terminology and their respective interrelationships with other components of social organization.

Eastern Baluch: the Marri Baluch

The Marri Baluch are presently found in Sibi District in the northeastern corner of Pakistani Baluchistan. Traditionally tent dwellers, the Marris subsist on agriculture and the mixed herding of sheep and goats. The area has always lacked any important sedentary component. It was reported in the early part of this century that the territory supporting the Marris and their traditional enemies, the Bugti Baluch, measured over 7,000 square miles with only five villages. The town of Sibi, on the perimeter of this territory, was a creation of British occupation and was largely in-habited by a non-Baluch population (*Baluchistan District Gazetteer* 1907, vol. 3, pp. 37–38).

British colonial attempts at domination of the warlike Marris appear to have greatly influenced Marri political organization, and the effects have carried over into the Pakistani era since Partition. Nonetheless, the traditional status of the Marri tribe is still evident in its political structure today. The original concept of the Marri tribe (*tuman*) was that of a military and looting organization, with chiefs functioning as warrior leaders for raiding and for looting caravans (Pehrson 1966: 103). It was the military character of the Marri which allowed them to occupy the territory they now inhabit. Tribal councils and echelons of leaders served as a means of coordinating warrior leaders, although notions of contract and consent from below were also key components. While the colonial administration stimulated a freezing of positions of authority, the prin-ciple of contract between a leader and his followers continued to function. The formal charter of the Marris consists of "a merging series of sections with a congruent series of offices, occupied by a hierarchy of leaders of sections," and while recruitment is patrilineal, the "crucial principle" is still the political contract (Pehrson 1966: 17).

There are three main social strata among the Marri Baluch: a majority group of commoners, an upper elite of title-holders, and a lower, "des-pised," group of serfs and emancipated slaves. The lines separating this last category from the other two are clear-cut, but there is room for achievement criteria between the categories of elite and commoners

(Pehrson 1966: 29). The dynastic lineage of the *sardar* [tribal leader] is included in the elite group of nobles. Traditionally, the *sardar* headed the *jirga* [tribal council] made up of a hierarchy of sectional and subsectional tribal leaders. The *sardar* is described by Pehrson as "the central and unifying leader" who "by his existence creates the Marri tribe," and who holds "an exalted position of authority" (Pehrson 1966: 20). The "considerable wealth" of the *sardar* comes mainly from landed property and taxes from tribesmen. While succession to the post of *sardar* is patrilineal, more specifically it passes to the eldest son of "a mother of clean caste."

Agnation plays a key role in Marri social organization. Local groups (camps) are based on patrilineage, with rights to property being clearly agnatic. The differences between patrikin and matrikin are expressed metaphorically by the difference between milk and urine, the former constituting mother's side and emphasizing laterality; the latter being father's side with the emphasis on lineality. The only invariant framework of rights and duties is the patrilineage. As far as the organization of the tribe as a whole is concerned, it "can...be thought of as an enormous agnatic lineage," although its structure is based on named groups and not on one all-embracing genealogy (Pehrson 1966: 18).

Makran

Pakistani Makran (an area of 23,000 sq. miles), is situated in the southwestern area of Baluchistan, bordered on the west by Iranian Baluchistan and shares with it a seacoast on the Arabian Sea. It is separated from the territory of the Marris and other eastern Baluch by the aforementioned corridor of Brahuis. While fishing on the coast and dry-crop cultivation and pastoral nomadism in the interior are important subsistence activities, the political and social history of Makran has long been dominated by oasis centers which, through ancient forms of irrigation, have supported quite large populations based on date cultivation. Such population centers mark the area as very different from Marri territory, with resulting apparent differences in social organization.

A feudal structure predominates in Makran, based on the extraction of revenue and the operation of patron-client ties between three ascribed social strata: the *hakim*, the Baluch, and the *hizmatkar*. The *hakim* represent a traditional ruling elite of sedentary landlords; the Baluch consist of a broad middle layer of cultivators and pastoral nomads; and the *hizmatkar* include tenants and craftsmen (*nakibs*) and ex-slaves (*ghulam*). The *hizmatkar* and many of the sedentary Baluch are ethnically distinct due to a negroid strain. However, all three of the major social strata share many elements of Baluch culture, including the Baluchi language.

Each of these ideally endogamous units of social stratification constitutes a *kom*, a term with similar connotations among the Marris. In Makran, *kom* also applies to named Baluch tribes, each with its own agnatic charter. The *hakim* maintain pedigrees which include maternal links. While these pedigrees are important to the maintenance of the elite character of the *hakim*, particularly with regard to marriage alliances, genealogies play little role in Baluch organization. They do not generate corporate groups and have not played as important a role in social organization as economic interests, residence, and political factors. The latter reflect long periods of rather chaotic political history in Makran. Prior to and including a period of domination by the Brahui Khanate of Kalat in the eighteenth century, later supplemented by British control in the nineteenth, politics were marked by a continual jockeying for power in the major oasis centers by various factions primarily represented by the *hakim*. The fluidity which marked alliance formation during this long era is clearly marked in kinship organization. The economic and techno-logical aspects of irrigation agriculture were, and still are, also influential, with the same result of minimizing corporate kin activity in general and agnation in particular. The complexities of subsidizing the construction of irrigation channels and the subsequent allotment of water rights in-volved (and involve) individualized economic activities which do not rest upon the functioning of lineages or of other forms of corporate kin groups (Pastner and Pastner 1972).

Bilaterality is evident in both kinship organization and kinship termi-nology. Metaphorically, matrikin and patrikin are described respectively as *lap* [belly] and *posht* [back]. Rights and duties emanating from these kin categories generally apply at the farthest to common great-grand-parents, although there is often a good deal of ambiguity as to the nature and extent of obligations to either side. This is frequently expressed in the dilemma as to whether *hak* [obligation] or *marzi* [free choice] is in-volved in specific instances.

A cognatic emphasis in social organization is relevant not only to the sedentary, oasis-dwelling populace of Makran but to pastoral nomadic communities as well. Unlike Marri camps, which revolve around patri-lineages, Makrani camps are formed around cores of bilateral consan-guines. Bilateral ties provide one major means of access to pasturage as well as the source of personnel for the realignment of groups (Pastner 1971). A bilateral kinship terminology system is shared by oasis center and nomadic camp alike.

Western Baluch: the Yarahmadzai

The Yarahmadzai are one of four major tribes in the highland Sarhad region of northern Iranian Baluchistan. Unlike the situation in Makran and the southern sector of Iranian Baluchistan, feudal structures are absent and tribal structures predominate. Pastoral nomadism and raiding, as well as limited irrigation agriculture, make up the traditional economy of the Sarhad. Lineages are politically important to tribal structure, being invested with the functioning of blood vengeance and the payment of bloodwealth (Salzman 1971: 435). Shallow lineages form the core of pastoral nomadic camps, the prime units of residence in the Sarhad. Yarahmadzai political organization revolves around headmen of camps and a *sardar* [chief] of the tribe. However, the authority of the *sardar* appears to be nowhere as strong as that of the chief of the Marris. In describing the *sardar* of the "pre-Persian" period before 1935, when the central government began effective domination, Salzman indicates that his resources were "not especially great" and "his sanctions were limited" (Salzman 1971: 437).

Several things are consistent with the absence of a strong, centralized authority in the Yarahmadzai tribe. One was the lack of intratribal corporate conflict and the availability of resources outside the Sarhad territory, primarily obtained through raiding. Secondly, there was the absence of feudal structures and of the more "urbanized" settlements that accompany them. In fact, their territorial mobility within the Sarhad (facilitated by their nomadic economic base and political structure) made the Yarahmadzai "less vulnerable" to outside political control (Salzman 1971: 443). By the same token, they were "constrained" from expanding outside the Sarhad by the presence of neighboring tribes and of the feudalized khanates to the south (Salzman 1971: 436).

Rend, or the concept of patrilineal descent, applies to all levels of Yarahmadzai social and political organization, from the extended family to the lineage, the three major sections of the tribe, and the tribe as a whole. Corporateness exists on the level of the tribe, the section, and the lineage; sections and lineages are structurally equivalent (Salzman 1971: 435). As in Makran and the Marri area, there are also endogamous groups consisting of tribesmen, *luris* [gypsies], agriculturalists, and slaves, although in the Sarhad the nontribal groups are small in number and less important in terms of social organization than in Makran, especially, where they are crucial to a feudalized economy.

In spite of the political significance of patrilineality among the Yarahmadzai, especially in terms of recruitment functions, bilaterality is very evident and contrasts with the heavy agnatic bias in Marri kinship organization. The concept of the bilateral Ego-centered network (*kom*) plays an important role. So, for example, one's *kom* ties are sometimes identified before those of *rend* (Salzman 1972: 163). Finally, the symmetrical kinship terminology in the Sarhad is more consistent with the bilateral notion of *kom* than with the patrilineal one of *rend* (Salzman 1972: 203).

BALUCH KINSHIP TERMINOLOGY[1]

A long tradition of kinship studies in anthropology has demonstrated that the terminological component of kinship is in no simple way reflective of other aspects of social structure. Time and again it has been shown that the basic types of kin terminological system delineated by anthropologists correlate with different kinds of sociopolitical systems. Fried, for example, concludes that "kinship terminology has little or no diagnostic value as a criterion of egalitarian, rank or stratified organization" (1967: 121). In an earlier evolutionary discussion, Service (1964: 192) finds the relation between kinship terminology and society "complicated," since terminologies are not made up of systematically related parts and are differentially affected by other (nonkin) social statuses.

On the other hand, controlled comparisons on a regional basis and outside an evolutionary framework can be useful in the analysis of interrelationships between kinship (including its terminology) and other aspects of social organization. There are important differences in social organization between the three regions in Baluchistan described here. Some of these differences are more obvious than others. So, for example, a long tradition of extensive irrigation agriculture and accompanying feudal order in Makran is consistent with the use of aristocratic pedigrees and cognatic structures on most levels. Makran contrasts with the Marri and Yarahmadzai situations, which are dominated by pastoral nomadic traditions and tribal forms of social organization. The differences between the Marri Baluch and the Yarahmadzai are more subtle and derive, it is suggested, from important cultural-ecological factors.

Looking at a summary of the basic consanguineal terms for all three areas (Table 1), it is evident that each system emphasizes sex, generation, and collaterality, while the Marri system also emphasizes lineality. All three systems are typical of Middle Eastern kinship terminologies in the use of extension. The only primary terms are Fa, Mo, Br, Si, So, and Da; all other consanguineous terms can be used in an extended sense, particularly in lineal fashion (e.g. in the Makrani system *pirǝk* [FaFa] also labels FaFaFa and so on). The use of extension is also seen in the tags *-sag*, *-zad*, *-zak*, and *-zakht* [child of].

Apart from certain minor differences in dialect and usage, the Makrani and Yarahmadzai terms are essentially the same, bilaterality manifesting itself clearly in both cases. Marri terminology, on the other hand, is clearly agnatic. The terms for grandparents, uncles and aunts, and cousins make this evident. More importantly, in paralleling the social environment, the agnatic principle emerges most clearly in Ego's own generation, where politics and property are most relevant (Pehrson 1966: 49). While

[1] Kin terms for the Marri Baluch are derived from Pehrson (1966); those of the Yarahmadzai from Salzman (1972). Makrani terms were collected by the author.

Table 1. Baluch consanguineal kin terms

	Marri	Makran	Sarhad
Father	*pis*	*pes*	*pes*
Mother	*mas*	*mas*	*mas*
FaFa	*dada*	*pirək*	*pirək*
FaMo	*dadi*	*balək*	*balək*
MoFa	*nana*	*pirək*	*pirək*
MoMo	*nani*	*balək*	*balək*
FaBr	*babu* (*chacha*)	*nako*	*naku*
FaSi	*pupi*	*tru*	*tru*
MoBr	*mama*	*nako*	*naku*
MoSi	*masi*	*tru*	*tru*
Brother	*bras*	*bras*	*bras*
Sister	*gwar*	*gwar*	*gohar*
Son	*bač*	*bačok*	*zag*
Daughter	*janik*	*jenek*	*dotag*
Grandchild	*nawasagh*	*nemasag*	*noasag*
BrCh	*brazakht*	*brazak*	*brazad*
SiCh	*gwarzakht*	*gwarzak*	*goharzad*
FaBrCh	*nakozakht*	*nakozak*	*nakuzad*
MoBrCh	*trizakht* (*mamachuk*)	*nakozak*	*nakuzad*
FaSiCh	*trizakht* (*pupichuk*)	*truzak*	*truzad*
MoSiCh	*trizakht* (*masichuk*)	*truzak*	*truzad*
FaBrChCh	*parnakozakht* (*nakozakht*)	*nakozak* (*parnakozak*)	*rand*
MoBrChCh	*waldein trizakht*	*nakozak* (*parnakozak*)	*rand*
Fa SiChCh	*waldein trizakht*	*truzakezak*	*balukzad*
MoSiChCh	*waldein trizakht*	*truzakezak*	*balukzad*

it should be noted that all the Marri collateral terms in the first ascending generation reflect heavy linguistic borrowing from Sindhi, Punjabi, and Brahui, the more significant point is that MoBr and FaBr are differentiated, which is not the case in Makran and the Sarhad. In addition, Marri cousin terms are descriptive, with FaBr children clearly distinguished from the politically less important MoSi children and from cross-cousins. Makrani and Yarahmadzai parallel and cross-cousin terms are also descriptive but reflect only the difference in the sex of the kin link, not whether the relationship is patrilateral or matrilateral.

Marriage patterns in all three instances are consistent with differences in cousin terminology. The Yarahmadzai depend on preferential bilateral kin endogamy, as do the Makranis; although, in the latter case, among the sedentary population, there is a wide gulf between this stated cultural ideal and actual marriage statistics, which indicate that the rate of endogamy is actually quite low (Pastner and Pastner 1972). The Marris, on the other hand, maintain a preference for FaBrDa marriage, the classical form of Islamic endogamy; and the actual rates of such marriages, as well as those with other agnates, are very high (Pehrson 1966: 57). The connection between marriage forms and cousin terminologies in all three cases is clear-cut.

A comparison of affinal terminologies is somewhat less revealing for

our purposes here (see Table 2), although the Marri terms for MoBrWi
and FaBrWi indicate an agnatic bias not present in the other two systems.
The absence of Marri terms for FaSiHu and MoSiHu can be attributed
to the facts of patrivirilocality (see Pehrson 1966: 49).

Table 2. Baluch affinal kin terms

	Marri	Makran	Sarhad
Wife	*zal*	*janen*	*jan (halk)*
Husband	*halk*	*mard*	*mard*
WiFa/HuFa	*waserk*	*nako*	*waserk*
WiMo/HuMo	*wasu*	*tru (wasu)*	*wasi*
BrWi	*nišar*	*nešar*	*nešar*
SiHu	*zamat*	*zamas*	*zamas*
WiBr	*wasirzakht*	*waserk*	*waserk*
WiSi	*doškiš*	*duskinč*	*dozkeč*
HuBr	*wasirk*	*waserk*	*waserk*
HuSi	*doškiš*	*duskič*	*dozkeč*
FaBrWi	*čači*	*tru*	*nešar*
MoBrWi	*mami*	*tru*	*nešar*
FaSiHu	—	*nako*	*zamas*
MoSiHu	—	*zamas (nako)*	*zamas*

Finally, while Pehrson's account does not set out address terms in
systematic fashion, it should also be pointed out that both Makrani and
Yarahmadzai address terms are also bilateral.

ANALYSIS AND CONCLUSION

The political independence of the Marri Baluch and the Yarahmadzai
Baluch, both pastoral nomadic tribes, contrasts with the situation in
Makran, where political centralization dominated by feudalism and irrigated agriculture has long played a key role, if at times a precarious one.
The Makrani situation is analogous in many respects to that in neighboring southern Iranian Baluchistan as described by Spooner. In that
area "where political leadership relies on an income from settled agriculture, there is a definite social differentiation into classes and cognatic
values are given to kin relationships" (Spooner 1969: 139). Pastoral
nomadic tribal groups which ordinarily rely on agnation come to develop
cognatic organization if they have traditional relations with a *hakim*, or
leader, from an irrigated settled community (Spooner 1969: 142). The
major difference between tribal and feudal organization here rests on the
reckoning of descent, since kinship terminology is shared by all Baluchi
speakers in the area, feudal and tribal alike. The terminology appears to
share the same principal features as that found in Makran and the Sarhad:
it "distinguishes only between cousins born of aunts and cousins born of

uncles [*sic*], and makes no distinction at all between patrilateral and matri-lateral relatives" (Spooner 1969: 141). Pedigrees serve as important adjuncts to the legitimization of feudal leaders. Ultimately, Spooner suggests, the differences between cognatic and agnatic orientations and political organization rest on cultural-ecological factors.

Salzman's analysis (1971) of the difference between the Sarhad and Spooner's area is also ecologically minded. He concludes that the lack of irrigated agriculture in the Sarhad, partly due to environmental reasons, prevented the development of a resource base for the feudal type of political leadership and class structure found southward (and to the east in Makran).

Nonetheless, it should not be concluded that the Yarahmadzai have always been totally isolated from the influence of feudal powers. It seems that the Yarahmadzai migrated to the Sarhad relatively recently, tradition being that they came from the Pakistani side (then the khanate of Kalat) in the late eighteenth and early nineteenth centuries, although how far to the east they had been is unknown (Salzman 1972: 210). There is archae-ological evidence of more agricultural, irrigated settlements in the Sarhad, which are believed to have been the resources of more "highly organized" groups to the north in Sistan (Salzman 1971: 443). Date groves in the Mashkel region of the Sarhad were suggested (by late nineteenth-century writers) to have belonged at that time to other groups, including Panj-guris (Makranis) and Kharanis (from north of Makran). There was a good deal of activity and movement back and forth between Persia and the western fringe of the khanate of Kalat throughout the nineteenth and early twentieth centuries. British intelligence reports are dominated by the problem of the border, generated in part by "disturbance and anarchy" among the Persian Baluch desirous of "throwing off the Persian yoke" (Saldanha 1905). Included in Makrani politics of the late nineteenth century were attempts at alliance formation with Persian Baluch by aspiring leaders (Saldanha 1905). Meanwhile, the British were attempting to offset Persian claims to the frontier in hopes of stabilizing the situation between Afghanistan and the British Indian Empire. A special boundary com-mission was established for this purpose in the 1870's. Nonetheless, prob-lems continued. During World War I, British reports are replete with accounts of raiding across the border from the Persian side, instigated, it was believed, by German agents (*Administration reports of the Balu-chistan agency* 1916). A British general was despatched to the Sarhad in order to put a stop to this infiltration. In the late 1920's and early 1930's, political refugees from Persian Baluchistan continued to cross the fron-tier, many, in fact, settling in Makran while en route to points farther east *Administration reports of the Baluchistan agency* 1934). During this same period, attempts to end slavery in the khanate of Kalat were hampered by the instability of the border and the continued smuggling of slaves from Makran to the Persian side (*Administration reports of the Baluchistan agency* 1928).

These brief examples of contact between the Persian and Pakistani (then British) halves of Baluchistan, as well as the sharing of many elements which make up the cultural identity of the Baluch, attest to the fact that modern-day political boundaries can serve to mask situations which are not as frozen as they might at first appear. In spite of a relatively (viz. continued smuggling) closed border today, geographical proximity alone would certainly suggest greater continuity between Persian Baluchistan and western Pakistani Baluchistan than between either of these and the Marri and other Baluch groups separated by the Brahui corridor.

The Yarahmadzai, while traditionally politically independent and reliant on the office of chief, have neither expanded beyond the Sarhad nor absorbed non-Baluch into their tribe. Barth (1969) described how eastern Baluch (such as the Marris) have continually absorbed new members and encroached on other territories, including those of neighboring Pathans. Their effective hierarchical and centralized political structure has made this possible. The Marris retained their independence, even in the face of British intervention, through their superior strength. The Yarahmadzai retained their independence until relatively recently by attempting to keep themselves apart from feudal powers (Spooner 1969: 151). The differences in political structure between the two tribes reflect the difference between the two means of maintaining independence, the Yarahmadzai exhibiting a far less autocratic and centralized type of leadership.

Differences in the locations of the two tribes are significant. The Marris inhabit a highland territory on the very edge of the Indus River valley, and perhaps their form of political organization represents a necessary adaptation to the fact of long proximity to powerful lowland-based systems, from the Moghuls to the Pakistanis. The traditional warfare between the Marris and neighboring Baluch tribes (such as the Bugtis) would also have served to reinforce the development of strong forms of leadership (in fact, the Bugtis themselves are even more tightly organized than the Marris). The Yarahmadzai, on the other hand, originally refugees from the khanate of Kalat, were not engaged in continuous conflict with other groups in the Sarhad. Salzman (1971: 436) indicates that rivalry between tribes was more often over prestige than over scarce resources. At the same time, the Yarahmadzai were constrained from expansion by the presence of other tribes and by feudal groups surrounding the Sarhad.

Bilaterality in the Sarhad might be a recent response to a decline in political power, and hence in the importance of lineages, since pacification by the Persian government in this century (Salzman 1972: 189). There are two other possible explanations which are neither mutually exclusive nor contradictory to the above suggestion but which indicate greater historical depth and continuity with other western Baluch groups. One is that bilateral terminology, a cultural accretion, reflects long-term exposure to feudal communities which surround the Sarhad and perhaps surrounded the Yarahmadzai prior to their migration to the Sarhad. Second, the terminology may reflect the importance of bilateral forms of alliance. Salzman notes (1972: 189) that the Yarahmadzai practice of preferential (as opposed to prescriptive) bilateral endogamy provides structural flexibility by serving either to coalesce near groups or to permit alliances with distant groups.

Such a bilateral emphasis need not detract, however, from the importance of the ideology of agnatic descent as the primary means of political recruitment. In fact, such a use of descent is what characterizes the Yarahmadzai as a tribal organization, in contrast to the use of descent in the form of pedigrees among feudal leaders in Makran and southern Persian Baluchistan. In the former case, descent serves as a means of political integration; in the latter, it serves to legitimize political authority.

Kinship itself relates particularly to the makeup of local and domestic groups and their social and economic needs. But kinship also articulates with other components of social organization; varying uses of the concept of descent represent an important mechanism of such articulation in Baluchistan and in many other areas. In conclusion, it is evident that there is no easy formulation of the relationship between kinship terminology, political organization, and cultural-ecological factors, even where it is possible to control partially for some cultural and historical elements. There are also a number of other considerations (for which much of the data is as yet nonexistent) which might have been introduced into this discussion. The historical question itself is unresolved, since the complexity marking the movement of groups throughout Baluchistan will perhaps never be fully unraveled. Nonetheless, we can conclude that kinship terminology in Baluchistan is related to the mosaic quality of social organization reflected in the various ways in which tribal-pastoral-nomadic and feudal-agricultural communities interact in specific regions. It is also evident that the traditional separation of western and eastern Baluch by the Brahuis affects terminology to the extent that western Baluch, feudal and tribal communities alike, share the same principles of kinship terminology.

REFERENCES

Administration reports of the Baluchistan agency
   1916 *Administration reports of the Baluchistan agency, 1915–1916, Calcutta.*
   1928 *Administration reports of the Baluchistan agency, 1926–1927, Calcutta.*
   1934 *Administration reports of the Baluchistan agency, 1932–1933, New Delhi.*

BACON, ELIZABETH
1958   *Obok*. Viking Fund Publications in Anthropology 25. Boston: Little, Brown.
Baluchistan District Gazetteer
1907   *Baluchistan District Gazetteer*, volume three: *Sibi*. Bombay.
BARTH, FREDRIK
1953   *Principles of social organization in southern Kurdistan*. Oslo.
BARTH, FREDRIK, editor
1969   "Pathan identity and its maintenance," in *Ethnic groups and boundaries*. Viking Fund Publications in Anthropology 43. Boston: Little, Brown.
COON, C. S.
1951   *Caravan: the story of the Middle East*. New York.
DAMES, M. LONGWORTH
1904   *The Baloch race: a historical and ethnological sketch*. London: Royal Asiatic Society.
FIELD, HENRY
1959   *An anthropological reconnaissance in West Pakistan*. Cambridge, Mass.: Harvard University Press.
FRIED, MORTON
1967   *The evolution of political society*. New York.
MURPHY, ROBERT, LEONARD KASDEN
1967   Agnation and endogamy: some further considerations. *Southwestern Journal of Anthropology* 23: 1–14.
PASTNER, STEPHEN
1971   Ideological aspects of nomad-sedentary contact: a case from southern Baluchistan. *Anthropological Quarterly* 44 (3).
PASTNER, STEPHEN, CARROLL M. PASTNER
1972   Agriculture, kinship, and politics in southern Baluchistan. *Man* 7 (1).
PATAI, RAFAEL
1962   *Golden river to golden road: society, culture and change in the Middle East*. Philadelphia: University of Pennsylvania Press.
1965   The structure of endogamous unilineal descent. *Southwestern Journal of Anthropology* 21: 325–350.
PEHRSON, ROBERT
1966   "The social organization of the Marri Baluch," in *Ethnic groups and boundaries*. Edited by Fredrik Barth. Viking Fund Publications in Anthropology 43. Boston: Little, Brown.
PETERS, E. L.
1967   Some structural aspects of the feud among the camel-herding Bedouin of Cyrenaica. *Africa* 37 (3).
SALDANHA, J. A.
1905   *Précis of Makran affairs*. Calcutta.
SALZMAN, PHILIP C.
1971   Adaptation and political organization in Iranian Baluchistan. *Ethnology* 10 (4).
1972   "Adaptation and change among the Yarahmadzai Baluch." Unpublished Ph.D. dissertation, University of Chicago.
SERVICE, ELMAN R.
1964   *Primitive social organization*. New York.
SPOONER, BRIAN
1969   Politics, kinship, and ecology in southeast Persia. *Ethnology* 8 (2).

The Promotion of Suzerainty Between Sedentary and Nomadic Populations in Eastern Ethiopia

WOLFGANG WEISSLEDER

In the east-central regions of Ethiopia, geography underscores the distinction between sedentary agricultural and nomadic pastoral modes of life. There, the cool high plateaus and mountains of the Abyssinian highlands, homeland of the agrarian Amhara, drop sharply to the sere and arid deserts of the Great Rift Valley, grazing grounds of the Adal pastoralists. (The Adal ought properly to be called "Afar," but in the Ankober region they are always called "Adal.") The region's cultural and polit_ical boundaries obey geographical and climatic imperatives, which have virtually separated disparate populations and kept interactions to an intermittent and sporadic minimum. The specific area to be discussed, now a part of Ankober *woreda* [district] of Shewa *teklay qezat* [province], once belonged to the kingdom of Ifat. It conclusively became a part of the Ethiopian Empire during the last two decades of the nineteenth century, in particular through the ejection of Egyptian occupation forces and the conquest of the city of Harar during the reign of Emperor Menelik II. The land beyond the city, Hararge province, remained largely unpenetrated by Amhara settlement and administration. The primary reason was the nature of the country itself, an uncompromising desert totally unsuited to the type of agriculture which is the Amhara's primary economic activity. It was an environment that could not be transformed by the technologies then available.

Purposeful interest on the part of the central government had to await a redefinition of "suitability" and could hardly be contemplated until advanced technologies presented new options and avenues for action. Once such options began to appear practicable, urgency was lent to schemes for making virgin desert lands productive; for instance, through

Information upon which this paper is based was gathered in 1963 during a field study in Ankober district of Shewa province under the sponsorship of the Foreign Area Training Fellowships (Ford Foundation).

the introduction of commercial and industrial crops, especially sugar and cotton. The control and exploitation of the Awash River water resources was a precondition for any development. It involved large-scale power, irrigation-reclamation, transportation, and settlement projects. At the time when material for this paper was gathered, most of the measures and programs, generically known as the Tendaho Project, were in various stages of planning and discussion; several have since been initiated and some have been completed.

Drastic effects upon preexisting local cultures were foreseen by the government, and preliminary steps were taken to facilitate the transition and to avoid unnecessary harshness and abruptness in the inevitable confrontations. Although the underlying problems may have been primarily of an economic, social, and cultural nature, regulatory measures had, of necessity, to assume political form.

The intricacies inherent in the greatly increased interaction between the relatively distant, and predominantly Amharic, central government and the nomadic Adal populations present intriguing parallels with the conditions and situations which Owen Lattimore (1962) described for the inner-Asian frontiers of China. The parallels apply no less to the statement of problems than to governmental measures deliberately employed and to the resultant sociopolitical situations which rapidly evolved into at least temporary solutions. For once, both inner-Asian and inner-Ethiopian societies can pause and look back upon almost endless sequences of frontier friction and upon the hostility of centuries. In both instances, the difficulties were caused as much by cultural incompatibility as by any other factor.

The diametrically opposed religious affiliations and commitments of the Christian Amhara and the Muslim Adal produced and aggravated conflicts in their interaction. The mutual distrust between Amhara and Adal is firmly founded in and reinforced by remembered reality. During their long and often painful history, both peoples engaged in endemic raids and wars, with ever-fluctuating success. But behind the historical events and their traditional consequences, nurtured and elaborated by the militant spirit of Adal and Amhara alike, is something more fundamental: the abiding aversion which pastoral nomads and sedentary farmers reserve for each other. This aversion reaches beyond rational and practical considerations into the realm of visceral attitudes and values, permitting little maneuvering room for social or political accommodation. As Professor Lattimore has phrased it, nothing can compensate in Chinese eyes for the "wickedness of being nomads," in which their Mongol neighbors persist (1962: 415). And as Lattimore states elsewhere, "All policies toward the Mongols. . .appear to start from a common premise: that something must be done about the nomadism of the Mongols. If, in other words, the Mongols can only be cured of being Mongols, all will be well..." (1962: 415). Indeed, "an entirely artificial line was drawn between 'civilized' agriculture and 'primitive' pastoral economy, dependent on livestock" (1962: 417). As far as the sedentary farmer is concerned, be he peasant or lord, there is "a kind of social crime" (1962: 417) associated with being a nomad, a disparagement of the nomadic way of life, balanced, it seems, to me, only by the nomad's own profound distaste and contempt for all those who commit agriculture.

Although the Adal are nominally and in fact subjects of the Ethiopian Empire, their way of life is largely a mystery to their Amhara neighbors, who generally regard them with fear, incomprehension, and aversion. Few actual facts are available to the Amhara beyond their awareness of the Adals' nomadism and of scattered customs which are usually not understood in context. Opportunities for developing better insight are not plentiful. Toward the end of the rainy season in the highlands, when the runoff in the lower reaches of the Awash tributaries gradually diminishes, the Adal migrate from pasturelands near the banks of the Awash into the foothills of the Abyssinian Escarpment in pursuit of the receding water, to supply themselves and their herds. Only then can the two groups acquire impressions of each other, for only then do contacts between nomads and sedentary farmers normally occur. Traditionally, this has taken place at markets, such as the one held every Friday in the large village of Aliu Amba and in several smaller locations.

Even on such occasions, both parties have tended to keep contacts to a minimum. The Amhara, thus, have had few opportunities to correct their image of the Adal, and the Adal have lacked opportunity and any sense of urgency about adjusting their view of the Amhara.

It might be conjectured that a third distinct population inhabiting the contact region between Amhara and Adal could fill the role of go-between for the two intransigently juxtaposed cultures. Interposed in the mid-altitudes live the "Argobba," as they are called by the Amhara. (Precisely applied, the term should designate a linguistic grouping not all of whose representatives live in the Ankober region. Although in this particular setting the language is said to be on the wane, the name continues to be applied to the population itself.) The Argobba are Muslim, like the Adal, and sedentary farmers, like the Amhara. This overlapping would seem to make the Argobba ideally suited to assume the role of brokers between the disparate cultures. Nothing, however, could be farther from the fact. The Amhara no less than the Adal tend to focus on the "negative" characteristics of Argobba culture, rather than on the potential which it might have for bridging the gap between the two groups. The Adal look down upon the Argobba, their fellow Muslims, because they are farmers; the Amhara distrust and dislike the Argobba, their fellow farmers, because they are Muslims. A doubling of culture contrasts results, which rules out the Argobba as potential mediators.

Rather than relying on intermediacy to provide a linkage through typological gradation, the Ethiopian central government evidently saw greater promise in and found that better results could be obtained by drawing the two extremes of the confrontation into a dyad for productive interaction. As has often happened in the distant and recent past, extremes that might appear logically incompatible can be brought into cooperation, while subtler and more nuanced cultural differences defy bridging.

The government, in fact, used expedients which made the separation of populations even more explicit, thereby creating the basis for a new synthesis. First, existing political boundaries were redrawn in such a way that traditional Adal lands were less directly administered by Amhara officials. Second, market patterns were so reoriented as to minimize the need for large-scale Amhara, Argobba, and Adal intercontact. Most important, however, were new measures which relied on a factor common to the Amhara and the Adal worldviews, the belief that events are moved by great men. The major thrust of change was placed in the hands of known and esteemed individuals and was entrusted to the realm of particularistic relationships. Interpersonal dealings at the leadership level were given preference over bureaucratic procedures. It was at this level, then, that interaction was increased to the same extent that population contacts were restricted. The process manifested itself in two ways, employing the traditions of both groups to effect change. First, an Adal "officialdom" was created by imperial fiat and appointment, relying on established leadership patterns. Second, the central government chose to represent itself in the newly formed political subunit through a commanding personality, who fulfilled the Amhara and Adal images of what a leader ought to be.

THE REDRAWING OF POLITICAL BOUNDARIES

One of the initial steps marking the new policy of fuller integration of the vast and always peripheral Awash River region into the centralized political and economic structure of Ethiopia was wholly under government control and could be accomplished without participation by local populations: political boundaries within the subprovincial district of Ankober could readily be readjusted. Ankober *woreda* [district] had originally been divided into five subdistricts (*mikitl woreda*), some of which extended from the Amhara highlands through the mid-altitudes and the desert lowlands to the west bank of the Awash River. Much of the lowland region, home for almost the entire Adal population of Ankober *woreda*, was combined into a sixth *mikitl woreda*. A new settlement and a new *mikitl woreda* capital were established in 1958 at a place called Duletcha, overlooking a ford across the Gatchane River, a tributary of the Awash which provides a reliable year-round supply of water. Five years after its beginnings, the settlement consisted of very few structures, only one of which – the Public Health Clinic – could be called substantial and permanent.

The forces of government are locally represented by the *mikitl woreda gezhe* [subdistrict governor], about whose personality and function more will be said later. The *gezhe* has one lieutenant, who also acts as his secretary. Among the government's salaried staff are a *hakim*, a mission-trained medical orderly who operates the clinic, and ten armed men (eight Amhara and two Muslim) whose official title is "game warden" and who at the same time constitute the local militia (*netch labash* [the white-clad ones]).

Apart from the clinic, there are hardly any consolidating institutions. Even taxes must officially be paid at the *woreda* capital in the highlands. The clinic was established at least partly in the hope that medical services would attract the shy Adal and would help to gain their confidence. The investment is only now starting to pay off. The Adal are beginning to bring in their sick, though hesitantly and only in desperate cases.

There is no Christian church at Duletcha; the Ethiopian Orthodox Church has no representation there, although substantial portions of the land and the people have been assigned *semon* [church tax obligations]. Most of the Muslims' hereditary land-holdings and Adal pasturelands are taxed about equally on behalf of Church and State.

Only the market which was assigned to Duletcha operates to bring Amhara, Adal, and Argobba into purposeful, regular, and controlled interaction. It attracts the Adal, since its location and isolation benefit their purposes more than the older market at Aliu Amba did. Besides, it can serve them throughout the year, while Aliu Amba was convenient only at the height of the dry season. However, the government's aims are also served; not only does the market regulate contacts with the nomadic Adal, but the time dimension of control is extended significantly.

When data were collected, Duletcha's permanent population was nearly one hundred, reckoning all the men and their wives and children. Ten of the inhabitants were Adal who had accepted a more or less seden-tary life, acting as traders and taking merchandise into the far reaches of Adal territory. About sixty Argobba dealt in grain, coffee, or cloth. The Amhara numbered no more than thirty. The *gezhe* himself maintained a small household there.

The entire population is undergoing adaptive change through separa-tion from its previous socioeconomic practices. All are beginning to look on trade as their main activity and as the foundation of their community rationale, though they were previously herders, farmers, or weavers. The young community already shows signs of acting in a spirit of separate identity, asserting and pursuing its special interests against "outsiders" of all kinds under the forceful and aggressive leadership of its own *gezhe*. Not surprisingly, these rudiments of community organization are showing signs of developing into the societal model which Owen Lattimore recognized in the inner-Asian setting:

In the mingling that takes place on such a frontier there is a tendency toward the formation of a frontier people, having not only identifiable geographic location, but also recognizable political characteristics, different from the two adjoining "standard" peoples. These peculiarities are registered in our vocabulary as "Borderers," "Marchmen," and "Grenzleute," echoing the fact that historically the political loyalties of frontier populations have on occasion been of decisive importance (Lattimore 1962: 166).

This point will be elaborated when I deal with factors which make for cohesion and a measure of stability along a traditionally unruly and militant frontier.

THE REORIENTATION OF MARKET PATTERNS

To understand the importance which the new market location at Duletcha holds for the Adal, the nature of the earlier market system must be understood. While a few minor trading locations had existed in the lowland areas for as long as memory can recall, the only significant trading and market location was at the large, permanent settlement at Aliu Amba.

The place and its market have a long history. Sixteenth-century travelers mentioned it, though not by its present name. It is probably identical with a place in that general region which is said to have existed in the twelfth century. Aliu Amba is situated on a bluff about one third of the distance and one third of the altitude that separates the edge of the Abyssinian highlands from the banks of the Awash River. The village, largely inhabited by Muslim Argobba farmers, lies close to the limits of arable land. Eastward lie the pasturelands of the Adal. Farther to the east, vegetation grows ever sparser, ending in the arid wastes of the Danakil Depression. Until the end of the nineteenth century, Aliu Amba was the western terminus of caravan routes from the seaports of Tadjoura (Djibouti) and Zeila and the eastern terminus of slave-trading routes which started in Wollega and Kaffa, traditional reservoirs of slaves for the Arabian trade. It was famous as one of the great inland ports of Africa, where commodities imported from Arabia, India, and China were reloaded from camels onto donkeys and mules for transshipment to the interior; the slaves had to continue on foot to their coastal destinations. Following Emperor Menelik II's abandonment of Ankober as his capital, and with the gradual suppression and attrition of the slave trade, both commercial routes fell into disuse. Aliu Amba turned into a market of only regional importance.

In its new role, the market at Aliu Amba assumed a very different significance. Prior to its decline, it had been a contact point between the Amharic rulers of the highlands and the strong and powerful rulers of the kingdom of Ifat. It marked a quasi-international boundary and developed a frontier population in its own right. The Adal, by controlling the long and dangerous access routes from the East, could participate from a position of strength. In the new setting, on the other hand, with the regionalization of the Aliu Amba market, the Adal became peripheral participants, their status now determined by their economic role alone. Aliu Amba became a market of farmers and remains a market of farmers to this day. Highland farmers, all of them Amhara, bring wheat, barley, peas, and *gesho* [a shrub used as flavoring in beer]. Amhara, as well as Argobba, trade several kinds of millet, peppers, tomatoes, bananas, honey, eggs, and so forth. Many Argobba and a few Christian weavers sell cotton cloth that is widely famed and in great demand. Aliu Amba is a major center for buying and selling *t'eff* (*Eragrostis teff*), the cereal preferred by great numbers of Ethiopians and always in demand. Craftsmen sell pottery, ironware, and leather goods and buy hides for tanning and resale. Outside traders "import" manufactured goods and specialties such as bulk-spun cotton, machine-woven cloth, ready-made garments, rubber and canvas shoes, flashlights and batteries, Coca-Cola, plastic hats, etc. The Adal contribute a highly prized and high-priced commodity, longhorn cattle, which the Amhara hold in high regard as a source of meat. (The Amhara farmer prefers to keep bovine animals in pairs, mainly for plowing.) The Adal also bring to market their sole manufactured product, ropage made from the fibers of desert plants. They occasionally bring hippopotamus hide, from which whips and shields are made.

In the past, the Adal attended the Aliu Amba market mainly as a matter of necessity. They knew themselves to be barely tolerated there and were ill at ease. They were therefore the first to welcome the realignment of market patterns that followed upon the restructuring of political boundaries and the establishment of the settlement at Duletcha. Not only was the new location nearer their main migration grounds, but contacts with other populations were more or less within their own control. At the same time, the new market was once more, as in the historic past, in the boundary territories where the influence of their own leadership could be trusted to be more effective.

The switch to Duletcha, welcome as it was, was not left entirely up to the Adal themselves, The newly appointed *gezhe* let it be known immediately upon the founding of the new *mikitl woreda* capital that he expected all Adal to come to its market in the future. There was to be no market at Meteclea, one of the traditional outlying minor markets; and to reinforce his edict, the Duletcha market was set for Tuesday, the day which had always belonged to Meteclea. The *gezhe* urged his people to go to Aliu Amba only as buyers and only as long as Duletcha lacked permanent stores (because of the Adal's almost negligible consumption needs) and remained too far off the beaten track for professional traders. The *gezhe* "forbade" the Adal to sell their cattle and rope at Aliu Amba and required that all transactions take place at Duletcha. Most of the Adal keep faith with him, for only a few are seen nowadays at the Aliu Amba market; this is remarkable in view of the fact that their cattle would fetch a better price there, as the distance to the highlands is only half that to Duletcha.

The Duletcha market, however, offers one major incentive. There, neither buyer nor seller pays the market fee which he would be required to pay at the older established markets in the *woreda*. This is a significant concession which the *gezhe* extracted from the higher authorities in furtherance of their policy of administrative penetration. The Adal leadership was naturally happy with the new arrangement, and the fact that several individuals in the Amhara hierarchy were less so only strengthened the position of the *gezhe* who, though an Amhara, could show himself protector of the Adal and guarantor of their interests and safety. At the same time, the older balance was at least partially restored. Amhara and Adal leaders again deal with each other in a situation of virtual equity, if not equality, along a more or less defined frontier.

THE CREATION OF AN ADAL OFFICIALDOM

Some of the processes by which the Ethiopian government instituted new authority in the Adal territories are reminiscent of those which Lattimore describes for the Chinese-Mongolian paradigm:

The character of the new authority seems to be directly related to the function of the chief as representative of his tribe, recognised by the Chinese in order to provide institutions and conventions for the coexistence of the Chinese community and the tribal communities. The fact that the Chinese make him their go-between reinforces the power of the chief over his own people (Lattimore 1962: 476).

As a first step, traditional leaders of the Adal, such as sheikhs or lineage heads, were given Amhara titles (some of which carry small incomes), thereby confirming and reinforcing their seignorial position among their own people. In the records, the title conferred is usually *balabat*, which designates a landlord among the Amhara. As a mark of office, the Emperor granted these officials a black cloak (the *kaba*), a white shirt, and white trousers, a garb which, as the Amhara point out, "makes them easy to confuse with Ethiopian priests." It also obliged them to wear "proper" clothes when their duties took them to the courts, offices, and markets of Amhara villages. Upon the Adal *balabat* devolve many obligations which the *melkenya* [lord] discharges among the Amhara. He is primarily a judge and at times also a tax collector; generally speaking, he acts as the responsible spokesman for his people in all dealings with the government, be it at subdistrict, district, or subprovincial level. At tax time, for instance, each Adal cattle owner is expected to pay his assessment at the *woreda* capital, Gorebela, in person. Often, however, the *balabat* collects taxes from individual family heads, which he remits in their stead. In turn, governmental power in the person of the local *gezhe* [governor] will assert itself over the Adal solely through the person of the *balabat*. Being the sole point of contact with the ruling Amhara adds to the *balabat*'s stature, importance, and usefulness among his own people, while shielding them from unnecessary involvement with highlanders, whom they view with apprehension.

The confirmation and even enhancement of status which the Adal *balabat* gains entails certain obligations toward the government and its local functionaries, obligations which can be interpreted as restrictions on traditional degrees of freedom. Their newly acquired responsibilities require the leading men of the Adal to be available to the government whenever the necessity arises. Thus, every *balabat* is obliged to report to the local *mikitl woreda gezhe* [subdistrict governor] all changes of location of his group, so that he himself, at least, may be easily found.

Actually, this requirement need not amount to a major imposition and does not even run totally counter to the conventions and practices of Adal culture. The migration patterns of many Adal subgroups come close to what should be called transhumance rather than pure nomadism, i.e. a patterned movement among several regularly visited locations, at least one of which either is permanently occupied by some part of the population or is improved by some structure – a house, a corral, a storage bin, or the like. Encampments established during seasonal migrations are often no more than lean-tos of brush and grass, while the group has a more permanent homestead elsewhere with fairly large beehive or oval habitations, surrounded by thorn-and-brush fences. Often, only the younger people go on seasonal migrations, taking the valuable camels and cattle to higher pastures, while sheep and goats are left behind in the care of the older folk. In this sense, the obligation of maintaining a fixed and defined habitation is not of itself innovative or unusual; neither does it automatically carry with it the onus of enforced sedentariness that would run counter to Adal cultural sensibilities. Even the relatively permanent homestead is subject to being picked up and carried to a new location, in which case the subdistrict governor is, of course, to be informed. Were this not done, "he would think the people have something to hide." Mobility is in no way rigidly curtailed, and even if "strict" nomadism, to the extent that it ever existed, were to be modified, the basic mode of Adal life remains definitely pastoral.

In practice, the traditionally established powers of Adal leaders over their communities remain essentially untouched by the duties they have to discharge to the central government so long as (a) they do not contravene central government policy as it expands into the region; (b) tax obligations are fulfilled; and (c) the security and political tranquility of the region are assured. The traditional power of the leaders may in fact be increased or restored compared with the situation in the recent past, before the creation of the largely Adal-inhabited subdistrict of Duletcha.

The aspects of security and political tranquility include measures for the control of major crime, especially murder, which tended to be associated with widespread feuding within and between Adal groups and also with non-Adal peoples. Murder, and particularly murder involving trophy-hunting, is rigorously investigated and punished by the Amhara authorities, curiously without normally becoming a major cause of friction and unrest between them and the Adal. The Adal have, of course, always possessed customary laws for the redress of all sorts of grievances, but it now appears that they tend to submit the settlement of some of their most serious internal conflicts to the coercive apparatus provided by the Amhara outsiders, so long as the latter also assume responsibility for the harshness of the retribution. When specific cases are brought to their attention, the police and the government courts are often successful because the Adal show an awareness that their own best interest is served when the culprit is handed over to the nonkin authority. There is a tendency to direct to the "government" those situations which, according to tradition and experience, would be likely to proliferate into protracted internal hostility and feuding. Lesser matters are solved through the mechanisms of traditional Adal law.

In one specific instance, a *balabat* was placed in the dilemma of having either to shield a man who had killed a member of their lineage or to hand him over to the police. Uncertain of his *balabat*'s decision, the murderer fled and tried to find refuge with another group. The culprit's own group, which was also the victim's group, had at first been reluctant to seek direct retribution but now felt free to accuse and denounce the sheltering group. The latter's *balabat* was also in a dilemma, for he would have to either call in the police or assume the consequences of a conflict with the offender's people, who, of course, relished his position. In this instance, the murderer's own kin finally broke the impasse, urging that he should be given up to the authorities. It is revealing that the primarily involved group took no action until the offender felt constrained to leave. Then they even menaced those who gave him shelter and did not object to having him apprehended by the police. If they were reluctant at first, it was evidently not from loyalty to a fellow member of the group but from fear of internal dissension and its consequences. Once the offender moved outside his immediate community, he was a fair victim of the more abstract and neutral government police force. His ultimate fate could then be blamed on alien institutions, beyond the reach of the feuding mechanisms and outside their system of imperatives.

From the standpoint of traditional Adal leadership, the new power constellation would appear to offer additional modalities for the settlement of grievances, by permitting transfer of critical, troublesome cases into the hands of forces whose detachment need not, and could not, be interpreted in terms of conflicting kin loyalties. Two essentially discrete political communities are thereby placed side by side. The traditional leadership of the Adal forms the connecting link, in quite the sense in which Owen Lattimore (1962) speaks of the role of Mongolian princes and members of the nobility, who acted as "wardens of the marches" on behalf of the Chinese sovereigns and their bureaucracy. This approach upholds, for a time at least, the integrity and autonomy of pastoral culture, by ensuring that a measure of actual power is retained in the hands of the established leadership, thus offering the nomad population a powerful argument in favor of the status quo against the potential threat of complete absorption. To a certain extent this is undoubtedly self-serving, for, as Lattimore points out,

In this way the hereditary principle is strengthened and a family of chiefs may come to have a vested interest in perpetuating the subordination of the people as a whole, in order to sustain their authority (Lattimore 1962: 476).

If this vested interest and its coalition with the vested interest of the central government were to dissolve, most of the safeguards for the pastoral way of life would likewise disappear.

THE CHARTER OF LEGITIMATE RULE

Modernization tends to be expressed by tables of organization and administrative codes, which are considered representative of new power relationships and jurisdictions. As in most modernizing countries, in Ethiopia such codes exist and are effectively applied in many of the internal operations of government. It must therefore have been a matter of choice if the letter of the administrative code was not always enforced in the particular situation of the Amhara-Adal frontier. Actual practice indicates that the government presence was extended along those conceptual lines by which dominion has traditionally been sanctioned in Amhara and Adal culture alike. An option was exercised in favor of particularistic authority, embodied in men whose background, personal history, and actions conformed to those established criteria by which a mandate to command and rule has traditionally been recognized. These criteria are cohesive sets or syndromes of the ascribed statuses of birth and origin, augmented, in each case, by a reputation for military valor and by other achievements. All these factors ought to be present if a leader's or officeholder's claim to dominion over men is to be fully sanctioned and supported by the people.

The biography of the man who was projected into the governance of the frontier region supplied the charter of legitimacy which the situation demanded and to which Amhara as well as Adal could subscribe:

Shambal Wolde Maryam (not his actual name) was born in about 1924 in Dibbi *mikitl woreda*, on his father's land. Later, however, he identified himself with the *melkenyenat* [seigniory] of his estate in Galla *mikitl woreda*, inherited through his mother, whose father's father had established a church there. Wolde Maryam received a good traditional church-school education but is not a member of the clergy in any capacity. He served for almost five years with the guerrilla forces of Woheni Azaj Haile during the Italian occupation, although he was little more than twelve years old when the war began to reach into his homeland. He participated in the fighting at Fikre Gemb, Gendeberet, and Kassam, and all over Galla. In 1944, when only twenty years old, he was given the rank of *shambal*, a relatively minor rank in the militia which he still holds. At some time in his military career, he acquired the reputation of possessing a "medicine" which makes him invulnerable to bullets; this, combined with a well-attested history of courage and daring, won him widespread respect.

The years between 1944 and 1953 were a period of unrest in Ankober *woreda*, partially an aftermath of the kaleidoscopically shifting alliances and antagonisms of the war years. Former guerilla fighters now fought each other in many parts of Dibbi and Galla; several *shifta* groups had put themselves beyond the control of constituted government. In this difficult situation, the young *shambal* demonstrated remarkable gifts as a peacemaker and managed to persuade hostile groups and their leaders to accept his services, first as go-between and then as guarantor of their settlements. This naturally enhanced his personal position and importance. It is said that on his word alone, two thousand men in the region would take up arms in his support. However, the power with which the *shambal* has surrounded himself need not necessarily be a threat to the undisturbed exercise of the authority of others.

Possessing this power and being the man he is, the *shambal*'s real strength now lies in the growing number of lesser men who look to him as their informal patron and potential spokesman in dealings with higher authorities, even as far afield as Addis Ababa. Men of substance throughout the region speak highly of him and actively seek his favor. This explains the size of his following among the local militia leadership, quite out of keeping with his minor title and rank. The fact is that when his admirers claim and his enemies admit that the *shambal* is "the most powerful man in Ankober," they are making a statement not only concerning power but also concerning authority. His more recent reputation among the Adal is built on a very similar foundation.

Because the *shambal* had contributed so significantly to the pacification of Amhara regions, the central government called upon him for similar service in the eastern reaches of Ankober *woreda*, the desert lands inhabited by the Adal nomads. The Amhara had never established firm control and had preferred to conclude that it was impossible for them to reside there. No Amhara would think of traversing any part of the country with fewer than ten armed men. A governor or judge might try to impose Amhara law and order when Adal internecine warfare or conflict with neighboring Galla produced unusual dislocations and casualties. Then the Amhara would venture into the lowlands with sizeable forces of police and militia, but they usually returned without achieving permanent changes in the political situation.

Because of the Adal, and the threat of malaria, any order to venture into the Awash desert lands was considered a death sentence by the highland farmers. Into this region came Shambal Wolde Maryam, preceded only by his reputation for courage and for invincibility and invulnerability. To this day, when a case of insubordination or recalcitrance comes to his attention, he shoulders his rifle and personally walks or rides out to confront his man, followed by only one or two of his lieutenants. The *shambal* was the first Amhara administrator of the region to make a sustained effort to acquire knowledge about the Adal and their ways. He achieved facility in their language and gained some insight into their social organization and system of internal rule. Most important of all, he established serviceable and durable lines of communication with the Adal's leading and important personages.

The effective strength of Wolde Maryam in his broker's role between two cultures rests upon his reputation, which is the common "knowledge" that the *shambal* is a great and courageous warrior; that he is invulnerable to bullets; that in his own house are stored 250 rifles and ammunition for them; that two thousand militia men would instantly rise to his call (although the militia is nominally under the *woreda* governor's command); and that the *shambal* has powerful friends in Addis Ababa. Not the least of the considerations which strengthen the *shambal*'s position as an intermediary is the respect and support which he receives from the dreaded Adal. Clearly he enjoys considerable freedom of action and decision which he uses to maintain contacts and to reach agreement by persuasion.

CONCLUSION

To sum up, there seems to be a good deal of similarity between the Ethiopian experience and the solutions applied historically in parallel situations by imperial Chinese governments along their inner-Asian frontiers. Many problems and some of the attempted resolutions have significant features in common, and Lattimore's analysis sounds as true for the Ethiopian case as it does for the inner-Asian:

The system was one of the standard expedients in Chinese history, whatever the ruling dynasty, and by no means a Manchu invention. It kept the peace at an expense that was very small compared with the cost of frontier wars, and it stabilized the normally nomadic society of the Mongols, because the regular payment of subsidy according to a classification of greater or lesser chiefs demanded a fixed habitat for each chief and his tribe. This promoted the demarcation of tribal boundaries, converting what had once been tribal followings into territorial principalities, in which the chiefs were no longer leaders of war bands, but hereditary wardens of the "peace and order" which is always the frontier fetish of the central government of great empires (Lattimore 1962: 442).

The full range of consequences of such a system may extend well beyond what Lattimore chooses to consider a fetish. In our instance, the potential for renewed conflict between Adal and Amhara was evident from the first intrusion of localized and sedentary communities, designed to serve an agricultural-industrial complex, into a region hitherto the sole province of desert and steppe pastoralists. Until very recently, contacts between sedentary and nomadic societies had been just that: contacts, by definition intermittent, temporary, and optional, whether they happened to be peaceable or hostile. Contact is rapidly becoming interaction, implying sustained and constant dealings across cultural and political boundaries, which call for similarly permanent and durable institutions.

Through the new political constellation promoted by the central government, the nomadic Adal have reacquired a certain measure of autonomy. It is expressed in the institutionalization of the broker role of the leaders, which has been added to their traditional position of leadership over their own people. The central government evidently saw advantages in resorting to particularistic role models when it proceeded to create integrative political mechanisms. As a result, there is at least a possibility that a measure of cultural pluralism may persist intact along the frontier. Whatever inevitable changes may be wrought in time by social, economic, or technological imperatives, the system does not preclude development along plural paths through a mutuality of accommodations.

REFERENCE

LATTIMORE, OWEN
1962 *Studies in frontier history, collected papers 1928–1958*. London: Oxford University Press.

Biased Symbiosis on the Tana River

NORMAN TOWNSEND

The literature on the Horn of Africa contains many references to various helot groups, despised castes, client peoples, etc., all living in a situation in which pastoralists are given the greatest prestige and privileges. Some of these people are farmers, others blacksmiths, craftsmen, and so on. Uniformly, the pastoralists hold them in contempt, yet would not try to do without them. There are many explanations for this contempt, but one of them surely must be that sedentarization is an option only for someone who has failed at herding; personal prestige is therefore at stake. Also, of course, there is the prestige attached to war and raiding, for which the nature of their economy forces pastoralists to acquire a greater aptitude than is the case with settled agriculturalists.

Our knowledge of the economic, political, and status relations between the (predominantly Bantu-speaking) farmers of the Tana, Juba, and Shebelle rivers on the one hand and the surrounding Galla and Somali on the other is scanty and impressionistic, and we know next to nothing about how these relations have changed and developed over the last 500 years. One thing does seem clear, however, and that is that the use of violence by pastoralists against farmers has been confined to periods when the pastoralists have fought among themselves. In more recent years, violence has been associated with the rise of Somali nationalism. On Tana River, the agricultural Pokomo seem to have no tradition of enslavement, capture, plunder, or even clientship in their relations with the Galla, although tempers may flare occasionally when Galla cattle stray onto Pokomo crops. It was only against Somali attacks, in the later nineteenth

1 am happy to acknowledge the assistance of the Canada Council (Doctoral Fellowship), the International Studies Programme of the University of Toronto, and the Institute of African Studies, Nairobi, under whose auspices the data for this paper were collected.

century, that the Pokomo felt compelled to build elaborate palisades, ambush pits, underwater spikes, etc., to protect their villages.

Early white travelers were very free with words like "slaves," "serfs," and "vassals" on the one hand and "kings" and "chiefs" on the other when they described the peoples they encountered in their wanderings through Africa. In true nineteenth-century authoritarian style, they exalted the wealthier of the Pokomo, and particularly the Galla, along the Tana River, into "chiefs" and "sultans." Many of them recorded that the Pokomo were "subjects" of the Galla; phrases such as "absolute slavery," "periods of long subjection," and "a state of vassalage" occur frequently in their writings of the 1880's and 1890's. Yet on the other hand, in 1858 Krapf recorded repeated Pokomo attacks on the Galla. As a result of these attacks, a peace agreement was reached between them, with the Galla promising to reform. From the limited data available, I would suggest that the bonds between the two peoples have been less precise than has often been believed.

The Pokomo number twice as many as the neighboring Galla but inhabit an area only a fraction of the size of that used by the Galla, for they farm only the land which is flooded periodically by the Tana River. They have no use for the land farther than about two miles from the river, and in fact most of the time they use an area within a hundred yards or so of the banks. Temporary Galla villages are sometimes built within approximately a mile of the river, but for the most part the Galla bring their cattle to water in the river only in the dry seasons and only at certain fixed places. These watering places have been authorized by the government, and the Pokomo refuse to allow the Galla access to the river through their land at any other point. Galla women bring milk daily to the larger Pokomo villages and sit with their containers under a large shade tree. They also go to the houses of individual Pokomo women whom they know. The smaller villages are visited on a more irregular basis, but even in the largest ones there is no fixed market location. The Galla do not dispute the Pokomo's claim to the land in the river valley, and their appearance near the river is only intermittent. Pokomo and Galla thus do not conflict over land ownership and rarely come into really close contact. The Pokomo do not envy the Galla way of life, nor the Galla the Pokomo way of life.

Before the decline in Galla fortunes in the final quarter of the nineteenth century, relations between Pokomo and Galla had probably stabilized over the centuries into something along the lines of those described for the Arusha and the Masai by Gulliver. That is, the Galla were confident of their superiority to the Pokomo, while the Pokomo accepted their inferiority but endeavored in many ways to orient their culture along Galla lines. If the Pokomo formed a lower stratum, then it was stratification based on status more than on wealth or power. That many Pokomo clans claim Galla ancestors is probably evidence of intermarriage between early-immigrating Pokomo and, among others, sedentary (and therefore poor) Galla in the Tana valley. The dialects and languages of the Pokomo contain many borrowings from the Galla, and in fact the Korokoro Pokomo speak Galla only. In general, it seems that the farther upriver one goes, the greater the borrowings from the Galla language. Many items of material culture, such as house style and furniture, are identical. All Pokomo have Galla personal names (as well as their Muslim or Christian ones), and in the middle and upper reaches of the river all Pokomo clans have Galla names. Like the Galla, the Pokomo (except for the Lower Pokomo) have adopted the customs of circumcision and organization into age-sets (*luva*), though these may be evidence of pre-Galla Cushitic influence in the area. (The Cushitic fish taboo is not shared by the two peoples.) Despite all this, we have no evidence that any precise obligations or contracts of personal dependence ever tied the Pokomo to the Galla, and, although there may seem to be echoes of feudalism in their relationship, the superiority of the Galla does not appear to have been institutionalized.

The most clearly substantiated form of Pokomo subordination, judging from the reports of early travelers and from Pokomo tradition, seems to have existed on certain reaches of the river only, namely near the river mouth and at the farthest inland point inhabited by Pokomo. But even for these places the reports are unclear. It is important to remember that accounts by whites of Galla-Pokomo relations must inevitably have been colored by the fact that nearly all employed Galla guides and Galla or Swahili interpreters. Early missionary efforts in the area were aimed primarily at the Galla, and it might not be going too far to suggest that whites in Africa generally showed a greater respect and admiration for pastoralists than for farmers (cf. the Masai).

The Lower Pokomo, living near the mouth of the river, have a tradition that records how the Galla took away all the cattle of the Pokomo when they were at Shungwaya, and that the Pokomo migrated southward under Galla harassment, ultimately settling along the Tana. Again coming under Galla pressure and also, for the first time, under Swahili rule, they agreed to submit to the Galla and to the Swahili (the words used translate as "to be the defeated of the Galla"). They are said to have paid tribute to the Galla in food and cloth and to the Swahili in slaves. New, on his visit to the area in 1867, mentioned only that the Galla regularly took a percentage of any ivory or other trophies of the hunt from the Pokomo. He noted, too, that the Pokomo "complain of the Galla, call them the worst of men, but resistance does not appear to enter their minds." In like manner the Galla also took from the Sanye a heavy proportion of the latter's ivory. The local Pokomo reaction, according to New, was to give up hunting (which would seem to indicate the absence of any necessity to supply regular tribute). The lack of strong resistance is perhaps to be accounted for in two ways. Throughout northeast Africa it is held that possession of cattle brings prestige as much as it does material advantage, so that having no cattle is shameful everywhere. The social superiority of the Galla was not questioned. Also, as pastoralists, the Galla were organized for plundering (facilitated by their organization into age-sets), and sedentary or hunting peoples could not hope to resist their demands for livestock or ivory.

Nearly all subsequent white visitors remarked on the oppressive demands made on the local Pokomo by the Swahili of Kau and Witu. For example, Bird-Thompson noted in 1891, "When a Swahili wants rice he goes to a Pokomo village, and sitting down by a hut, gun in hand, tells a Pokomo to cut him as much rice as he requires, and afterwards makes him row him back to his house." There are no parallel mentions of Galla exactions in this manner, and we hear nothing of even the cloth or food tribute. By that time, of course, the number of Galla on the lower Tana was no more than a few hundred.

Among the Korokoro Pokomo, living on the river some 200 miles inland, early travelers noted what seemed a similar kind of subjection. Chanler described it as follows:

They [the Galla] keep the Pokomo in a state of subjection, forcing them to give them a certain portion of their crops, and convey them up and down the river when they so desire. This state of affairs has evidently lasted for many years; for at present the Pokomo, although preserving their racial characteristics, have not only adopted the language of the Galla, but have lost all remembrance of their own tongue. The distinction between the two tribes is, however, clearly maintained, and they never intermarry. In return for the tribute above mentioned, the Galla protect the Pokomo from the raids of the Somali on the left bank, and the attacks of the Wakamba on the right.

That the Galla enjoyed some such privileges is confirmed by the visit, three years after Chanler, of Ormerod, who spoke Galla; he noted that they helped themselves to the corn, peas, honey, and even ivory of the Korokoro.

But it seems that the protection offered by the Galla was merely illusory, for they were mortally afraid of the Kamba, being convinced, as Chanler noted, that within a few years the Kamba would wipe them off the face of the earth. "I never saw a people so convinced of their evil fate." As a result, both Galla and Korokoro had their villages and plantations on islands in the river. (Elsewhere on the river, the Somali and the Masai induced the same fear in the Galla.) Portal, on his way to the coast from the Uganda Mission of 1893, took the local Galla as natural masters of the Korokoro and was greatly annoyed that a Galla "chief" was unable to command a fleet of twenty Korokoro canoes to convey his party downriver. In the end only the threat of force produced some canoes.

Complementing Pokomo acceptance of the superior status of the Galla was the Galla fear of Pokomo sorcery. Pokomo traditions record that whenever the Galla's cattle fell sick they called in the Pokomo to apply medicine (just as the Masai came to the Meru). Ormerod found that the upriver Galla greatly feared Pokomo medicine men, holding that some of them had bewitched their country; they threatened to kill his Pokomo companions from downriver for this reason.

The region most independent of Galla economic pressure was the stretch of river between the areas inhabited by the Lower Pokomo and the Korokoro; and this was (and is) the most densely populated part of the river. Here also, from Mwina to Milalulu, all but one of the largest villages were found. It was this area that the Swahili did not dare to raid, for fear of Pokomo archery, and it appears that only rarely did any non-Pokomo pass through. One European traveler recorded that the "sultan" of one district refused him help, "assigning as the reason that it was his custom to hinder all Europeans, Arabs and Swahilis from passing up-river." The Pokomo here preferred to transport and sell their ivory by themselves, rather than to allow middlemen to enter the trade. Neither the Galla nor the Swahili succeeded in interfering with the trade of these Upper Pokomo. In fact, the Galla seem to have had no power to interfere in any aspect of Pokomo social, political, or ritual life anywhere on the river; even the Korokoro, who speak only Galla, have always maintained politico-ritual contact with the other Pokomo groups and intermarry only with them.

Following the decline in Galla power, relations between the Lower Pokomo and the Galla changed to the middle-river pattern of tolerance and noninterference. In the Korokoro area, the Galla seem to have moved away as the Somali moved in. So great was the reverse suffered by the Galla at the hands of the Somali that the Pokomo claim that but for their protection the Galla would have been wiped out. Certainly the Galla were greatly reduced in numbers. The *Book of Zenj* relates that ironically the Pokomo in fact "enslaved" some Galla at that time. Today, now that the Galla have lost their social superiority, the exemplars and preceptors for the Pokomo are whites, "black Europeans," and Swahili.

I am arguing that relations between the Galla and the Pokomo were probably more nearly equal than often claimed. The advantages of maintaining a free exchange of goods has probably always been obvious to both sides: the Galla acquire bananas, maize, rice, gourds, honey, beer, tobacco, and grazing, while the Pokomo acquire much-needed meat and milk. Bargaining over these items occurs only within fairly narrow limits. At the present moment, with the Somali on one side of the river and the Galla on the other, the Pokomo are in the fortunate position of being able to choose and bargain. And now that hunting has been banned, the Pokomo are forced into closer dependence on their neighbors as suppliers of meat. The Galla do not covet Pokomo land, nor do the Pokomo covet Galla land, and there is no marginal land over which quarrels could begin. At times, Galla and Pokomo attend one another's feasts. Pokomo often have their own few livestock grazed by the Galla at certain times of the year, such as Ramadan. There are many cases of close friendship between individual Pokomo and Galla.

Yet both sides are cautious, for people have been killed when cattle strayed onto crops. The Galla and the Somali give the Pokomo nothing in exchange for the right to pasture their herds on Pokomo fields after harvest. When they have meat or milk to sell, it is the women who bring it to the Pokomo villages (cf. the privileged position of Masai and Kikuyu women in the last century). There is still virtually no intermarriage between the Pokomo and the others. No Somali or Galla seem able to speak Pokomo, yet nearly every older male Pokomo can speak Galla and many know Somali also. Even now, most Pokomo villages are on the west bank and out of range of Somali attack, for memories are still fresh of Somali raids during the 1890's and again during the Shifta emergency of the 1960's. Somali attacks on Bantu villages in Kenya have not yet ceased. In recent years, the descendants of Pokomo and Galla captured by Somali in the 1890's have been returning to their homes in small numbers. The Pokomo are under no illusions, however, as to the ultimate intentions of the Somali.

Only in recent years have the Pokomo begun to own cattle in any numbers. A commonly expressed view among them on this point is that in the remote past there was an agreement by which the Pokomo would stick to farming and the Galla to herding, for the mutual benefit of both peoples. This is in line with Pokomo traditions of intermarriage with sedentary Galla (even now, occasionally, a few impoverished Galla settle down to till the soil), and with a story claiming that the two founders of the Pokomo and Galla peoples were brothers, who split up in the style of Cain and Abel. On the other hand, we have early reports from some areas of the river that the Pokomo never kept livestock for fear of tempting Galla (and later, Somali) raiders; any sheep or goats acquired in trade were at once slain and eaten. Perhaps we should regard these traditions of an agreement between Galla and Pokomo and their common ancestry as attempts by the Pokomo to rationalize their inferior status. The position is not entirely clear, but the division between the two peoples was clearly horizontal rather than vertical. Unfortunately no ethnographic study of the Tana Galla has ever been carried out, and we lack information on *their* views of the development of relations with the Pokomo. But the sparse data we do have would generally seem to indicate that there was little in common between the situation on the Tana River and that in Ankole, for example.

What seems to have existed in this part of Africa, then, is a situation in which a very small-scale society of farmers acknowledged their social inferiority, but not their political inferiority, to a numerically smaller, neighboring, uncentralized, pastoral people. That this relationship was marked by very few occasions of violence may be attributed to agreement among all parties as to the esteem that cattle ownership brings. Tribute relations seem to have been very localized, intermittent, and undeveloped. Nowhere in this part of Africa were farmers and pastoralists ever united in any statelike political structure; the reasons for this, I suggest, may be in large part ecological.

REFERENCES

KRAPF, J. L.
  1858   *Reisen in Ost-Afrika.* Stuttgart.
PRINS, A. H. J.
  1952   *The coastal tribes of the north-eastern Bantu.* London: Ethnographic Survey of Africa.

Changes in the Family Structure of the Pamir Nationalities in the Years of Socialist Construction

L. F. MONOGAROVA

The Pamirs (or the Pamiri Tajiks) – Yazgulems, Bartangs, Rushans, Shugnans, Ishkashims, and Vakhans – present a group of kindred nationalities whose mother tongues, the so-called Pamiri languages, belong to the East Iranian group. In the Soviet Union they live in isolated, almost inaccessible, canyons or valleys of the West Pamirs, a part of the Gorno-Badakhshan Autonomous Region of the Tajik Republic.

According to the All-Union Census, including the Pamir Tajiks, there were 65,534 Tajiks in 1959 and 89,314 Tajiks in 1970 in the Gorno-Badakhshan Autonomous Region. In 1959, more than 42,000 people considered the Pamiri languages their mother tongue. The religious Pamir Tajiks belong to the Ismaelites, one of the Shiah sects of Islam. They differ considerably from the Tajiks of other Tajikistan regions in their language and religion.

A predominantly natural economy, extreme backwardness and a secluded life in the past, and an oppressed semidependent and even dependent position contributed to the preservation of patriarchal and feudal relations among the Pamir nationalities in the first decades of the twentieth century.

Descendants of the oldest settled agricultural population of Central Asia, who had preserved archaic survivals in economy, material culture, and social and family relations, received, as a result of the great October Socialist Revolution, a national state organization in the form of an autonomous region within Tajikistan. With the help of the Soviet Union's fraternal peoples, especially Russians and Tajiks, they underwent the deepest socialist reforms leading to their transition to socialism.

The changes in their family structure were related to the socialist transformations in the economic and cultural life of the Pamir nationalities, with the gradual overcoming of alienation from the surrounding world.

All investigators note numerous families among the Pamir nationalities. The collected field and archival materials indicate that the number of family members does not always determine its form. The factor determining what form a family takes is not the numerical composition of the family or the number of generations dwelling together but the relationship of the family property to land and personal belongings and the number of married couples. The large patriarchal family community is based on a collective communal form of property, whereas the undivided family, the last stage in the development of the large patriarchal family, is characterized by the appearance of the rudiments of private property in the family couples which form small individual families within this large family. A numerous family (ten to fifteen persons) may consist of two generations only: parents and their little children, i.e. it is a small individual family. At the same time a nonnumerous family (six to eight persons) consisting of two, seldom three, generations and incorporating parents with children and one married son, or parents and two married sons and grandchildren – such a family is an undivided family by its form because their land is common, they cultivate it together, and they eat together, though each married couple has its own personal belongings.

The large patriarchal family, often in its later form of an undivided family (*ibyna*, *ashgol*, or *vokh*) consisting of two or more married couples usually of two to three generations, was, as a rule, a primary social and economic unit of society in the nineteenth century.

The population of the Pamir regions in the seventeenth to nineteenth and beginning of the twentieth centuries paid duties to and sharecropped for the ruler of Badakhshan or Darvaz or for the Bukhara emir: in addition they did forced labor for local feudal proprietors and collected *sarkory* from every household for their religious leader Aga Khan. A tax collected from every family irrespective of its numerical strength undoubtedly contributed to the preservation of undivided families.

Family kinship groups including a number of large patriarchal undivided families and some small families (not many), formed the basis of the *kyshlak* community in the West Pamirs. The families included in these patronyms were called *avlod* (the Yazgulems called them *kaum*; the Shugnans, *gru*; the Vakhans, *tukhm*) and were agnatic. Large family kinship groups living near each other had close neighborly relations; they rendered mutual help (*kyryar*) in agricultural work, pasturing cattle, battue hunting, construction of dwellings and farm premises, etc. In addition, members of one patronym helped each other in conducting family rites (weddings, childbirths, circumcisions, funerals, etc.).

The ideological community of a patronym was expressed by recognizing the authority and power of its head – the oldest relative. The heads of all families consulted him on various economic and everyday problems; his house was the place for praying to the "ancestors' spirits" because all successive heads of the particular patronym were descendants of their common forefather, who really lived a few (usually five to seven) generations ago. Each patronym had its own cemetery, or a special burial-ground at the cemetery if a settlement was rather large with two or more patronymic groups. In Yazgulem the patronym head's duty even in the 1950's was to personally lower the dead male into the grave. The members of the same patronym were supposed to come to the funerals and the funeral repasts of a family's relatives as well as to any other family occasions without any special invitation.

The economic unity of a patronym came from the fact that the land was formerly considered an undivided common property of the *kaum* (*avlod*). With an increase in the number of patriarchal families the arable land was divided among them, and by the middle of the nineteenth century it had become their private property; but up to the thirties and forties of our century, when collective farms were organized there, pastures, forest, and water remained in common use belonging to the whole patronym (if the settlement was small and members of one patronym lived there) or to the whole *kyshlak* community (if the settlement was large and several patronyms lived there). The economic basis of the family in any of its forms was land and other means of production. The family represented a production team in which, by order of the family head, each member fulfilled a certain task depending on his abilities. It is interesting to note that after the father's death it was not the eldest brother who was chosen as the family head but the one who could run the household best. If the brothers could not come to an agreement they did it in succession: each brother performed the family head's functions for a year. All of the family means including movable property were at his disposal. This testifies to the survival of democratic principles in the patriarchal family structure of the Pamir population.

Usually informants name two factors that cause family divisions: (1) numerical increase of the family which, for example, can cause lack of space for sleeping; and (2) quarrels between women, mainly between the brothers' wives. But the real cause of divisions lay in the further social and economic development: in the introduction of commodity-money relations, an increased part played by seasonal work, and, as a result, a possibility for individual married couples to accumulate private means. The separating family received, depending upon the fortune, several sheep, goats, and cows and a few yaks, as well as several carpets, a cauldron (*dig*) for cooking, and wooden and earthenware crockery. All the men of the family together built a house for the separating family.

When dividing the arable land, the best plot, according to the common law, was allocated to the eldest son, whereas the farm and the father's house went to the youngest son. According to custom, the parents went to live with the latter.

In the past mutual relations between the sexes of the Pamir nationalities were characterized by more freedom than among the Tajiks. Archaic
survivals in matrimonial and family relations existed among the Pamir
nationalities much longer than among the Tajiks, including the mountain
dwellers, not only because of their extreme geographical isolation from
the cultural centers of Central Asia and the neighboring countries but to
a considerable extent because further development of marriage and family
was influenced by Ismaelism (Bobrinskoj 1902: 259; 1908: 55). Ismaelism
absorbed various popular pre-Islamic beliefs and rites of which Ismaelism
is more tolerant than Sunnism. Women in the Pamir countries were not
separated from male society in either family or social life. They always
walked with unveiled faces. Seclusion of women was unknown, whereas
it was typical of the Tajik neighbors, where it was "legalized" by Islam.
Pamiri women lived on the same premises as men and participated with
men not only in family but in social entertainments and festivals as well.
Absence of the custom of mutual avoidance of the husband's (wife's)
relatives by the engaged couple and absence of the rite of ascertaining in
public the bride's virginity speak, in our opinion, in favor of more equality
of rights between women and men. Andreev, one of the most prominent
investigators of the everyday life of the Pamir nationalities, noted

...absence in the wedding rites of the official identification of the bride's virginity....This custom penetrated as high as the upper reaches of the river Panj
in the Yazgulem Valley where it came with Sunnism and where the old men
still remember the stories about the time when this custom did not exist there
(Andreev 1953: 176).

After these valleys were joined to the Bukhara Khanate, Sunnism, at
the end of the nineteenth century, penetrated to Yazgulem. That the family
head's wife could participate in the village gathering in case of his
absence, and in case he had no grown-up brothers or sons; that women
could take part in the night parties organized by relatives or neighbors;
that a woman on equal terms with a man could become the *murid* of one
or another *pir* [an Ismaelite spiritual tutor]; that the women who performed a certain rite and became the *murids* of some *pir* always took part
together with the male *murids* of the same *pir* in special parties organized
by the *pir* (when he visited his *murids* at other *kyshlaks*) or organized by
some more prosperous *murid* – during these parties where they spent
time talking about religion, they also shared the general meal; all these
testify to the greater freedom of the Pamiri women.

Women took part in various popular festivities (*khijvest* [the first
ploughing festival] and others). The Rushans differed from other Pamir
nationalities in their highly developed arts of dancing and singing; men
and women gathered in the moonlit nights by whole *avlods* and sang and
danced in the gardens or in the *kyshlak* center.

According to the common law the blood feud demanded equal revenge for both a murdered male relative and a female relative, and later the "paying off" that substituted for the blood feud was also equal.

And yet the woman did not have absolutely equal rights with the man. As a member of the family she was bent to the will of the family head – her father or her brother and, after marriage, her husband. "A husband for the woman is her god, her tsar, and then – her husband." The choice of a husband for a young girl was in the hands of the family head.

There were no equal rights with the man in the property and inheritance. The daughter inherited only one-fourth of the property. If a man had two wives (it should be noted that polygamy was a rare case, an exception), and each had children, the children of one wife inherited the same as the children of the other wife, the land being divided among the sons; the daughter in this case did not get any land. The son who had small sisters living with him inherited more cattle when the property was divided because he had to marry his sisters off, providing each of them with a certain number of cattle as a dowry.

If one wife had only one daughter and the other had many children, the property and land were divided into two equal parts – one part was inherited by the single daughter, the other was successively divided among the second wife's children. They tried to marry the heiress of land (*dokhtary surbi*) to her cousin – the son of the father's brother – or to some other relative from her *avlod*, though every young man was eager to marry such a girl even if she was not pretty. If the girl was a single child in the family her husband had to move to her parents' house, becoming a so-called *primak* [husband living in the wife's family].

Fundamental changes in the economic and social life of the Gorno-Badakhshan Autonomous Region (GBAR) took place during the years of Soviet power. The Soviet marriage legislation and the introduction of compulsory education radically changed the status of the woman. The Women's Soviets that actively helped women during the first years of Soviet power in achieving real equal rights in society and in the family continue to defend women's interests, especially those of mothers and children. The Women's Soviets carry on the work of drawing women into production and are also engaged in women's political education.

In the GBAR, as all over the country, the bearer of new ideas in family life is the intelligentsia, fighting survivals of the past that are incompatible with the new social and family relations and the Soviet morals.

Different social status of family members on the collective farms of the Pamir nationalities is now a usual thing. There are collective farmers, workers, employees, pupils, and students in almost every family. There are more workers and employees in the families of those collective farms that are situated at or near regional centers.

The formation of socialist forms of economy and participation of family members in the public production resulted in the economic independence of individual married couples within the undivided family and speeded up the formation of small families inside the undivided family and its subsequent division during the first years of socialist construction.

Small families now usually consist of parents, their small or unmarried children, elderly mother or father of the family head (or both), and small or unmarried brothers and sisters of the family head.

The data allow us to assume that a change has taken place in the main family form of the Pamir nationalities during the last sixty years. The small family was gradually replacing the undivided family that was predominant at the beginning of the twentieth century. But at the same time our data show the existence of some undivided families, especially in mountain areas of Shugnan and Vakhan.

The data gathered in 1966–1967 at three collective farms, i.e. the data taken from the farmstead registers, show ninety-one Vakhan households in the Lenin collective farms, Vrang village Soviet, Ishkashim district; 163 Shugnan households in the Sole collective farm, Rosht-Kalinsky village Soviet, Shugnan district; and 205 Rushan households in the Rushan collective farm, Rushan village Soviet, Rushan district. Analysis of the data collected at these three places shows a certain local peculiarity in the family development process.

At the Lenin collective farm an average Vakhan family numbered 11.7 persons; the largest family was thirty persons; the smallest was two persons. It was found that there were many undivided families in this collective farm: fifty-four, or 59.3 percent. Fifteen, or 27.7 percent were families with married sons living with their fathers, and in 72.3 percent of families, married brothers kept a common household.

In the Sole collective farm, Rosht-Kalinsky village Soviet, Shugnan district, in the Shakh-dary valley, an average Shugnan family numbered 1.01 persons (1967 data). The largest family consisted of twenty-three members (two cases), the smallest of two members (two cases). There were ninety-seven (59.5 percent) undivided families. Among the undivided families, married sons lived with their fathers in fifty-three families (54.6 percent), and married brothers lived in forty-four (45.4 percent) of undivided families; out of this number four married brothers lived in one family and three married brothers lived in five families.

The size of the undivided family differs: there is an undivided family of five persons (two married brothers, one of them having a child); another family of eight persons (two married brothers with wives and children); a third family of ten persons (three married brothers with wives and children). There is a family that consists of two brothers with wives and children – twenty persons in all. The thirty-member family consists of four married brothers with wives and children, and the twenty-four-member family consists of five brothers and their families.

In the Rushan collective farm, Rushan village Soviet, Rushan district, in 1967, an average Rushan family numbered 6.2 persons. The largest family consisted of twenty-four persons, the smallest families had two persons (ten families).

There are thirty-nine undivided families (19 percent) at this collective farm. The overwhelming majority here consists of Rushans, but there are several Bartang and Shugnan families. The families in which married sons live with their fathers run to twenty-five (64.1 percent), and there are fourteen families of married brothers (35.8 percent). Among those twenty-five undivided families in which married sons live with their fathers, there are seventeen families consisting of the father's family and one married son; there are nine families with two or more married sons. Among the fourteen families in which married brothers live together, there are two families with three married brothers; others consist of two brothers.

Thus two family forms – undivided and small – existed among the Pamir nationalities in the 1960's.

The structure of the undivided families is interesting because it shows the violation of the common law. According to the common law, the children of the family head's daughter (a widow or a divorcee) cannot live in the family – they should live in their father's family; neither can the sister of the family head's mother live in the family. At the present time such families consist of parents and their small children, married sons (including their children), and sometimes grandfather or grandmother (sometimes both), brothers and cousins of the family head, his sister or daughter, or other collateral relatives – the brother's wife with children, the mother's sister, or nephews (children of the dead or departed brother of the family head or, occasionally, his sister's children of the first marriage).

Living in an undivided family of collateral relatives (especially cousins with families) can be considered as one of the substantial survivals of the patriarchal family community.

With the establishment of Soviet power the land was expropriated from the secular and ecclesiastic feudal owners; the peasant families (first of all poor families) were given allotments of land which made it possible, for those families that felt it necessary, to separate. The collectivization was completed in the GBAR by the end of the 1940's. The collective farms allotted personal plots to the separated families out of the whole stock of land; this furthered the separation process. As a result the small family became predominant in the 1950's in spite of the fact that undivided families still exist in some mountain areas.

The economic basis of such a family, especially when young married couples have, because of their professions, little or no connection with agricultural labor, is formed not by common household and labor but by the fees given by the separate married couples (often out of their earnings) into "the common purse," a considerable part of the earnings of the

married couples remaining at their personal disposal. This factor under-
mines the economic unity of the family and gives an impetus to accumulating means for independent housekeeping. The functions of the family
head decrease, and very often only the traditional respect toward older
relatives, mainly the attachment to the father, helps to maintain the
temporary unity of such an undivided family during the final period in its
existence. Thus the undivided family of our days differs strikingly from
the prerevolutionary undivided family.

In spite of survivals of a large patriarchal family's traditions in the form
of the undivided family and its coexistence with the small family, the
urge toward family separation in the undivided families is a clear sign of
the fact that the process of the formation of small families – the main
Pamiri Tajik family form – is gradually being completed everywhere in
the western Pamirs.

Our data show that the traditional patriarchal survivals in the Pamiri
family incompatible with the equal status of husband and wife and old
and young members of the family are vanishing. The family relations of
the Pamir nationalities are now based on equality of all family members
who reach mature age and who have equal rights and opportunities to
participate in public production and to receive an education.

The Pamir nationalities were among the most backward and oppressed
nationalities in the colonial outskirts of tsarist Russia. Thanks to the
achievements of the great October Socialist Revolution these nationalities,
during the years of Soviet power, have passed from patriarchal and feudal
relations and natural economy toward socialism, by-passing the capitalist
stage of development. All this has brought about deep changes in the
family structure of the Pamir nationalities during the years of socialist
construction.

REFERENCES

ANDREEV, M. S.
   1953   *Tadzhiki doliny khuf*[Tajiks of the Hup Valley], vyp. 1, 176. Stalingrad.
BOBRINSKOJ, A. A.
   1902   Sekta Izmail'ja [The Ismael sect]. *Etnograficheskoe Obozrenie* 2 (1).
   1908   *Gortsy verkhov'ev Pjandzha* [Mountaineers of the upper Pyanj].
            Moscow.

Problems of Social Change Among the Asiatic Nomads

G. E. MARKOV

A considerable number of special studies deal with the history of nomadic cattle breeding. Nevertheless, most of the problems concerning nomadism are still far from being solved. We do not yet know how it came into being and what caused its emergence. Questions about the development of the nomads' social organization and structure are still unanswered.

In special studies one cannot even find generally accepted meanings for such terms as "nomadism" or "nomadic," "seminomadic" or "semi-sedentary" cattle breeding. Sometimes only the very mobile "pure" cattle breeders are reckoned among the nomads, but sometimes semisedentary groups are too. Usually a society is or is not considered nomadic depending on the extent of migrations in search of grazing lands. Yet it is well known that this extent varies a great deal according to the geographical environment: in a year the nomads may cross either thousands of kilometers (Arab Bedouins, Mongols, a considerable part of the Kazakhs in the past, and others) or only some dozens (some Turkmen in the past, Kurds, and others). The extent of mobility of the pastoral peoples is a variable, subject to change depending on season, weather, and local environment. Pastoral economy is always complex.

The overwhelming majority of the nomads were occupied to a certain degree not only with cattle breeding but also with domestic crafts, caravan trade, primitive agriculture, etc. But extensive cattle breeding was the basis of their subsistence. That is why the term "nomadism" should be applied only to those societies for which extensive mobile cattle breeding was the main economy, the main source of all the necessary wealth. Depending on the environment, nomadism took various forms. One can single out a true nomadic subtype (Bedouins of Arabia, Gobi-Mongols, and others) and a seminomadic subtype (sheep breeders of Arabia, some Turkmen and Kirghiz in the nineteenth century, and some groups of the

Pathans). But the difference between nomadic and seminomadic cattle breeding is not fundamental. The former is more mobile, the latter is less so. Agriculture as a rule is more widely spread among the seminomads than among the nomads. But in their main social and economic traits both types of cattle breeding, nomadic and seminomadic, are similar.

The following kinds of nomadic economy were (and in some places still are) generally prevalent: the meridional, the vertical, the desert, and the stationary (the latter being a variety of the desert type, if the cattle breeders roam with their flocks around a reservoir of water, thus covering a short distance in a year).

The role of cattle breeding differs in the semisedentary and the sedentary economy. In the former it takes the form of herding, which is as important as or subordinate to agriculture; in the latter it is but a minor branch of the economy.

Archaeological, historical, and ethnographic data show that nomadism has covered a long path of socioeconomic development. Now it may be considered as fixed that nomadism originated in the Bronze Age, at the end of the second millennium B.C., among tribes of the mountains and steppes of Eurasia who had had a complex agricultural-pastoral economy since the Neolithic period. The causes of development of mobile cattle breeding into a separate economic type for considerable groups of peoples were very complex and manifold. This process represented the next stage of the division of labor proceeding under the impact of socioeconomic, political, and, probably, natural factors.

The emergence of mobile cattle breeding in the beginning of the first millennium B.C. probably proceeded polycentrically. It was accompanied by important changes in the social organization and structure of the farmers-herdsmen who shifted to extensive nomadism.

Little is known about the social organization of the tribes that inhabited the "mountainous steppe belt." Judging by remains of their settlements they were organized in small communities, most probably clan communities. Apparently there were also certain kinds of tribal organization, as indicated by archaeological cultures that sometimes covered vast areas. But we do not know what the functioning of this social organization was nor to what extent all these primitive clan-tribal institutions preserved their functions.

The development of mobile cattle breeding and the emergence of nomadism caused profound changes in social organization. Old territorial and clan connections were broken, and a need arose for establishing new kinds of connection and social organization. New forms of social organization came into existence, and the old forms became filled with a new content. A revolutionary collapse caused the establishment of a new social-tribal organization specific to nomadism. The more the cattle breeders separated themselves from other barbarian peoples, the more the primitive communal character of their society decayed, the more there emerged a political organization of nomads which was neither a replication nor a continuation of the organizational structure of the primitive society. The historical sources about the ancient nomads (the Huns, the Scythians, etc.) allow us to distinguish a mature tribal structure among them.

Social organization of any society is based on various kinds of relation. Some relations are minor and do not determine social structure. Only particular relations and phenomena constitute its distinguishing nature. The social organization of the nomads founded itself on economic, political, military, cultural, linguistic, ethnic, and kinship ties, although the importance of these factors varied.

The decay of the primitive communal system of the tribes engaged in a sedentary or semisedentary economy and the emergence of a nomadic organization resulted in the establishment of a structure based on economically independent extended families of cattle owners. But, because of economic and military-political factors, the families could not live independently together with other families; nomadic groups formed communities, tribal subdivisions, and tribes. The emergence of nomadic communities and tribal subdivisions was also caused by segmentation of the families. Each social structure of the mobile cattle breeders, from nomadic community up to tribe and tribal union, was regarded by them as a result of the segmentation of a primordial family, thus giving ideological substantiation of the concept of communal-tribal unity, of the common descent of all their members united by genealogical kinship. The unity of a tribe was strengthened by endogamic regulations. But the communal-tribal structure was not really based on kinship ties. Both the tribes and their large subdivisions were, as a rule, historically established complicated ethnic units which had been consolidating, sometimes over a long period of time. Nevertheless the idea about "genealogical" kinship enabled groups not connected by kinship ties to unite. Artificially they traced their genealogies back to a common "ancestor," a real or imaginary forefather of the nuclear group of the new unit. This was enough to justify a newly formed idea about the unity of the group and "consanguineous kinship" existing between the social units. The latter in its turn justified the violation of endogamic taboos, which necessarily happened when marriages took place within the multiethnic nomadic social units. The socioeconomic and political conditions of the nomadic cattle breeding presupposed tribe structure as the only possible form of social organization of the mobile nomads. Principles of tribal organization were very expedient under conditions of a mobile way of life, when there were no lasting interrelations on a territorial basis, when wars were innumerable, and when some nomadic units broke down and others emerged in the form of genealogical communities. Real kinship or consanguinity was of practical importance only within families or within small nomadic communities. But even there kinship ties were sometimes subordinate to economic and other practical interests.

Genealogical "kinship" and genealogical tribal structure existed and were of importance as long as they formed an ideological framework for real political, military, economic, and other relations. Their decline and the emergence of new nomadic units led to the creation of new genealogical structures. The mobile social organization of cattle breeders was very flexible and lent itself to regeneration in the face of the vicissitudes of nomadic life.

Communal-tribal organization appeared in various forms depending on political, social, and other conditions. During wars or great migrations the tribal structure was molded into a "military nomadic" form, based on a military organization. Moreover, in such cases the tribal subdivisions became elements of the military structure of the tribal army.

The "nomadic empires" were the acme of military and political consolidation of the mobile nomads. These "empires" temporarily acquired the character of a state (the Huns, the T'ü-k'ü Turks, and the Mongols). But many relevant features differentiated them from the sedentary cultivators' states. In particular, they were transient and short-lived and had no economic and social base in the steppe. The communal-tribal structure survived within nomadic empires and outlived them.

In relatively peaceful periods the tribal organization as well as the military one tended to become amorphous. Separate families and small nomadic communities became more self-sufficient, and that resulted in an emergence of a "communal-nomadic aggregative mold." It should be emphasized that such aggregative molds never appeared in a pure form but always included transitional and compound variations.

The involvement of the nomadic peoples in the socioeconomic network of the neighboring states also influenced their social organization. But both in antiquity and in the Middle Ages the communal-tribal structure of the mobile cattle breeders survived in one form or another as long as extensive nomadic cattle breeding continued to be the basis of their economic activity. The decline of nomadism was accompanied by the emergence of a territorial organization. Capitalistic conditions strongly influenced the organization of nomadic societies as well as other aspects of their life and caused a quick collapse of the nomadic economy and tribal organization.

The transition in a remote antiquity of some "steppe/mountainous bronze-using" tribes to mobile cattle breeding brought about deep changes in their social structure. Direct indications of the socioeconomic state of the mountainous/steppe tribes before they began to practice extensive mobile cattle breeding are scarcely available. Indirect data from investigating burial sites and settlements of mountainous/steppe tribes indicate that there were already some traits of social and property differentiation. But this process most likely had just begun, and the remnants of primitive communal social structure were still strong.

The emergence of mobile cattle breeding induced revolutionary changes in the social structure and a collapse of primitive remnants. Among many factors that stimulated these processes, one that should be mentioned is the establishment of the concept of private property in one of the main means of production: cattle. Before the emergence of the mobile cattle breeding economy, cattle could be owned by the community or by families. We suppose that cattle had become private property at an even earlier stage of mobile cattle breeding development. Nomadism arrived at its maturity under conditions of private ownership of domestic animals. It is impossible to assume that during an extensive mobile cattle breeding economy the cattle still continued to be communal property. Seasonal care of the flocks, the pasture, utilization of animal products – all this could be handled only by families. In case of need the families could unite their flocks (e.g. during summer migrations or war) or disperse (during the spring lambing or in the winter when it became difficult to merge the pasture of all the flocks).

Private familial cattle owning engenders property and social differentiation. Cattle become a commodity and acquire the functions of money. The development of exchange in its turn engenders the further stratification of the society and sometimes stimulates the growth of various kinds of contact with near and distant neighbors. The mobile, well-armed cattle breeders were often involved in armed conflicts. In certain periods, war became the main occupation for nomads.

The pastures, unlike the cattle, were in communal-tribal ownership and use. Nomadism can exist only if the pastures are used extensively. In each stage the nomads exploited the pastures collectively. Each deviation from this rule brings on the decline of the mobile extensive cattle breeding economy and the emergence of various types of semisedentary economy. Ethnographic and historical evidence and the customary law of the nomadic peoples (*adat*) confirm that pastures were not private property. *Adat* regulations, even fixed at the end of the nineteenth century according to statements of the ruling tribal elite (e.g. the Kazakhs) make no provision for private property in pastures. It is important to stress that at the same time the *adat* examines in every detail all the problems concerning cattle, house property, and cultivated land as private property. The only thing that was usually fixed by common law was the traditional possession of certain pastures by certain tribes or tribal subdivisions. In the case of pasture distribution, either the tradition served as a regulator or the first seizer got the right to use it (for instance, among the Kazakhs). Only under conditions of the decline of nomadism can winter pastures be assigned to private households.

The chiefs and rich cattle breeders had preference in using the pastures because of their prestige and economic superiority. The chiefs often supervised pasture distribution and, like the rich people, could seize the best parts of the pastures. It is known that sometimes the chiefs seized the best pastures for long-term use. But in all cases these pastures were used exclusively for the needs of one's own household, and no special rights to own pasture land or new means of production arose thereby. Not only had the chiefs and the rich no right to appropriate the pastures of the common cattle breeders, but, on the contrary, such actions would have contradicted their own interests. Loss of pastures implies reduction and disease of the flocks and destruction of the nomadic society led by the chiefs and the rich.

Social stratification of the nomads is caused not only by property differentiation but also by military tribal subordination. The chiefs of the nomads acted as civil, military, and economic leaders, thus constituting the elite of the society. One of their main duties and privileges was to conduct external relations with their nomadic and sedentary neighbors. A person could obtain the position of chief either through elections or heredity. But even in the latter case the appointment had to be approved by a popular assembly or by a council of elders. In relatively peaceful periods the power and influence of the chiefs were based on their personal prestige, knowledge, and ability to execute tribal rites, and on the support of their relatives. The chiefs had no other forces at their disposal than tribal home reserves. Total armament of the people forbade the usurpation of power and the use of extraeconomic forms of exploitation. However mighty the chief might be, the armed nomads would support him only as long as his politics and activities did not contradict the common law and the intrinsic interest of his tribesmen.

The situation was different when the leaders could be supported by the forces of army and state which dominated the nomads. Because of this support the chiefs succeeded in plundering the people and making them subject to extraeconomic exploitation.

Various forms of exploitation derived from free hiring (of shepherds, herdsmen, etc.) were widespread among the nomads. Rich cattle breeders exploited the poor by leasing to them animals for grazing. But the property stratification among the nomads could not exceed a certain limited degree. If the majority of the common people were alienated from the means of production, they would have to look for means of subsistence outside the steppe, because the manpower need is not great in mobile extensive cattle breeding. And this led to a decline of the tribal and military organization and the decay of the nomadic society.

Although the nomadic society was distinctly stratified from the point of view of property and social status, it was not arranged in classes or estates owning the means of production in a monopolistic way. The history of nomads does not contain data on peasant uprisings like those which so often occurred among the sedentary cultivators against slave owners and feudal lords. This is an indication of a less-developed class stratification.

The nomads knew the institution of patriarchal slavery, but the slaves were not numerous and were exploited mainly in the household. Nevertheless a considerable slave trade existed there. A tribute system was also practiced by nomadic tribes. Restraints on personal liberty, such as bondage or serfdom, did not exist. Some limited forms of bondage were found only when they were fixed by the legislation of a sedentary state which had subdued the nomads (e.g. the Mongols in the eighteenth and nineteenth centuries).

The social structure of the nomads was determined by a lack of adequate development of productive forces and of division of labor, private property in cattle and communal property on pastures, and considerable social and proprietary stratification. In the period of early nomadism as well as in its prime, the socioeconomic system of the pastoral nomads represented a type of the "military democracy." As Lenin pointed out, in the course of the further development of nomadism marked by a decline of nomadic empires, submission to agricultural states and the gradual decay of extensive cattle breeding, its socioeconomic system acquired patriarchal traits among its predominant characteristics. Besides these predominant socioeconomic structures, other types of structures also occurred in nomadic societies: slaveholding, tributary, feudal, etc. To a great extent such structures could develop due to the interconnection with neighboring advanced sedentary agricultural nations. Mature feudal or other class structures emerged within a nomadic society only in the course of its sedentarization.

Scientific research on nomadic peoples shows that they developed in accordance with the general socioeconomic laws developed by Marxism. At the same time their development, as well as the development of all other peoples of the world, was marked by specific historical factors.

Cognition, Values, and Religion

The Segmental System: Native Model or Anthropological Construction? Discussion of an Iranian Example

JEAN-PIERRE DIGARD

The arid and semiarid regions extending from western Africa to Central Asia are a principal domain of what anthropologists have called "segmental societies." These societies feature

1. An organization of unilinear, usually patrilinear, type, with preferential marriage of a male Ego to his father's brother's daughter, leading to a split of the lineages into lineage segments (segmentation).

2. The formation of these segments into interlocking elements which increase in number when one moves from the largest social unit – the tribe – to the smallest units – the nuclear families.

3. A system for maintaining internal order and political stability based on the balanced opposition of equally powerful elements (lineage segments or lineage-segment groups).

I apologize for this extremely diagrammatic illustration, which I have used to save time, and I would like to refer to the recent work of Gellner. We will deal here with the last of the three points mentioned above, namely the system for maintaining order in segmental societies. We are especially concerned with the following questions: which part of the system can be traced to native thought; which part stems from the anthropologist's ideas; and how much is derived from actual description of such systems in the specialist literature?

The level of awareness members of a society have of the way in which their society and its institutions operate seems to me to constitute for the anthropologist an important key to an understanding of that society's "politics." This awareness can be expressed in the most varied forms: proverbs, laws, myths, etc. For instance, all the specialists in the regions we are dealing with are well acquainted with this Bedouin saying:

Me against my brother,
Me and my brother against my cousin,
Me and my cousin against the stranger,

and with the concepts it refers to. I recently discovered among the Bakhtyari (highland nomads of the Iranian Zagros) an important point of law
which has not, curiously enough, been mentioned yet, to my knowledge,
by any of the travelers who have recently been in contact with this tribe.[1]
This is the "rule" of the *khin-cuq* [literally, in Lori, "blood stick"], the
operation of which can be summed up as follows: suppose there are four
individuals or groups – A, B, C and D; if A and B enter into open conflict, and if C takes sides with A, for example, D *not only* must take sides,
but also must take B's side. D is therefore said to be the *khin-cuq* of B.

This legal point calls for two comments:

1. I was greatly impressed in field investigations by the clear and
accurate way this rule was explained to me by my Bakhtyari informants
and by their awareness of its social "function," which was, they said, to
prevent an isolated group's being attacked and overrun by a larger group.
In fact, the *khin-cuq* rule encourages parties in a dispute to seek a solution
by arbitration instead of resorting to open conflict. But I would add that
if arbitration is unsuccessful and conflict does arise, the operation of this
same rule leads to a rapid extension of hostilities to a larger number of
groups. Thus, any group which is liable to be involved, though not itself
one of the primary parties to the conflict, should choose its allies at once;
if it does not, it is liable to be the *khin-cuq* of a group to which it is not
related, as was the case with D in our example. An exploration of this
phenomenon might help to explain what classical literature calls, for lack
of a better term, the "warlike tradition" of the nomadic pastoral tribes.

2. I was also impressed by the nature of this "rule" (*ravesh*) that my
informants in the field mentioned and on which they laid great stress.
And in fact there are many cases of conflict where the *khin-cuq* rule prevails even over the ties created by filiation, and its application therefore
involves related groups in conflicts with each other. But there are also a
number of examples which demonstrate that this "rule" is far from being
as binding as the Bakhtyari would lead one to believe. It is quite significant that examples of this nature should have been more numerous
in the second half of the nineteenth century, sometimes leading to extensive changes in a tribe's system of organization. In the Bakhtyari tribe,
this period represents a decisive stage in the historical process of autono-
mization and of concentration of political power in the hands of a dominant class of chieftains (*khan*). The latter development brought considerable economic advantages. At the beginning of the twentieth century, this
process resulted in the emergence of a hierarchically structured political
system affecting segmental levels and controlled at the top by one chief-
tain, the *il-khan*. This was a real state system through which the dominant
class could block or manipulate, at its pleasure, the law-enforcement

---

[1] The legal point concerned here was studied during my last stay in the field, in the
spring of 1972, unfortunately too late to discuss more fully in this article.

agencies of the segmental system. For further details on this evolution, I would like to refer to the works by Layard (1848), Curzon (1892), and d'Allemagne (1911). For more recent results, see Digard (1973 and i.p.).

We are therefore confronted both with a legal system, clearly stated and understood to the extent of its so-called social implications – which I will call the "native model" – and with a *de facto* system, operating on radically different premises, which the members of the society are aware of only in a vague way. The superimposition of these two apparently contradictory types of system in the Bakhtyari tribe (and, in various degrees, in other societies, in particular industrialized ones) suggests that the validity of a social model, for the anthropologist, varies as an inverse function of the degree of awareness displayed by members of the society of the social phenomenon it illustrates. The *khin-cuq* rule, corresponding here to the "native model," or at least to one of its aspects, must be considered as an "ideological" model in Marx's sense of the term; that is, as a model whose major result is to mask the effective laws of operation of the system. I now feel that anthropologists have been too long content to take the native model and develop it more or less accurately. Especially in their studies covering a number of the so-called segmental societies, they have perhaps not differentiated these various levels clearly enough; nor have they tried to produce a really operational model – i.e. a model applicable to all societies. This, I feel, is one of the most urgent tasks of an anthropology which claims to be a science.

REFERENCES

CURZON, G. N.
1892 *The Persian question*. London.
D'ALLEMAGNE, H. R.
1911 *Du Khorassan au pays des Backhtiaris*. Paris.
DIGARD, J.-P.
1973 "Techniques et culture des nomades Baxtyari d'Iran." Microfilm. Institut d'Ethnologie, Paris.
i.p. "Problèmes d'anthropologie historique des sociétés de pasteurs nomades: le cas d'une tribu d'Iran," in *Les Annales: Économies, Sociétés, Civilisations*. Paris: École Pratique des Hautes-Études.
LAYARD, L. H.
1848 *Early adventures in Persia*. London.

The Gnawa of Morocco: The Derdeba Ceremony

VIVIANA PAQUES

Throughout Morocco, the Gnawa are known for their public performances; they dance to the sound of drums and iron rattles, calling down divine blessings upon the passersby in return for alms. Generally, these dancers are blacks. They often wear a white uniform, set off by a double sash crossed in front and decorated with cowrie shells, and a military cap with a long black tassel, items provided by the Bureau of Tourism. At other times they dress in brightly colored robes and make the public laugh at their pranks.

Who are the Gnawa?

The name "Gnawa" was applied to the blacks, presumed to be former slaves, who made up the principal armed forces of the sultan Moulay Ismaïl. It has been claimed that the name derives from the appellation "Guineans," but this is doubtful since the majority of these blacks came not from Guinea but from the Sudan. It seems more convincing to us to derive the term "Gnawa" from the Tamazirt *igri ignawan* [the field of the cloudy sky], an expression implying a turbulent wind. In fact, the Gnawa do call themselves "the people of turbulence." Moreover, the expression "field of the sky" is a circumlocution for the star Aldebaran, which is found at the center of Gnawa cosmological representations and is also called *amzil* [the blacksmith].[1]

Indeed, the Gnawa form a religious order which does not include only blacks, or even only former slaves, but also adepts from the white race – Arabs, Berbers, Jews – who all call themselves "sons of Sidna Bilal," the black slave of the Prophet, the Christian Ethiopian who was converted to

---

[1] Father Foucauld gives, for the Ahaggar dialect, the terms *dar gennaouen* (*dar* [space] and *igennaouen* [mass of clouds]; by extension "rain") and *dar tgînîn* [whirlwind; a mass of air traveling restlessly with a double motion of rotation and translation] (*Dictionnaire touareg-français* vol. 1, p. 578).

Islam. Because of this, every Gnawa considers himself a slave and a black, no matter what his ethnic and social origins may be.

The Arabic-speaking Gnawa can be characterized, as can a number of other orders, by the particular musical instruments they use. Besides drums and rattles, they also play a three-stringed guitar, the *gumbri*, whose music causes the adepts to be possessed by genies. The Gnawa are in fact masters of the possession rituals practiced during ceremonies which last throughout the night. They cure people who are victims of genies or who suffer from diseases or internal disorders by wrapping them in colored veils.

There is, however, another order whose members also call themselves slaves and blacks. They are also called Gnawa, but this is not strictly correct, for they are devotees not of Sidna Bilal but of Lalla Mimuna or Lalla L'Krima. They use the same musical instruments, except for the *gumbri*. However, although they go into trances during certain meetings, where they eat sacrificial meat and bread together, they cannot organize dances of possession or make the genies (*muluk*) manifest themselves. They play during the day and stop at sunset, at the very moment when the Gnawa are beginning their possession rituals in the *derdeba* ceremony. They cannot "enter into the night." These adepts of Lalla Mimuna have inherited a platter which received the first silver offerings of the Companions of the Prophet. They go from town to town collecting alms, and the money they receive represents compensation for the blood shed during the primordial sacrifice, the blood of the deflowered virgin, the dowry money. They are selected from among the Berbers of the Atlas region and the southern oases. Their group constitutes the feminine side of the *derdeba*, the real slaves, belonging to the king.

The Gnawa order is found, with identical beliefs and rituals, throughout northern Africa, from the Mediterranean to Timbuktu, from Libya to Chad and the Sudan. The order includes all the children of Sidna Bilal (Paques 1964).

While the slaves of Lalla Mimuna and those of the *derdeba* form the two complementary parts of a large order of slaves (*'abid*), the latter also stand in a complementary relationship to other orders, the 'Aissawiya and the Qadriya. This relationship is felt quite profoundly by the Gnawa. They explain that when the first being was sacrificed, his body was divided into seven parts (in reality, nine), and each order received a portion. The skin, divided up in the same fashion, was used to make musical instruments for each order. The Gnawa still say that Sidi 'Abdelqader el Jilani, the founder of the Qadriya, was the first *bu derbala*, i.e. the first to wear the patched woolen robe that Sidi Heddi, founder of the Heddawa order, received as an inheritance from heaven when he was a child. This *derbala*, which was crawling with vermin, was seen by Sidi Heddi washed and patched together in heaven (Brunel 1955); it has become the model for the patched woolen tunics which the adepts have worn ever since. The Gnawa say that it was worn by Sidna Bilal, the *mueḍḍin* of the Prophet; made of red, white, and blue squares of material, "it contains the sky and the earth"; it is the union of the seven heavens and the seven earths, whose origin is explained by the myth of the creation of the world, as we shall see later on. Briefly summarized, this myth involves the intervention of three sorts of characters, who form a single ontological being: the Chorfa, who offer sacrifices and who in everyday life are sometimes butchers and barbers; the 'Aissawa, who with the Hamača are members of the complementary feminine order and are most often blacksmiths; and finally, the Gnawa.[2]

BASIC SYMBOLIC ELEMENTS IN GNAWA BELIEFS

The beliefs of the Gnawa are expressed in terms of a certain number of basic symbolic elements, which they share with the other orders.

1. The primary symbol is the blacksmith. On the mythic level, he is the "ever-living one." He is the perpetual motion representing the uninterrupted cycle of deaths and resurrections. His rising and falling motion causes him to be called "the monkey," which has become a euphemism for the male sexual organ. This blacksmith's anvil is his wife; she is also his head, which fell from heaven when the blacksmith was decapitated during the primordial sacrifice that foreshadowed all circumcisions.

The blacksmith has another aspect as well, that of woodworker, the one who cut down the tree to make ploughs and bent it in order to put together a drum. By thus attacking the cosmic tree, he took hold of space, which was originally as upright as a tree, and transformed it into a curved space like the body of a drum. Under yet another guise, the blacksmith is identified with the fellah, who opens up the earth, his mother, with the plough – his sexual organ – and later cuts off the ears of barley, which contain the souls of the dead, and spreads them over the grain market.

The blacksmith, the "ever-living," is given the name *el buḥari* among the Gnawa (for no one, when speaking about religion, will ever utter the word *haddad*, which technically means "blacksmith"). What is the *buḥari*? This word has a whole range of meanings for the Gnawa. In the first place, it is the book of Muslim traditions collected by the scholar who died at Bukhara (see Abu 'Abdullah Muhammed ben Ismaïl 1906). It discusses, in particular, the Prophet's ascension to the sixth level of heaven and his vision of the celestial tree, the *ṣedr* [Mediterranean jujube tree] mentioned in the Star *sura* of the Koran. It was upon this book, and

[2] Popular tradition, differing from historical tradition, makes Sidi ben 'Aïssa a blacksmith.

not upon the Koran itself, that the black guard of the sultan took the loyalty oath. Every year, from the month of Shaaban until the feast of Ashoora, it is solemnly read by the *tolba* of the *zawiya* of Tamegrout. This order was founded by a carpenter, the *qebab*, and was organized by Sidi ben Naser, a disciple of El Ghazi. Among the Gnawa, it has the reputation of having the "ever-living" in its keeping. Sidi ben Naser, who died on the first day of the Ashoora, is thought to rise again on the tenth day, when the reading ends. At this time, a plate of barley semolina, also called a *buḥari*, is brought out of the *zawiya* and is presented to the pilgrims, who fight over it. When the Gnawa have conjured up all the various types of genies during their dances of possession, they say that they have made "a *buḥari* ring," since, for them, the book contains them all.

The *buḥari* can also be a horse. Just like Buraq, the mare who carried the Prophet into heaven and will appear again at the end of time ridden by Jesus, the "ever-living," this mythical horse carried off the possessed during their mystical trances.

Buḥari is also the name given to the master of the royal stables, the *qaïd* of the *mechouar*. This man has the privilege of helping the king to mount one of the seven horses which precede him when he goes in official procession from his palace to the mosque. He is also the master of all blacksmiths in the palace; accompanied by two of his assistants, carriers of "flyswatters," he walks behind the king's horse. One of his most important duties seems to be the removal of any dead person from the palace. Traditionally, this *qaïd* would be provided by the *zawiya nasiriya* of Tamegrout.

The Gnawa also call their incense burner a *buḥari*. The incense, either black or white, is used to saturate both the seven colored veils covering the heads of the possessed and all other objects used in the *derdeba* ceremony. This is the same incense that the possessed must breathe when entering a trance.

Buḥari is also the name given to the banner (*'alam*) commemorating Sidna Bilal, the standard-bearer who gathered the combatants together during the holy wars. The fighters had been divided into seven small groups, each following a flag of a different color. These seven flags recall the seven veils used in the *derdeba*; together, they form the *sutra*, the white veil which Bilal wore on his head when he pierced the sky, as we shall see later.

Finally, the *buḥari*, the "ever-living," has a human incarnation in the person of Ibn Abbas el Qutam, who is buried at Samarkand in the province of Bukhara. According to local legend, this cousin of the Prophet, the ancestor of the Abbassids of Baghdad, was decapitated – or, according to other versions, decapitated himself – before disappearing, carrying his head, under a boulder which closed over him. Ibn Abbas still lives there for all eternity, next to a subterranean river called the Or. This location was used as a burial ground for the wives of the Timurids and is still a shrine for all Muslims.

The symbolism of the "ever-living" is also expressed astronomically. From the point of view of relationships between heaven and earth, the "ever-living" is represented by the sun, conceived of as the severed head of the red-light serpent which surrounds the earth at dawn and dusk. Its sacrifice took place at night, and the sun only rises from the dead at daybreak: this is why the *derdeba* is still called *lil* [night] and lasts from sunset to sunrise. From a cosmic perspective, the blacksmith is represented by the Milky Way, which rises to the horizon in the summer sky only to go back below it during the winter months. It is divided by the ecliptic traveled by the sun and by the planets, (*hajaj* [wandering ones]), which have come out from the cosmic tree of Sidi Mussa; the cross thus formed has become the identifying mark of the Gnawa order. Finally, among the planets, the role of one who dies and rises from the dead falls to *Qibla* (Venus in the east), the one who offers sacrifices and the star of the Prophet, and to *Zohrah* (Venus in the west), the one sacrificed and the star of Lalla Fatima.

The same symbolism is also expressed on earth in terms of a number of basic elements, first and foremost the *şedr* [Mediterranean jujube tree]. This tree, mentioned in the Koran, is the sacred tree of the Gnawa, as it was for the Chorfa before the reformist persecutions in Islam. It is *şedr* branches that are made into hedges (*zeriba*) around houses, enclosures, and sheaves of barley piled up to be taken to the threshing floor; the *zeriba* mark the boundaries within which the spiritual powers of the family (*horma*) are operative. For the Gnawa, the *şedr* is divided into three parts, a red trunk with three branches, each of a different sort: on the left, a yellow branch, bearing apricots; in the center, a black branch, bearing figs; and on the right, a white grapevine, which twines around all of the branches to insure their unity. Each part of the tree lets genies of the corresponding color pass through. Beneath the tree are various levels: the *segya*, representing all the *mrabtin* [*marabouts*], which flows over the *dunya*, an image of twilight, itself placed upon the black earth, out of which come all the genies of the underworld, the genies of the Sudan, who may be red, black, or white. One or several of these trees is present in all Gnawa sanctuaries, depending upon the genies with whom the sanctuaries are particularly associated. Let us note that it was the grapevine, the tree of Lalla Myriam [Mary], which, according to legend, was cut down and sacrificed.

Another basic part of this symbolism, summing up the same representations, is the mountain, together with the stream which rushes down it. South of Marrakesh, it is represented by the Atlas mountain range. For the Gnawa of the Marrakesh area, it takes the form of three rocky peaks: Sidi Fars, an image of the foreskin (the head of the male organ), a shrine of the Hamača order; Mulay Brahim, an image of the body (and thus of the sex organ), a shrine of the 'Aïssawa; and finally, in the plains, the Tamesloth boulder, an image of the tree root and a shrine of the Gnawa. For these three orders, pilgrimages are obligatory, although others may participate in them as well. At the foot of the Mulay Brahim peak flows the Gheghaya wadi, one of the three branches of the wadi Sidi Chamarouch (the king of the genies), whose source is in Toubkal, still called the mountain of the Glaoui, the high point of the Atlas range.

2. All of the representations described are connected with an interpretation of the "ever-living" as a blacksmith. But we have also indicated that this being could be conceived of as a fellah, and this opens the way to a new cycle of representations, establishing an identity between tilling the soil and weaving, between the ear of barley and man. For the Gnawa, the first fellah was the *mueḏḏin* of the Prophet, who cultivated his field by irrigating it through three *segyat* and by dividing it into squares, as peasants from the valley of the Draa wadi still do in Ternata and Zagora. Each *segya* divides the field into halves, then into quarters; then each quarter is in turn divided, giving a total of twenty-four squares bounded by earthen levees, or *gemun*. South of Marrakesh, where the fields are irrigated only by rainwater, tilling is done in a different direction every year, from west to east one year, from north to south another, so as to clearly identify the furrows with the threads (woof and warp) in weaving. According to the Chorfa, cultivation and weaving appeared on earth at the same time, when the first *shereef* burned all of the *ṣedr* covering the area. One particular version of the myth states that the first field descended from heaven after the sacrifice of Shaaban, a feast celebrated by all the Gnawa.

The ear of barley is identified with the initiate who must suffer all the grain's vicissitudes during the dances of possession. Just as the barley stalk is composed of seven parts, so man possesses seven souls. In imitation of the plant's cycle, the initiate, during these dances of possession, is put to death and divided up, and is then reborn via the intervention of the *moo addem*, representing the blacksmith and the fellah in the order. Just as the seeds in the plant's stem come out of the ground upon germination and become receptacles for the souls of the dead, so the initiate, in going through all the stages of the dance, reassembles the great body of the blacksmith, through which will pass the subterranean souls of the dead and the celestial souls of those to come in the great cosmic union which we shall describe below.

The fellah begins by ploughing, i.e. by slaughtering the sterile earth, his mother; then he sows and reaps, dressed in a skin apron similar to that of the blacksmith, the *tabenda*, a religious symbol. He gathers the ears of barley, carries them to the threshing floor, and separates the grain from the chaff just as man is separated from woman in the *zawiya*. He tosses the straw into the air with his pitchfork, in the sunlight; some of the seeds stay trapped there and thus die in the sunlight. The others are collected for the *rahba* [grain market], to be sold and then buried in silos. After the grain has been brought up by basket, it is divided into stacks and then sifted, to separate the wheat from the chaff. The flour can then be boiled or grilled to prepare *smeita*, a staple of desert peoples' diets. Thus grain nourishes the blacksmith and all the men of his various embodiments. These individuals are considered dead men; the living souls locked within the seeds are then saved because they give life to the great dead: man, the blacksmith, who will thus be able to rise up towards heaven and bring about the great mystical union by means of his dance.

3. The grain market (*rahba*) is a holy place throughout all Morocco; to make an oath there is equivalent to swearing upon the Koran. At Marrakesh, it is also a wool market in the morning and was formerly a slave market in the afternoon. It has thus quite naturally become the basic symbolic element in their religious representations. People know that if a child who is not himself a Gnawi enters the Gnawa order, he is a "bought" child. This sham purchase has already been described many times by those who have studied this order: the child's relatives make him go inside the *zeriba* [sheep fold], a term applied to all the *zawiya* of the Gnawa, and the Gnawa assemblage sells the child back to them for a preposterously low sum.

In the eyes of the Gnawa, the market, where business is always done in the daytime, represents the sky and all the stars. Symbolically, selling goods at market means the rising of a star just at sunrise; the sun is the buyer. In the same way, marriage symbolizes the conjunction of two stars, and childbirth the moment when a star falls in the west. The sale of wool has also become part of these beliefs: wool (*soff*) has become the symbol of knowledge, of mystical communion (Sufism is externally represented by the woolen robe or the simple woolen bonnet worn by the adepts of Sidi Bunu). For the Gnawa, wool worn on a man's body is identified with the hair and fur which stand on end (just as the spiny branches of the *şedr* straighten up towards heaven) when an initiate "rises" (*tatla*) during possession. The counterpart of the grain market is the slaughterhouse (*gurna*) and the meat market, where the first sterile cow (*agra*) was sold as a substitute for a slave and made fertile by the wind; under the name of *dada stra*, she was slaughtered and butchered by the blacksmith, her son and her spouse. She is the sexual organ of the sleeping earth, the fallow land covered with *şedr*.

4. Meat leads us to another basic symbol of the ever-living blacksmith: sacrificial animals. The cow symbolizes the *dunya* which comes out of

the earth and swells up; the billy goat is the top of the *dunya* when it rises towards the sky; two chickens represent the two whirlwinds which turn in opposite directions, the *hajaj* which make the *dunya* rise and fall. The *dunya* is conceived of as a serpent of red light or as the *zeriba* [spiny branches of the *şedr*].

5. At the heart of the order itself, the "ever-living" is symbolized by the *gumbri*, the musical instrument used to summon the genies. This represents the very body of the sacrificed blacksmith. It looks like a three-stringed guitar, has a boat-shaped resonance chamber, and is covered with a skin that the player can beat while he plucks the strings. The *gumbri* is the sultan, or Allah, and the player is Bilal, his slave. The instrument is identified with death, with the possessed (*jdeb*), and with barley seed. It can only be played at night, inside the sanctuary. It is accompanied by two drums, its "wives," only played outside the sanctuary, and by *karkabou* [iron clappers], which keep a rhythm like that of a horse's gallop.

All these basic mythic elements underlie the exhibitions during pilgrimages, which are a concrete expression of the cosmology revealed through religious feasts.

These pilgrimages are directed toward the sepulchres of particular saints, honored on set dates by the groups who have them as patrons. These saints or *marabouts* have many different characteristics, but all occupy a position after that of the triad composed of the Prophet, Lalla Fatima Zohra, his daughter, and Sidna Bilal, his *mueḍḍin*. The Prophet is identified with the cosmic blacksmith; Bilal is his word, his spittle, which makes Lalla Fatima Zohra laugh and which, according to legend, acts as a connection between her and her spouse, Sidna 'Ali, or between her and the Prophet, for in the popular mind the Prophet is often confused with his son-in-law.

The two canonical feasts celebrated by all the Gnawa are first Shaaban, preceding the month of Ramadan, and then the Mwulud. Shaaban is celebrated at the time when Bilal rises to the heavens and dies; the Mwulud is the time when he comes back to earth after the head of the blacksmith which has fallen to earth and become his anvil. These events are brought to mind in the course of every *derdeba*. To understand them properly, one must try to make a synthesis of Gnawa cosmology by relating it to the various steps in the creation.

GNAWA COSMOLOGY

In the beginning, there was nothing but the black earth, which was sterile, the sea (firmament), and night. Our world came out of a serpent's egg which was placed upon the sea and covered by the night, which made it fertile. Two whirlwinds turning in opposite directions made the egg crack open: the white fell first and then evaporated and rose beyond the darkness; the "red" (yolk) sank into the black earth, the rock which rested upon the subterranean waters. There, like the white, it was divided into seven parts, so that there are now seven earths and seven heavens (or, more precisely, seven celestial earths).

The efforts of the cosmos were thenceforth to be directed toward reuniting the black and white earths. The red was to come out of the black earth like a serpent from a cave: this serpent of light, which surrounded the earth, is the *dunya*. Its sex is female, but its head is male. The rising whirlwind lifted it towards the sky, like a *ṣedr* tree; it then penetrated the celestial sea at night, in the region of Aldebaran, in order to reach the white earth. This was the first marriage, consummated at night. As a result of this defloration, several new entities were born: blood, drunk by the black earth; the *sutra*, or hymen of the sky; the veil of white wool which contained the seven colors and was stuck like a turban on the spiny head of the *dunya*; milk; water; and the tree of Sidi Mussa, a tree with seven levels set in the firmament with the seven planets. Following this mythical marriage, night cut off the head of the *dunya*; it caught fire and became the sun, which fell back from the cosmic world to the terrestrial heaven. This operation was the first circumcision; it is considered to be the birth of the Islamic world and occurred at a time commemorated on earth by the Mwulud.

This union also had the effect of setting the genies (*mulik* or *jwed*) in motion. The black genies of the depths went back up into the *dunya* and, by way of its head, penetrated into the white earth. On the other hand, the white genies of the celestial earth remain attached to the hair of the *dunya*, which was taken into the *sutra*, which became the first cultivated field when it fell to earth. This grandiose cosmological conception is transposed into religious ritual by the Gnawa: Bilal, the voice of the Prophet, went up to the minaret to pronounce his profession of faith, *la illah llah*. His voice pierced the firmament, but he himself fell to his death, pierced by the arrows of the Jews. He landed at the feet of the Prophet, who brought him back to life. The minaret is thus an image of the *dunya* lifted up toward heaven. Bilal is its spouse: he is the black genie who rises up to heaven.

All the *derdeba* ceremonies were organized in terms of these mythical events, which we have too briefly summarized. The *derdeba* is night and the mystical marriage of heaven and earth. Like human marriage, whose stages it reproduces, it is a feast lasting three days. The first day is that of the *tengya* [sifter]. Invitations, gifts from adepts in the form of food, of chickens and other sacrificial animals, or even of silver, are given to the *moqadma*, who remains shut away inside the *hajba*, an image of enclosure in a *ṣedr* hedge, just like a married girl when the *gumbri* player comes to her home. She embodies the celestial earth and he the black-smith; the silver is the price of blood. Gifts of clothing pay for the use of veils with the genies' colors, worn by the adepts. The ceremony takes on meaning when the good grain is separated from the tares with the aid of a sifter. The second day is that of the nocturnal ceremony, the *lilah*. At sunset the cow is slaughtered, an image of the *dunya*, the egg fertilized by night. On the third day, the *halu* ["sweet" or "sugared"], they eat the he-goat, which represents the head of the *dunya*, and also the chickens, which represent the two opposing whirlwinds. The food is always pre-pared without salt, for salt is life; without salt, food is dead, and this is why souls are attracted to it. (The name *halu* is also given to the meal eaten by the husband on the morning after the marriage.)

It is during the night of *lilah* that the great possession ceremony, the *derdeba*, takes place. It is made up of two parts, one profane and external, the other sacred and internal; the latter is performed first. Its function is to give present form to the cosmic events that made the world break into seven parts parallel to the seven colors. The other part of the ceremony has the goal of reuniting disparate elements by means of the journey to be undertaken by the souls of the possessed through all the stages of the world, so as to permit penetration into the celestial earth, behind which is God. It is through the body of the *moqadden*, who is the blacksmith, that all the souls of dead adepts rise up to the celestial earth and the souls of future adepts descend, in an eternal cycle of reincarnation. The purpose of the night ceremony is thus to sacrifice the adepts and then to cut them up into seven pieces, like the *dunya*, parallel to the seven types of genies subdivided according to the seven colors which are representative of the seven categories of the universe which must be traversed by the *dunya* so as to arrive in heaven. Then all the souls of the possessed come back together to make up the body of the cosmic blacksmith, who, through his dance, will make all dead souls come back to life and all future souls come back to earth. This great spiritual force only lives to the extent that he feeds on souls by killing personalities.

The profane part of the nocturnal ceremony is made up of two ele-ments: the *uqba* and the *nuqša*. During the first of these, the musicians sing about the creation of the world; they divide a communal meal just as they would for a marriage ceremony; the tea they drink is reminiscent of the water of the earth drunk by the *dunya* before being slaughtered. Next comes the *ftaɔ el rahba*, the opening of the grain market. The male adepts go out into the streets, accompanied by two drums; they are now identified with the *dunya* when she seduced the celestial earth, producing the *sutra*. The Milky Way is symbolized by a cortege of women, each carrying two candles. At the head of the group is the *tabieka*, a platter bearing milk and dates, symbols of sperm and blood; this platter is identified with the head of the *dunya* when it came under the power of the two opposing whirlwinds. The celestial and subterranean worlds are henceforth open, one through the heavenly sacrifice of Lalla Fatima Zohrah and the other through that of the blacksmith-*dunya*. Consequently, the communication of the genies is made possible, space is no longer closed, adepts may enter the sanctuary just as the husband comes to his wife, and possession by the genies may begin. The possession will continue through seven stages, conducted by the *gumbri*, the dead blacksmith, until daybreak; daybreak marks the resurrection of the demiurge, when he lifts up his head, the sun.

REFERENCES

ABU ʿABDALLAH MUHAMMED BEN ISMAÏL
  1906 *Les traditions islamiques*. Translated by O. Houdas and W. Marcais. Paris: Imprimerie Nationale.
BRUNEL, R.
  1955 *Le monarchisme errant dans l'Islam. Siddi Heddi et les Heddawa*. Paris: Emile Larose.
Dictionnaire touareg-français
  1951 *Dictionnaire touareg-français*, volume 1. Paris: Imprimerie Nationale.
PAQUES, V.
  1964 *L'arbre cosmique dans la pensée et la vie quotidienne du nord-ouest africain*. Paris: Institut d'Ethnologie.

Marriage and Marriage Rites Among the Kazakhs in the Nineteenth and Early Twentieth Centuries

KH. ARGYNBAEV

Abundant and extremely interesting factual material in the works of pre-revolutionary authors and in local archives provides an excellent source for the study of various stages in the history of family and matrimonial relations among the Kazakhs. Kazakh wedding rites during the Soviet period have been analyzed by Soviet ethnologist N. A. Kisljakov (1969: 98–114), who used literary sources.

The abundant ethnographic material at our disposal concerning marriage forms among the Kazakhs and the various customs and rites connected with them, which often retain archaic elements, allows us to trace the evolution of these marriage forms and to understand the long and complicated history of Kazakh family development.

One of the most widespread forms of marriage among the Kazakhs was marriage by matchmaking and with a *kalym* [bride-wealth] payment. For very young people, the matchmaking was done by parents or older relatives. At a more mature age, the young people often contracted marriages by their own free will. Even in such cases, however, the customs connected with matchmaking had to be followed.

Before the official matchmaking talks, the parties involved would find out, through various family ties or other connections, all the pros and cons of the intended match. Even a preliminary bride-show was often held. If such private reconnaissance showed both parties favorably disposed, the suitor's father could send his *zhaushi* [confidential agent] to make an official proposal (Altynsarin 1870: 104).

When a general agreement had been reached and the consent of the bride's father obtained, the confidential agent was presented on his return with *shegé shapan* [robes] (Divaev 1900: 15). The very meaning (*shegé* [a nail], *shapan* [a robe]) of this gift testifies to the wish of both sides to make their preliminary talks firmly binding, as though fixed with nails.

After the confidential agent had undertaken a successful mission, the suitor's father would send matchmakers, varying in number from three to thirty. Their leader was an experienced matchmaker, a close relative, or the suitor's father himself.

On the arrival of the matchmakers, and after a proper reception, there were usually official talks between the matchmakers and the bride's side concerning the amount of bride-money, expenses for the wedding arrangements and dowry, preliminary terms of the bride-money payment, and the date of giving the daughter in marriage.

The mutual consent was sealed by reading a prayer called *ak bata* [white prayer]. After the prayer, all the matchmakers present took a sip of water from an *aiak* [wooden cup], and the matchmaker-in-chief on the suitor's side announced the *bata aiak* [quantity of cattle given as a present] on this occasion.

Before the Kazakhs converted to the religion of Islam, the parties to a forthcoming marriage sealed their agreement by sacrificing a sheep and swearing on its blood. For this purpose, a wooden cup was filled with the animal's *bauyz daukan* [arterial blood], and the cup was immediately handed to the *bauyzdau kuda* [matchmakers-in-chief of both sides] who simultaneously dipped their fingers into it. In more ancient times, they dipped the sharp points of their lances into the cup and each in turn would take a sip of the still-hot blood (Kudaiberdyuly 1911). Both sides thus pledged to keep their oath, and anyone who did not keep faith was punished with the lance of the insulted party, which had been dipped in the sacred blood of the sacrificed animal. Such rites vanished long ago.

In honor of the promised bride, her father was presented with a special *kargybau* [a collar] or *ouky tagar* [a mark], which signified that his daughter had already been promised to someone. Only after this had taken place could the contracting groups be considered legal matchmakers and be treated to a special dish (*kuiryk-bauyr*) prepared from fresh boiled tail-fat and liver. Mutual treating of each other by the matchmakers was a symbol of the families' having entered into a relationship which was expected to endure for many years. While doing this they kept repeating, "*Kuieu zhuz zhyldyk, kuda myn zhyldyk*" [Son-in-law for hundreds of years, and related parents of the husband and wife for thousands of years] (*Polevye zapisi* 1966–1970). This meant that family relations could continue far beyond the life of one generation. It is possibly an indication of the endogamic customs that once existed among the Kazakhs.

In case one of the sides broke the marriage conditions announced at the matchmaking talks, the mutual acknowledgment of this action before the *bii* could serve as direct proof of one party's guilt in breaking an absolutely legal matchmaking agreement.

The end of the matchmaking was celebrated with entertainment and feasts, at which the newly related parties were put to various tests by women simply for fun. They were forced to sing, to play musical instruments, or to tell legends, and if they could not, they had to pay a forfeit with *kède* [gifts].

Before his or her departure, each matchmaker was given a *kiyt* [present]; if the fiancé's father was not present among the matchmakers, a good saddlehorse or a full-grown camel covered with a large *kaly kylem* [pile carpet] was sure to be sent to him as a gift (*Polevye zapisi* 1966–1970). Such presents and gifts sometimes amounted to *ush togyz* [thirty head] of camels or horses (Ibragimov 1872: 130).

Some time after the matchmaking, the bride's father paid a return visit at the invitation of his related matchmaker, the groom's father. The aim of this visit was for them to get to know each other, and for the bride's father to receive the bulk of the bride-wealth. For this reason, before the matchmakers of the bride's side left, the necessary quantity of cattle was taken out of the total herd of sheep and horses to pay the bride-money. Usually, when showing the animals to the matchmakers, the shepherd had the right to one sheep and the horse-herder to one horse for their respective services in *kosak bau* [tying up sheep] and *kuryk bau* [catching horses]. In addition, one animal was taken for the *korymdyk* [fiancé-show] (Kustanaev 1894: 27) and one to insure that the bride would speak pleasingly, i.e. that she would not be *kelyn tyly* [boring or talkative] (Levanevskii 1895: 77).

Shortly before the wedding, when the bride had come of age, most of the bride-money had to be paid and the fiancé had to pay his first official visit to his bride (*uryn baru*). This was usually the first time that the couple had met, and the visit was therefore of great importance for their future life. They could get to know each other, have a talk, get accustomed to each other, and even fall in love – which was the parents' goal. Bearing in mind the main goal of this official visit, it should be noted that the Kazakh word *uryn* is probably a derivative of the old Turkish word *urun* [to nestle close to; cuddle up to]; the still-older Turkish expression *bayir-sagnï bulsa bayirga urun* [if you find a merciful one, nestle close to his breast] (*Drevnetjurkskii slovar'* 1969: 615) testifies to this assumption.

In this connection, it is necessary to note that the now-popular view of this visit as a secret meeting between fiancé and bride does not correspond to its real sense and meaning. The outer form of this visit was far from being secret (Grodekov 1889: 63; Kustanaev 1894: 27; Malyshev 1902: 24; Dinaev 1900: 15; *Narody Srednei Azii* 1963: 434; Kisljakov 1969: 104–105). If we also take into account the fact that sometimes such visits could prevent unsuitable matches, their main aim and significance become still clearer. So both sides did their best to conduct such a visit in the appropriate manner.

The fiancé's experienced *kuieu zholdas* [best man] led his suite of five or six persons on this trip. The party was provided with numerous gifts:

ylu [a gift to the future father-in-law's home], *esyk ashar* [a gift on the occasion of entering his home], *zhyrtys* [several score of "scraps of different cloth" to distribute among those gathered], and many other small things, presented to observe various customs and rites during the visit.

A special yurta was erected for the fiancé's suite at the bride's *aul*; they were permanently among young people, but at this time the bride was, as a rule, at her relatives', where a *kyz kashar* [traditional party] was organized on the next day. At the end of the party the older women pretended to capture the bride, while her girl friends tried to prevent such "violence." The women then took the bride to her father's house, where a bed for the young couple had been prepared beforehand. Then a few young women from among the bride's relatives (her elder brothers' wives or other relatives) brought in the fiancé, who gave them presents for the invitation (*kuieu shakyru*). Meanwhile other women put artificial obstacles in his way by throwing under his feet a long pole (*bakan*), used to erect the cupola ring of a yurta, and by stretching before him a rope which was used for tying up *zhely* [foals]. According to popular belief, these implements were considered sacred, so they could not be stepped over, and in this case they could not be gone around either. So the fiancé gave presents to the women, thus persuading them to take away all the obstacles and allow him to proceed further. An elderly woman opened the door of the yurta of the bride's father, receiving a special present (*esyk ashar*) for this service (Altynsarin 1870: 110; Kustanaev 1894: 28; *Obychai Kirgizov* 1878: 35; *Polevye zapisi* 1966–1970). The bride's mother met the fiancé in the yurta, helped him to place *otka mai kuiu* [fat in the hearth], and then treated him to a cup of milk, known by the collective name *ak* [white] (Ibragimov 1872: 138). These rites accomplished, she wished the young couple happiness and went to her bed on the other side of the partition.

Then the young women attending the bride left the fiancé alone with her, after he had given them presents for *shymyldyk ashar* [opening the curtain], *tesek salar* [making the bed], *kol ustatar* [shaking hands with the bride], and *shash sipatar* [stroking her hair]. On this occasion, the fiancé and bride could sit until morning and admire each other, speak in whispers, even sleep side by side, but they had no right to the intimacy of husband and wife. Early in the morning the fiancé had to leave for his yurta before his future mother-in-law and father-in-law arrived. After this imitation of a traditional first nuptial night (which really took place later during the wedding feast), the fiancé could repeatedly meet his bride in secret (*kalyndyk oinau*) until the wedding day. It sometimes happened that, in spite of the prohibition, the fiancé and the bride lived as husband and wife during these secret meetings (*Polevye zapisi* 1966–1970).

Even the *bii*, when solving disputes about bride-money, in cases in which the prospective match had failed to take place for some reason, took into account the fiancé's official visit; this is a significant fact, attesting to the great importance of the first official visit paid by the fiancé to his bride. Even if, after the visit, the wedding settlement was broken by the bride's father, he kept the bride-money that had already been paid. All the ceremonies, rights, and duties connected with the fiancé's visits, both secret and official, were nothing but survivals from the earlier matriarchal system.

After a successful official visit by the fiancé, both sides started wedding preparations. The fiancé's father paid off the remainder of the bride-money and sent the previously determined quantity of cattle for the wedding feast (*toi maly*) and some parts of the wedding yurta agreed upon by both parties. In his turn, the bride's father prepared the main part of the wedding yurta, a *sèukele* [wedding headdress], and many other dowry articles.

Having received a formal invitation, the fiancé went to the wedding feast given by the bride's father (*uzatu toiy*). His party was led by his mother. They had a special present for the bride's mother: payment for her milk (*sut aky*), various cloth scraps to distribute (*zhyrtys*) (Grodekov 1889: 66; *Polevye zapisi* 1966–1970), and many other small things, plus some money for bribes (*kède*) if necessary.

Before the wedding began, the wedding yurta (*otau*) was erected. The women who took part in the erection of the yurta got presents from the fiancé's mother for helping to put up the *shanrak koterer* [cupola ring], for covering the yurta (*otau zhabar*), and for the *otau korymdyk* [yurta show]. When the yurta had been erected, a sheep was sacrificed and all the women were treated to the meat. The fiancé and his best man usually took part in this entertainment.

By nighttime a nuptial bed had been prepared at this yurta, where the newlyweds were to spend their first matrimonial night (Levshin 1832: 107; Makovetskii 1886: 12; Kustanaev 1894: 32; Levanevskii 1895: 84; Izraztsov 1897: 77; Divaev 1900: 12–13; Divaev 1889). Everything was repeated: an imaginary fight for the bride, an invitation to the fiancé, the setting up of artificial obstacles of all kinds with payments exacted for their removal, and the giving of presents for making the nuptial bed, for organizing the meeting, etc., exactly as had been done during the fiancé's first visit to the bride.

The difference was that during the first visit they met at the yurta of the bride's father and had no right to engage in intimacy, whereas this time their meeting was in private at the wedding yurta and was, in fact, the beginning of their married life. If the bride was not a virgin and the fiancé was not to blame, he could give her up. In the seventeenth and eighteenth centuries, if this happened, the best men would rip open a horse's belly, cut a saddle in two, and tear the fiancé's clothes. Such a display of protest did not usually end well. Insulted by the loss of his daughter's honor, her father could sentence the one guilty of her defloration (if he was in the *aul*), and the girl herself, to death (Andreev 1796: 43–44; *Pozorishche strannykh* 1797: 201–202; Spasskii 1820: 154; Levshin 1832: 106). But by the beginning of the nineteenth century, such extreme measures were very seldom taken, and by the end of the century most cases were solved peacefully by means of penalties imposed for the daughter's behavior.

To avoid such disgrace, the Kazakhs were very strict with their daughters. Not without reason did a popular saying run, *kyzga kyryk uiden tyiu* [a ban is imposed on the girl by forty families].

If the bride was a virgin everybody was glad, and both sides would begin immediately to prepare the wedding feast with great enthusiasm. Many neighboring *aul*s were invited to participate. After feasting on the abundant food, they started various national games, wrestling, and *bèige* [races]. Poor families held more modest feasts.

Immediately after the *bèige*, the ceremonial song *zhar-zhar* was sung. The *djigit*s congratulated and consoled the bride, and she, in turn, expressed her regret at leaving her family home, native area, and relatives.

On the eve of departure, the bride and her girl friends made the rounds of all her relatives, saying goodbye to their homes (*kyz tanysu*). In the remote past, she was carried on a carpet from one yurta to another on this occasion (Levshin 1832: 105). The relatives made her memorable presents of carpets, robes, and various decorative items (Altynsarin 1870: 114; Grodekov 1889: 73; Ibragimov 1872: 143; Izraztsov 1897: 79; *Polevye zapisi* 1966–1970). In the evening, the *neke kyiu* [wedding ceremony] took place at her father's yurta according to the Muslim rite.

On the day of the bride's departure, the dowry was shown to the matchmakers, the wedding yurta was dismantled, the wedding caravan was prepared for the journey, and presents were given to the matchmakers, the fiancé, and the bride. Then at a special yurta the bride changed into the costume of a young wife. Her head was decorated with a *sèukele* [wedding headdress] with a *zhelek* [special veil] in which she would enter the fiancé's *aul*. This traditional headdress was a symbol of her consecration into the group of *kelynshek* [young wives]; a young wife was usually known by this veil.

The customs connected with the preparation of a wedding yurta (*otau*) deserve special attention. One can trace survivals of the matrilocal marriage (Bonch-Osmolovskii 1926: 109) in the inclusion of the yurta in the dowry. And the Kazakh material yields a very interesting detail: one-half of the *koshma* [felt cover], the *shanrak* [cupola ring], and the *bosaga* [door-posts] for the wedding yurta were supplied by the fiancé's father, in order for the dowry to include a complete yurta. We think that this has a special meaning connected with the supremacy of the patriarchate. Let us assume that if the fiancé's provision of half the *koshma* [felt cover] had some economic significance, then the provision of a cupola ring and door-posts symbolized the husband's right to consider himself, in future, the rightful owner of the wedding yurta. And it is perhaps not without reason that expressions formed in the language for determining the ownership of the yurta: "Look at the *shanrak*" (*shanrakka kara*); "Whose is the *shanrak*?" (*shanrak kymdyke?*); and so on.

The bride's caravan was colorfully decorated, and she set out on her journey on one of the "happier" days of the week (Tuesday and Friday were considered bad days for traveling). The bride's mother and some of her close relatives accompanied her.

Approaching the fiancé's *aul*, the bride and her *zhenge* [sister-in-law] waited while the rest entered the *aul*. The women of the *aul* began at once to sort out the dowry and to erect the wedding yurta; the young women and girls met the bride and formed a circle around her, hiding her under a *shymyldyk* [wedding curtain] lest the fiancé's elder relatives should see her. The elderly women of the *aul* organized a *shashu* [shower] expressing their best wishes.

Before the *uilenu toyi* [wedding feast] began, a special ceremony, the *bet ashar* [bride-show] took place, to introduce the bride to the fiancé's relatives. For this ceremony, the honorable people of the *aul* assembled at the yurta of the fiancé's father; then the bride was brought in in full wedding dress, and the mother-in-law helped her to add fat to the hearth. After this ceremony, the *djigit* [improvisor] sang the traditional everyday song (*bet ashar*). Its content met the requirements of patriarchal family standards. The near-relatives present at the bride-show ceremony publicly announced what presents they were giving the new family.

After the wedding feast the bride's relatives returned home with *kiyt* [presents].

Some time after the mother's departure, the bride changed *sèukele* for *zhaulyk* [woman's headdress]; this change was also accompanied by rites marking her transition into the group of married women. And, after her first child was born, on solemn occasions she would wear a *kundyk* [turban] made of cotton fabric, connected with her transition into the next age group.

According to custom, the bride had no right to visit her parents (*terkyn*) until the birth of her first child. Only after the birth could she and her husband go to her parents' home with the baby, carrying presents (*torkyndeu*) for the relatives (*Polevye zapisi* 1966–1970). This custom is a direct survival of matriarchy. During this visit the bride's father or his heir had to allot to her an *enshy* [a piece of land] out of his fortune. With this visit all customs, ceremonies, duties, and rights connected with the marriage came to an end.

Let us briefly describe some universal rites repeated more than once at all stages of the matchmaking and wedding:

The *shashu* [shower] rite was very popular; it was performed on any occasion during the matchmaking and wedding, both at the bride's *aul* and at the fiancé's *aul*, by women of a venerable age. They usually showered the bride with *sykpa* [small cheeses], *bauyrsak* [pieces of fried bread], sweets, sugar, and small coins, pronouncing benedictions upon the young couple. Judging by the expression, *nur zhausyn* [let the light come onto you from heaven], often repeated during "showering," the rite was connected with popular cosmological beliefs. According to popular notions, this "showering" as though by the rain could bring the young family happiness, wealth, and posterity. During the rite, all those present had to pick up everything thrown as *shashu*, because it was considered sacred and could bring happiness.

During the first official visit of the fiancé to his bride, and during the wedding feasts at the bride's and the fiancé's *aul*, hundreds of yards of various kinds of cloth were torn into *zhyrtys* [scraps] and distributed among those present. These scraps had no utilitarian significance at all; they were connected with a magic notion that a *zhyrtys* could bring happiness to those who kept it as a relic.

During the matchmaking and the wedding, only those women were allowed to associate with the fiancé and the bride and participate in erecting the wedding yurta who were exemplary in all respects, leading a happy family life and having many children. This was to insure that the young couple would be equally happy and would have many children. Childless women were especially feared and were not allowed to provide any services.

All the rites described above were connected with magic. During the first visit of the fiancé to his bride at her father's home, the fiancé put fat into the hearth under the guidance of the bride's mother. On the arrival of the bride at the fiancé's *aul*, this rite was performed by the bride at her father-in-law's yurta under the guidance of her mother-in-law. The rite of adding fat to the hearth fire is connected with the cult of ancestors. According to a popular notion, this act could both gain the dead ancestors' favor and cajole the sacred fire to make the young couple happy in all respects. Since this rite was performed by the fiancé at his father-in-law's hearth and by the bride at her father-in-law's hearth, it is worth noting that this evidently mutual appeal to the ancestors was meant to join a stranger to one's family. There is no doubt as to the connection of this ancient rite, in one way or another, with the cult of ancestors.

The popular traditions, customs, and rites described above and existing among the Kazakhs before the October Revolution have been transformed beyond recognition during the years of Soviet power. Long-standing customs and institutions (e.g. *kalym*, betrothal of small children) have disappeared without a trace. But many traditional customs and rites have been preserved and are developing under new conditions. Among them, matchmaking is worth mentioning; it is now performed only on the initiative of the young people themselves, who agree to marry and then announce it to their parents, who carry out the official matchmaking. But the old complicated matchmaking process has become much simpler as the main, decisive condition is now the mutual love and disposition of the young people. The first official visit of the fiancé to the bride (*uryn baru*) has also lost its former meaning. And not only are the rites not performed, but the term itself has gone out of use. Instead, a new term (*korzhyn aparu*) has appeared; it indicates the bringing of gifts in a *korzhyn* [saddlebag] by the fiancé to the bride's family after the matchmaking. Now these gifts are often brought in suitcases, but the term *korzhyn aparu* still exists. Thus the custom *korzhyn aparu* is a surviving element of the former first visit paid by the fiancé to his bride – *uryn baru*. Earlier, the feast organized on this occasion was called *uryn toi*; now such a feast is called *korzhyn toi*, which shows once more that the former meaning and significance of the whole ceremonial have changed.

Great importance is now given to the wedding that takes place either at the bride's father's (*uzatu toiy*) or at the finance's father's (*uilenu toiy*). These wedding feasts are accompanied by traditional folk and modern games, songs, and dances. New versions of the ritual songs are performed: *zhar-zhar, bet ashar* – their content now reflects modern life.

Many wedding ceremonies connected with the dependent state of the bride have disappeared; other elements are slowly disappearing. Thus, for example, very sad parting songs of the bride (*synsu*) performed before her departure, the bride's avoidance of the suitor's older relatives, the wearing of traditional headdresses connected with the transition from one age group to another, and so on, have only survived in the memory of old people.

Mutual gifts (*kiyt*) among matchmakers and the tradition of giving a dowry to the bride have been kept and developed under new conditions. Ready-made clothes and material for dresses are now given. The dowry includes only the most necessary articles and belongings for a young family.

All this is indicative of a correct and organic combination of popular traditions and modern life in the family and matrimonial relations of the Kazakh people.

REFERENCES

ALTYNSARIN, I.
1870   *Ocherki obychaev pri svatovstve i svad'be u kirgiz Orenburgskogo vedomstva* [Essays on the customs of matchmaking and the wedding among the Kirghiz of the Orenburg department]. Zapiski Orenburgskogo Otdela PGO, I.

ANDREEV, I.
1796   Opisanie srednei ordy kirgiz-kaisakov [Description of the Middle Horde of the Kirghiz-Kaisaks]. *Novye ezhemesjachnye sochinenija* 112. St. Petersburg.

BONCH-OSMOLOVSKII, G.
1926   Svadebnye zhilishcha turetskikh narodnostei [Wedding dwellings of the Turkish ethnic groups]. Leningrad.

DIVAEV, A.
1889   Zhenshchina v kochevom bytu [The woman in nomadic life]. *Turkestanskie Vedomosti* 33–34.
1900   Neskol'ko slov o svadebnom rituale kirgizov Syr-Dar'inskoi oblasti [A few words on the wedding ritual of the Kirghiz of the Syr Darya region]. *Uchenye Zapiski Kazanskogo Universiteta*, volume four.

Drevnetjurkskii slovar'
1969   *Drevnetjurkskii slovar'* [Old Turkish dictionary]. Leningrad.

GRODEKOV, G.
1889   *Kirgizy i karakirgizy Syr-Dar'-inskoi oblasti* [The Kirghiz and Karakirghiz of the Syr Darya region], volume 1. Tashkent.

IBRAGIMOV, I.
1872   Etnograficheskie ocherki kirgizskogo naroda [Ethnographic essays on the Kirghiz people]. *Russkii Turkestan*, volume one. Moscow.

IZRAZTSOV, N.
1897   Obychnoe pravo (adat) kirgizov Semirechenskoi oblasti [Customary law (*adat*) of the Kirghiz of Semirechensk region]. *Etnograficheskoe Obozrenie* 34 (3).

KISLJAKOV, N. A.
1969   *Ocherki po istorii sem'i i braka u narodov Srednei Azii i Kazakhstana* [Essays on the history of the family and marriage among the peoples of Central Asia and Kazakhstan]. Leningrad.

KUDAIBERDYULY, SHEKERYM
1911   *Kazak, kyrgyz, turyk zhene khandar schezhyresï* 2, Orynbor [Orenburg].

KUSTANAEV, KH.
1894   *Etnograficheskie ocherki kirgiz Perovskogo i Kazalinskogo uezdov* [Ethnographic essays on the Kirghiz of Perov and Kazalin districts]. Tashkent.

LEVANEVSKII, M.
1895   Ocherki kirgizskikh stepei (Embenskogo uezda) [Essays on the Kirghiz steppes (of Embensk district)]. *Zemlevedenie* 2–3.

LEVSHIN, A.
1832   *Opisanie kirgiz-kazach'ikh i-i kirgiz-kaisatskikh ord i stepei* [Description of Kirghiz-Kazakh or Kirghiz-Kaisak hordes and the steppes], part 3. St. Petersburg.

MAKOVETSKII, P. E.
1886   *Materialy dlja izuchenija juridicheskikh obychaev kirgiz* [Materials for the study of the juridical customs of the Kirghiz], volume one. Omsk.

MALYSHEV, N.
1902 *Obychnoe semeinoe pravo kirgizov* [Customary family law of the Kirghiz]. Jaroslavl'.

Narody Srednei Azii
1963 *Narody Srednei Azii i Kazakhstana* [Peoples of Central Asia and Kazakhstan], volume two. Moscow.

Obychai kirgizov
1878 Obychai kirgizov Semipalatinskoi oblasti [Customs of the Kirghiz of Semipalatinsk region]. *Russkii Vestnik* 137.

Polevye zapisi
1966–1970 *Polevye zapisi v Tselinogradskoi, Karagandskoi, Semipalatinskoi, Alma-Atinskoi, Chimkentskoi i Gur'evskoi oblastjakh Kazakhstana* [Field records in the Tselinograd, Karaganda, Semipalatinsk, Alma-Ata, Chimkent and Gur'ev regions of Kazakhstan].

Pozorishche strannykh
1797 *Pozorishche strannykh i smeshannykh obriadov pri brakosochetanijakh* [Spectacle of strange and mixed rites during the marriage ceremony]. St. Petersburg.

SPASSKII, G.
1820 Kirgiz-kaisaki bol'shoi, srednei i maloi ordy [The Kirghiz-Kaisaks of the Greater, Middle and Lesser hordes]. *Sibirskii Vestnik* 9–10. St. Petersburg.

Interaction of Cultures Among Peoples of the U.S.S.R.

YU. V. ARUTYUNYAN

Integration is the dominant process in mankind's present-day cultural development.

The growing dimensions of ethnic communities, the formation of large nations, the increasing communication among nations, the fall of religious and other barriers; all these promote a steady, if difficult, process of integration of peoples, through which the elements of a future culture common to all mankind are gradually being formed. What are the real prospects for the formation of such a common culture?

This is the most important question for ethnographers and sociologists; it can be answered not only by pure theorizing but also, using concrete historical material, through a retrospective analysis of the road covered by mankind, and through a study of the contemporary processes of the cultural interaction of different peoples. This second method is particularly effective, since a comparison of historical phenomena would be difficult, and since the cultural interaction of peoples in this era of scientific and technical revolution is unprecedented. The rapid spread of the new common elements of culture through the mass media have made this interaction extremely broad and all-embracing.

It is natural that the present-day cultural interaction of peoples attracts the particular attention of researchers, both in the U.S.S.R. and abroad. But perhaps no other country has as wide a field for this research as the U.S.S.R., so Soviet science has a particular responsibility.

It seems as if history itself has staged in the Soviet Union a large-scale experiment on the interaction of different cultures, formed on different social, economic, and ideological bases. The historical heritage of the Soviet peoples is extremely varied, ranging from patriarchal society to developed capitalism, from the Muslim East to the Christian West. The cultural contacts of these peoples are of different durations; they have different experiences in historical communication. The processes of interaction of genetically different cultures increase when the peoples form one state and have a joint economy and the same ideology. It would not be an overstatement to say that no country in the world, no matter how large, has such a great variety of cultures and, at the same time, such close cultural interaction as the Soviet Union. Because of this, the summing-up of the experience of cultural development of the U.S.S.R. is important not only for the understanding of present-day reality, but also for the understanding of processes common to all mankind.

Cultural interaction can be studied in two ways, which supplement one another. One is the study of the cultural fund of different peoples: their songs, dances, rites, customs, and so on. The simplest elements of every kind of culture are then compared and the similarities or differences of the interacting cultures and the degree of their mutual penetration established. This method is effective enough when the traditional folk culture is studied, and when the researchers have the task of reconstructing ethnogenesis, but it is less productive for the study of contemporary societies, in which professional culture plays a great role.

In those societies in which the state of the cultural fund is largely determined by the development of professional culture, cultural production and consumption do not coincide. In such cases, the similarity of the cultural fund does not imply similarity in the cultural makeup of the peoples. The question remains: to what degree has a people acquired certain features of professional culture? Therefore, when studying contemporary societies, it is more expedient to use a different method: to analyze cultural consumption and not the cultural fund; that is, to analyze how widespread certain features of culture are.

The Institute of Ethnography of the U.S.S.R. Academy of Sciences has undertaken this kind of research into the cultural interaction of the nations of the Soviet Union. These studies make it possible to solve a number of specific fundamental problems:

1. In what way are the development and the growing closeness of nations influenced by specific features of their culture history, by the degree of development of their national cultural fund, and by the nature of the historical experience of relationships among peoples?

2. In what way is the cultural development of a nation influenced by the degree of industrialization and urbanization and by the development of mass media and international contacts?

3. What are the interdependencies governing the changes of the inner structure of national cultures (infrastructure: the correlations among material culture, language, art, and values in a given society); and what are the specific features and rates of internationalization in different fields of culture which vary in their development and types?

4. What are the specific common features in the cultural makeup of different peoples?

The scope and nature of the comparative research conducted on a countrywide scale determined the methods used and the organization of the research. In order to reflect the multifariousness of the Soviet nations, the sample had to be large enough even if this involved a breakdown into several stages. The sample therefore included some 40,000 people. By taxonomic analysis, on the basis of thirty-five specific features, republics were chosen which would offer examples of economic development and urbanization, historical experience, and cultural history. Moldavia, Georgia, Latvia, Uzbekistan, and the Russian Federation are being surveyed. The summing-up of the material on the social and cultural development of the native populations of these republics will, we hope, considerably enrich the theory of culture.

It is planned to use research methods that have rarely if ever been used in either ethnography or sociology. The new methods involve the combining of the material describing an individual, obtained through polling, with objective data describing the environment. All the information is fed into a computer and processed, making it possible to obtain a clear-cut picture of the influence of the environment on the cultural development of the individual.

One of the main research instruments is a questionnaire which formalizes the biography of the person polled. The interviewer obtains information about the social and cultural development of the individual, the factors and the channels of this development (school, family, environment), and so on. This enables the researchers to judge the relative importance of certain factors in the social and cultural development of the individual. The selection also enables the researchers to create a combined portrait of a nation and of its social or other groups. The specific social and cultural features are judged not only on the basis of formal signs, such as the level of education, but mainly on the basis of the nature of cultural and national orientation. The actual behavior of the individual and his cultural values are established. Orientation to national cultural features only is regarded as highly national orientation.

In some republics the research has already been completed. The material obtained makes it possible to say that a common culture exists in the U.S.S.R., within every nation and in society as a whole. It is based on the uniform social structure of the Soviet population, in which every nation is made up of the same social groups. The objective basis for a common culture for the whole of Soviet society has been created by industrialization and urbanization. These are historical processes that take place all over the world, but in the Soviet Union their effect is qualitatively heightened by a number of specific factors which accelerate cultural integration.

The most important of these factors is the unity of economy that serves to change the configuration of culture in different nations. It is known that the specifically national features of life lose their importance and play a secondary role in all industrially developed countries. In the Soviet Union, with its unified economic system and countrywide division of labor, this process is very rapid. Large-scale industrial production of consumer goods provides a wide choice of goods, with which locally produced handicrafts cannot compete. Mass production can certainly reflect national traditions – in architecture and construction, for instance. But national preferences in material culture have a limited spread. In every case, practical considerations win out. It is more important that things should be comfortable, cheap, and durable. Tastes are relatively stable only in the choice of food, the sphere in which the competition from mass production has thus far been less keen. With reference to other elements of material culture – housing, interior decoration, clothes – the advantages of industrial production are obvious to all, and the higher the degree of urbanization of the people, the weaker the national preferences. For instance, 18 percent of the Moldavians and only 5 percent of the Russians in the city of Kishinev would like to have national features in interior decoration. National foods make up 36 percent of the favorite dishes of the Moldavians and 13 percent of those of the Russians.

The countrywide development under uniform economic conditions of industrialized material culture leads to the development of a uniform material culture as it spreads increasingly beyond national limits. Thus, the economic unity which increases the similarity of the material culture of the developed nations of the Soviet Union promotes the formation of a culture common to the entire Soviet Union.

Another important factor in the development of one common culture is connected with the unified Soviet political system, which leads specifically to a uniform cultural policy. The Soviet cultural policy is essentially the same with regard to every nation and nationality. A single educational system operates all over the Soviet Union: there are the same cultural standards for every people; secondary education is equally obligatory for every nationality; and so on. The single cultural policy brings closer together the standards of cultural consumption of different peoples. The differences in cultural consumption between urban and rural populations and various social and professional groups are not directly connected with specific national features.

Unity of ideology is an equally important condition of the creation of a common culture. All the religious and other ideological barriers that in the past separated one people from another have been removed. Even among peoples that in the past professed Islam, which, as is well known, played a particularly great role in their lives, the influence of religion has been reduced to a minimum. Thus, in the rural areas of the Tatar Autonomous Soviet Socialist Republic, only one-third of the population think of themselves as believers. Most of these are people of advanced age, illiterate and unskilled.

The single system of social and moral standards and values is typical for every nation and nationality of the Soviet Union. The distinctions in this respect, too, are the distinctions between urban and rural populations, between different classes and social and professional groups. But the same system of values is accepted in identical social and ecological spheres and in similar social groups in different nations.

Thus intensive international communication and the unity of ideology and outlook of the Soviet people create the basis for the development of processes of integration in spiritual culture. A uniform system of values and common moral standards has developed. This is the sign of the moral unity of the new historical formation which everyone comes to regard as the Soviet people. This unity is manifested with particular clarity in the coincidence of social and moral values in peoples living under similar conditions, such as the Moldavians and the Russians living in Kishinev.

There are no differences in social and moral values. However, certain differences in values still exist in family life and daily living. For instance, 67 percent of the Russians believe that it is better for a woman to work than to run a house, while this view is held by only 57 percent of the Moldavians. Correspondingly, the Russians value a woman's professional abilities more than her being a good housewife.

The present-day professional forms of culture play an important role in creating a common culture for the entire Soviet Union. The development of national professional culture takes place in the Soviet Union under conditions of unity of ideology and of social and moral values which increase the integrating functions of professional culture.

Evidence shows that it is precisely professional forms of culture and not folk culture that play a special role in the processes of the mutual penetration of cultures. Nations that have a developed fund of professional culture have more opportunities to exert a cultural influence on other peoples. On the other hand, when the cultural fund is less developed, a nation more readily assimilates other peoples' cultures. The historical logic of cultural development is such that the nations that formerly had a less-developed culture now have more rapid cultural development. The process of the leveling-off of various national cultures takes place. This also promotes the development of a common culture.

The fact that the Soviet nations are developing a common culture does not mean that they are culturally homogeneous. Certain national distinctions remain, including social, class, socioecological, and professional distinctions. The nations that were more highly developed in the past have a relatively higher percentage of intelligentsia and workers, while the nations that were backward in the past have a higher percentage of peasants. The nations also differ in the ratio of urban to rural population. These social distinctions determine the different levels of actual consumption of culture by the peoples and are reflected in professional culture, the standards of consumption of culture, and the system of values. The nations of today are complex historical formations that differ not only ethnically (although many ethnic distinctions are being increasingly erased) but also in their specific combinations of social and cultural features, determined by different levels of economic and social development.

It stands to reason that these distinctions will gradually disappear, since the main trend of the development of Soviet society, aimed at the liquidation of major distinctions between urban and rural populations and between classes and social and professional groups, will gradually lead to the complete social and cultural leveling-off of the nations. How will this affect the ethnic peculiarities of the peoples?

To answer this question, we shall use the data from a homogeneous social and ecological environment, where different nationalities already have essentially the same social structure: the Moldavian capital, Kishinev. The Russians and the Moldavians living in Kishinev have a similar social and professional structure and a similar level of education (the Moldavians, on the average, have nine years of schooling, and the Russians ten), they have the same standards of consumption of culture and the same ways of spending free time. In their leisure time they read books (88 percent of the Russians and 78 percent of the Moldavians) and go to the theater (70 percent of the Russians and 60 percent of the Moldavians).

At the same time, national cultural orientations continue to differ greatly. The Moldavians give preference to national Moldavian types of art (74 percent have national preferences in music and 81 percent in dance). The majority of Moldavians (58 percent) give preference to the national wedding ceremony with its archaic features. As for the Russians, they are much less oriented to folk rites and folk art; only 40 percent of them prefer a national wedding. The Russians have a strong orientation to professional types of Russian art.

The leveling-off of consumption of culture, therefore, does not lead to the restriction of national forms of culture: cultures with a progressive character are being preserved, and thus the cultural range of the peoples widens. This can be seen in linguistic processes. The Moldavians study Russian intensively. In Kishinev, with its mixed ethnic environment where contacts between the nationalities are very active, 70 percent of the Moldavians speak fluent Russian. Every new generation contains a larger proportion of people with a good command of Russian, demonstrating the intensity of the linguistic process. While only 32 percent of Moldavians above sixty speak Russian well, nearly all the Moldavian young people in Kishinev, 82 percent, speak fluent Russian.

But, as is seen in their contacts with Russian culture as a whole, the Moldavians do not lose touch with their own national (mainly folk) culture; the Moldavian language is not forced out of use by the Russian language. Eighty-nine percent of the Moldavians in Kishinev have a good command of the Moldavian language. It is particularly important that all professional and age groups of the Moldavian population have a constant percentage of people with a good command of Moldavian. This percentage does not drop below 80 to 90 percent in any of these groups. Thus, under conditions of the most active international contact, the Moldavians, while acquiring the culture of another people, continue to enjoy the wealth of their own cultural fund. This is a sign of the optimum cultural development of the Moldavian people.

National psychology, based on an awareness of national interests and a national self-awareness, helps preserve the ethnic elements in the culture of a nation.

The growing cultural similarity does not weaken solidarity within a nation or the intensity of national feelings. Depending on the stage of cultural development, different mechanisms come into play to preserve and strengthen national solidarity. The scientific and technical revolution exerts a twofold influence on national social and cultural development. On the one hand, it increases national similarity, equalizes, and promotes mutual understanding. On the other hand, due to the development of mass media and other cultural channels for the purpose of national consolidation, it leads to the growth of national self-awareness in the broad masses of the people.

Thus, even in the Soviet Union, where there exist strong accelerators of cultural integration, it is a common culture and not a homogeneous ethnic culture that is being formed; cultures are growing closer but not blending. Cultural integration is a long and complex process which dialectically combines international and national features and common and specific features. In the long run, the rates of ethnic integration depend on the intensity of social processes, on the breakdown of social distinctions, and on the creation of economic abundance as the condition for complete merging of specific interests, including national interests.

Ethnic Traditions in Agriculture in the Northern Caucasus

B. A. KALOEV

The study of agriculture in all its aspects has always been a major task of Soviet ethnographic science. Research in this area has been intensified of late, as part of the work on historico-ethnographic atlases covering the entire territory of the Soviet Union (Bruk and Rabinovich 1964). This has been vividly illustrated by the appearance of the Siberian (*Istoriko-etnograficheskii atlas Sibiri* 1961) and Russian (*Russkii istoriko-etno-graficheskii atlas* 1967) atlases, as well as by a great number of mono-graphs and publications, some of a general theoretical nature and others devoted to specific peoples and regions of this country. Of great methodo-logical importance for the solution of the whole problem was a discussion sponsored in 1967–1968 by the journal *Sovetskaja Ethnografija*, which brought to light two opposing viewpoints about ethnic traditions in agri-culture. Some authors (Shennikov 1968) either absolutely deny the exis-tence of such ethnic traditions or regard them as being of minor con-sequence (Gromov and Novikov 1967), while others (Cheboksarov and Chesnov 1967; Saburova 1967), on the contrary, believe that agriculture is marked by important ethnic features. We share the latter point of view and will corroborate it with some material on the northern Caucasus.

The Caucasus is one of the world's oldest agricultural areas. It pro-duced a number of highly important cereals (barley, wheat, and rye), developed fruit and wine culture, and evolved unique agricultural im-plements showing the influence of local and ethnic traits. Agricultural traditions in the Caucasus evolved over thousands of years, from the Neolithic period to the Middle Ages. Archaeologists have discovered a great number of agricultural implements in different parts of this terri-tory. The finds date back to different historical periods (Alfimov 1953: 48–53; Krupnov 1960: 312–316; Lavrov 1952) and bear witness to a gradual change from hoe farming to plow farming, which reached the peak of its development in the flatland areas of the Caucasus in the Middle Ages. The appearance in these areas, prior to the Mongol invasion, of the heavy carriage plow (Krupnov 1957; Minaeva 1965: 62–65), designed for plowing large plots of land, and of a number of implements for harrowing, reaping, threshing, etc., as well as the cultivation of various cereals, especially millet, are all indicative of an intensive development of agriculture in the northern Caucasus. An indirect corroboration of this development is provided by the Ossetian epic, which mentions a number of important agricultural implements and processes, and also cultivated plants (*Osetinskie nartskie skazanija* 1948: 68, 78, 137). The devastating Mongol invasion resulted in a decline in agriculture, especially in flatland areas, and dramatically changed the ethnic map of the northern Caucasus. Only the Kabardians survived in the flatland areas, while some West Adygei tribes and the Nogai nomads, the ancestors of the present-day Ossets, Balkarians, and Karachaev, were driven to the mountains of the Great Caucasus where, together with the Chechens, Ingush, and West Adygei, they lived in almost inaccessible caynons, continuously suffering from the acute shortage of land.

Following the Mongol invasion, the economic life of these peoples was marked by intensive agriculture under alpine conditions. Terraced farming was widespread, and the basic modern systems of farming (a fallow period, cutting, and crop rotation) emerged, as well as local varieties of vital cereals (wheat, barley, rye, etc.) and new methods and skills. In any case, until the 1870's, cultivation was better developed in the mountains (Gardanov 1967: 61–87) than in the neighboring fertile plains, whose population, both Caucasians and Russian Cossacks, for the most part engaged in cattle breeding as a more profitable occupation.

In the 1870's and 1880's, however, the situation was reversed as a result of capitalist penetration into the countryside and of the expansion of sown areas, which called for improved agricultural implements and new methods of cultivation. The development of farming in the plains was boosted by the influx of landless peasants from the southern provinces of Russia, who settled down in the Stavropol region and in the Kuban and Terek valleys. They brought with them improved implements (Shatskii 1970: 188–215; *Obzor Kubanskoi oblasti* 1886: 5–6) and rich traditions of cultivation, which they shared with their new neighbors, the Caucasians and the Cossacks. On the whole, the development of farming in the plains, which started in the first half of the nineteenth century, and a mass resettlement of farmers from the mountains, in particular the Ossets, the Chechens, and the Ingush, brought about a decline in alpine-type cultivation. Down in the plain, the mountaineer could buy any quantity of cheap bread; for this reason he abandoned his terraced fields and took little pains to cultivate his other sown areas (Kaloev 1972:

92–96). His chief occupation became cattle breeding, because of a growing market demand for animal produce.

The nature of farming and its development in the northern Caucasus, as in other regions of the Caucasus, depended upon altitudinal sequence as well as upon socioeconomic, historical, and ethnic factors. The entire territory under review may be divided into three zones: (1) the mountainous zone, at altitudes from 1,500 to 3,000 meters above sea level; (2) the highland zone, at altitudes not greater than 1,500 meters; and (3) the flatland zone. Each zone is marked by specific climatic and soil conditions calling for appropriate crops and even varieties of cultured plants, as well as for specific agricultural implements, methods, and know-how. In the region under review, we also distinguish three groups of peoples related in their origin and culture and having specific ethnic traditions in farming: the Adygei-Abazin, the Osset-Balkarian-Karachaev, and the Chechen-Ingush.

The Ingush occupied an intermediary position between the Chechen and the Adygei-Karachaev group; in some cases they identified themselves with the former, in others with the latter, due, in our opinion, to the presence of the common Alan element in the ethnic origin of these peoples. As for the settled Nogai of the Stavropol region, their farming traditions were influenced by those of the Adygei-Circassians. The former borrowed from the latter their agricultural implements, including the heavy carriage plow, as well as cultivated plants and agricultural methods and know-how.

It should also be noted that, unlike other ethnic groups, most of the Adygei-Abazin peoples inhabited the fertile plain of the northern Caucasus and were in a far better position for the development of farming.

The ethnic traditions of each of these groups are especially apparent in their agricultural implements, which we shall now describe in some detail. The oldest and most widespread plowing implement in the mountains and, to a lesser extent, in the plain, where it was used for second plowing, is the *ralo* [plow] which is still erroneously referred to in literature on Caucasian studies as the "wooden plow" (*Narody Kavkaza* 1960: 175, 204, 473). Its origin in the northern Caucasus dates back to the first half of the first millennium B.C. (Krupnov 1960: 314). This implement comprises a runner, a handle, a dowel, a beam, and an iron moldboard. Despite a substantially uniform design, it is marked by a number of local and ethnic features, observed for each group of related peoples under review. The Ossets, the Balkarians, the Karachaev, and the Ingush used similar types of *ralo*; the first three even used common Ossetian names for some of its components: the *glush* [handle], the *chino* [furrower] (Kaloev 1971: 76). At the same time, for each of the above-mentioned peoples the *ralo* had specific features due to altitudinal sequence. The *ralo* of the Balkarians, for instance, in some cases had a long beam connecting it to the yoke, while in others the beam was replaced by a belt. To plow virgin or long-fallow land, the Ossets often complemented the *ralo* with a cutter fixed in the furrower perpendicular to the moldboard. The *ralo* of the Chechens was different from the above types (Zaks n.d.: 163); it was closer to the Daghestan *ralo* than to that of the peoples of the northern Caucasus (Nikol'skaja and Shilling 1952: 98). Apart from this implement, the mountaineers also used a plow without a forecarriage, drawn by two pairs of oxen, as well as another type of *ralo*, a long pole provided with a massive cutter. The latter was drawn by two oxen and was placed in front of a plow for horizontal cutting. For the most part, the distribution of these implements was confined to mountainous Chechnya, good reason to identify the Chechens with the Vainakh ethnic group.

Tillage, especially in terraced fields, was also done with different types of hoe; these, in turn, had a number of local features. Thus, the massive elongated hoe with a broadened end was found only among Balkarians in the villages of the Bezenginskoye Canyon. Farmers in other parts of Balkaria and in neighboring areas used totally different types of hoe. The pick-mattock with a sharp flat end was used only by the Ossets of Digoria.

Cutting-farming implements were also of a unique nature. Cutting-farming was most widely practiced among the West Adygei and in the foothills of Chechnya, where it was marked by long-standing ethnic traditions; these were manifest in all aspects of farming, especially in cutting and tillage implements. Thus, the West Adygei used peculiar types of cutters and hatchets for brush-cutting; their tilling spade with foot support was in many respects different from that used by the Chechens. At the same time, these peoples had a number of similar implements for cutting-farming. These included, in particular, the digging stick for covering seeds, the massive mattock with one flat end, and the stubbing crowbar.

Finally, there was one more implement with pronounced ethnic features, the Adygei (Circassian) heavy carriage plow which doubtless emerged in the Middle Ages (Minaeva 1965: 62). It was used by almost all the Caucasians inhabiting the north Caucasus plain; the Adyg peoples (Kabardians, Circassians, Adygei, Abazin, Nogai), as well as by Ossetian, Balkarian, and Karachaev migrants from the mountains, and to some extent by the Ingush and the Chechens. There is every reason to believe that this implement belongs to the Adyg ethnic group; the Adyg peoples, in particular the Kabardians of Greater Kabardia, still used it in the first years of Soviet power.

The long-standing use of the heavy plow by the Adyg may also have been due to the fact that, in keeping with an old tradition, they did not use horses as draft animals. A Kabardian proverb says, "It is a sin to eat bread from a horse-plowed field." The Adyg believed that a horse was only to be used for riding. Apart from the Adyg plow, the mountaineers, especially the Ossets, the Chechens, and the Ingush, also used the Ukrainian heavy plow, brought to this area by migrants from southern Russia in the eighteenth century.

Similarities and differences are observed in implements for sowing, harrowing, threshing, etc. The most commonly used sowing implement was an elongated twig basket with a plank bottom; it was held in front of the sower by a rope across his shoulder. In some parts of Chechen-Ingushetia, however, saddlebags were used instead of baskets, while in other parts of that territory the ordinary Caucasian *bashlyk* [hood] was used for the purpose. Local and ethnic peculiarities of sowing implements are also observed among other peoples of the north Caucasus. Of considerable interest in this respect is the drag harrow, one of the oldest types of harrow in the Caucasian highlands, also used to some extent in the plain of the north Caucasus. In contrast to the form it took among other peoples of the north Caucasus, the drag harrow of the Chechens had a massive forebar with several rows of wooden teeth; this was used in the cultivation of corn. Of great interest from the point of view of ethnic traditions is the double-edged scythe, commonly used by the Ossets, the Balkarians, and the Karachaev, which doubtless descended from the Alans.

A number of peculiar features are also observed in threshing, generally done by animals' hooves throughout almost the entire region under survey. The Chechens and Ingush used only oxen for threshing; the Ossets, the Balkarians, and the Karachaev used all kinds of cattle; the Adyg peoples used only horses for the purpose. The West Adygei also used wooden and stone rollers for threshing; in some parts of eastern Chechnya this was done with a wooden board, as in neighboring Daghestan.

Thus, an analysis of agricultural implements and techniques of the mountaineers of the northern Caucasus reveals a number of local and ethnic features due to natural, geographic, and socioethnic factors and to ethnic traditions.

The region under survey was also marked by specific local varieties of basic cereals, such as barley, wheat, and rye, described by Vavilov as having no equivalent anywhere in the world (1967: 596).

The highlanders in general grew barley as the most frost-resistant plant; the only cereal grown high in the mountains was an early double-row variety of barley, the mountaineers' staple food. Over the centuries, each culture in the region under survey evolved its own varieties of this crop. Wheat and barley cultivation was highly developed in the mountains; it is curious that these crops, especially wheat, were unknown in the plain of the northern Caucasus until the 1870's to the 1890's. The basic and predominant cereal in the plain was millet, the oldest local crop, grown only in this zone of the region because of climatic conditions. It can therefore be stated with good reason that millet culture descends from the Adyg of the plain. Other Caucasian peoples first saw millet much later, approximately in the eighteenth century, after they came down from the mountains. According to informants, until recently the West Adygei grew some fifteen different varieties of millet. In Greater Kabardia, millet remained the predominant crop until the early twentieth century and played a major role in the evolution of the national foods and beverages of the Adyg at a certain stage of their historical development.

In the latter half of the nineteenth century, due to the development of agriculture and the expansion of sown areas in the plain, the mass of plains people started growing wheat and corn. It is noteworthy that wheat, one of the oldest cereals in the Caucasus, was little known to inhabitants of the plain, especially to the Kabardians, although it had been grown in the mountains of the north Caucasus since ancient times. The mountain varieties of spring and winter wheat were of an exceptionally high quality; migrants from the mountains brought these varieties down to the plain and shared them with their new neighbors, the Caucasians and the Russian Cossacks.

Another widespread crop in the plain of the northern Caucasus was corn, which appeared there much later than the other above-mentioned crops, coming to Georgia in the seventeenth century (Dekaprelevich 1960). About that time it also reached the West Adygei from Turkey. Corn made a tremendous impression on the mountaineers, who described it as the bread of the *narts* [legendary heroes]. The Adygei name for corn is *natryf*; the Circassian and Kabardian, *nartykhu*; the Ossetian, *nartkhor*. Corn was so named due to the size of its cobs and grains and to its high yields, intensified by the local climatic and soil conditions.

In spite of all this, corn remained a ridge crop with almost all the peoples of the north Caucasus until the 1880's. The Chechens were an exception; as far back as the first half of the nineteenth century they grew corn on such a scale that it called for irrigation canals and special implements, among them wooden harrows of a specific type and iron hoes.

Because of its large areas sown with corn, Chechnya became a bread basket for the entire east Caucasus. The corn bazaars in a number of large villages provided bread not only for the mountaineers but also for the Russian Cossacks.

In the late nineteenth and early twentieth centuries, corn became the predominant, and, in some cases, the only crop in the plain. It became a traditional crop of such peoples as the Chechens, the West Adygei, the Ossets, and, to some extent, the Ingush. Corn cultivation stimulated the development of a number of new types of implements and barns, each people producing specific types and considering corn its own national crop.

Farming in the mountain areas of the northern Caucasus was marked by the presence of the basic farming systems (cutting, fallow, and rotary), unknown in the mid-nineteenth century as a result of the inhabitants of the plain losing their farming traditions during the post-Mongol period.

Irrigation and fertilizers were of great importance for farming. Yet as far as the plain of the northern Caucasus is concerned, irrigation there was practiced only by the Chechens, who had built some irrigation canals as far back as the first half of the nineteenth century. Neither was artificial irrigation widespread in the foothills of the region under survey. Special irrigation systems were built by the Balkarians and the Karachaev (*Tjurkskoe plemja* 1910: 292; Shamanov 1971: 50–55) and also in some places in eastern Chechnya. Yet while irrigation in its classical form is only observed among these peoples, fertilizers were used throughout the highlands of the Caucasus; at the same time they were not used at all in the flatland areas of the northern Caucasus.

Regular application of organic fertilizers was a major cause of high yields in the mountains. It is notable that, along with manure, wild pigeon dung was also used as fertilizer in some places, especially in Ingushetia, another (indirect) indication of the long-standing nature of the mountaineers' farming.

Thus, as we have tried to show, farming by the peoples of the northern Caucasus was not uniformly developed in the mountains and in the plain and was influenced by ethnic traditions as well as by natural, geographic, and socioeconomic factors.

REFERENCES

ALFIMOV, N.
  1953 *Drevnie poselenija Kuban'ja* [The ancient settlements of Kuban']. Krasnodar.
Arkheologicheskie raskopki
  n.d. *Arkheologicheskie raskopki v raione Zmeiskoi Severnoi Osetii* [Archaeological excavations in the Zmei district of northern Ossetia]. Ordzhonikidze.
BRUK, S. I., I. G. RABINOVICH
  1964 Istoriko-etnograficheskie atlasy [Historico-ethnographic atlases]. *Sovetskaja Etnografija* 4.
CHEBOKSAROV, N. N., JA. V. CHESNOV
  1967 Nekotorye problemy agro-etnografii jugo-vostochnoi Azii [Some problems of the agroethnography of southeastern Asia]. *Sovetskaja Etnografija* 3.
DEKAPRELEVICH, L. L.
  1960 Iz istorii kul'tury kukuruzy v SSSR [From the history of maize culture in the U.S.S.R.]. *Materialy po istorii sel'skogo khozjastva i krest'janstva SSSR*, coll. 4. Moscow.

GARDANOV, V. K.
1967   *Obshchestvennyi stroi adygskikh narodov* (*XVIII–pervaja polovina XIX v.*) [Social composition of the Adyg peoples (the eighteenth to the first half of the nineteenth century)]. Moscow.

GROMOV, G. G., JU. F. NOVIKOV
1967   Nekotorye voprosy agroetnograficheskikh issledovanii [Some questions of agroethnographic research]. *Sovetskaja Etnografija* 1.

Istoriko-etnograficheskii atlas Sibiri
1961   *Istoriko-etnograficheskii atlas Sibiri* [The historico-ethnographic atlas of Siberia]. Moscow and Leningrad.

KALOEV, B. A.
1971   *Osetiny: istoriko-etnograficheskoe issledovanie* [The Ossets: historico-ethnographic research]. Moscow.
1972   Itogi izuchenija zemledelija u narodov Severnogo Kavkaza v plane istoriko-etnograficheskogo atlasa [Results of the study of agriculture among the peoples of the northern Caucasus in the framework of a historico-ethnographic atlas]. *Tezisy dokladov na sessii i plenumakh, posvjashchennykh itogam polevykh issledovanii v 1971 g.* Moscow.

KRUPNOV, E. I.
1957   *Drevnjaja istorija i kul'tura Kabardy* [The ancient history and culture of Kabardia]. Moscow.
1960   *Drevnjaja istorija Severnogo Kavkaza* [The ancient history of the northern Caucasus]. Moscow.

LAVROV, L. I.
1952   Razvitie zemledelija na severo-zapadnom Kavkaze s drevneishikh vremën do serediny XVIII v. [The development of agriculture in the northwestern Caucasus from the most ancient times to the middle of the eighteenth century]. *Materialy po istorii zemledelija SSSR*, coll. 1. Moscow.

MINAEVA, T. M.
1965   *Ocherki po arkheologii Stavropol'ja* [Essays on the archaeology of the Stavropol' region]. Stavropol'.

Narody Kavkaza
1960   *Narody Kavkaza* [The peoples of the Caucasus], volume one. Moscow.

NIKOL'SKAJA, Z. N., E. M. SHILLING
1952   Gornoe pakhotnoe orudie terrasovykh polei Dagestana [Mountain plowing implements of the terraced fields of Daghestan]. *Sovetskaja Etnografija* 4.

Obzor Kubanskoi oblasti
1886   *Obzor Kubanskoi oblasti za 1886* [Survey of the Kuban' region for 1886]. Ekaterinograd.

Osetinskie nartskie skazanija
1948   *Osetinskie nartskie skazanija* [Ossetian Nart legends]. Dzaudzhikau.

Russkii istoriko-etnograficheskii atlas
1967   *Russkii istoriko-etnograficheskii atlas* [The Russian historico-ethnographic atlas]. Moscow.

SABUROVA, L. M.
1967   Po povodu stat'i G. G. Gromova i Ju. F. Novikova "Nekotorye voprosy agroetnograficheskikh issledovanii" [Rejoinder to G. G. Gromov and Ju. F. Novikov's article "Some questions of agroethnographic research"]. *Sovetskaja Etnografija* 6.

SHAMANOV, I. M.
1971   Zemledelic i zemledel'cheskii byt karachaevtsev [Agriculture and agricultural way of life of the Karachaev]. *Iz istorii sel'skogo khozjaistva Karachaevo-Cherkesii*. Cherkessk.

SHATSKII, P. A.
1970   Sel'skoe khozjaistvo Predkavkaz'ja v 1861–1905 gg. [The agriculture of Ciscaucasia from 1861 to 1905]. *Nekotorye voprosy sotsial'no-ekonomicheskogo razvitija jugo-vostochnoi Rossii*. Stavropol'.

SHENNIKOV, A. A.
1968   Rasprostranenie zhivotno-vodcheskikh postroek u narodov Evropeiskoi Rossii [The distribution of cattle-breeding buildings among the peoples of European Russia]. *Sovetskaja Etnografija* 6.

Tjurkskoe plemja
1910   *Tjurkskoe plemja* [The Turkic tribe]. *Kubanskii sbornik* 4.

VAVILOV, N. I.
1967   Gornoe zemledelie Severnogo Kavkaza i perspektivy ego razvitija [Mountain agriculture of the northern Caucasus and the prospects of its development]. *Izvestija AN SSSR* 5.

ZAKS, A. B.
n.d.   Severo-Kavkazskaja istoriko-bytovaja ekspeditsija Gosudarstvennogo istoricheskogo muzeja 1936 g. [The north Caucasian cultural-historical expedition of the State Historical Museum in 1936]. *Trudy Gosudarstvennogo istoricheskogo muzeja*, vyp. 15.

Settlement and Traditional Social Institutions of the Formerly Nomadic Kazakh People

G. F. DAKHSHLEIGER

The transition from extensive animal husbandry and a nomadic or semi-nomadic way of life to an intensive type of economy and a settled way of life takes different forms under different social conditions. Under one set of conditions we have the forced ousting of nomads and seminomads from their cultivated pastures, the preservation of private ownership of the means of production, an increase in property inequality, and juridical and actual national discrimination. This was the case with the Kazakh people before we had the establishment of juridical and actual national and social equality, taking into consideration the psychological readiness of the bulk of the population, active participation in changing the archaic forms of property and economy, and the purposeful assistance (material and ideological) of the state. This was the case in the sedentarization of the nomadic and seminomadic Kazakhs after the revolution. The comparison of these two variants clearly shows the advantage of the second.

Here I intend to examine the changes in the traditional social institutions of the Kazakh people as they made the transition to the settled way of life in terms of the organic connection with the basic reorganization in the system of the social relations. The changes are in many ways typical for the people of the Soviet Union who practiced nomadic or seminomadic animal breeding in the near past and in part typical for all people with a predominantly precapitalist structure who are shifting to a new social system and bypassing capitalism.

This report is based on historical and ethnographic literature and investigations, taking into consideration the social affiliation of the informants, their sex, age, and urban or rural place of residence.

The first Kazakh scientist and researcher, Chokan Valikhanov, wrote, "We [the Kazakhs] organized our life adapting ourselves to the requirements of animal breeding." Let us add – nomadic or seminomadic.

The origin of the ethnically peculiar features of the economy, of the everyday life of the Kazakh people and their ancestors, and of their social institutions goes back to the preclass society and the formation of a nomadic and seminomadic animal-breeding economy as an economic-cultural type in the historical and ethnographic region that became the Kazakh ethnic territory. With the transition to a class society and the development of ethnogenetic processes which led to the formation of the Kazakh nationality, the institutions and forms underwent a transformation.

For a long time the pastoral-nomadic community was the main form of social organization of the nomadic and seminomadic Kazakhs. It inherited many important institutions and customs from the remote past and represented a stable community very closely connected with the type of economy. The community in many ways retained its basis of blood relationship, yet it was no longer a simple union of blood relatives. The class factors became determinant, though they were concealed by a patriarchy that penetrated all areas of production and social and family life. The community was an intact body, the reproduction of which was conditioned by a continuous struggle for existence in the difficult natural conditions, by a specific type of economy, by a need for cooperation, and by the practical impossibility for a lone man to survive outside this collective body. Using the economic cycle, roaming from place to place, pasturing, cattle breeding, sharing a common economic territory, and defense against enemy forays united all the elements of the tribal structure – aouls, subdivisions, divisions, and tribes. The common-law provisions sanctified the idea of the subordination of the young to the old, of the poor and common to the noble and rich – and, in fact, they substituted the institution of noneconomic compulsion. In spite of great mobility, mainly within the economic cycle, the community remained a comparatively secluded world.

A most important and long-lived social institution of the Kazakh community was communal-tribal land tenure. Monopolistic feudal land property was not juridically fixed (with very rare exceptions) in the complex of ancient seasonal pastures. In reality the communal land tenure that had developed with the growth of property inequality became a fiction, concealing an inequality in land ownership determined by the ratio of property to cattle. An increase in population density, an increase in livestock in the pasturable area, wars and raids of neighbor sovereigns (for example, the invasion of Dzungar feudals in the seventeenth and eighteenth centuries), withdrawal of the Kazakh lands by the tsarist administration, penetration of capitalism, and migration of the Russian and Ukrainian peasantry to the territory of Kazakhstan (in the second half of the nineteenth and beginning of the twentieth centuries) – these and other factors inevitably sharpened the struggle for pastures and slowly destroyed the institution of communal land tenure. Yet only after the Revolution and the nationalization of land (which returned to the Kazakh working people the land taken by tsarism) and the growth of a tendency to lead a settled life did the question face them in all its magnitude: how to overcome completely the communal-tribal land tenure by equalizing reallotment of the arable land and a part of the livestock that had belonged to rich semifeudal *bais* [rich landowners in Central Asia]. Living conditions determined the destruction of the institution of communal land tenure and the development of a mass cooperation among the Kazakh animal breeders (*sharoua*) and of a planned, settled life, taking into consideration the folk traditions in land tenure and filling them with a new content. Both animal husbandry and agricultural land tenure are now of a really communal character, and social and national inequality are nonexistent.

The reciprocal tribal aid (*zhardem*) was part and parcel of the Kazakh nomadic pastoral community. It developed of necessity in a community of pasturers and cattle breeders as a way of helping a poor neighbor in years of cattle sickness with his expenses for feasts, hospitality, or funeral rituals, and in making payments in cases of murder, mutilation, or insult to avoid the blood feud (*koun, ayip*). The reciprocal aid at first was not conditioned by any commitments for reimbursement. Yet with the development of patriarchy and feudal relations many forms of reciprocal tribal aid acquired class implications. Such institutions as lending draft animals such as a camel or a horse (*kolyk mayin berou*), livestock with the right to use milk and wool (*saoun, mal shounyn berou*) and other forms of aid (*zhourt shylyk, zhylou* – communal aid to one who suffered from some natural calamity), though still under patriarchal sanction, as a rule became means of exploiting the poor (*kedeya*) by the *bai*. For such "aid" there was an obligatory return of the livestock with an increase; the *bai* received an almost gratuitous and almost permanent work force in payment by imposing work conditions unequal to the "aid." In this paying in work, the surplus labor was not separated from the necessary labor, and not only the head of the family who had received the "aid" but often the family members participated in working off the assistance – so the possibilities for the *bai*'s accumulation grew while the exploitation was concealed.

Among the seminomadic, semisettled population there were similar forms of "aid": when building a house, laying in fodder, tilling crops for temporary use of the agricultural implements, giving seeds under metayage conditions (*asar* [literally "aid"]; *ortak* [literally "common, companion"]). With penetration of capitalist relations the working-off by poor villagers at the *bai*'s farm existed side by side with, or was even replaced by farm laborers' work which was paid in kind, and the scale of *saoun* relations shrank. The agrarian reforms of the Soviet State giving privileges and preferences to the poor in taxes, the system of land tenure, aid with crops and animals and, as a consequence, the predominance of middle peasants at the *aoul*, revealed the class meaning of the "reciprocal tribal aid" forms.

After planned mass sedentarization and cooperation of the Kazakh peasants, when their true social equality in labor and distribution of its products became firmly established, when the level of well-being and culture increased, the *saoun* relations completely lost their meaning. Yet the sense of the need for mutual aid remained both among blood relations (not tribal) and in production and social life. Now it is especially apparent in collective work in the collective farm, the Soviet farm, the team, the shop, and the factory, and in cases of natural calamities, for example, a serious illness.

The process of transforming the Kazakh nationality into a nation had not been completed before the Revolution. The 1926 census clearly showed that the time had come for the Kazakhs to be affiliated with one or another tribal group. Strengthening of the Soviet national state system and reunion of the Kazakh land, rapid industrial development, collectivization together with settlement, and a golden age of culture proved decisive in overcoming the remnants of the tribal structure and tribal ideology and consolidating the Kazakh nation. The economic unity of the nation, formed on the basis of revolutionary reforms in the economy, social relations, and culture, in close connection with a settled life, resulted in territorial relations completely replacing tribal relations. Rotation within a limited seasonal succession, combined with a certain secluded community life and comparatively restricted contacts with other communities, were changed by the high mobility of the nation within the borders of not only the Kazakh Soviet Republic but the whole Soviet Union. Permanent contacts were established by the Kazakh nation with all the peoples of the Soviet State, with all ensuing consequences in economic, political, and cultural life and a leveling of local differences in material and spiritual culture inside the Kazakh nation. Settlement in small nomadic or semi-nomadic *aoul*s where the blood ties were still in force gave way in the rural areas to large, well-built, modern, Soviet and collective farm settlements with all the amenities, while rapid industrial development resulted in a resettlement of a considerable part of the Kazakh population in urban areas. This also contributed to the destruction of the remnants of tribal structure and its influence on the life of the people.

The importance of intertribal estrangement, the complex of tribal duties and rights, the dependent state of a stranger (*krme*), the "tribal peace" idea (*intymak*) were all replaced by self-consciousness about nationality, a sense of national pride on the international basis of the common interests shared by the Kazakh nation and the peoples of the Soviet Union. Glorifying one's own tribe to the detriment of another tribe disappeared from oral competitions of *akyn*s (*aytysov*); now the songs are about the social and political unity of the nation, its cooperation with friendly nationalities and nations, the exploits of laboring people – all fighters for a bright future, irrespective of their tribal affiliation.

Now, when meeting each other, people are interested not in tribal origin but in where a person is from – in what Soviet farm, collective farm, town, district, region he lives, what his profession is, where he works, and what his position is. The exogamy barrier has become less, though it has not lost its role (*kyr alyspaymyn zher*). The consciousness of tribe affiliation still exists, but it is not opposed to the consciousness of belonging to the nation.

The qualitative changes are inseparably connected with the social and cultural progress of the Kazakh nation as a whole, with the transition to settled life in particular, and with forming the national working class, collective farmers, and intelligentsia – changes that have taken place in the evaluation of man's social rights and his place in society. The sense of traditional forms of respecting a man's labor, his professional skill, his knowledge, intellect, wit, honesty, decency, faithfulness to his word, responsiveness, delicacy, military valor, courage, exploits – this sense is constantly growing; and this respect has nothing to do with tribal ideals; it is in the name of the ideals of the society that is free of exploitation and is built on internationalist principles of a new system of national relations. Animal husbandry (but not nomadic or seminomadic), as before, is the main occupation of a considerable part of the Kazakh working people. Keen knowledge of folk meteorology, astronomy, veterinary medicine, phenology, and botanical lore accumulated by the people over the years is highly valued by society. The twelve-year animal cycle once used to register a man's age, and a reliable way of measuring the economic cycle is not forgotten.

The new social system and settled mode of life led to some terms losing their significance; such notions are *ak-acuyek* [a white bone] and *kara-kalyk*, *kara-boukara* [black people] – the categories of social hierarchy based on noble descent, wealth or, on the contrary, on dependency and poverty – *khan, sultan, bai, tyulengout* [servant, combatant], *alypsatar* [second-hand dealer], *saoudeger* [tradesman], *konsy* [dependent], *malay* [servant], *baygoush* [beggar], etc. Also the derogatory shade of meaning was lost in the notions *zhatak* [not roaming], *otrykshy* [settled]. Among the *aoul* nobility these words formerly underlined the advantages of wealthy livestock owners who could roam from place to place. The layer of *atkaminers* [literally "on horseback"], in a social sense very close to that of the Russian *podkulachnik* [a rich peasant], formerly used by *bai*s to fortify their influence in the community, has also disappeared. Now one can find only in the dictionary the term *barymta* – a Kazakh common law institution according to which a man revenged himself upon his offender by stealing his livestock up to the limits of material damage caused to him; this institution in the past served as a way for the rich and noble to strengthen their privileges and power. Social equality and equality before the law, a high cultural level of the population, standards of comradely community, and law and order put an end to all kinds of penalties that had been substituted for the blood feud. Conditions that made various presents to the rich and noble almost compulsory on gay or sad occasions were done away with. For example, it was once a compulsory custom to make a gift of meat at cattle slaughter, sometimes in the form of livestock (*sogoum*). Yet the custom of making gifts to relatives, close friends, and friends at work continues. More than that, the traditional institution of hospitality (*konak asy*) is still preserved but now free of any self-interest. The popular custom continues of organizing feasts for close relatives and friends on happy occasions: weddings, childbirths, state decorations (*toy*), for new neighbors (*eroulik*), or on mournful occasions – for example, a funeral repast (*as*) – all of which are accompanied by typical rites, songs, and competitions.

At the very start of the Kazakh Republic the law forbade payment of the bride price (*kalym*) in all its varieties, but a certain period of time was required for the elimination of this payment as a social institution. Establishing juridical and social equality of the Kazakh woman, giving her opportunities to participate in socially useful work and in social life and to get an education helped destroy the significance of the *kalym*. The bargain, including such peculiar cases as a paying-by-work marriage (*koush kouyeou*), gave way to marriage by free choice. A betrothal from the cradle (*besik kouda*), matchmaking of yet unborn children (*bel kouda*), and other everyday forms violating the will of the young all disappeared. The remnant of the levirate, a survival according to which the brother of a dead man had a right to take the widow as a wife (*amengerlik*) also disappeared. But at the same time the role that the parents and close relatives of the fiancé play in preparing and organizing the wedding, in creating the necessary material conditions for the future family, and that of the bride's parents in preparing the bride's dowry (*zhasaou*) is still very important. The monogamous family is firmly established, whereas the polygamy that was a privilege of the rich has ceased to exist. At the same time, the idea of numerous progeny as the most important index of the real wealth of a family and its love for children is well preserved. One proof is the high birthrate. During the period from 1959 to 1970 the Kazakh population of the Republic grew from 2,723,230 to 4,161,164 people. The institution of matchmaking (*kouda*) still exists, though now it has a more ritual character; in any case, it never replaces the decision of the young to join their lives. The relations between the parents and relatives of the young ones who are going to marry are still as important as before. The past custom of successive marriage of elder sons or daughters has practically no real importance today.

Emancipation of the Kazakh woman was clear with regard to inheritance (*entsi alou*). The almost monopolistic right of succession only by the male line was replaced by the Soviet equal rights legislation. The custom of making a show of the dead person's inheritance, used by the *bais* to inspire respect in his family and descendants, does not exist any longer.

The popular tradition of respecting and taking care of old people (including the forms of addressing them) has now acquired new social content. Now it is free of its formerly absolute authoritarianism, of the elements of violating the feelings and demands of the younger generation.

The authority of parents and older members of the family now rests not on the common law ("son before father as slave before master") and not on force, but reflects the new moral principles. It is a response to the parents' care of the children, their health, up-bringing, and education. At the same time people are aware of the division of relatives into the father's line and the mother's line (ascendant and descendant), the division into close and distant relatives, and their classification according to age; the traditional terms of relationship are used in everyday life.

It is very interesting to trace the face of such an institution as *kara shanyrak* [the father's *yurt*], which envisaged assigning the father's *yurt* and the succession rights to the father's hearth to the youngest son (*kenzhe*) after the apportionment for the elder children; the institution predetermined the authority of his hearth and obliged the relatives to present him with gifts. Many centuries ago, this institution originally served to prevent the bases of a large patriarchal family from disintegrating. Sanctified by time, it acquired an economic basis. The youngest son and his family took upon themselves the obligation to help the father and mother, grandfather and grandmother who as a rule lived with them. This institution did not completely disappear. Today the parents usually live with the youngest son who inherits the father's house (*settle*) and who takes upon himself the care of the parents in their old age.

But modern social conditions have changed, both in the country and in the urban areas, where we have separate dwellings, old-age and disability pensions, and a high level of material well-being. Furthermore, there are new forms of population mobility. Often the younger sons, as soon as they have finished their education, or after active service, or for a job or other reason leave the parents' residence for another place, go from the *aoul*, collective farm, or state farm settlement to the city, whereas their parents stay in the same place with one of the older sons or even daughters, living either with them or separately. All children, irrespective of age or sex, help their parents and get together periodically. As to the rites connected with *kara shanyrak*, they no longer exist.

In this report I have analyzed only some traditional social institutions of the Kazakh nation as they are related to changes in social relations and their organic connection with settlement. But even these few examples permit us to point out that the traditional social institutions of the Kazakh nomadic and seminomadic *aoul* did not stagnate but rather evolved together with the social and economic structure of society. After the Revolution some institutions died out; these institutions are those that were directly or indirectly exploitative or were directly connected to a nomadic or seminomadic mode of life; other institutions that had none of those elements or got rid of them were preserved and strengthened, incorporating people's experience of many centuries, their knowledge and wit. Fundamental social changes introduced by the Soviet State in connection with the transition to settled life sharply speeded up the selection of social institutions from the past but did not discard them entirely. All that was really valuable was naturally introduced into today's material and spiritual life of the people. Dialectically contradictory negations of conservative outlived principles and the preservation and renewal on new social grounds of progressive, really popular principles were naturally joined with the birth of new social institutions and customs, and these innovations gradually turned into traditions. The Kazakh Republic is a model in this field because it is multinational, and the Kazakh nation developed not in isolation but in continuous economic, political, and cultural intercourse with all peoples of the Soviet Union. New social ideals were born and firmly established; for example, submission of personal interests to social ones, a new attitude of man to man and man to labor, new social psychology, morals, and standards of behavior, friendly feeling for fraternal peoples, patriotism, and a sense of the Kazakh nation belonging to the new multinational community of people – the Soviet people.

Investigations show a direct connection between the age of a man and his knowledge of traditional social institutions and customs: the ones that have become obsolete are as a rule known only to the older generation; the positive ones are known to both old and young people. Thus the continuity of generations in real ethnic and cultural values of the past is never broken. There are not many changes in the geographical environment that supposedly doomed people to an internal nomadic and seminomadic livestock-breeding economy; but the social conditions underwent qualitative changes. Hence there was a sharp increase in the productive forces, a change in the people's mode of life and well-being, and thus a change in social institutions. The planned mass settlement in cooperation with the revolutionary reforms in the economy were the powerful catalysts of the social and cultural progress of the Kazakh nation.

REFERENCES

ARGYNBAEV, KH.

1969 *Etnograficheskie ocherki skotovodstva kazakhov* [Ethnographic essays on Kazakh cattle breeding] (in Kazakh). Alma-Ata.

1970 *Bibliography on land tenure in Asia, the Far East and Oceania.* Food and Agricultural Organization of the United Nations. Rome.

1970 *VIII International Congress of Anthropological and Ethnological Sciences*, Symposium: 8–10, Eurasian nomads, Tokyo.

1966 *Inter-regional study tour and seminar on the sedentarization of nomadic populations in Soviet Socialist Republics of Kazakhstan and Kirghizia.* Geneva.

1964 *Kul'tura i byt kazakhskogo kolkhoznogo aula* [Culture and daily life of the Kazakh kolkhoz *aul*]. Alma-Ata.

1960 *V. I. Lenin o Srednei Azii i Kazakhstane* [V. I. Lenin on Central Asia and Kazakhstan]. 1960. Tashkent.

1970 VII Mezhdunarodnyj kongress antropologicheskikh i etnograficheskikh nauk. Moskva [VII International Congress of Anthropological and Ethnological Sciences. Moscow] 10. Symposium *Vzaimootnoshenija kochevogo i osedlogo naselenija* [Interrelationships of nomadic and settled populations]. Moscow.

SHAUMJAN, M. KH.

1961 *Ot kochev'ja – k sotsializmu* [From nomadic life to socialism]. Alma-Ata.

TOLYBEKOV, S. E.

1971 *Kochevoe obshchestvo kazakhov v XVII – nachale XX vv.* [Nomad society of the Kazakhs from the seventeenth through the beginning of the twentieth century]. Alma-Ata.

VALIKHANOV, CH. CHR.

n.d. *Sobranie sochineniy* [Collected works], volume one: *O kochevkax kirgiz* [On the nomadic life of the Kirghiz].

VOSTROV, V. V., KH. A. KAUANOVA

1972 *Material'naja kul'tura kazakhskogo naroda na sovremennom etape* [Material culture of the Kazakh people at the contemporary stage]. Alma-Ata.

ZHDANKO, T. A.

1968 *Nekotorye aspekty issledovanija nomadizma na sovremennom etape* [Some aspects of research on nomadism at the contemporary stage]. Moscow.

Patronymy Among the Peoples of the Caucasus

A. I. ROBAKIDZE

The peoples of the Caucasus are genetically very close to each other. All belong to the same language family, and for thousands of years there have been close and multiform links between them. The natural and historical conditions of their evolution have been very much alike. All these factors have contributed to their integration, so that a typologically uniform cultural world has been formed in the Caucasus. The features of this common culture are particularly obvious in the population of the mountain regions of the Caucasus.

At the same time, the process of socioeconomic evolution of the Caucasian peoples, like that of other regions of the world, was not uniform in its progress. It was a specific factor which determined the different levels of social progress, each pertaining to a particular stage (Barabash 1971). This general regularity is well traced at the earlier evolutional stages in the peoples of the Transcaucasus (Melikashvili 1970: 89), and also in the history of mountaineers of the northern Caucasus up to the time of their joining Russia (Anchabadze and Robakidze 1971).

The above-mentioned has opened vast opportunities for a comparative and historical study of the most valuable elements of culture and everyday life, as well as the patronymic organization of the peoples of the Caucasus on a common general scale, taking into account all phases of their existence.

The concept of patronymy is known to have been suggested by Kosven, who defined it as groups of families formed through the segmentation of family communities, and to some extent preserving their economic, social, and ideologic unity (Kosven 1963).

Further investigations in this field have proved that all peoples of the Caucasus, without exception, in their past everyday life regarded patronymy as a form of social interrelations and a universal stage of common evolution. It was found, however, that in the plains of Azerbaijan, Armenia, and Georgia by the middle of the nineteenth century the specific features of patronymy had been either completely lost or radically transformed, whereas the mountain regions of the Caucasus still preserved some of the traits which, though largely decayed, permit us to reconstruct its general features.

The form of settlement, the way in which the filial families settle down around their father's home, has proved to be the most stable feature of the community. This order of settlement is regulated by the close socioeconomic interests of the patronymic principle and, to a certain extent, reflects the degree of preservation of other aspects of this patronymic unity.

A comparative analysis of patronymic forms of settlement of the peoples of the separate regions of the Caucasus Mountains provides for possible variants which reflect the subsequent stages of patronymic development.

The simplest form of patronymic settlement is found in the Chechen-Ingush variant. It is a complex of dwelling and economic constructions grouped around a tower used for dwelling and for defense. These complexes were formed over a very long period of time, which suggests a multistage segmentation of families. At the initial stage of the process the filial families settled down inside the dwelling complex, never leaving its limits (Khristianovich 1928). But when this complex failed to house the next generations of filial families, the latter had to leave their father's home and settle down in separate dwellings built in the direct vicinity of the old house.

In this process of expansion, the territorial unity of patronymy gradually vanished. At the same time other links uniting it into a single whole were broken. In this process patronymy of the first range developed into patronymy of the second range and so on. There came into being concentric circles of kin organizations which, within the wider circle of relatives, were characterized by a decrease in the strength of this link of relations.

To qualify the above-mentioned concentric circles of relatives there gradually developed a corresponding differentiated terminology. For instance, in the Ingush language, the starting point of patronymy, a big family was specified by the term *dezal*. When segmented, patronymy of the first range became *naykie* and that of the second range became *vayr*. At this evolutional stage the patronymic system is represented by two groups, depending on the degree of relationship – *iykhera doal* [close by their father] and *gaynar doal* [distant from their father]. In the further course of its development there appear *voshal* [brotherhood] and, finally, *teipa*, meaning a circle of people who were either really or supposedly of common origin (Kharadze 1968).

A similar situation has been observed in the Chechen language (Rossikov 1888). Here the corresponding terms are dialect forms of the Ingush ones, and they repeat the principal links of the Ingush patronymic structure: *doyzal-nekkyu* (Mamakaev 1962), which in its turn had two sequent stages: *genara doish* and *gargara doish*, then *vezheralla* and *taip*.

The Karachaev-Balkar variant of this patronymic settlement developed somewhat differently. Initially there would be a one-room dwelling made of logs; it had a central hearth and a double-pitched roof. When the family expanded and new married couples were added, each of the latter built onto the initial house its own one-room dwelling. The next generations to follow went on adding such rooms to those built before, so that the exit came to face an inner yard. In this way the settlement presently acquired a U-shape, with only one exit from the yard. The initial one-room building was called *uluyu* [big house] and was meant for the first generation of the family, i.e. the elder parents (Robakidze 1960).

The Ossetic variant is more developed. As the Ossets hold, "it is impossible to light two candles in one house" except when there is a death in it. The family segmentation here resulted, as a rule, in building a new dwelling in the immediate vicinity of the father's home. There appeared patronymic nests which, when developing, resulted in branched patronymy, forming new nests and later on even whole villages. At the same time the structure of the kin organization also became more complicated.

The center of a patronymic quarter, as a rule, was a complex built as a dwelling and defense tower. The additional buildings were more simplified dwelling structures.

Southern and northern Ossets reveal an identical structure of patronymic organization. The initial cell was also the family (*khadzar*). Patronymy developed in the course of the family segmentation, acquiring the name *dyggag khadzar* [the second home, the second family]. In some cases patronymy of the first order was called *eu artai baiyarga* [gone away from the same one fire]. A more distant collective of relatives, including descendants up to the ninth generation, was termed *eu fydy fyrt* [sons of one father]. Descendants of one of the brothers after an interval of time would form a kin group called *fydy fyrta*. There is a group which forms the widest possible circle of relatives with the same original patronymy known as *rvad* (Gagloeva 1964), which means "a relative," originating from the ancient Iranian *bhrata* (Abaev 1962).

In its concrete meaning, *rvad* corresponds to the Chechen-Ingush term *taip* or *teip*, because it embraces all true or supposed relatives.

The mountaineers of Georgia also had a widespread patronymic form of settlement. Its main features reveal much in common with the forms of settlement in Ossetia and Chechen-Ingushetia. These common features are first of all found in Khevsureti, where the bulk of alpine settlements formed and developed immediately around the defense tower of the father's home, with additional houses built on later in accordance with the developed patronymy of later origin. These were the very settlements which have been ethnographically fixed as the most ancient ones in Khevsureti.

Of similar structure is the patronymy of the Khevsurians. Upon the segmentation of the family, which was not large in members but big in its social importance, there formed a group of filial families called *mamani* [fathers], which had two stages – *akhale mamani* [new fathers] and *dzveli mamani* [old fathers]. With the further expansion of the circle of relatives there formed a kindred organization called *dziri* [root] which by its degree of kinship corresponds to the Chechen-Ingush idea of brotherhood. The widest circle of relatives is called *gvari* (Kharadze 1971) which by its place in the system of kindred organizations corresponds to the Chechen-Ingush term *taip* or *teip* and the Ossetic term *rvadalta*.

Among Mtiulians, as well as among some Khevsurians, the ancient forms of settlement have been replaced by comparatively new ones. Yet in villages which are now deserted there are still some traces of patronymic settlements, developed upon the old scheme of the dwelling-and-defense tower in the center. These traces make it possible to reconstruct the old scheme of patronymic settlement and the very process of the building of villages.

Patronymy among Mtiulians is termed *komoba*. It evolved around the segmentation of the family *komi*. A wider circle of relatives of the same origin is called *dziroba* or *budoba*, from the word *bude* [a nest]. It corresponds to the Khevsurian *dziri* and, together with the range of *budoba* of kindred origin, it makes up the widest circle of relatives, called *gvari* (Robakidze 1971).

The farmstead form of settlement on the west Georgian coast of the Black Sea differs considerably from the dwelling complexes of the highland Caucasus. However, the patronymic scheme of settlement can be well traced here, too.

Analyzing the Abkhazian ethnographic material, we find that here the basic element in the evolution of patronymic organization is a big family, called *atatsea du*. Upon its segmentation there evolved a patronymy *abitsara*, which was, however, not of two but of several stages, such as *khabitsara*, *oybitsara*, *khyabitsara*, etc. The system of the above-mentioned *abitsara* is also called *ashiara* [brotherhood], and, finally, *azhela* (Bakhija 1970), which corresponds to the Chechen-Ingushian *taip* or *teip*, the Ossetic *rvadalta*, and the Georgian *gvari*.

As to the form of the patronymic settlement, the Abkhazian ethnographic material reveals some new features, of certain interest for the general rules of the evolution of patronymic organization. The dwelling complex in Abkhazia, besides its main house and auxiliary buildings, included a separate structure, namely a round hut called *amkhara*, usually placed behind the big main house. In this hut the young people had their dates before marriage; it was here that the newly weds spent their first night. *Amkhara* was built in the family for future married couples ("He has built his *amkhara*, now he can bring himself a wife"). But the family was not yet divided, and all its members lived together.

Upon the segmentation of the family the filial families settled down on their own around the father's house, not in the *amkhara* but in solid houses (Inal-Ipa 1954).

This form of a big family's dwelling in the Abkhazians differs considerably from the Adjar one. The latter was characterized by an extremely segmented dwelling, so that separate chambers were designed beforehand for future married couples, who, as a rule, settled down under the same roof together with other members of the family; but each had its own separate room.

There were two forms of patronymic settlement in Svanetia. The more ancient of the two repeats in the main the Khevsurian and the Mtiulian forms. But the newer form of patronymic settlement differs considerably from the older one. It has no additional buildings attached to the main house by the filial families, but complete dwelling complexes of the same type and size as the father's house. According to Svan customs it was possible to divide the family only after all conditions for the filial families' independent life were met.

The Svan patronymic structure does not show any special differences. Here, too, a big family (*kor*) was the initial cell of the patronymic organization. Upon its segmentation there developed a group of filial families: *samkhub* [brotherhood]. *Samkhub*s, in their turn, had two stages, *dzirish* [indigenous] and *kyakhiba* [distant] brotherhoods (Kharadze 1939). In its further evolution the system developed the widest circle of relatives, called *tem*. This term is borrowed from the Georgian language, where it means "community." But in the Svan language it acquired the meaning of "family," and, hence, by its place in the patronymic structure, it corresponds to *taip* or *teip*, *azhyola*, *rvadalta*, and the Georgian *gvari*.

Despite some local peculiarities (the degree of differentiation in the patronymic structure, the order of names of its separate links, the specific forms of settlement, etc.), all these structures are built upon the principle of the kinship degree. In this feature they somewhat resemble the norms of the Roman inheritance law, which distinguished between *sui heredes* [one's own heirs], *agnati proximi* [close relatives], and *gentiles* [all relatives]. When referring to the Roman nomenclature of kindred systems built upon their degree of genetic closeness, we do not mean any successive links but only their typological similarity, which is quite natural in view of the general regularities.

The above-mentioned variants of patronymic settlement of the Caucasian mountaineers reveal sequential stages in the evolution and transformation of the patronymic system as a specific form of social organization. However, in all of its phases, at the first segmentation of the family and the division of the family property, i.e. when patronymy of the first range was formed, it was always only the principal items of property that were subject to division: the house in the first place, then the land and the cattle. The other less-significant items of property remained in common use by the filial families, making up the patronymic property.

The part of the property that was patronymically owned (the cattle-shed, summer and winter cots in pastures, the mill, the threshing floor, the brewery boilers, the apiary, the loom, sometimes the hayfields, even certain plots of plowing land, etc.) made up the economic basis which determined the common work and consequently the common economic interests. Some part of the property (the tower, the family sanctuary, the jugs for the sacrificial wine, etc.) ideologically strengthened the social and economic community of the patronymic settlement.

An analysis of the patronymic system in the Caucasus in all its successive phases shows such a system to be a specific universal form of social organization and not a subdivision of a family. The patronymy originates from the evolution of a family, which is a kind of successive process of numerous divisions. Its initial cell could be only the family community or its alternate form, based upon family communal ownership, which was universal in the late Middle Ages, and in some places even later, as was the case in the Caucasus (Itonishvilj 1969) and elsewhere (Bromley 1968). It is because of its origin that patronymy has common features in social life, economy, and ideology which made it possible to regard it as a family organization or a family subdivision. The universal nature of patronymy and its stability are due to its important functions for so long in both the family and the social life of the Caucasian mountaineers.

This long preservation of traditional forms of everyday social life, patronymy in particular, among the peoples of the Caucasus was in some cases due to the lack of a state system there, and in other cases due to the fact that the influence of the central power upon the social life of the people in the distant regions was weak.

In these conditions the most important criterion of the social life of the Caucasian mountaineers was the *adat*: either a written or an unwritten code of norms of common law by which the degree of relationship was accentuated as the basis of regulation of the estate and legal property relations (the order of inheritance, the questions of marriage relations, etc.). Marriages were allowed only after the ninth generation, even for those of different families. The *adat* also settled questions of blood revenge, since responsibility for murder was directly proportional to the degree of kinship with the guilty person.

It was the vital importance of patronymic organization in the everyday social and family life of the Georgian mountaineers and especially their peculiar natural and historical environments which maintained this patronymic organization up to the middle of the nineteenth century.

REFERENCES

ABAEV, V. I.
1962   Proiskhozhdenie i kul'turroe proshloe osetin po dannym jazyka [Origin and cultural past of the Ossets according to language data]. *OJAF* 1. Moscow.

ANCHABADZE, Z. V., A. I. ROBAKIDZE
1971   K voprosu o prirode kavkazskogo feodalisma [On the question of the nature of Caucasian feudalism]. *Tezisy dokladov sessionnykh i plenarnykh zasedanij.* Tbilisi.

BARABASH, I.
1971   Prostranstvo i vremja v istoriko-etnografiches kom issledovanii [Space and time in historico-ethnographic research]. *SE* 1.

BAKHIJA, S. I.
1970   *Abkhazskaja abipara* [Abkhaz *abipara*]. Tbilisi.

BROMLEJ, J. V.
1968   *The archaic form of the communal family.* Moscow.

GAGLOEVA, Z. D.
1964   *Osetinskij "rvaldata"* [Ossetian *rvaldata*]. Moscow.

INAL-IPA, SH. D.
1954   *Ocherki po istorii sem'i i braka u abkhazov* [Essays on the history of the family and marriage among the Abkhazians]. *Sukhumi.*

ITONISHVILJ, V. DZH.
1969   *Semejnyj byt gortsev tsentral'nogo kavkaza* [Family life of the central Caucasian mountain people]. Tbilisi.

KHARADZE, R. L.
1939   *Perezhitki semejnoj obshchiny u svanov* [Vestiges of the family community among the Svans]. Tbilisi.
1968   Nekotorye storony sel'sko-obshchinogo byta gornykh ingushej [Some aspects of village community life of the mountain Ingush]. *KES* 2. Tbilisi.
1971   Khevsurskoe "dziri" i "gvari" [Khevsurian *dziri* and *gvari*]. *Mimomkhilveli* 1. Tbilisi.

KHRISTIANOVICH
1928   *Gormaja Ingushija* [Upper Ingushia]. Rostov-on-Don.

KOSVEN, M. O.
1963   *Semejnaja obshchina i patronimija* [The family community and patronymy]. Moscow.

MAMAKAEV, M.
1962   Chechenskij taip /rod/ i protsess ego razlozhenija [Chechna *taip* (family) and the process of its decline]. *Prilozhenie* 1. Groznyj.

MELIKASHVILI, G. A.
1970   Osnovnye etapy drevnejshej i drevnej istorii Gruzii [Basic stages of the very ancient and ancient history of Georgia]. *Ocherki istorii Gruzii* 1. Tbilisi.

ROBAKIDZE, A. I.
1960   Formy poselenija v Balkarii [Forms of settlement in Balkaria]. *MEG* 11. Tbilisi.
1971   Nekotorye storony mtiul'skogo "komoba" [Some aspects of Mtiulian *komoba*]. *KES* 3. Tbilisi.

ROSSIKOV, K. N.
1888   Poezdka v jugo-zapadnuju chast'gornoj Chechni v zapadnyj Dagestan [Journey to the southwestern part of mountainous Chechnja in western Daghestan]. *IKORGO* 9. Tbilisi.

Tradition and Innovation in Family Rites in the Northern Caucasus

YA. S. SMIRNOVA

All traditions are characterized by a certain degree of stability. As Marx observed (Marx and Engels 1930: 119–120), tradition generally outlives the conditions from which it sprang. Nevertheless, under certain historical circumstances marked by major and fast-moving upheavals in the material, cultural, and psychological spheres, traditions become less stable. Such epochs provide an excellent demonstration of how tradition falls to pieces and is replaced by innovation. It is the object of this paper to have a look at the mechanism of this process, taking as an example the family rites in the northern Caucasus.

On the eve of and immediately after the establishment of Soviet rule in the northern Caucasus, local family customs and rites reflected and strengthened the patriarchal tradition which dominated the family life of the Caucasian peoples. Thus, there still existed marriages by purchase, which were very humiliating for the women and which were often associated with a large age difference between spouses, marriages involving adolescents, and polygamy. Even more humiliating for women was marriage by abduction. The marriage price and other expenses connected with the wedding rites constituted a heavy financial burden for the families of brides and bridegrooms. The wedding rites included oppressive and unpleasant customs of hiding, wedding obstruction, and numerous magic rites. In fact, the wedding was a feast for the distant relatives and the whole community, rather than for the newlyweds and their next of kin.

The customs and rites of childhood also featured negative aspects, such as the inequality of the sexes, the parents' and children's avoidance of each other, and well-developed religious and magic rites. Under such conditions, even some positive popular traditions were carried to their absurd extreme and became negative: the attitude toward weddings or funerals as social affairs involved inordinate, even ruinous spending;

respect for elders inculcated in the children acquired abnormal proportions and turned into blind obedience.

Since the 1920's and particularly the 1930's, the general transformation
of the economic, social, and cultural life of the northern Caucasian
peoples has triggered a relatively fast process of modification of family
customs and rites. This process features three main trends.

First, there was further development of the positive popular traditions
compatible with the new conditions, such as social resonance of major
family events, respect for elders, moderation and modesty in relations
between the sexes, and so forth. The second trend consisted of the withering away of obsolete negative traditions incompatible with the requirements of the new times, such as the marriage price, abduction, avoidance,
magic midwifery, and the religious rituals of weddings and funerals. The
third trend consisted of the emergence, on the common socialist basis and
as a result of close interpeople contacts, of day-to-day family innovations
common to all Soviet peoples, such as solemn registration of marriages
and births, celebrations of children's birthdays, and nonreligious funeral
rites (*Kul'tura i byt* 1968: 185).

One will readily see that while the first aspect of the process in question
is relatively independent, there is a negative feedback loop between the
other two trends: innovation (say, solemn marriage registration) takes
root only with the dwindling of tradition (in this case the former marriage
rites). This is a commonly known fact, but it is of a too-general nature to
provide an answer to the question of how the transition from tradition to
innovation takes place.

Some authors believe that innovation is altogether incompatible with
tradition in the social and family spheres, as distinguished from the
material or spiritual cultural spheres. This belief was most succinctly
expressed by Lavrov, a prominent figure in Caucasian ethnography.
Studying the upheavals in the culture and daily life of the Adyghes over
the years of Soviet rule, Lavrov came to the conclusion that

> ...one of the specific features of the family customs and standards of behavior
> in society consists in that as the new appears, the old is generally given up;
> therefore, the new not so much overlaps the old as destroys it. Thus, a marriage
> without a price or with the bride violating the custom of avoiding her father-in-
> law signifies not only the emergence of new forms of relations, but also the
> renunciation of the old customs. In such cases, the old and the new are mutually
> excluding. At the same time, a person donning new clothes is not necessarily
> expected to discard his old clothes if they are not worn, and one singing a new
> song may sing an old one right here (Lavrov 1962: 18–19).

As we see it, the theory of incompatibility of tradition and innovation in
family customs and rites is not borne out by facts, not even in the above
examples of marriage price and the custom of avoidance. Indeed, the
marriage price was legally banned in the northern Caucasus as far back as
the early 1920's, yet it persisted for at least another three decades in a

modified compromise form of "gifts" in goods or money presented to the bride's family (Chistjakova 1940: 29; Kulov 1941: 16). The same occurred in the custom of avoidance of the father-in-law by his son's wife: the old avoidance, which lasted in some form throughout the whole lifetime, and the present-day relatively decisive deviation from this custom spanned a range of attenuated, compromise forms. For instance, renunciation of the ban on seeing each other went together with preservation of the talking ban (Smirnova 1961). Thus, the relationship between the new and the old in family customs and rites is governed by compromise, and adaptation is to be singled out in the mechanism of transition from tradition to innovation.

The role of adaptation in the transformation of family rites is best illustrated by the so-called "dual" and "semitraditional" weddings, birth celebrations, and funerals, widely popular among the peoples of the northern Caucasus.

Wedding hiding, from which the subsequent avoidance originates, is the most characteristic trait of the traditional wedding in the region in question. Indeed, the Soviet linguist and ethnographer Sigorskij suggested that this feature be used as a basic element in the classification of the wedding rites of the entire Caucasus (Sigorskij 1930). Neither the bride nor, particularly, the bridegroom would take part in the wedding. The bride would be in the premises set aside for her, or behind a curtain, and even when appearing before the wedding gathering, she would invariably station herself in a corner, her face covered by a cape. The bridegroom, after his journey for his bride, would be hiding at one of his friends' or junior relatives' homes. And it was only in the closing phase, after the wedding celebration, that the bridegroom officially returned home, where a ceremony of his "reconciliation" with his parents was held; some peoples of the region also practiced a ceremony of the bridegroom's "reconciliation" with the village folk. The bride's parents also took no part in the wedding and in general were barred from intercourse with the bridegroom's parents.

In this case we shall not consider the historico-cultural origin of these customs (the problem of diffusion in the Abkhazian-Adyghian wedding cycle) or their historico-sociological origin (the problem of transition from matrilocality to patrilocality); we confine ourselves to mentioning the indisputable fact of wedding hiding. Among other important elements of the traditional rites two should be mentioned: the religious registration of the marriage (Muslim for the overwhelming majority of the region's population), and the giving of presents, mostly to the bride's and bridegroom's closest relatives rather than to the newlyweds.

In contrast with this tradition, the new wedding rites of the northern Caucasus peoples which have sprung up under Soviet rule are characterized by rejection of the hiding custom, a feature taken from the modern urban wedding. Thus, the central episode of the new wedding – civil registration in the solemn atmosphere of a wedding house, a club, or a village Soviet – calls for the presence of both newlyweds, who arrive to have their marriage registered accompanied by their relatives, friends, and comrades. Another important element of the new rites – wedding festivities – also requires the presence of the heroes of the festivities. The giving of presents has been retained as an element of the new wedding rites, but nowadays presents are given to the newlyweds rather than to their relatives.

One may think that observance or violation of the hiding custom, religious or civil registration of marriage, and the like render the traditional and the new wedding incompatible with one another. Indeed, in the prewar period and in the years immediately after the war the two sets of rites were practically isolated from each other. Most people, particularly in the countryside, adhered to the tradition, whereas some people in urban areas, generally the most advanced and cultured, limited the wedding ceremony to an act of official civil registration and a subsequent banquet. Recently, however, there has been a widely popular trend toward renovation of the obsolescent rites. Accordingly, two kinds of adaptation have emerged – "double" and "semitraditional" weddings – which have spread to even the remotest rural areas.

In our opinion, the "double" wedding can be regarded as the first step of adaptation; it is characterized by both sets of rites – traditional and new – being observed at the same wedding. This reflects a measure of cultural and psychological collision between the older and younger generations within a family or even a broader group of kinsmen. The young and many middle-aged people already prefer the new rites, but the emphatic respect for elders, inherent in the people of the northern Caucasus, forces them to take into account the views of their grandparents and other old relatives. As a result, the wedding is in effect celebrated twice. The bride and bridegroom, accompanied by their younger and sometimes older relatives, friends, and comrades, have their marriage solemnly registered according to the civil pattern, whereupon they sit down to a feast together with the guests and accept congratulations and presents. But in the bridegroom's parents' house, another wedding ritual is held, this time conforming to the traditional pattern with its attendant hiding of the newlyweds, giving of presents to the relatives, and sometimes even religious registration of the marriage. In other cases, the traditional wedding precedes rather than follows the new one; but the particular variations are irrelevant, for the important thing is that tradition and innovation coexist in a "double" wedding, not interacting and not interpenetrating.

The next step of adaptation – the "semitraditional" wedding – exhibits features of interaction. This kind of wedding is characterized by a blend of new features and old rites, although it is free from the most unacceptable vestigial forms. The "semitraditional" wedding exists in numerous versions, differing in form from one people of the region to another, from one stratum of the urban and rural population to another, and even among families of different cultural standing. Nevertheless, its most characteristic and widespread components can be singled out: (1) solemn registration of marriage according to the civil pattern, which, however, is not attended by the parents and other older relatives of the newlyweds because of avoidance; (2) a wedding feast during which the newlyweds together with the younger guests sit at one table and the elder relatives and guests at another (in more traditional families the two groups are placed in different rooms or even houses); and (3) wedding presents which are given both to the newlyweds by their relatives and friends and to the bridegroom's and bride's relatives by the bride's and bridegroom's relatives respectively. Thus, in a "semitraditional" wedding, tradition (vestiges of avoidance and mutual giving of presents by the relatives) is closely intertwined with innovation (solemn registration of marriage, participation of the newlyweds in the wedding, giving of presents to the newlyweds). The result is a peculiar transitional set of rites with the old being progressively superseded by the new.

As far as the chief rite of childhood, the birth celebration, is concerned, the situation is essentially the same. The peoples of the northern Caucasus used to have several traditional celebrations on the occasion of a birth. If a son was born, particularly if it was a first-born, the father lavished gifts on the bearer of the glad tidings; the relatives and the village folk came to offer their felicitations and were treated to food and drink. Actually, this tradition was supported by the legislation of the Russian Empire, whereby only male babies were entered on the family lists. The birth of a girl was not celebrated, but on the day the mother left her bed for the first time, the women of the family, irrespective of the sex of the baby, would sometimes call together their relatives and female neighbors and treat them to a modest feast during which one of the old women would offer a thanksgiving prayer for the saved lives of the mother and child.

The main festivities on the occasion of a birth, also purely feminine in character, were held several days later and were connected with the placing of the newborn in a cradle. On that day, female relatives and neighbors, mostly aged, were again called together; the mother-in-law had her first look at the baby and begged her daughter-in-law to appear in her presence without feeling shy. In keeping with the avoidance custom, the close relatives of the young mother stayed away but had to send presents, including the very cradle, as was the custom among many peoples of the region. Among certain peoples the baby was given its name that same day, whereas among others this rite was held at various later times. (Pchelina 1937; Smirnova 1966; Aliev 1968).

Under Soviet rule, even before the war but mostly in the last fifteen to twenty years, two main trends have appeared in the development of birth rites: (1) a merger of the once-numerous rites and celebrations marking the birth into a single social-familial celebration on the occasion of the birth of a baby, whether boy or girl; and (2) the weakening and gradual withering away of those avoidance customs which prohibit the young spouses from appearing together, particularly with their baby, before the older relatives and outsiders. The new tradition has taken almost complete hold; the old one is less pronounced. At present, on a day soon after the mother and child leave the maternity home, the family holds birth celebrations attended by young relatives and friends of the parents and, not infrequently, by many older relatives. The father-in-law and the mother's parents, however, rarely take part except in urban areas. The guests congratulate the young parents and offer presents to the baby. The chief present, a cradle, is traditionally sent by the mother's mother. In many rural families the baby is solemnly placed in the cradle the same day and given its name.

Since the mid-sixties, first in urban and then in rural areas, birth celebrations have come to include another important innovation – solemn registration of births in the local house of culture, club, or village Soviet. As distinguished from purely formal registration, this solemn occasion is attended by both parents, rather than just one, as well as by their relatives and friends and representatives of the public. This practice of solemn registration of births and marriages, now widely popular in the northern Caucasus, has been made possible only by the weakening of the avoidance traditions. Nevertheless, in rural areas the specially avoided older relatives, above all the father-in-law and the parents of the young mother, participate in the solemn birth registration as infrequently as in home birth celebrations.

An interesting fact is that the transition from the old to the new in the birth cycle of the northern Caucasus immediately takes the form of "semitraditional" rites, bypassing the logical predecessor – "double" rites. The reason for this phenomenon lies in the fact that the birth rites in the region in question apparently had no significant social import as compared with the rites, which accompanied the two other main events in a human life – marriage and death.

On the other hand, the transition from tradition to innovation in funeral rites has so far been evident only in the early form – "double ritual." The reason is clear: funerals constitute the most religious and conservative part of family rites. Even those who would reject a traditional wedding or birth ritual can hardly be expected to challenge the feelings of their religious relatives by arranging a funeral without the appropriate rites. That is why, though many of them have turned atheist, the peoples of the northern Caucasus still stick to the traditional funeral ritual (Muslim among all but the Christian Ossets): the women are barred from the cemetery; the deceased is wrapped in a shroud but buried without a coffin, in a prescribed position, before sunset; and often a mullah or one of the pious elders offers prayers. Equally popular is the traditional funeral repast, held several times, with the guests being treated to special ritual food and sweetmeats and sometimes being offered money (Avksent'ev 1966; Aliev 1968).

At the same time, in more advanced and cultured urban strata, the civil funeral ritual is steadily gaining ground. This is characterized, first, by the absence of any religious acts, speeches, or symbols, and, second, by the presence of general Soviet funeral attributes, such as the laying of the body in a coffin; the wearing of crape armbands, the laying of wreaths and flowers, and funeral music; funeral orations by relatives, friends, and colleagues; and also a one-time funeral repast in the home of the deceased immediately following the funeral. Lately, this sort of ritual has been making inroads in rural areas, a process which is facilitated in part by the common tradition of burying the remains of a deceased urban dweller in his native village. In such cases the funeral ritual is mostly of a "double" nature: after the civil burial rites in town, it winds up in the countryside on a more or less traditional note.

To summarize, the family rites, like other spheres of culture and daily life, gradually change through intermediate, compromise forms – adaptation. The adaptation of rituals may be broadly classified into early "double" forms, in which tradition and innovation coexist side by side, and later "semitraditional" forms, in which tradition and innovation blend into a single set of rites. In the complex: tradition – adaptation – innovation, the adaptive component constitutes a necessary intermediate form instrumental in the replacement of old rites with new ones.

REFERENCES

AVKSENT'EV, A.
1966 *Koran, shariat i adaty* [Koran, Shariahs and Adats]. Stavropol.
ALIEV, A. K.
1968 *Narodnye traditsii, obychai i ikh rd' v formirovanii novogo cheloveka* [Folk traditions, customs and their role in the formation of the new man]. Makhachkala.
CHISTJAKOVA, E.
1940 Religija i bytovoe polozhenie zhenshchin u shapsugov [Religion and the position of women in everyday life among the Shapsugs]. *Religioznye perezhitki u cherkesov-shapsugov. Materialy Shapsugsko ekspeditsii 1939 goda.* Moscow.
KULOV, S. D.
1941 *O nekotorykh perezhitkakn feodal'norodovogo byta i kapitalizma v severnoj Osetii* [On some remnants of feudal-tribal life and capitalism in northern Ossetia]. Ordzhonikidze.

Kul'tura i byt
1968   *Kul'tura i byt narodov severnogo Kavkaza 1917–1967* [Culture and daily life of the peoples of the northern Caucasus 1917–1967]. Moscow.

LAVROV, L. I.
1962   Izmenenija v kul'ture i byte adyqejtsev za gody Sovietskoj vlasti [Changes in the culture and daily life of the Adyghes during Soviet rule]. *Sovetskaja Etnografija* 4.

MARX, K., F. ENGELS
1930   *Sochinenija* [Works], volume eight.

PCHELINA, E. G.
1937   Rodil'nye obychai u osetin [Birth rites among the Ossetians]. *Sovetskaja Etnografija* 4.

SIGORSKIJ, M.
1930   Brak i brachnye obychai na kavkaze [Marriage and marriage rites in the Caucasus]. *Etnografija* 3.

SMIRNOVA, JA. S.
1961   Obychai izbeganija u adyqejtsev i ikh izzhivanie v sovetskuju epokhu [Avoidance customs among the Adyghes and their gradual elimination in the Soviet epoch]. *Sovetskaja Etnografija* 2.

1968   Vospitanie rebenka v adyqejskom aule v proshlom i nastojashchem [Childrearing in the Adyghian *aul* in past and present]. *Uchenye zapiski Adyqejskogo nauchno-issledovatel'skogo instituta jazyka, literatury i istorii* 8. Maikop.

Cultural Diversity, Conflicting Ideologies, and Transformational Processes in Afghanistan

M. JAMIL HANIFI

The problem of sociocultural development in Afghanistan has not received sufficient study by those anthropologists in whose primary field such a study would logically rest. In the absence of an analysis in depth conducted by trained academicians, the present paper will give a broad outline of some of the problems arising from cultural diversity within the country. It will also examine the breakdown of loyalties to varying, and at times conflicting, political-cultural ideologies in relation to the modernizing efforts of the Afghan government in recent years.

Afghanistan is a nation which is heterogeneous in many important ways. The artificiality of Afghanistan's boundaries and the sharp cultural differences among its peoples point up the fact that Afghanistan is a colonial creation – British and Russian – and that the concept of an Afghan nation is the result of political arrangements between Britain and Russia, who never colonized the country but merely created it as a buffer between conflicting colonial appetites.

The existence of this cultural heterogeneity has not stopped the political leaders of Afghanistan from espousing, creating, and encouraging nationalistic ideologies, although it has undoubtedly hindered them in realizing these goals.

Afghanistan's estimated population of 16 million represents many cultural groupings. Most of these fall into one or the other of the two major groups – the Indo-Europeans, and those who only recently emigrated into the country from Muslim Soviet Central Asia. People of the first of these large groupings are concentrated in the eastern, southern, and southwestern parts of the country, while those of the second occupy northern and northeastern Afghanistan (Wilbur 1962).

In the first group, the great majority, including the Pashtuns and the Tajiks, speak an Iranian variant of the Indo-European language family and have common cultural characteristics with groupings to the west, southwest, and east of Afghanistan. Those of the second group, including the Uzbeks and the Turkmen, speak a Turkic language belonging to the Ural-Altaic family. They have ties with cultures in Central Asia and Mongolia.

Of the various cultural groups, the largest are the Pushtuns and the Tajiks, followed by the Uzbeks, the Turkmen, the Hazaras, the Chahar Aimaks, and small pockets of Nuris, Hindus, and Jews. Pushtuns make up over half the population and dominate the cultural scene. The Tajiks provide the second largest and the dominant merchant class, while the Pushtuns make up the political elite and predominate in the small educated class.

Islam is the religion of 98 percent of the Afghan population. Almost all Pushtuns are Sunni, as are the Turkmen and the Uzbeks, while the Tajiks and the Hazaras are substantially Shia. All the religious cultural groups in Afghanistan have corresponding and numerically larger counterparts in close proximity outside the territorial boundaries of the country. This, in addition to the heterogeneous character of Afghan society, makes the reality of cultural integration and subscription to and identity with a national ideology imperative for the successful implementation of the modernizing efforts of the Afghan government. To this date, no deliberate, systematic effort has been made to provide a viable, uniform focus for the fragmented subnational loyalties and thus generate and maintain a national collective conscience for all Afghans. Only Islam as a religion has been able to provide the basis of a (rather loose and at times self-defeating) cultural unity at the national level. Though the penetration of Islam into various cultural planes in Afghanistan is quite deep and can be considered a kind of national cultural common denominator, one cannot expect it to provide by itself the rallying point for an all-transcending national conscience.

This penetration by Islam has provided the legitimization of the present Afghan political structure, but such unity of state and Islam has seriously impeded the development of modernizing attempts, because the continuity of the throne – the Afghan monarchy as sanctioned and validated by the Islamic dicta – has and does take priority over other national concerns. Thus, attempts to uproot and to modernize the mass of Afghans have always been a secondary consideration. It should be pointed out, however, that the continuity of the monarchy has been instrumental in providing a degree of stability necessary for modernization. But the paramount imperative is, has been, and perhaps will always be a national identity overriding other kinds of identities and loyalties, i.e. loyalty to kinship and other smaller sociocultural spheres. This may be construed to mean nationalism, as defined by Coleman (1958: 425):

Broadly, a consciousness of belonging to a nation (existent or in the realm of aspiration) or a nationality, and a desire, as manifest in sentiment and activity, to secure or maintain its welfare, prosperity and integrity, and to maximize its political autonomy.

In addition to the secular-theocratic, multicultural character of Afghan society, an examination of some of its other significant features is necessary for the proposition of a modernizing model. The Afghan individual is surrounded, as it were, by concentric rings consisting of family, extended family, clan, tribe, confederacy, and major cultural-linguistic group. The hierarchy of his loyalties corresponds to these circles and becomes more intense as the sociocultural circle gets smaller. To his kin and his cultural group he gives service, cooperation, and, in time of danger, perhaps his very life. From these groups he derives protection, a livelihood, and, above all, a sense of belonging. As was already mentioned, an Afghan is expected to adhere strictly to traditional Islamic tenets, especially in the realm of politics at the national level (Caroe 1958).

But seldom does an Afghan, regardless of cultural background, need the services and/or the facilities of the national government. Thus, in case of crisis, his recourse is to the kinship and, if necessary, the larger cultural group. National feelings and loyalties are filtered through the successive layers surrounding the individual and tend to become meaningful to him only to the extent that they happen to coincide with the interests of his cultural setting, corresponding to a subnational group.

The structure of the Afghan society described so far has resulted in conflicting cultural and social values and loyalties such as exist today in that country. Inevitably, they bring in their wake a host of problems, among them significant and irreconcilable dichotomies. And, as time passes, these gaps tend to become wider and less susceptible to being bridged. Correspondingly, the process of modernization becomes increasingly impeded and the possibility of further fragmentation increasingly high.

The process of modernization and development in Muslim Afghanistan being considered here involves changes in value systems as well as economic, political, educational, and social structural changes. In traditional Afghan society the value system tends to be "prescriptive" rather than "principial" (Becker 1957: 128). A prescriptive system is characterized by a comprehensiveness and specificity of the value commitments and by its consequent lack of flexibility. In the Afghan Muslim cultural systems loyalties are frozen, so to speak, through commitment to a vast range of relatively specific religious and subnational norms governing almost every dimension of life. Islam is characterized by such a range of norms. Most of these specific norms are thoroughly integrated with the religious system (Islam), which invokes ultimate sanction for every infraction and deviation from the norm. Thus, changes in Afghan economic, political, educational, and other institutions that are the targets of modernizing efforts tend to have religious implications. Furthermore, because of the very close nature of state and religion mentioned earlier, any change or other form of innovation in Muslim Afghan society can be considered not only as a political revolt but also as a religious sin. In other words, modernization will and must involve Islamic religious sanctions.

And yet, Afghan Islamic society, when faced with grave dislocation consequent on modernizing attempts, must make certain major alterations in its institutional structure, operationally and symbolically, if it is to be progressively transformed. What changes must be made in the organization of the structure of Afghan society and also the cultural value system therein so that modernizing changes must and can succeed?

It is proposed that the cultural value system and structure of traditional Islam must change from a "prescriptive"–Islamic to a "principial"– secular type in accordance with the aforementioned usage by Howard Becker. Afghan society, as we have briefly examined, tends to have an Islamic normative system in which a comprehensive, codified Koranic (*sharia*) and an uncodified (*hadith*) set of relatively specific norms govern concrete behavioral categories of individual Afghans. But in the already modernized and technologically advanced societies, an area of flexibility must be gained in the various dimensions of sociocultural life in which specific norms may be determined in considerable part by short-term exigencies in the realm of behavior, or by functional requisites of the relevant social subsystems.

Ultimate or religious values may lay down the basic principles of sociocultural behavior – thus, such a normative system is called "principial" – but the religious system does not attempt to regulate the dynamics of the social structure in its every detail, as in Afghan Muslim society. Looking at this process in another way, we may say that there is a differentiation between religion and ideology, between ultimate values and suggestedpreferred ways in which these values may be put into effect.

In Afghan society there is no such discrimination. Differences of opinion on political, legal, economic, and other matters of policy are taken to mean differences in religious commitment. Thus, the Afghan "innovator" becomes a religious heretic. But in systems where the distinction between political ideology and religion is legitimate and realized, there is a differentiation between the levels of religious and national politico-cultural ideology which makes possible greater flexibility at both levels (Horowitz 1964: 363).

How is the normative system in Afghan Islamic society to be transformed from prescriptive to principial, and how is the differentiation of the religious and ideological levels to be achieved, especially in the face of the staunch Islamic local cultural barriers and in the light of the vast intranational cultural diversity in Afghan society? It is proposed that a new religious reformist initiative, such as the one which transpired in Turkey (Berkes 1964; Lewis 1961) be undertaken. Such a movement will

claim religious ultimacy for itself and can successfully challenge the in-
hibiting nature of the old and diverse value systems and their Islamic
and/or subnational cultural base. The new movement, which arises from
the necessity to make drastic cultural changes conducive to the successful
modernization of Afghanistan, in the light of new conditions, is essentially
ideological and political in nature.

But, arising as it does in an Afghan society in which the ideological
level is not yet recognized as having independent legitimacy, the new
movement must take on a religious coloration in order to meet the old
Afghan-Islamic social system on its own terms. Even when such a movement is successful in effecting major structural and symbolic changes in
Afghan society and freeing formerly subdued motivation and narrowly
derived and defined loyalties, so that considerable flexibility in economic
and political life is attained and a national conscience articulated, the
problem posed by its own partly religious origin and its relation to the
traditional Afghan Muslim religious system may still be serious indeed.

It seems worthwhile to stress that the process of secularization – as
the basic prerequisite for modernization – suggested for Afghan national
society, which is, in part, what the transition from prescriptive to principial society is, does not mean that Islam as a religion should disappear
from Afghanistan. The function of religion in a principial society is
different from that in a prescriptive society but not necessarily less important. Moreover, in the very process of transition Islam may reappear in
many new guises on the Afghan national cultural plane. Perhaps what
makes the situation so unclear is its very fluidity. Even in highly differentiated societies, traditional religion so deeply associated with the prescriptive past is still in the process of finding its place in a modern, technologically advanced sociocultural setting.

Nevertheless, what is proposed here is a feasible alternative at the
present time for theocratic and multicultural Afghanistan. The stark
reality is that xenophobic nationalism in Afghanistan is gaining ground
because of, and at the expense of, Islam. If this trend continues, some
basic rethinking will be needed if Islam in Afghanistan and in other
similar settings is to survive at all.

One final note might be added. Although certain religious conservatives
and secular extremists continue to blame modernization for the fact that
they must face the issue now in becoming party to the process of secularization before the caravan of technological sophistication is too far ahead
to catch, the fight is no longer between local cultural dictums and the need
for a collective Afghan national culture. The conflict now takes place
within Afghan society itself, and until Afghanistan has dealt with the
roots of retarding elements in the path of modernization, change in that
country will continue to be unnecessarily painful, haphazard, slow-paced,
and, at times, bloody and violent. Afghan Islam must be transformed

before its outdated feudal aspects disable and obliterate those dimensions of Islam which are still healthy and repairable. Such transformation must above all be adaptive to a national Afghan cultural psyche which can, collectively and with the force and enthusiasm of its variety, succeed in its eventual attempts to modernize its past.

REFERENCES

BECKER, HOWARD
  1957   "Current sacred-secular theory and its development," in *Modern sociological theory in continuity and change*. Edited by Howard Becker and Alvin Boekoff. New York: Dryden.
BERKES, NIYAZI
  1964   *The development of secularism in Turkey*. Montreal: McGill University Press.
CAROE, OLAF
  1958   *The Pathans*. New York: St. Martin's.
COLEMAN, JAMES S.
  1958   *Nigeria: background to nationalism*. Berkeley: University of California Press.
HOROWITZ, IRVING L.
  1964   Sociological and ideological conceptions of development. *American Journal of Economics and Sociology* 23.
LEWIS, BERNARD
  1961   *The emergence of modern Turkey*. London: Oxford University Press.
WILBUR, DONALD H.
  1962   *Afghanistan: its people, its society, its culture*. New Haven: HRAF Press.

The Mimouna Festival Among the Moroccan Jews

ISSACHAR BEN-AMI

While Jews around the world are ending their Passover holidays, the Jews of North Africa are making intensive preparations to welcome the Mimouna festival.

What is the nature of this Mimouna festival, which begins on the eighth day of Passover? What are its expressions, its symbols, its sources? Do vestiges of this festival exist in other Jewish communities? Is this an ancient custom or is it the creation of later generations?

DESCRIPTION OF THE MIMOUNA

On the eighth day of Passover, just before the festival begins, the Jews hurry to acquire flowers, grains of wheat and barley, milk, butter, honey, and other things from Arab merchants who come to the Jewish quarters especially to supply these items.

In the Jews' houses, which are decorated with flowers and greenery, tables are set with green lima beans, farina, milk, honey, dates, lettuce, and a fish. On this night, neither salt, pepper, nor cured meats are eaten. Everyone must visit friends, acquaintances, and family. The benedictions *Tarbah* or *Tassad* [succeed and be happy] are repeated while the visitors dip their fingers in the milk and honey. These visits continue all through the night. Groups of young people in Arab dress stroll through the *mellah*; bands of musicians gather and travel about, blessing the families. They sing

Ah Lalla Mimouna	Oh, Lalla Mimouna
Ah mbarka mes'ouda	The blessed, the happy
O Tarbho o tssa'do	Succeed and be happy
Ah ya oulad lihud	Oh, Jews
Ah ya oulad Israel	Oh, Children of Israel

The following morning, as early as possible (since, according to the Jews of southern Morocco, he who rises late on this day will be lazy all year long), people go to the seashore, to the river bank, or to the country-side and spend the day there. In Marrakesh, mothers slap the water seven times with their hands while they murmur a prayer; men take off their shoes, soak their feet for a long time in the running water (a symbol of abundance), and moisten their faces and chests. In Tafilalet, the Jews spill water on their doorsteps while saying, "We cast away all harm and hindrance."

ORIGINS OF THE MIMOUNA

The Moroccan Jews have several different explanations for this festival. One explanation associates the Mimouna with the Arabic word *mimoun* [good luck or happiness]. All the actions performed on that night are intended to express the desire for a blessed and happy year.

A second explanation relates the festival to the Hebrew word *emuna*: the Jews were saved in the month of Nissan and will be saved again in the month of Nissan. To mark their faith in this salvation, the Jews have dedicated a special festival, the festival of *emuna* [belief].

A third explanation associates the festival with what is said in the Talmud about the fate of the year's harvest being at stake at Passover, when a green and successful year is hoped for.

It is also said that the festival is celebrated in honor of the death of Rav Maïmon, father of Maïmonides, who died on that day.

Yet another explanation: it was only after their festival just after the exodus from Egypt that the Jews were able to see the booty seized from the Egyptians. As they burned it, they saluted each other with the words, "Succeed and be happy" (Hirschberg 1972: 210–211).

Slouschz (1927: 208) speaks of a town called Timimona, in the country of Tovat, which was destroyed at the end of the fifteenth century. The residents of Timimona who migrated to Tafilalet say every year, "Next year in Jerusalem, next year in Timimona."

Another researcher (Noy, personal communication, 21 April 1968) tells of all the Jewish traditions relating to water on the last day of Pass-over; traces of these traditions can be found in the customs of North African Jews.

Einhorn (1972: 211) has also proposed an enticing solution, but it does not fully resolve the problem. According to Einhorn, Mimoun is the king of the spirits, to whom the Jews dedicate a meal on the last day of Pass-over. This tradition has been maintained among the Moroccan Jews, and the table which is prepared for the Mimouna festival is for the spirit Mimoun, so that he will do them no harm throughout the rest of the year.

But this solution fails to account for all the other Mimouna customs which I have described (Ben-Ami 1972: 36).

None of the cited authors has been able to resolve the linguistic problem posed by the use of the feminine form of the word *mimoun* ("Mimouna"); but, nevertheless, "Mimouna" is an actual name. There exists a spirit named Mimoun, found, among other places, in the stories of the *Thousand and one nights*. There also exists a cult of Lalla Meimouna among Moroccan Muslims (see Dermenghem 1954: 69).

An interesting legend was gold by a French traveler at the beginning of this century (Aubin 1903: 97–98) concerning the *koubba* of Lalla Meimouna, which he saw before his arrival at Larache à Fès:

There once was a holy man named Sidi Bou-Selham, who lived at the seashore and had a companion named Sidi Abdel-Aziz El Tayar. One day while Sidi Bou-Selham was enjoying himself fishing, El Tayar approached him and, to amuse his friend, plunged his hand into the water and immediately pulled it out full of fish. Each hair on his hand had served as a hook for this miraculous catch. Sidi Bou-Selham, in turn, wanted to prove his own skill. He gestured with his *selham* and dragged the sea along behind him, vowing that he would transport it to Fès so that the girls of the town might wash their hands in it. Followed by the docile sea, he arrived in this manner at the *douar* where Meimouna lived. In the face of imminent disaster, the holy woman told Sidi Bou-Selham that he was about to inundate the habitation of a friend. Sidi Bou-Selham protested that he had made a vow. Lalla Meimouna then gestured and several girls were transported into their presence as if by magic. They washed their hands in the sea and returned to their homes. Thus the threatened *douar* was spared and the vow kept. The name of Lalla Meimouna has been preserved among the people, who venerate her *koubba* [grave].

The motifs shared by this legend and the Mimouna festival are remarkable. For the first time, we find the name "Mimouna" in its feminine form. The miracle of salvation from the sea is reminiscent of the one that took place in the time of Moses. The link with the town of Fès is important; and the ablutions in water are also found in the legend.

But even then, the problem is not completely resolved. What is the actual relationship between the Muslim Saint Meimouna and the Mimouna festival? Indeed, many parts of the Middle East (Syria, Kurdistan, etc.) have customs parallel to those of the North African Jews, and it is an obvious possibility that this was a common tradition, a tradition which has resulted, in North Africa, in an important development.

Without doubt, we need more thorough research before the enigma of Mimouna can be solved.

REFERENCES

AUBIN, EUGÈNE
1903   *Le Maroc d'aujourd'hui.* Paris.
BEN-AMI, ISSACHAR
1972   La fête de Mimouna. *Yeda Am* 39–40: 36–44.
EINHORN, ITSHAK
1972   The origin and nature of the Meimouna. *Tarbiz* 2: 211–219.
HIRSCHBERG, HAIM-ZEEV
1972   "La Mimouna et les festivités de la fin de la fête de Pâques," in *Zakhor le-Avraham. Mélanges Avraham Elmaleh.* Edited by H. Z. Hirschberg, 206–237.
SLOUSCHZ, NAHUM
1927   *Travels in North Africa.* Philadelphia.

Biographical Notes

SAUL M. ABRAMZON (1905–) is Doctor of Historical Sciences, ethnographer, and Orientalist-Turkologist. From 1926 to 1931, he organized and directed the first scientific institutions in Kirghizstan, and since 1931 he has worked at the Institute of Ethnography at the U.S.S.R. Academy of Sciences in Leningrad. From 1933 to 1935 and from 1968 to 1973 he was Head of the Department of Near and Central Asia and Kazakhstan and, from 1940 to 1943, was Scientific Secretary and Deputy Director of this institute. From 1950 to 1952, he lectured on the ethnography of Central Asia at Leningrad State University. He is specifically interested in the ethnic and social history of the nomadic and seminomadic peoples of Central Asia and Kazakhstan, including their modern history. Main publications include *Rodoplemennaia organizatsia kochevnikov Srednei Azii* [Lineage-clan organization of the nomads of Central Asia] (1951), *Die Stammesgliederung der Kirgisen und die Frage nach ihrer Herkunft* (1962), *The impact of sedentarization on the social structure, family life, and culture of former nomads and seminomads, an example: the Kazakhs and Kirghis* (1966), and *Formy sem'i u dotiurkskikh i tiurkskikh plemen Semirech'ia, Tian'-Shania i Iuzhnoi Sibiri v drevnosti i srednevekov'e* [Forms of family among the pre-Turkic and Turkic tribes of the Aral Basin, Tian Shan, and southern Siberia, in antiquity and the Middle Ages] (1973). He was also one of the editors of the two-volume work *Narody Srednei Azii i Kazakhstana* [Peoples of Central Asia and Kazakhstan] in the series *Narody mira* [Peoples of the world] (1962, 1963).

S. G. AGADZHANOV. No biographical data available.

S. ANNAKLYCHEV. No biographical data available.

KHALEL ARGYNBAEV (1924–   ) was born in the Baian-Aul District of the Pavlodar Region. In 1961, he successfully defended his Candidate of Sciences dissertation in ethnography and became a Senior Research Fellow. He defended his Doctor of Sciences dissertation in 1976 and has been Head of the Departmentof Ethnography at the Institute of History, Kazakh S.S.R. Academy of Sciences since then. He is particularly interested in problems of Kazakh ethnography. His publications include: *Etnograficheskie ocherki o narodnoi veterinarii y kazakhov* (1963), *Etnograficheskie ocherki po skotovodcheskomu khoziaistvu kazakhov* (1967), and *Sem'ia i brak u kazakhov* (1973).

Y. V. ARUTYUNYAN. No biographical data available.

ISSACHAR BEN-AMI (1933–   ) was born in Casablanca. He received his B.A. from the Hebrew University of Jerusalem in 1962 and his Ph.D. in Folklore and Oriental Studies from the University of Göttingen in 1967. He is currently Senior Lecturer at the Hebrew University and Director of the Folklore Research Centre there, Director of the Centre for Research on North African Jewry, Director of Misgav Yerushalayim (an institute for research on Spanish and Oriental Jewry), and Secretary of the Folklore Society in Israel. He has been Editor of the Folklore Research Centre Studies since 1970 (5 volumes), and is author of the book *Études ethno-culturelles sur les Juifs marocains*. His present research interest is folk-saint veneration among North African Jews.

GRIGORII FEDOROVICH DAKHSHLEIGER (1919–   ) is Doctor of Historical Sciences, Professor, and Corresponding Member of the Kazakh S.S.R. Academy of Sciences. He has studied problems of the economic and social history of the Kazakh people, sedentarization of the Kazakh nomadic and seminomadic populations, and the history of historical science. Currently he is specializing in the history of peasantry. His published works include *Sotsial'no-ekonomicheskie preobrazovaniia v aule i derevne Kazakhstana?* (1965), *Istoriografiia Sovetskogo Kazakhstana* (1969), and *V. I. Lenin i problemy kazakhskoi istoriografii* (1973).

JEAN-PIERRE DIGARD. No biographical data available.

CHARLES FRANTZ (1925–   ) received his Ph.D from the University of Chicago in 1948 and is currently Professor of Anthropology at the State University of New York at Buffalo. Previously he taught at Portland State University, the University of Toronto, Howard University, and Ahmadu Bello University, Nigeria, and was Executive Secretary of the American Anthropological Association. His research and publications – concerning Russian Doukhobor sectarians in British Columbia (Canada);

interethnic relations in Zimbabwe; pastoralism, ecology, and social organization in Africa, especially in Nigeria; and the history of anthropology in the United States – include *Racial themes in Southern Rhodesia* (1962, co-authored), *The student anthropologist's handbook* (1972), and *Pastoral societies, stratification, [and national integration in Africa* (1975).

MARCEAU GAST (1927–), born in Chéragas, Algeria, is a Doctor of Ethnology presently in charge of research at the Centre National de la Recherche Scientifique (CNRS). A specialist on the populations of the central Sahara, he has concentrated on the study of their diet (*Alimentation des populations de l'Ahaggar, étude ethnologique*, 1968; *Mils et sorgho en Ahaggar*, 1965; *Le lait et les produits laitiers en Ahaggar*, 1969) and their socioeconomic structures (Matériaux pour une étude de l'organisation sociale chez les Kel Ahaggar, *Libyca* 22, 1976; Les Kel Rela: historique et essai d'analyse du groupe de commandement des Kel Ahaggar, *Revue de l'Occident Musulman et de la Méditerrané* 21, 1976). Most recently he has studied the Republic of Yemen and worked on a comparative analysis of the social structure of various Touareg societies.

M. JAMIL HANIFI (1935–) was born in Kabul, Afghanistan, and is a native speaker of Pashto and Dari Farsi. A resident of the United States since 1957, he studied at Michigan State University (B.Sc. in Social Science, 1960; M.A. in Political Science, 1962) and Southern Illinois University, Carbondale (Ph.D in Anthropology, 1969). He has taught at California State University in Los Angeles and at Northern Illinois University, where he has been Associate Professor of Anthropology since 1974. In 1975–1976 he served as Chairman of the Executive Committee of the Afghanistan Studies Association and as Chairman of the Afghanistan Committee of the South Asian Regional Council (SARC) of the Association for Asian Studies. Author of many scholarly works, including *Islam and the transformation of culture* (1974) and the *Historical and cultural dictionary of Afghanistan* (1976), his special interests include culture, process and change, urbanization, comparative political systems, religion, and Islamic law.

B. A. KALOEV. No biographical data available.

A. KAVRYEV. No biographical data available.

ANATOL M. KHAZANOV (1937–) was born in Moscow. He received his Candidate of Historical Sciences degree in 1966 from the Moscow State University and his Doctorate in Historical Sciences in 1976 from the Institute of Ethnography at the U.S.S.R. Academy of Sciences. He is a

Senior Member of the Institute of Ethnography. His special interests include anthropology, archaeology, and history of the Eurasian nomads (especially the Scythians); general theories of nomadism; the social organization of primitive society and its evolution; the origin of the state and early statehood; and ecological anthropology. Recent books include *Essays on the history of the Sarmatians' military art* (in Russian, 1971), *The social history of the Scythians: main problems of the development of the ancient nomads of the Eurasian steppes* (in Russian, 1975), *Primitive society: main problems of evolution* (in Russian, co-authored, 1975), and *The gold of the Scythians* (in Russian, 1975).

RAIL' KUZEEV (1929–   ) finished his aspiranture at the Institute of Ethnography in Moscow in 1954. Currently, he is Professor of History of the U.S.S.R. at the Paedagogical Institute in Ufa (Bashkirian, A.S.S.R.) and Head of the sector of archaeology, ethnography, and folk art in the Bashkirian branch of the U.S.S.R. Academy of Sciences. He is primarily interested in historical ethnography and the medieval history of Turkic peoples. He has published books and articles on the structure of tribal organization, ethnic history, the history of the culture of the Bashkirs and of other Eurasian nomads of the medieval epoch, Turkic onomastics, textology, and archaeography. He is President of the Volga–Ural Coordination Committee on Archaeology and Ethnography, and Chairman of the South-Uralian division of the Archaeographical Commission of the U.S.S.R. His most recent publications are *Bashkirskie rodoplemennye nazvaniia i ikh altaiskie paralleli* [Bashkir lineage-clan names and their Altai parallels] (1971), *Proiskhozhdenie bashkirskogo naroda* [Origin of the Bashkir people] (1974), "Etnonim tarkhan u baskhir, chuvashei, vengrov i dunaiskikh bolgar" ["The ethnonym *tarkhan* among the Bashkir, Chuvash, Hungarians and Danubian Bulgarians"] (1975), and "Ob istoricheskom sootnoshenii territorii Drevnei Bashkirii i Velikoi Vengrii" ["On the historical correlations of the territory of ancient Bashkiria and Great Hungary"] (1976).

GENNADII IEVGENIEVICH MARKOV (1922–   ) was born in Moscow. He studied ethnography, history, and archaeology at the Moscow State University and graduated in 1951. Since 1948 he has done extensive fieldwork in Central Asia and western Siberia. In 1954, he received his Candidate of Historical Sciences degree for his studies on the origins of the Northern Turkmenians, and in 1968 he earned his Doctorate of Historical Sciences for studies on the nomads of Asia. Since 1954, he has worked at the Moscow University, where he became professor in 1970. He is currently Head of the Department of Ethnography. His major works include *Ocherk of the history of the Northern Turkmenians* (1961), *Narody Indonezii* (1963), and *Kochevniki Azii* (1976).

EMANUEL MARX (1927–   ) was born in Munich. He studied sociology and Oriental studies at the Hebrew University (M.A., 1958), and social anthropology at the University of Manchester (Ph.D., 1963). Currently he is Associate Professor at Tel Aviv University and Head of Research on Bedouin settlements at the Desert Research Institute, Ben Gurion University, Beersheba. He has carried out field research among the Bedouin in the Negev and in South Sinai, in a new town in northern Israel, and in Palestinian refugee camps. His publications include: *Bedouin of the Negev* (1967), *Some sociological and economic aspects of refugee camps on the West Bank* (with Y. Ben-Porath, 1971), and *The social context of violent behavior* (1976).

LIDIIA MONOGAROVA (1921–   ) was born in Moscow. She studied ethnography in the Department of History of Moscow State University where she graduated in 1946. In 1951, she received her Candidate of Historical Sciences. She worked as a Senior Editor of *Bolshaia Sovietskaia encyklopediia* from 1952 to 1959 and has worked at the Institute of Ethnography of the U.S.S.R. Academy of Sciences in Moscow, where she has been a Senior Research Fellow of the Central Asia and Kazakhstan division since 1956. She worked as Deputy Editor of Sovietskaia Ethnografiia (1960–1972) and is currently a member of the editorial board. She is engaged in research on the ethnography of the peoples of Central Asia, with an emphasis on Iranian-speaking populations. Her works include *Preobrazovaniia v bytu i kul'ture pripamirskikh narodnostei za gody sotsialisticheskogo stroitel'stva* (1972); Kompleksnaia tipologiia gorodoc Tadzhikskoi SSR v svete problem etnicheskoi mozaichnosti ikh naseleniia, *Sovetskaia Etnografiia* 2, 1972; "Etnicheskii sostav i etnicheskie protsessy v Gorno-Badakhshanskoi avtonomnoi oblasti Tadzhikskoi SSR," in *Strany i narody Vostoka* 16, 1975; and Sovremennye etnicheskie protsessy na Zapadnom Pamire, Sovetskaia Etnografiia 6, 1965.

VIVIANA PAQUES (1920–   ), Docteur ès-lettres, is Professor of Ethnology and Directress of the Institut d'Ethnologie of Strasbourg. Her extensive fieldstudy on the different black and white riverine populations of North Africa has resulted in *L'arbre cosmique dans la pensée populaire et dans la vie quotidienne du Nord-Ouest africain* (1964). As a specialist on the black populations of North Africa, she has published numerous articles concentrating on their spiritual and religious worlds. A collection of these articles – *La religion des esclaves* – is in preparation. Other publications include *Les peuples de l'Afrique* (1974); *Les sciences occultes d'après les documents littéraires italiens du XVI siècle* (1971); and "La religion africaine," in *Croyants hors frontières* (1975).

STEPHEN L. PASTNER received his Ph.D. from Brandeis University in 1971 and is presently Assistant Professor of Anthropology at the University of Vermont. He has conducted fieldwork in Baluchistan, Pakistan; Trinidad, West Indies; and eastern Ethiopia, and has, since September 1976, been carrying out maritime anthropological research in Pakistan. He has published articles in *Man, Anthropological Quarterly, Asian Affairs,* and *International Journal of Middle Eastern Studies.* With Carroll Pastner, he has jointly authored papers on the Baluch for *Man, Anthropologica,* and *Pakistan: the long view.*

CARROLL McC. PASTNER received her Ph.D. from Brandeis University in 1971 and is presently Assistant Professor of Anthropology at the University of Vermont. She has conducted fieldwork in Baluchistan, Pakistan; Trinidad, West Indies; and is currently, as of September 1976, carrying out further anthropological research in Pakistan. She has published articles in *Anthropological Quarterly, Journal of Marriage and the Family,* and in the forthcoming *Beyond the veil: women in the Middle East.* With Stephen Pastner, she has jointly authored papers on the Baluch for *Man, Anthropologica* and *Pakistan: the long view.*

RAPHAEL PATAI was born in Budapest and studied in Budapest (Dr. Phil., 1933) and Jerusalem (Ph.D., 1936). He lived and taught in Jerusalem until 1947, when he settled in the United States. There he taught anthropology at Columbia University, Princeton University, the University of Pennsylvania, Ohio State University, New York University, etc. His special interests are the anthropology of the Middle East and the cultural history of the Jews. He has published more than twenty-five books, including *The Hebrew goddess* (1967), *Myth and modern man* (1972), *The Arab mind* (1973), *The myth of the Jewish race* (1975, with Jennifer P. Wing), and *The Jewish mind* (1977).

ALEXY ROBAKIDZE (1907–   ) holds the titles of Doctor of Historical Sciences, Professor, Meritorious Science Worker of Georgia, and Head of the Department of Ethnography of the Caucasus at the Institute of History, Archaeology, and Ethnography of the Georgian Academy of Sciences. He has dealt with the problems of material culture of Caucasian peoples in his *Settlements as a basis for the study of social conditions* (1964), of economical being in *Hunting in Racha* (1941), of apiculture in *The history of apiculture* (1960), of social relationships in *The social structure of the Caucasian mountaineers* (1968), of patronomy in *Patronomy among the peoples of the Caucasus* (1973), of feudalism in *Towards the problem of mountain feudalism among the Caucasians* (1971), of the history of ethnographic thought in Georgia in *Besarion Nizaradze – the ethnographer* (1964) and of the theory of survivals in *Caucasiological problems of the Georgian ethnography* (1972).

YA. S. SMIRNOVA. No biographical data available.

SUSAN E. SMITH. No biographical data available.

NORMAN TOWNSEND (1940–   ) was born in England and educated at the London School of Economics (B.Sc. Econ. 1962), McMaster (M.A. 1969), and the University of Toronto (Ph.D. 1976). He has taught for some years in schools in East Africa and at the University of Western Ontario. Currently he is an Assistant Professor of Anthropology at Trent University. He has done field work in Kenya and specializes in economic anthropology.

SEV'IAN IZRAIL'EBICH VAJNSHTEIJN was born in Moscow. He studied ethnography and archaeology at the Moscow State University, from which he graduated in 1950. In 1969 he took his Doctor of Historical Sciences for his work on the ethnography of the Tuvinians. Since 1959 he has been working as a Research Fellow at the Institute of Ethnography of the U.S.S.R. Academy of Sciences. All his field studies have been carried out among the Ket, the Tuvinians, the Tofalars, and other peoples of Siberia. He has published more than 100 works on the history of nomads of Siberia and Central Asia, the origin of peoples of Siberia, and other special problems of ethnography and archaeology. His main works include *Tuvintsytodzhintsy* (1961), *Tuvinskoe shamanstvo* (1964), *Isoricheskaia etnografiia tuvintsev. Problemy kochevogo khoziaistva* (1962), and *Istoriia narodnogo iskusstva* (1974).

WOLFGANG WEISSLEDER (1920–   ) was born in Germany. His early education was in Germany however in 1957 he turned to the study of anthropology. He received a B.A. from Columbia University in 1960 and an M.A. from the University of Chicago in 1962. After fieldwork in Ethiopia from 1962–1964 he received his Ph.D. from the University of Chicago in 1965. He is currently a Professor of Anthropology at the University of Toronto, Canada. His current interest is in peasantry in general and Medieval European peasants in particular.

T. A. ZHDANKO. No biographical data available.

BIGTARMA JEAN ZOANGA. No biographical data available.

Index of Names

Index of Subjects

Index of Names of Places